WOMEN'S FOOTBALL

The global increase in viewership of and participation in women's football means that, to continue with this growth, we need to appreciate the specific scientific and health issues that determine successful performance for women. *Women's Football* provides a thorough, yet straightforward and accessible, analysis of the key physiological, biomechanical and social-psychological issues that can be applied to achieve women's footballing development.

This cutting-edge text puts developing elite women footballers at the front and centre of its core aim, through the delivery of evidence-based, scientific information focusing on best practice. As such, each chapter is co-written, where possible, by a scholar and a practitioner or player (e.g. coach, footballer), meaning that the scientific principles and research presented within are translated clearly into practice.

Women's Football is essential reading for anyone who is involved with the game, including footballers themselves, as well as strength and conditioning coaches, physiotherapists, medics, nutritionists, sport psychologists, sports scientists, coaches, coach developers, technical directors, general managers, governing body personnel and club owners, from grassroots to elite level. The book is also invaluable to students and academics in sport and exercise, who are studying this topic.

Jacky J. Forsyth, PhD, is an exercise physiologist and has worked in various roles in academia, undertaking both teaching and researching. Her main priority and drive in research are about promoting, raising awareness and advancing understanding of the key influences which impact women in sport and exercise. She has published research articles on improving the health and exercise status of pre- and post-menopausal women. She co-founded the Women in Sport and Exercise Academic Network with Claire-Marie Roberts for the purposes of connecting like-minded academics to promote and strengthen research into women in sport and exercise.

Claire-Marie Roberts, PhD, is a Chartered Psychologist, Chartered Scientist and BASES Accredited Sport & Exercise Scientist who is the Performance Director at Coventry City Football Club. She has worked in various roles in men's and women's professional football for 20 years, including nearly a decade at the Premier League, leading transformational change in elite football development. She is a senior research fellow at the University of the West of England, a special advisor to Nike on women athletes, and a Trustee of Restart—the official charity of The Rugby Players Association dedicated to supporting elite men's and women's rugby players suffering from serious injury, illness or hardship. She has published over 40 peer-reviewed research articles and authored and edited three books.

WOMEN'S FOOTBALL

From Science to High Performance

*Edited by Jacky J. Forsyth and
Claire-Marie Roberts*

Routledge
Taylor & Francis Group

NEW YORK AND LONDON

Designed cover image: Getty images

First published 2025
by Routledge
605 Third Avenue, New York, NY 10158

and by Routledge
4 Park Square, Milton Park, Abingdon, Oxon, OX14 4RN

Routledge is an imprint of the Taylor & Francis Group, an informa business

ISBN: 978-1-032-46488-6 (hbk)
ISBN: 978-1-032-46485-5 (pbk)
ISBN: 978-1-003-38191-4 (ebk)

DOI: 10.4324/9781003381914

Typeset in Times New Roman
by Apex CoVantage, LLC

CONTENTS

FIGURES

TABLES

CONTRIBUTORS

Roar Amundsen
Norwegian School of Sports Sciences, Norway

Paul Ansdell
Northumbria University, Newcastle-upon-Tyne, United Kingdom

Francisco Ayala
University of Murcia, Spain

Polly Bancroft
Manchester United Football Club, United Kingdom

Ali Bowes
Nottingham Trent University, United Kingdom

Millie Bright, OBE
Chelsea Football Club Women, London, United Kingdom
England Women's Senior National Football Team

Emma Brockwell
Physiomum, Independent Private Practice, Surrey, United Kingdom

Daniel Broman
The Football Association, London, United Kingdom

Nicola Brown
St Mary's University, Twickenham, United Kingdom

Sean Carmody
Department of Orthopaedic Surgery, Amsterdam Movement Sciences, Amsterdam, UMC, University of Amsterdam, Amsterdam, The Netherlands

Francesca M. Champ
Football Exchange Women's Network, and Liverpool John Moores University, United Kingdom

Beth G. Clarkson
University of Portsmouth, United Kingdom

Tom Clifford
Loughborough University, United Kingdom

Rosalyn Cooke
Centre of Precision Rehabilitation for Spinal Pain (CPR Spine), School of Sport, Exercise and Rehabilitation Sciences, University of Birmingham, Birmingham, United Kingdom
   Bisham Abbey National Sports Centre, English Institute of Sport, London, Buckinghamshire, United Kingdom

Charlotte Cowie
The Football Association, London, United Kingdom

Alex Culvin
FIFPRO

Naomi Datson
Manchester Metropolitan University, United Kingdom

Margie Davenport
Program for Pregnancy and Postpartum Health, Physical Activity and Diabetes Laboratory, Faculty of Kinesiology, Sport and Recreation, Women and Children's Health Research Institute, Alberta Diabetes Institute, University of Alberta, Edmonton, Alberta, Canada

Mark De Ste Croix
University of Gloucestershire, United Kingdom

Barry Drust
University of Birmingham, United Kingdom

Sinead Dufour
McMaster University, Hamilton, Ontario, Canada
   The World of my Baby, Pelvic Health Division, Ontario, Canada

Stacey Emmonds
Leeds Beckett University, United Kingdom

Adam Gledhill
Leeds Beckett University, United Kingdom

Amal Hassan
HCA Healthcare UK, London, United Kingdom
Harlequins FC, Guildford, United Kingdom
Kynisca Insights and Innovation Centre, Falls Church, VA, United States

Kirsty Marie Hicks
Northumbria University, Newcastle-upon-Tyne, United Kingdom

Lisa Hodgson
Medical Education Lead, The Football Association Group; Leeds Beckett University

Jonathan Hughes
University of Gloucestershire, United Kingdom

Melissa Jones
University of Portsmouth, United Kingdom

Ross Julian
Department of Neuromotor Behavior and Exercise, University of Münster, Germany, University of Gloucestershire, United Kingdom

Katrine Okholm Kryger
St Mary's University, Twickenham, London, United Kingdom
Sport and Exercise Medicine, Queen Mary University of London, Sport and Exercise Medicine, London, United Kingdom
FIFA Medical, Fédération Internationale de Football Association, Zurich, Switzerland

Dave Lawrence
Head of Talent Management/Sporting Group International-Sports Management

Lawrence Mayhew
Leeds Beckett University, United Kingdom

Rebecca McConville
Private Practitioner, United States

Kristin McGinty-Minister
University of South Wales, Australia

Kelly Lee McNulty
Technological University of the Shannon, Athlone, Republic of Ireland

Ritan Mehta
The Football Association, London, United Kingdom

Samantha L. Moss
University of Chester, United Kingdom

Maria Luisa Fernanda Pereira Vargas
Loughborough University, United Kingdom

Carly Perry
University of Central Lancashire, United Kingdom

Hanya Pielichaty
University of Lincoln, United Kingdom

Rebecca K. Randell
Gatorade Sports Science Institute, United Kingdom

Monica Rho
Shirley Ryan AbilityLab, Northwestern University Feinberg School of Medicine, Chicago, IL, United States

Ian Rollo
Gatorade Sports Science Institute, United Kingdom

Craig Rosenbloom
Sport and Exercise Medicine, Queen Mary University of London, Sport and Exercise Medicine, London, United Kingdom

Debby Sargent
University of Gloucestershire, United Kingdom

Alice Stratford
Football Exchange Women's Network
Liverpool John Moores University, United Kingdom

Melissa Streno
Private Practitioner, United States

Solveig Thorarinsdottir
Norwegian School of Sports Sciences, Norway

Kevin Till
Leeds Beckett University, United Kingdom

Maurizio Valenti
Manchester Metropolitan University, United Kingdom

Joanna Wakefield-Scurr
University of Portsmouth, United Kingdom

Matthew Wright
Teesside University, United Kingdom

FOREWORD

You can't be what you can't see.

Propelled onto the pitch by a header from Zidane in the 1998 World Cup final, influenced by *Bend It Like Beckham* and motivated by Mia Hamm, I enjoyed playing football in my beloved Evreux (Normandy), for Paris Saint-Germain in the first division and all the way to the French national team.

Football has sharpened my character, my way of being in the world. It has not simply been a goal in itself, or a direction to take with or without a ball, but it has been and continues to be a tool serving my development and my freedom. Football is in my DNA.

Tomboy in the playground

Team player

Coach, physical education and sports teacher

Manager: General Secretary of the Amateur Football League at the French Football Federation (Fédération Française de Football)

Sportscaster and football commentator on Eurosport then Canal+

Co-director of the documentary Little Miss Soccer, "The world tour of women football players"

Operations Manager for the Paris Saint-Germain Foundation.

As a true adventurer in the world of women's football, I continue to explore its contours to better determine my place in its environment, seeking to understand what's at stake.

Finding one's place and space—isn't that an issue that concerns us throughout our lives? What is the place of women's football? How do women carve out a space in a predominantly male environment? How do women appropriate the playing field, emancipating themselves from the codes of men's football, breaking free from its prejudices to play the game on their own terms? Women's football should not simply replicate the codes of men's football. Women's football must write its own story.

Succeeding in finding one's place means allowing yourself to dream, to learn, to set goals and putting yourself in the position to achieve them. Dreams are personal and can take different forms, such as playing at a high level, playing for leisure, being the best, scoring goals, winning individual or collective titles, succeeding at a beautiful gesture and/or a collective play or even maintaining a healthy mind in a healthy body.

The challenge here is to be enlightened on the different areas in which we can have an impact. The modern woman footballer is the one who decides their own standards to better redefine the boundaries of the game. She is tailor-made; she is her own self! The complete footballer is the one who studies subjects that optimise the achievement of their goals. Today's woman footballer is an enlightened, lucid and autonomous woman. Those who accompany her in her daily life and/or their performance also have a responsibility as they take part in her story.

This is why we need to have access to literature of *One's Own*,[1] specific and scientific writings that can help to shed light on the diverse aspects of the women's game. This book, *Women's football: From science to high performance*, presents an overview of essential data and elaborates on the key points in women's football today, with a view to improving how it is structured and the way women footballers are supported during their careers.

Candice Prévost

Note

1 Virginia Woolf, A Room of One's Own.

INTRODUCTION

Jacky J. Forsyth and Claire-Marie Roberts

Based on data published by the Fédération Internationale de Football Association (FIFA, 2023), money spent on international transfers for women, in the mid-year window of 2023, was just 3.0 million US dollars, compared to 7.3 billion spent in the men's game, so 0.04% of that spent for men. Despite the last two decades of increasing globalisation of women's football (explored in Chapter 1 of this book), there remain large disparities between men's and women's football in terms of funding, prize money for major tournaments, broadcasting and sponsorships deals (Archer & Prange, 2019; Coche, 2022). Research on women's and girls' football reflects this disparity, in that it is extremely limited compared to that carried out on men (Okholm Kryger et al., 2022). Beyond deliberating the historical and socio-cultural context of women's football to explain the disparity, in this book we focus on how we can develop footballers in the girls' and women's game, through putting into practice cutting-edge, evidence-based, scientific information. We want to highlight what is already "out there". What is the scientific research on women's football that determines successful performance and how is this used to inform current practice? What are practitioners (those working in women's football, such as coaches, support staff, managers) doing in the women's game to ensure that women perform at their optimum, physiologically, biomechanically and psychologically? The focus of our book is, therefore, on the key physiological, biomechanical and social-psychological principles and research that inform footballing practice and that determine success.

The lack of scientific research on women's football often means that research findings on, for instance, training programmes, injury rehabilitation, psychological skills training and nutritional strategies that have been conducted on men are simply transposed to women. In this book, we want to set the bar from which research, and its practical application, can develop, to help the women's game flourish. It is our hope, therefore, that the growth in women's football continues at the same pace as it has done in the last couple of decades, and that the scientific research explodes along with it. The information, which has been carefully constructed by the authors of each of the chapters, not only provides a thorough, yet straightforward and accessible, analysis of what research has been done to date, but also provides examples of how the science can be applied and actualised in the game to improve women's footballing success.

We have asked authors to avoid referring to women's or girls' football, and, where feasible, to simply to use the term "football" and "footballer". In some countries, such as in Finland and Spain, the equivalent translation of the word "women" has been removed from team and league names (Christenson, 2020; Robson, 2023). Since the entire book is about women's football, we did not feel the need to keep referring to women specifically, except where it was necessitated, such as when the research carried out on men versus that carried out on women needed to be distinguished. The book is, therefore, on football!

We subtitled the book, "From science to high performance". The rigorous science underpinning aspects of football based on innovative research is, therefore, critically evaluated, and include physiological determinants, match demands and talent identification physiological changes that occur due to exogenous and endogenous sex hormones, injury epidemiology, prevention and rehabilitation, concussion, nutrition, eating disorders, relative-energy deficiency in sport, psychosocial development, transitions in women's football, pregnancy, motherhood, breast health and mental health. These topic areas were felt to be of relevance at the time of writing, reflecting predominant themes in existing literature (Okholm Kryger et al., 2022). To the best of our knowledge, this book is the first text dedicated to the science of women's football.

We have advocated for use of the term "sex" when referring to biological attributes (Canadian Institutes of Health Research, 2023; Clayton & Tannenbaum, 2016; Gogovor et al., 2021; Heidari et al., 2016), which, in this book, are those associated with ovarian hormone function relating to the menstrual cycle, chromosomes and gene expression, and sex-related anatomy and physiology. We have recommended the use of the term "gender" when referring to a multidimensional, mainly sociocultural construct, encompassing gender identity, behaviour, expectations, perceptions, expression, roles and norms (Canadian Institutes of Health Research, 2023; Clayton & Tannenbaum, 2016; Gogovor et al., 2021; Heidari et al., 2016). We believe that gender is non-binary and socially constructed, and that gender and sex are not mutually exclusive (Clayton & Tannenbaum, 2016; National Academies of Sciences, Engineering, and Medicine & Education, 2022).

Owing to the global popularity of football generally and the growth in the women's game, we have asked authors to write chapters so that the content has worldwide appeal to a range of audiences. We realise, however, that, paralleling the success of football organisations in the Western nations (Culvin & Bowes, 2023; Lago et al., 2022), much of the literature in this area is dominated by researchers from the European democratic nations, the United States and Australia (Thomson et al., 2022; Valenti et al., 2018). Where possible, however, examples have been included from research conducted from across the globe.

A key feature of the book is that, when feasible, chapters have been co-written by a scholar and a practitioner or player (e.g. coach, footballer), so that scientific principles and research are translated clearly into practice. We realise, however, that there are challenges involved in transforming sport science research into practical solutions regarding athletic performance, health and training (Bartlett & Drust, 2021; Bishop, 2008; Coopoo et al., 2018). To partly address this challenge, we deliberately asked authors to include the practitioners' perspective, since we wanted the content not to be driven solely by what research has been published to determine best practice, but by what is being done in practice and what works. There are, therefore, two main themes of the book:

- Knowledge: What science is known already about women footballers and the industry? A clear, thorough analysis of the key scientific issues pertinent to women's football that will enable success is provided.
- Application: How is this knowledge applied in a practical setting? Case studies, examples and practical guidance are presented on how to implement scientific principles and knowledge in women's football into practice.

This book is essential reading for anyone who is involved with women's football, including footballers themselves, as well as strength and conditioning coaches, athletic trainers, physiotherapists, medics, nutritionists, sport psychologists, sports scientists, coaches, coach developers, technical directors, general managers, governing body personnel and club owners, from grassroots to elite level. The book is also invaluable to students and academics in sport and exercise, who are studying this topic.

This book is a call to action. We want more scientific research specifically on women's and girls' football. We want research to be applied to practice and we wish to learn from our combined best practices, sharing ideas in order to create a better future in the game and to achieve excellence in performance. We hope this text serves as a foundation upon which research into the women's game can be built further.

References

Archer, A., & Prange, M. (2019). "Equal play, equal pay": Moral grounds for equal pay in football. *Journal of the Philosophy of Sport, 46*(3), 416–436. https://doi.org/10.1080/00 948705.2019.1622125

Bartlett, J. D., & Drust, B. (2021). A framework for effective knowledge translation and performance delivery of sport scientists in professional sport. *European Journal of Sport Science, 21*(11), 1579–1587. https://doi.org/10.1080/17461391.2020.1842511

Bishop, D. (2008). An applied research model for the sport sciences. *Sports Medicine, 38*(3), 253–263. https://doi.org/10.2165/00007256-200838030-00005

Canadian Institutes of Health Research. (2023, May 8). *What is gender? What is sex?* Retrieved January 26, 2024, from https://cihr-irsc.gc.ca/e/48642.html

Christenson, M. (2020, February 27). Finnish FA drops "women's" prefix for league in push for equality. *The Guardian.* https://search.proquest.com/docview/2365938579

Clayton, J. A., & Tannenbaum, C. (2016). Reporting sex, gender, or both in clinical research? *The Journal of the American Medical Association, 316*(18), 1863–1864. https://doi.org/10.1001/jama.2016.16405

Coche, R. (2022). A new era? How the European ESPN covered the 2019 Women's World Cup online. *International Review for the Sociology of Sport, 57*(1), 73–91. https://doi.org/10.1177/1012690221992242

Coopoo, Y., Kubayi, A., & Toriola, A. (2018). Analysis of sports science perceptions and research needs among South African coaches. *South African Journal of Sports Medicine, 30*(1), 1–4. https://doi.org/10.17159/2078-516X/2018/v30i1a4240

Culvin, A., & Bowes, A. (2023). Introduction: Women's football in a global, professional era. *Women's football in a global, professional era* (pp. 1–13). Emerald Publishing Limited. https://doi.org/10.1108/978-1-80071-052-820230001

FIFA. (2023). *FIFA® report: International transfer snapshot.* https://digitalhub.fifa.com/m/2d3b5b32c3b965b9/original/International-Transfer-Snapshot-September-2023.pdf

Gogovor, A., Zomahoun, H. T. V., Ekanmian, G., Adisso, É L., Deom Tardif, A., Khadhraoui, L., Rheault, N., Moher, D., & Légaré, F. (2021). Sex and gender considerations in reporting guidelines for health research: A systematic review. *Biology of Sex Differences, 12*(1), 62. https://doi.org/10.1186/s13293-021-00404-0

Heidari, S., Babor, T. F., Castro, P. D., Tort, S., & Curno, M. (2016). Sex and gender equity in research: Rationale for the SAGER guidelines and recommended use. *Epidemiologia E Serviços De Saúde, 26*(3), 665–675. https://doi.org/10.1186/s41073-016-0007-6

Lago, I., Lago-Peñas, S., & Lago-Peñas, C. (2022). Waiting or acting? The gender gap in international football success. *International Review for the Sociology of Sport, 57*(7), 1139–1156. https://doi.org/10.1177/10126902211060727

National Academies of Sciences, Engineering, and Medicine, & Education. (2022). *Measuring sex, gender identity, and sexual orientation.* National Academies Press. https://doi.org/10.17226/26424

Okholm Kryger, K., Wang, A., Mehta, R., Impellizzeri, F. M., Massey, A., & McCall, A. (2022). Research on women's football: A scoping review. *Science and Medicine in Football, 6*(5), 549–558. https://doi.org/10.1080/24733938.2020.1868560

Robson, J. (2023, September 22). Spain removing "women" from national team name to show "conceptual shift". *The Atlanta Journal-Constitution (2001).* https://apnews.com/article/spain-women-rubiales-world-cup-30cac2479fe03b47c6dd32821ca916a6

Thomson, A., Hayes, M., Hanlon, C., Toohey, K., & Taylor, T. (2022). Women's professional sport leagues: A systematic review and future directions for research. *Sport Management Review, 26*(1), 48–71. https://doi.org/10.1080/14413523.2022.2066391

Valenti, M., Scelles, N., & Morrow, S. (2018). Women's football studies: An integrative review. *Sport, Business and Management: An International Journal, 8*(5), 511–528. https://doi.org/10.1108/SBM-09-2017-0048

1

GLOBAL CONTEXT AND ORGANISATION

Maurizio Valenti and Polly Bancroft

Introduction

Football is traditionally the most popular sport among men in many countries and regions of the world, while a minority of women play and follow the game globally (Bridgewater, 2018). Had women and girls not been formally prevented from playing football for about five decades (1921–1971), one may wonder whether the women's game would not currently be the most attractive and globalised team sport in the world. Before the ban was imposed in 1921, women's football attracted large crowds to stadia. Following the lifting of the ban, the women's game has entered a period of gradual development with significant institutional changes between the 1970s and the 1990s. These led women's football to enter a stage of starting globalisation in the 2000s, with international football-governing bodies progressively supporting the evolution of the women's game in the last two decades. In this chapter, we trace a brief history of women's football in the global context. We then critically review actions and strategies of stakeholders that contributed to improving the standards of women's football globally. Finally, we formulate recommendations for governing bodies and clubs to continue fostering the growth of women's football in the future.

The evolution of women's football in the global context

Origins of the women's game and the ban

Knowledge about the history of women's football is largely fragmented (Cooper, 2023). For example Williams (2006) reports that a "female form" of football was played in a British colony in Hong Kong in 1840, while Macbeth (2002) indicates

DOI: 10.4324/9781003381914-1

that the origins of women's football are to be located in Scotland. Sources indicate that the women's game was popular in Britain, China, Denmark, France, the Netherlands, Norway and Sweden between the end of the 19th century and the beginning of the 20th century (Dumas, 2019; Skogvang, 2019).

Regardless of the geographical location, the existing histories of women's football and of women in football are primarily stories of exclusion and marginalisation. Stemming from the interplay between gender perceptions and cultural norms, women playing football have historically been subject to social interpretation and judgement (Devonport et al., 2018), and have often been treated as the "outsiders" (Caudwell, 2011). The imposition of a ban by the English Football Association (the FA), which outlawed women from playing on its members' grounds in 1921, is viewed as a major representation of the enactment of traditional and inherent masculinity in the game (Harris, 2001). According to Cox and Pringle (2012), two-thirds of ruling national football associations both in Europe and worldwide banned women's football and forbade young girls to play in teams alongside boys during the first half of the 20th century. The ban was maintained in many countries until late 1960s, contributing to making women's football economically and politically marginalised for many years (Williams, 2011).

The involvement of women in non-playing roles in football has also been difficult, with research indicating that women have had limited opportunities to occupy administrative, coaching and leadership positions in the sport industry in general (Burton, 2015; Hancock & Hums, 2016; Norman et al., 2018; Welford, 2011). Leaving little or no space for women to participate in the evolution of the sport allowed hegemonic masculinity to be embedded within football culture (Connell, 1987, 2009; Knoppers, 2011). This situation has favoured the emergence of dominance and paternalism by men in their interactions with women in football (Allison, 2017; Sibson, 2010; Washington & Patterson, 2011). Therefore, advancements of women's football are often discussed as manifestations to politically challenge gender roles in favour of equality.

Post-ban institutional recovery

The persistence of women in the second-wave feminist movement of the 1960s influenced the lives of women in many domains, including their involvement in sport (Pope, 2011). Women's football has not progressed at the same pace worldwide. However, it can be argued that the 1970s triggered a recovery process at the institutional level. The 1971 Union of European Football Associations (UEFA) Extraordinary Congress in Monte Carlo represented a particularly important turning point for this process to begin, as most European national associations agreed to take the women's game back under their control. Prominent scholars discuss that football institutions continued to be active, historical opponents of the game for decades following the lift of the formal ban (Giulianotti, 1999; Williams, 2007).

Nonetheless, after years of isolation and hostility, this decision formed an initial basis for women's football to develop from organisational, managerial and technical perspectives.

During the late 1960s and early 1970s, women's national teams started to be established across the globe. Concomitantly, the launch of international competitions contributed to fuel the worldwide expansion of the game. For example the first non-official Women's European Championship in 1969 and the first non-official Women's World Cup in 1970 were organised in Italy. These were followed by unofficial international tournaments in Mexico in 1971 and the Mundialito in the 1980s. In Asia, a competition between 12 national teams was set up in 1975 by the Asian Ladies Football Confederation (later merged with the Asian Football Confederation [AFC]). The Oceania Football Confederation (OFC) Women's Nations Cup (previously named OFC Women's Championship) was established in 1983 with four teams qualifying to the final stage. In Europe, the first edition of the UEFA Women's European Championship (now the UEFA Women's European Championships) was played in 1984. Four years later, in 1988, the Fédération Internationale de Football Association (FIFA) organised an invitational tournament in China to test the viability of the first Women's World Cup with 12 national teams taking part in the competition (four from UEFA, three from AFC, two from the Confederation of North, Central America and Caribbean Association Football [CONCACAF] and one each from the Confederación Sudamericana de Fútbol [CONMEBOL], the Confédération Africaine de Football [CAF] and OFC). The opening match between China and Canada attracted 45,000 spectators and the average crowd for the competition reached about 20,000 spectators per match. The first official edition of the FIFA Women's World Cup was finally inaugurated in 1991. In the same year, the CAF started the African Women Cup of Nations, the CONCACAF established its Women's Championship, and the CONMEBOL introduced the Copa Américana Femenina (previously known as Campeonato Sudamericano de Fútbol Femenino).

Following the organisation of the first FIFA Women's World Cup, the women's game continued its progress in terms of recognition at the institutional level when the women's football tournament was added to the 1996 Olympic Games in Atlanta. This addition made women's national football teams gain more serious consideration by the public and the media. Furthermore, with the possibility of obtaining prestige and political credit through women's football in the Olympic Games, governments in many countries decided to support women's football in terms of budget and training provision.

Towards the globalisation of women's football in the modern era

The globalisation of women's football has been markedly underway in the last two decades. In its reports, FIFA (2019, 2022) indicates that over 13 million girls and women play organised football worldwide, 73% of its member associations have an active senior women's national team and 90% of top-tier women's football leagues follow a written strategy. Contributing to the process of globalisation, footballers in the women's game now move within and between continents, which results in an increase in the flow of capital, a higher number of transfers with fees and ultimately a larger overall spending at the global level (FIFA, 2022). Similarly, the flow of information, images and media content relating to women's football have reached an all-time high, with the 2019 FIFA Women's World Cup in France attracting over one billion viewers worldwide (FIFA, 2019). Finally, the expanded competition format seen at the 2023 FIFA Women's World Cup in Australia and New Zealand (from 24 to 36 teams) signals the entrance of women's football in a "modern era" and phase of starting globalisation.

Alongside international women's football gaining global momentum, considerable transformations are also seen at the club level. In Europe, in 2001–02, UEFA pioneered the launch of a continental club competition, the Women's Cup, a pan-European tournament for the best women's football clubs. In 2009, the competition was rebranded as the UEFA Women's Champions League and started including more entrants from the top eight European nations (the top 12 since 2016). In the same year, CONMEBOL incepted the Copa Libertadores Femenina for women's football clubs in South America. In Asia, the AFC launched the Women's Club Championship in 2019 as a pilot tournament for top Asian women's football clubs. The format was changed in 2023 to an invitation tournament, and in 2024 it is being replaced by the AFC Women's Champions League. In Africa, the CAF has been organising its version of the Champions League for the top eight clubs from the six CAF zones since 2021–22. In Oceania, the OFC announced that the first edition of the Women's Champions League is set to start in 2023. Finally, in 2022, FIFA announced plans to establish a FIFA Women's Club World Cup, although to date the FIFA Council has not yet officially approved the launch of the competition.

Overall, this progress provides ground to suggest that women's football has finally reached a stage of starting globalisation. However, despite the rapid expansion of women's football in recent years, the question of whether the women's game can be viewed as a truly global sport has remained the subject of much debate. The growth of women's football is mainly dominated by Western football organisations, with the international rank order of nations in the women's game reflecting power blocs along political, economic and cultural lines (Culvin & Bowes, 2023; Liston, 2023). These blocs position Western European and North American countries at the centre of the scene; Australia, Brazil, countries with former socialist governments and emerging nations (e.g. China and North Korea) represent the semi-periphery, whilst African countries form the periphery of women's football. A similar trend is also observed in academic literature where most research into women's football is predominantly informed by academics and contexts from Europe and the United States (Thomson et al., 2022; Valenti et al., 2018).

The global organisation of women's football

The role of (inter)national governing bodies

Institutions, and the policies that they formulate, play a key role in altering conceptions and influencing public attitudes and perceptions (Soss & Schram, 2007). In football, the role of governing bodies and policymakers, such as FIFA and its member confederations, resembles that of social institutions and is thus decisive for the advancement of women's football due to it being positioned within a complex and gendered environment (Allison, 2016, 2017; Pfister, 2010). In this respect, Gammelsæter and Senaux (2011) posed two critical questions on the role played by (inter)national football institutions in fostering the growth of women's football: (1) Is the recent development of women's football a result of the general shift towards a more "gender-neutral" society, or (2) is it an attempt by governing bodies to extend their influence beyond men's football, presenting themselves as promoters of sport-for-all?

The development of women's football in the last decade has seen active participation from FIFA and its confederations, as evident in their respective strategic plans (AFC, 2014, 2019; CAF, 2020; CONCACAF, 2019; CONMEBOL, 2020; FIFA, 2018; OFC, 2021; UEFA, 2019), which contributed to the setting of guiding principles and supporting transformations in the sporting, governance and commercial dimensions of the game. Interestingly, juxtaposing women's football strategies of FIFA and its confederations, five common goals can be identified: (1) increase participation; (2) change perception; (3) enhance visibility and commercial value; (4) professionalise standards and conditions for administrators, coaches, players and referees; and (5) increase representation of women and girls. As such, international football-governing bodies highlight their role as agents for change in relation to issues that women's football and its stakeholders face off the pitch. They clearly recognise their actions as being intertwined with broader societal concerns such as power, ethics or institutional behaviour and governance, by utilising keywords such as "gender balance", "empowerment", "social impact", which are typical of political and social institutions. Yet, while the recent, shifted focus of football institutions towards the women's game certainly represents a positive improvement globally, it is important to note that when it comes to a discussion of, for instance, the allocation of resources, sex disparity continues to be a prominent issue within the football world. For instance, the Equal Pay legal claim launched by the United States' Women's National Team in 2016 contributed to raising public attention on the pay gap that exists between the men's and women's game and to put societal pressure on football stakeholders to improve the standards and conditions for women players (Carrick et al., 2021).

Criticism was directed at FIFA for consistently providing inadequate funding and not properly recognising the value of the women's game. For example the prize money paid to the FIFA Women's World Cup has historically been considerably lower than that for the men's tournament. Also, FIFA used to bundle the rights of both women's and men's tournaments together and sold these as a package to broadcasters and other commercial entities. As such, this meant that there has never been a true valuation of the FIFA Women's World Cup as a stand-alone product, which instead has been offered to broadcasters as an add-on to the Men's World Cup for decades. Another key area of concern was raised by the Fédération Internationale des Associations de Footballeurs Professionnels (FIFPro, 2022) about the scheduling of international football, which has resulted in tensions between clubs and national teams over the release of players for international matches amid fears for their health and welfare. In an attempt to respond to some of these concerns, FIFA announced that the prize money for the Women's World Cup 2023 will total $110 million (FIFA, 2023), a significant increase for the women's game if compared to the $30 million and $15 million awarded in 2019 and 2015 editions, respectively. Moreover, FIFA doubled the sums allocated to preparation money (from $12 million in 2019 to $31 million in 2023) and the Club Benefits Programme (from $8 million in 2019 to $11 million in 2023). Finally, after his re-election in March 2023, the FIFA President Gianni Infantino called for broadcasters and sponsors to offer more lucrative deals for the rights to broadcast the FIFA Women's World Cup 2023, and committed to have equality in prize money for the next editions of the FIFA Men's and Women's World Cups.

The commercialisation of women's football

Women's football has regularly been considered as the "Next Big Thing" (Williams, 2006, p. 157) and yet finds itself in a period of transition in terms of commercialisation and financial sustainability. In 2016, FIFA noted that, despite significant growth, "the women's game has not yet realised its full potential" (p. 36). In a similar line, UEFA (2022) indicated that matchday revenue for domestic club games continues to be "inconsistent and relatively low" (p. 27). To explain how sports break through society's sports culture and become commercialised, Markovits and Hellerman (2001) put forward the notion of "sport space" as culturally contested territories where each "new" sport can only be accommodated once space has been made available by another "departing" sport. Above all, timing matters immensely. However, sport spaces are not filled simply on a first-come-first-served basis, but rather disputed by social groups and actors with particular sets of interests. In this respect, after a historical period of complete neglect, the overall positioning and accelerating commercial value of women's football in the global sport marketplace is reflective of changing power relations and ideological views, which gradually has led to emerging commodification for revenue generation in more recent years.

Currently, the financial structure of women's football clubs is mainly based on private donations and subscriptions, while a much less substantial contribution comes from prize money and gate receipts (European Club Association

[ECA,], 2014; FIFPro, 2017; Valenti, 2019). If we refer to models of finance prevailing in professional men's team sports (Andreff, 2017; Andreff & Staudohar, 2000), most women's football clubs are close to the so-called SSSL model (Spectators-Subsidies-Sponsors-Local) with the peculiarity of having a relatively smaller share for spectators. However, the rapidly expanding fan base of women's football is resulting in new revenue opportunities, driving commercial growth and providing the momentum towards further professionalisation and commercialisation of the sport (UEFA, 2022). In its 2022 report, FIFA indicated that between 2021 and 2022 the number of leagues with a title sponsor had grown by 11 percentage points, and that clubs had recorded year-on-year commercial revenue growth of 33%. Also, UEFA (2022) defined the current and potential future value of women's club football in Europe with commercial value being forecasted to an estimated €686 million by 2033 and the value of club sponsorship set to potentially increase sixfold in the next decade.

Women's football is now visible and building its own identity, with right holders seeking to unbundle the women's game from the men's product. As the sports industry moves towards an evolving direct-to-consumer media landscape and over-the-top (OTT) streaming services, digital and social media represent an opportunity for greater coverage of women's sports (Cooky et al., 2021). For example in 2016 the Swedish women's top tier, Damallsvenskan, launched its own free-mium streaming service to expand the league's audience reach. In England, the FA made the Women's Super League games available to livestream via the FA Player subscription streaming service before signing a deal with pay TV broadcaster Sky Sports and the BBC's free-to-air service in 2021. Following a similar approach, the OTT sports streaming service DAZN and the online video-sharing platform YouTube partnered with UEFA to stream the UEFA Women's Champions League fixtures live and free globally. In 2022, FIFA launched the platform FIFA+, offering over 100 free, live matches every week, including women's football games from leagues that do not have a TV broadcast deal in place.

Overall, increasingly higher media coverage contributes to the more general expansion of the social, cultural and economic significance of the game in the global context. Nonetheless, there are still substantial differences across countries and regions of the world in terms of how the marketisation of the game is progressing. This condition has inevitable impacts on the lives of players and the general pathway of the sport, also depending on how commercialisation manifests itself in a gendered environment such as that of women's football.

Towards "universal" football clubs

Over the last 15 years, several professional men's clubs have entered the women's football sector by establishing a link with and/or integrating women's team into their ownership structures. Collaborations with men's clubs are often associated with enhanced professionalisation, visibility and participation for women's football. As such, governing bodies aim to encourage men's clubs to embrace women's and girls' football (UEFA, 2019). Some national football associations (e.g. Brazil, China, Italy) and confederations (e.g. CONMEBOL) have even implemented a policy requiring men's clubs to invest in women's football as part of their licensing criteria in an attempt to build capacity and improve the conditions of women's football in their respective territories (Valenti et al., 2021).

Six distinct types of organisational structure exist in European women's football, depending on the level of involvement between men's and women's teams of the same club (Valenti, 2019; Welford, 2018). These range from "two separate entities with very little involvement" to "integrated at all levels with joint organisational structures". Among the areas that most integrated clubs usually share is the *identity*, meaning that both men's and women's teams play under the same crest and with the same colours. In this way, clubs can be recognised *universally*, regardless of whether their teams compete in men's or women's football. For example the recent launch of women's teams by long-standing men's clubs with considerable international reach, such as Juventus (Italy), Real Madrid (Spain) and Manchester United (England), epitomises such attempts by these clubs to becoming truly universal brands in both men's and women's football.

Among the factors influencing the decision of men's football clubs to start a women's section are institutional pressures (e.g. from local governments), the need to comply with regulation standards (e.g. licensing criteria), instrumental motives (e.g. opportunity to increase financial and non-financial performance), normative considerations (e.g. sense of responsibility and duty) and internal capabilities (e.g. slack resources and organisational values) (Valenti, 2019). Moreover, professional football clubs indicate that their organisation benefits from having a women's football section in various ways. These benefits include enhanced image, brand strength and reputation, increased attractiveness to new investors and the opportunity to reach an audience that encompasses potential fans with various interests and backgrounds (Valenti, 2019). Also, football-club executives argue that having a women's football section as part of the club improves the club's organisational capabilities and individual employees' development, particularly for areas relating to increased awareness among both playing and non-playing members about broader societal and gender issues (Valenti, 2019).

A long-lasting debate exists around the issue of integration in sport (Hargreaves, 1990) and on whether the development of women's football should be tied to the men's game (Welford, 2018; Woodhouse et al., 2019). Associating women's football with the men's game arguably results in a scenario where the women's game is provided the resources by the men's game to try and "catch up" in what remains a male preserve. This implies women's football potentially being seen as the "big brother's little sister" (Woodhouse et al., 2019). Also, with men's clubs entering the women's football market, similar financial and sporting inequalities displayed in the men's game risk being replicated in the women's sector. Notably, in the absence of training compensation and solidarity mechanism, a major threat posed by this scenario is market polarisation; the more dominant men's clubs from the more powerful football nations "cannibalise" the women's game at the expense of clubs and nations with limited resources in men's, and consequently, women's football (LTT Sports, 2020). Valenti et al. (2023) confirmed the existence of this scenario empirically as they show a clear domination by women's teams that are integrated in ownership structures of men's clubs based in the Big-Five leagues in the context of the UEFA Women's Champions League.

Concluding remarks: recommendations for the future of women's football

Football still represents a typical example of a strongly biased and gendered environment in many countries of the world. Therefore, the recent evolution of women's football at the global level may be best understood through gender and political lenses. The changing normative expectations from supranational political organisations about the role of sport-governing bodies in the fight against gender and sex inequalities has created pressure for entities such as FIFA and its member confederations to implement initiatives that fundamentally improve the positioning of the women's game. Overall, women's football has reached a phase of preliminary and uneven globalisation, although the sport continues to face challenges in terms of financial sustainability and commercial value at both international and club levels. Thus, given the current scenario, it is critical to pose a question as to whether women's football should seek to follow the path that will likely lead to hyper-commodification (with the related issues that this can generate), or instead, identify and follow a business model that features a different set of values compared to the one that is typical of men's professional sports. If the objective of football-governing bodies is to foster a sustainable and viable growth of the women's game, it is important that a co-ordinated approach is taken to improve the conditions and standards for women players, including the scheduling of the international match calendar and their remuneration scheme. Finally, there is a need to establish financial redistribution models and mechanisms, including solidarity payments and training compensation, to help protect clubs with no links to men's professional sides and/or that are based in relatively smaller football markets, which otherwise risk disappearing.

References

Allison, R. (2016). Business or cause? Gendered institutional logics in women's professional soccer. *Journal of Sport and Social Issues*, *40*(3), 237–262. https://doi.org/10.1177/0193723515615349

Allison, R. (2017). From oversight to autonomy: Gendered organizational change in women's soccer. *Social Currents*, *4*(1), 71–86. https://doi.org/10.1177/2329496516651637

Andreff, W. (2017). Le modèle économique du football Européen, *Pôle Sud. Revue de Science Politique de l'Europe Méridionale*, *47*(2), 41–59.

Andreff, W., & Staudohar, P. (2000). The evolving European model of professional sports finance. *Journal of Sports Economics*, *1*(3), 257–276. https://doi.org/10.1177/1527002 50000100304

Asian Football Confederation. (2014, March). *Women's strategic plan 2013–2019 unveiled.* https://www.the-afc.com/en/about_afc/technical/womens_football/news/womens_strategic_plan_2013-2019_unveiled.html

Asian Football Confederation. (2019, September). *Development programmes continue to strengthen AFC member associations.* https://www.the-afc.com/en/more/news/development_programmes_continue_to_strengthen_afc_member_associations.html

Bridgewater, S. (2018). Women and football. In S. Chadwick, D. Parnell, P. Widdop, & C. Anagnostopoulos (Eds.), *Routledge handbook of football business and management* (pp. 351–365). Routledge.

Burton, L. J. (2015). Underrepresentation of women in sport leadership: A review of research. *Sport Management Review*, *18*(2), 155–165. https://doi.org/10.1016/j.smr.2014.02.004

Carrick, S., Culvin, A., & Bowes, A. (2021). The butterfly effect? Title IX, the USWNT and the continued fight for gender equality. *Journal of Legal Aspects of Sport*, *31*(2), 289–311. https://doi.org/10.18060/25604

Caudwell, J. (2011). Gender, feminism and football studies, *Soccer & Society*, *12*(3), 330–344. https://doi.org/10.1080/14660970.2011.568099

Confédération Africaine de Football. (2020, July). *#ItsTimeItsNow for CAF women's football strategy.* https://www.cafonline.com/news-center/news/itstimeitsnow-for-caf-womens-football-strategy

Confederación Sudamericana de Fútbol. (2020, September). *El futbol es futbol.* https://www.conmebol.com/el-futbol-es-futbol/

Confederation of North, Central America and Caribbean Association Football. (2019, June). *CONCACAF announces strategic plan to develop women's football.* https://www.concacaf.com/article/concacaf-announces-strategic-plan-to-develop-women-s-football/

Connell, R. (1987). *Gender and power*. Allen and Unwin.

Connell, R. (2009). *Short introductions: Gender*. Polity Press.

Cooky, C., Council, L. D., Mears, M. A., & Messner, M. A. (2021). One and done: The long eclipse of women's televised sports, 1989–2019. *Communication & Sport*, *9*(3), 347–371. https://doi.org/10.1177/21674795211003524

Cooper, C. (2023). A reflection on contemporary myths of women's football: A historical analysis. *Accounting, Auditing & Accountability Journal*, *37*(2), 661–671. https://doi.org/10.1108/AAAJ-06-2022-5886

Cox, B., & Pringle, R. (2012). Gaining a foothold in football: A genealogical analysis of the emergence of the female footballer in New Zealand. *International Review for the Sociology of Sport*, *47*(2), 217–234. https://doi.org/10.1177/10126902114032

Culvin, A., & Bowes, A. (2023). Introduction: Women's football in a global, professional era. In A. Culvin & A. Bowes (Eds.), *Women's football in a global, professional era* (pp. 1–13). Emerald Publishing. https://doi.org/10.1108/978-1-80071-052-820230001

Devonport, T. J., Russell, K., Leflay, K., & Conway, J. (2018). Gendered performances and identity construction among UK female soccer players and netballers: A comparative study. *Sport in Society*, *22*(7), 1–17. https://doi.org/10.1080/17430437.2018.1504773

Dumas, E. (2019). *Le "football féminin": L'autre histoire du football*. Observatoire Géostratégique du Sport, IRIS.

European Club Association. (2014, May). *Women's club football analysis.* https://www.ecaeurope.com/media/1649/womens-club-football-analysis.pdf

FIFA. (2016, December). *FIFA 2.0: The vision for the future.* https://www.sportanddev.org/sites/default/files/downloads/fifa_2.0._the_vision_for_the_future.pdf

FIFA. (2018, December). *Women's football strategy*. https://resources.fifa.com/image/upload/women-s-football-strategy.pdf?cloudid=z7w21ghir8jb9tguvbcq

FIFA. (2019, June). *Women's football: Member associations survey report*. https://img.fifa.com/image/upload/nq3ensohyxpuxovcovj0.pdf

FIFA. (2022, August). *Women's football: Setting the pace*. https://digitalhub.fifa.com/m/70a3f8fbc383b284/original/FIFA-Benchmarking-Report-Womens-Football-Setting-the-pace-2022_EN.pdf

FIFA. (2023, March). *Gianni Infantino announces significant investment increase for FIFA Women's World Cup*. https://www.fifa.com/womens-football/news/gianni-infantino-announces-significant-investment-increase-for-fifa-womens

FIFPro. (2017, December). *Working conditions in professional women's football*. https://www.fifpro.org/attachments/article/6986/2017%20FIFPro%20Women%20Football%20Global%20Employment%20Report-Final.pdf

FIFPro. (2022, July). *UEFA women's Euro 2022 workload journey report*. https://fifpro.org/media/zjrjmtpi/fifpro-uefa-womens-euro-2022-report-eng.pdf

Gammelsæter, H., & Senaux, B. (2011). Understanding the governance of football across Europe. In H. Gammelsæter & B. Senaux (Eds.), *The organisation and governance of top football across Europe: An institutional perspective* (pp. 268–291). Routledge.

Giulianotti, R. (1999). *Football: A sociology of the global game*. Polity.

Hancock, M. G., & Hums, M. A. (2016). A "leaky pipeline"? Factors affecting the career development of senior-level female administrators in NCAA division I athletic departments. *Sport Management Review*, *19*(2), 198–210. https://doi.org/10.1016/j.smr.2015.04.004

Hargreaves, J. A. (1990). Gender on the sports agenda. *International Review for the Sociology of Sport*, *25*(4), 287–305. https://doi.org/10.1177/10126902900250040

Harris, J. (2001). Playing the man's game: Sites of resistance and incorporation in women's football. *World Leisure Journal*, *43*(4), 22–29. https://doi.org/10.1080/04419057.2001.9674246

Knoppers, A. (2011). Giving meaning to sport involvement in managerial work. *Gender, Work & Organization*, *18*, e1–e22. https://doi.org/10.1111/j.1468-0432.2009.00467.x

Liston, K. (2023). Power at play—women's football commercialisation as a sociological problem. In A. Culvin & A. Bowes (Eds.), *Women's football in a global, professional era* (pp. 175–189). Emerald Publishing. https://doi:10.1108/978-1-80071-052-8202300012

LTT Sports. (2020, November). *COVID Crisis 2020 in football—issue 4: Resilience and mitigation in women's football*. https://lttsports.com/Executive-Summary-Covid-Impact-on-Football.pdf

Macbeth, J. (2002). The development of women's football in Scotland. *Sports Historian*, *22*(2), 149–163. https://doi.org/10.1080/17460260209443387

Markovits, A. S., & Hellerman, S. L. (2001). *Offside: Soccer and American exceptionalism*. Princeton University Press.

Norman, L., Rankin-Wright, A. J., & Allison, W. (2018). It's a concrete ceiling; It's not even glass: Understanding tenets of organizational culture that supports the progression of women as coaches and coach developers. *Journal of Sport and Social Issues*, *42*(5), 393–414. https://doi.org/10.1177/0193723518790086

Oceania Football Confederation. (2021, July). *All in: OFC Women's football strategy 2027*. https://www.oceaniafootball.com/cms/wp-content/uploads/2021/07/All-IN-OFC-Womens-Football-Strategy-compressed.pdf

Pfister, G. (2010). Women in sport: Gender relations and future perspectives, *Sport in Society: Culture, Commerce, Media, Politics*, *13*(2), 234–248. https://doi.org/10.1080/17430430903522954

Pope, S. (2011). "Like pulling down Durham cathedral and building a brothel": Women as "new consumer" fans? *International Review for the Sociology of Sport*, *46*(4), 471–487. https://doi.org/10.1177/1012690210384652

Sibson, R. (2010). "I was banging my head against a brick wall": Exclusionary power and the gendering of sport organizations. *Journal of Sport Management, 24*(4), 379–399. https://doi.org/10.1123/jsm.24.4.379

Skogvang, B. O. (2019). Scandinavian women's football: The importance of male and female pioneers in the development of the sport. *Sport in History, 39*(2), 207–228. https://doi.org/10.1080/17460263.2019.1618389

Soss, J., & Schram, S. F. (2007). A public transformed? Welfare reform as policy feedback. *American Political Science Review, 101*(1), 111–127. https://doi.org/10.1017/S0003055407070049

Thomson, A., Hayes, M., Hanlon, C., Toohey, K., & Taylor, T. (2022). Women's professional sport leagues: A systematic review and future directions for research. *Sport Management Review, 26*(1), 48–71. https://doi.org/10.1080/14413523.2022.2066391

Union of European Football Associations. (2019, May). *#TimeForAction women's football strategy 2019–24.* https://www.uefa.com/MultimediaFiles/Download/uefaorg/Womensfootball/02/60/51/38/2605138_DOWNLOAD.pdf

Union of European Football Associations. (2022, August). *The business case for women's football.* https://editorial.uefa.com/resources/0278-15e121074702-c9be7dcd0a29-1000/business_case_for_women_s_football-_external_report_1_.pdf

Valenti, M. (2019). *Exploring club organisation structures in European women's football.* https://uefaacademy.com/wp-content/uploads/sites/2/2019/07/2019_UEFA-RGP_Final-report_Valenti-Maurizio.pdf

Valenti, M., Peng, Q., & Rocha, C. (2021). Integration between women's and men's football clubs: A comparison between Brazil, China and Italy. *International Journal of Sport Policy and Politics, 13*(2), 321–339. https://doi.org/10.1080/19406940.2021.1903967

Valenti, M., Scelles, N., & Morrow, S. (2018). Women's football studies: An integrative review. *Sport, Business and Management: An International Journal, 8*(5), 511–528. https://doi.org/10.1108/SBM-09-2017-0048

Valenti, M., Scelles, N., & Morrow, S. (2023). The impact of "super clubs" on uncertainty of outcome in the UEFA Women's Champions League. *Soccer & Society, 24*(4), 509–519. https://doi.org/10.1080/14660970.2023.2194514

Washington, M., & Patterson, K. D. W. (2011). Hostile takeover or joint venture: Connections between institutional theory and sport management research. *Sport Management Review, 14*(1), 1–12. https://doi.org/10.1016/j.smr.2010.06.003

Welford, J. (2011). Tokenism, ties and talking too quietly: Women's experiences in non-playing football roles. *Soccer & Society, 12*(3), 365–381. https://doi.org/10.1080/14660970.2011.568103

Welford, J. (2018). Outsiders on the inside: Integrating women's and men's football clubs in England. In G. Pfister & S. Pope (Eds.), *Female football players and fans: Intruding into a man's world* (pp. 103–124). Palgrave Macmillan.

Williams, J. (2006). An equality too far? Historical and contemporary perspectives of gender inequality in British and international football. *Historical Social Research, 31*(1), 151–169.

Williams, J. (2007). *A beautiful game: International perspectives on women's football.* Berg.

Williams, J. (2011). *Women's football, Europe and professionalization 1971–2011.* https://www.dora.dmu.ac.uk/bitstream/handle/2086/5806/Woman%27s%20football,%20Europe%20%26%20professionalization%201971-2011.pdf?sequence=1

Woodhouse, D., Fielding-Loyd, B., & Sequerra, R. (2019). Big brother's little sister: The ideological construction of Women's Super League. *Sport in Society, 22*(12), 2006–2023. https://doi.org/10.1080/17430437.2018.1548612

2

ADVANCING WOMEN'S FOOTBALL THROUGH STRATEGIC HOLISTIC WORKFORCE DEVELOPMENT

Payment, conditions and policies

Beth G. Clarkson and Ali Bowes

Introduction

The market for labour in women's football is high with the game fast growing; the Union of European Football Associations (UEFA) predicts the commercial annual value to surpass €686 million over the next decade (UEFA, 2022). During this pivotal expansion period, a talented and skilled playing workforce is needed to create a sustainable and successful women's football industry. Utilising data from two (semi-)professional footballers from England (pseudonyms are used), examples of existing policies and the emerging body of literature, we argue, for appropriate workplace conditions, now more than ever. The talent and skill of the playing workforce in women's football must also be combined with appropriate and sustainable payment conditions (e.g. wages and performance bonuses), working conditions (e.g. training facilities, travel and living arrangements) and workplace policies (e.g. maternity and motherhood, safeguarding) that place players at the centre of policy decisions to realise the economic potential UEFA predicted. Furthermore, a virtuous circle exists where player talent and skill are inextricably linked to player welfare and development, and arguably are collective signs of a well-functioning, strong workforce.

In England, three pivotal changes arguably indicate economic growth and the positive trajectory for the financial landscape of women's football: (1) The England national team won the UEFA 2022 European Championship tournament for the first time in their history, sparking widespread media interest; (2) the Women's Super League (WSL), the top-tier of women's football in England, has operated as a fully professional league since 2018–19, with the second-tier Women's Championship increasingly professionalising during this time period; and (3) Income

DOI: 10.4324/9781003381914-2

streams have diversified and grown from crucial commercial, sponsorship and broadcasting partnership agreements (Clarkson et al., 2023). This evolution has brought multiple positive remuneration changes for the footballers, including where the increased professionalism of the WSL has meant that footballers are now offered competitive, full-time wages. Football is a realisable career goal for girls in youth academies.

Players, scholars and journalists continue to advocate for, and hold governing bodies to account on, long-standing, working-condition issues (e.g. training facilities, travel and living arrangements) and lack of workplace policies (e.g. maternity and motherhood, safeguarding) that have not been fully resolved. As an illustration of this advocacy, the media have been heavily critical of subpar pitches within the WSL as one of the potential contributing factors to the large number of anterior-cruciate ligament (ACL) knee injuries seen in women's football in the 2023–24 season. Poor-quality training pitches have been identified by researchers as a significant injury risk factor in women's football (Geertsema et al., 2021). One outlet, "The Athletic", described the real impact of WSL player ACL injuries as "unemployment, isolation and no insurance" (Whyatt, 2023). Similarly, there is a varied body of research conducted within women's football to understand women's football power structures. Some of this work has served to amplify voices within existing patriarchal constraints, to highlight issues with payment and working conditions (Culvin, 2023), and to ultimately better inform the development and implementation of workplace policies. Women footballers are also leveraging their newly platformed voices to challenge inadequate working conditions and remuneration issues in traditional and social media spaces. How football-governing bodies address the needs of women footballers must therefore evolve, particularly considering this newfound spotlight on long-standing, gender-specific issues from multiple stakeholders, including the workforce themselves. While pregnancy discrimination is defined as a sex issue in the UK Equality Act 2010, it cannot be extricated from the extremely gendered inequalities in the organisation and institution of football (Bryan et al., 2021; Clarkson et al., 2023), and we argue the lack of workplace policy implementation by a male-dominated, hierarchical system is a gender issue.

Professional women footballers as a workforce are compromised by the juxtaposition of, for many in the game, inadequate working conditions and precarious financial health alongside an influx of fan interest, broadcasting agreements and league/club sponsorship deals. Some high-profile, international footballers secure individual sponsorship and endorsement deals; however, these arrangements are in the minority of the broader workforce. Without the players, leagues do not exist and unlike their counterparts, women footballers have typically played a vital, visible role in resolving working conditions and pay disputes. For example professional footballers competing in the National Women's Soccer League (NWSL) in the United States had to push the agenda via open media statements to demand that the league launch an independent investigation into abusive working conditions

(Reavis et al., 2022). Similarly, England's goalkeeper Mary Earps spoke publicly about a lack of equality from the national team's kit manufacturer Nike after goalkeeper jerseys were not made available for sale, later causing a U-turn. In the case of Mary Earps, this decision to speak publicly was because she had been "fighting behind closed doors" to find a solution with Nike and that she had "been trying to go through the correct channels as much as possible, which is why [she had] not spoken on it publicly" (Wrack, 2023a, para. 4). These examples are indicative of women footballers feeling or being required to advocate for change when perceived inequalities are not addressed within existing power structures.

As two current professional footballers explain in their own words, the consequences of the broader cultures of elite-level football, alongside current policies and policy decisions on the women's game (e.g. equal-pay policies, investment in facilities, maternity policies and safeguarding and player welfare), are very real. Women footballers can experience poor pay and benefits, inadequate training and match facilities, underfunded club staffing and even homelessness in extreme cases (see Notts County collapse in 2017, "Notts County Ladies", 2017) when ineffective (or perceived lack of) decisions are made at a governance level concerning the workforce. The UK Government's (2023) "Raising the Bar" review into women's football, led by former player Karen Carney, MBE, highlighted the potential for women's football to be "a billion-pound industry" (MacInnes, 2023, para. 9) as well as the financial investment required to raise standards. To raise player salary floors (i.e. a club requirement to pay players at least the UK Living Wage) or mental and physical health provisions (i.e. full-time, dedicated physiotherapists and psychologists) require greater income than some clubs currently generate through matchday, commercial and broadcasting revenue streams (Philippou, 2023). Club revenue in the WSL has increased 590% since the league was formed; however so too has club debt (1,351%), which has outstripped increases (Clarkson et al., 2023). Accordingly, we argue that strategic considerations are regulated and mandated to hold governing bodies accountable to better support women footballers, as standards remain disproportionately low.

Aims of the chapter

In this chapter, we summarise key issues for the strategic, holistic development of women footballers including payment conditions, working conditions, workplace policies in maternity and motherhood, and player welfare and safeguarding. To do so, we do the following:

(1) Examine current policies alongside key industry insights and research findings.
(2) Highlight the real-world impact of policy decisions on the lives of two current professional women footballers.
(3) Provide a summary of key holistic workforce-development considerations that could advance women's football.

Critical evaluation of evidence

Payment conditions

One of the biggest recent shifts in the women's game in England has been the organisation of the professional and semi-professional league structure, and subsequently opportunities for football to exist as work for women (Culvin, 2023; Culvin & Bowes, 2023; Williams, 2011). However, as the structuring of women's football becomes increasingly professionalised, discussions have shifted towards pushing for equitable payment of players, especially at the international level. Often, these debates have been stimulated by the players themselves in demands for equitable environments in elite sport (Bowes et al., 2023). For example the United States Women's National Soccer Team's (USWNT's) equal pay debate, first launched in 2016, was considered a landmark case for women's football with global implications (Carrick et al., 2021). The 2019 Fédération Internationale de Football Association (FIFA) Women's Football Convention, held before the 2019 Women's World Cup, was convened to discuss the key pillars of the FIFA Women's Football Strategy. One pillar was to establish pay equity with men, which had been absent from the game as it professionalised (FIFA, 2019). Bowes et al. (2023) document numerous international federations that have adopted equal payment of players, in some form, since the USWNT put the issue onto the agenda in women's football (Culvin et al., 2022). In 2023, professional women footballers, backed by the professional players' global union, Fédération Internationale des Associations de Footballeurs Professionnels (FIFPro), demanded equal World Cup prize money. Equal prize pots have since been committed by FIFA by the 2026 and 2027 World Cups with an increasing number of national football associations pledging to equal pay for men and women international footballers (Clarkson et al., 2021; Wrack, 2023b) (also discussed in Chapter 1).

While many leading international teams have adopted equal pay, a FIFPro player survey, completed by 362 international players prior to the 2023 Women's World Cup in Australia and New Zealand, highlighted inequalities within the women's game: 29% of players had not received any payment from their national team, and 66% of players reported having to take unpaid leave or paid leave from another employment to participate in tournaments (FIFPro, 2023). Both South African and Nigerian national teams held boycotts in the weeks leading up to the tournament over withheld payments, outstanding wages and a lack of written agreements over future payments (Michollek, 2023). While equal-pay steps have been made by (predominantly Westernised) national football associations, FIFPro's survey highlights that equitable pay compensation at the international level still has some way to go across the world.

At a club level, pay parity between men and women is a complex phenomenon. Professional football clubs are unlike national football associations that have social and ethical responsibilities to ensure: "football is for all" (see the English Football

Association [the FA] and the Football Association of Ireland [FAI] campaigns). Therefore, the equal pay argument in international football is clearer. Professional football clubs, however, are independent businesses, and more frequently multinational corporations, able to set their own budgets and player salaries. If men's player salaries and other football-related expenditure, like transfer fees, fit within UEFA's Club Licensing and Financial Sustainability Regulations (formerly Financial Fair Play), it is up to each club to determine what a player is paid on the basis of supply and demand. Women's football is an exempt cost from these financial regulations, meaning that European clubs do not incur penalties if women's football-related expenditure (such as salaries and fees) exceeds matchday, broadcasting and commercial income. This situation is, however, complicated by diverse accounting frameworks and limited football-accounting transparency in different countries, depending on the scale of the operation (Wilson & Plumley, 2018). This variance limits the level of transparency required in publicly reporting football club accounts related to the women's team (Clarkson et al., 2023).

In a rare study, in which the focus was on the financial health of any professional women's sports league worldwide, Clarkson et al. (2023) found English women's football exists at an important crossroads with precarious financial health, where the five-year growth of fan interest and commercial revenue streams are juxtaposed with increasing debt and poor financial health. This finding might help explain why women footballers' average annual salaries have only recently become higher than basic living, with estimates ranging from £25,000 to £47,000 (UK Sterling) (Atkin & Thomas-Humphrey, 2023; Read, 2022). Stories of English women footballers being paid £45/week were as recent as six years ago (Moore, 2017). Indeed, when considered against where women footballers' wages have come from, payments have significantly risen. The situation has been helped by the FA's professional club-licensing-criterion requirement for footballers to be on full-time contracts (part-time in the second tier). With the new income from commercial revenue streams—clubs have collectively generated £32 million in the past season (Deloitte, 2023)—players need to be rewarded for growing the game, but the distribution must consider salaries alongside the need to develop talent pathways (for future game success) and for the game to grow in a financially sustainable manner (Philippou, 2022).

Working conditions

While some employment concerns are not limited to women footballers and affect men too (e.g. post-career transition), women face additional precariousness in their working conditions due to vastly lower economic remuneration, poorer access to resources and shorter contract length (Culvin, 2023; FIFPro, 2017). As one player interviewed by Culvin (2023, p. 690) stated, "we're getting told to be professional, but they (club) don't provide us with the means to be professional." For this chapter, the footballer we have named "Hilary" highlighted deficiencies with a minimum requirements-based, club-licensing system:

> There's lots and lots of grey areas that probably need to be ironed out in terms of policy because it stops [at] the access that you have [to have] and other players like you have to [have like] facilities and training.
>
> *(Hilary)*

Women footballers still often receive short-term contracts (FIFPro, 2017), particularly in developing nations, though the practice is still common in countries with more established setups for women, like those seen in England. With player voices amplified in media spaces, as previously discussed, football-governing bodies, leagues and clubs must be cognisant of growing demand for change and the need for higher standards of practice among players and the increased media spotlight, should they not respond to open or closed (via union) concerns. While short-term contracts were a traditionally accepted practice, it is no longer sufficient for footballers to merely tolerate these norms with professionalisation and economic growth of the game. As a current player "Jocelyn" spoke to us, saying this:

> If you are a professional footballer, the bulk of what you do should be football but that isn't the case right now because it's not the reality that we have. So, for me it has to be about a consistent and steady income, and I think part of that has to be about security we probably haven't had previously; but giving [footballers] yearly contracts doesn't give them the kind of security they need to be able to do the life things people need to be able to do.
>
> *(Jocelyn)*

There are also player welfare concerns linked to working conditions. In a study on migration of Nigerian women footballers into Scandinavian football clubs, Engh and Agergaard (2015) uncovered instances of Nigerian players relying on compatriot Nigerian footballers for salary advice and other contractual concerns to translate, explain exchange rates and costs of living: "I don't know anything about money but [Wendy] tried to psych me up . . . to let me know how the money valued with Nigeria money, you know . . . So, it's not easy and I tried to catch up" (Michelle, in Engh & Agergaard, 2015, p. 988).

Short contracts may be perceived to benefit clubs that limit their long-term investment in players (and arguably the women's game), yet short-term player contracts pose strategic challenges to both club and footballer. In the WSL, a gap is starting to emerge between the established, financially stronger and more successful clubs and clubs lower down the table who do not generate as much commercial income and who are more dependent on playing performance for revenue (Clarkson et al., 2023). There is commonly more frequent player turnover in these less successful teams as clubs chase more financially lucrative league positions. Hence, it logistically follows that short-term contracts contribute to a more dynamic and potentially volatile transfer market, disrupting the product of women's football. In the English Women's Championship, the FA's licencing criteria state that clubs must provide a minimum of eight hours a week of player contact, but there is nothing to stop clubs from providing more contact hours. While greater resources in training, infrastructure and staff support are certainly welcomed by players, these are not felt across the league (or perceived down the football pyramid), creating an uneven competitive league balance:

> It's not as easy as just turning up and playing and not having to worry about anything else . . . You've got the top 12 [clubs], who are all contracted professionally and maybe three or four others in the [Women's] Championship at the moment but below that it is exactly the same as it was 10–15 years ago.
>
> *(Hilary)*

Addressing disparities in access to facilities, resources and training schedules is crucial for women footballers, and, as such, policies that centre on quality-assuring player development are strategically needed. At Jocelyn's club, she remarked, "we are very bound" when using the indoor training pitch as it was limited to a single 90-minute slot between the boys' academy evening sessions and closure of the training ground:

> You are constantly fighting against different people in the club to get access to other training slots that are reserved in case of use, preventing us from utilising the space even if we are there and [the other team] are not.
>
> *(Jocelyn)*

Access to training pitches is only part of the problem, as, at some clubs at the top of the women's game in England, footballers train on poor-quality pitches, play on artificial turf and are given inappropriate workloads (i.e. too much training, reduced recovery and hard tackles) that are important risk factors for injuries in women's football (Geertsema et al., 2021). Women footballers risking injury on short-term contracts are in a precarious position, impacting upon future contracts, chances of contract renewal, new contracts at other clubs and in some cases for footballers towards the end of their careers, livelihoods; Jocelyn asked, "Why don't we matter" in reference to this. Travel and accommodation are also particularly important welfare concerns for migrant, diaspora and transnational players (Tiesler, 2016), who have limited-to-no family- and peer-support networks, and these temporary accommodation and travel arrangements are only guaranteed for the length of their contract.

Workplace policies: maternity and motherhood

One of the most pertinent issues emerging in the professional women's game revolves around recognising and addressing the uniquely gendered nature of women as workers, particularly in the context of maternity and motherhood. As Culvin and Bowes (2021) state, "there are very real concerns for the diminished career prospects of professional women footballers who become mothers" (p. 11). Consequently, the number of mothers in the professional game is particularly low and is indicative of the number of mothers in elite sports more broadly (see Chapter 7 on pregnancy and motherhood). In 2007, a survey completed by over 540 elite female athletes in Norway, it was indicated that the number of mothers was only 4% (Bø & Backe-Hansen, 2007). Specifically related to football, based on data from FIFPro (2017), it was reported that only 2% of elite footballers were mothers and that 47% of footballers felt they would have to leave the game early to start a family. Such challenges are not limited to professional football, with demands experienced by elite athlete mothers being well documented (Roberts & Kenttä, 2018). At the time, the FIFPro report (2017) highlighted that 61% of women players were offered no childcare support, and of the players who had children, only 8% were provided with maternity pay from their National Governing Body or their club, and only 3% were provided with childcare support.

In response to some of these challenges, in 2020 FIFPro published their Player Pregnancy and Parental Management report, in line with the International Labour Organization convention number 183 from 2000. The policy guide outlined directions in both mandatory and guided forms for players and organisations on the contractual requirements and obligations for pregnancy and maternity, aiming to protect players against discrimination (FIFPro, 2020). Minimum conditions were then introduced by FIFA, coming into effect on 1 January 2021, including the following: The player shall be given a minimum 14-week period of maternity leave, of which at least eight weeks must occur after the birth of the child; the player shall be paid at least two-thirds of the salary, and the player is to remain registered (with a club), and, even outside of formal registration periods, is to be registered upon return of the maternity leave, unless mutually agree not to. Following birth, the club should reintegrate the player, whilst also providing medical support and opportunities to breastfeed and/or express milk. Significantly, there is also protection against the presumption that a contract terminated by the club in this period is due to pregnancy or maternity leave (FIFA, 2020). The regulations were described as a "first step", specifically around the length of time afforded to players postpartum (Wrack, 2020).

Even with provisions now in place, there is a need for cultural change in the acceptance of working mothers in football (sport and society more broadly). "Hilary" is a mother and semi-professional footballer who described her club as supportive:

> There's a fair bit going on, but it's all got to fit around my family [if it can]. So, I'm very grateful to [the club] for allowing me to do that with the training and the work side of it as well.
>
> *(Hilary)*

Despite the support of the club, the cultural shift required around motherhood and athletehood was still evident to Hilary:

> But they don't kind of understand that it's not just about training an hour a day. I need to find time to train for however long it is. But I also need to find the time, or I need to find someone else's time to have my kids if they're not at school.
>
> *(Hilary)*

Culvin and Bowes (2021) noted that even if maternity and parental policy were part of player contracts, it is not certain that women who have a desire for motherhood would utilise the policy, given genuine concerns over their bodies and highlighting a perceived incompatibility with motherhood and athletehood. As such, Culvin and Bowes (2021) highlighted three strategies: (1) Research should be conducted to explore and identify the best practice in relation to maternity for professional women's teams; (2) a framework should be developed that includes expected contractual conditions, including the rejection of pregnant women athletes as individualised, one-off success stories; and (3) compatibility of motherhood and athletehood should be advocation through organisations, such as FIFPro and individual unions and clubs.

Workplace policies: player welfare and safeguarding

Recognising the unique challenges that women footballers face in their careers in the male-dominated sport of football, it is important that governing bodies create safe, supportive and inclusive working environments for women footballers. We will refrain from detailing explicit cases to ensure the wellbeing of the reader and avoid potential triggers, appreciating the sensitive content of high-profile examples of some safeguarding issues in women's football. In this section, we focus on the safeguarding, career transitions and healthcare support and measures needed within women's football, aspects that have received limited attention in existing literature.

Public discussions about women's safety in work, public and digital spaces and the safeguarding of girls in schools have heightened awareness of the extent of abuse and harassment across institutions and in public life. The role of sport and exercise is increasingly featured in these conversations about inequality, discrimination, violence and overt and subtle forms of abuse faced by women and girls, mostly through calls for sport to "acknowledge its duty to address the issue of violence against women" (McElwee, 2021, para. 1).

The FA's Safeguarding Framework contains a three-part strategy to safeguard across the game: implementing preventive safeguarding measures (e.g. safer recruitment practices), simplifying reporting mechanisms to make it as easy as possible and ensuring swift safeguarding, child protection and adult-at-risk investigations in conjunction with statutory agencies. However, in Sport England's (2022)

Active Lives Survey, it was revealed that 100,000 more girls were playing football than they were five years previously. Questions of safeguarding in this newly professionalising domain are comparatively under-researched in relation to men's youth football (see Brackenridge et al., 2004; Platts & Smith, 2009). Such research in women's football is especially pressing, given the speed of professionalisation in the game and the aforementioned issues connecting to the inadequacy of gender- and sex-specific policy and practice.

Lewis et al. (2023) highlighted the challenges associated with the cultural climate of *care* (or lack of) in coaching in the context of women's football. They emphasise that the results-driven nature of elite sport can be attributed to a failure of care, or superficial care, for women footballers. Lewis et al. (2023) also noted the coaching challenges involving touch and consent, which can be deemed uncomfortable and intrusive for players. Some issues connected to safeguarding relate to player–coach relationships, a phenomenon seen in women's football readily, notwithstanding the precarious nature of work that is football for women (Culvin, 2023). In a BBC report, the issue of coach–player relationships in women's football was described as inappropriate, due to the power imbalance between the player and the coach, which could lead to a potential abuse of players (Sanders & Magowan, 2022). This "grey area"—which clubs often try to address with codes of conduct—highlights the need for further education within clubs for both players and coaches as they navigate expected and/or accepted standards of behaviour. As it stands, players have a lot to lose, such as their livelihoods, in reporting inappropriate behaviour, and "whistleblowing" is risky business in the context of short-term contracts and with accommodation and travel often bundled in with direct wages for migrant players (Engh & Agergaard, 2015). Clubs need to continue to develop support for players connected to safeguarding, especially around reporting, alongside educating coaching staff on the power dynamics at play.

Summary

In this chapter, we utilise data from two professionalising footballers, examples of existing policies and the emerging body of literature to show that the talent and skill of the playing workforce must also be combined with appropriate payment conditions (e.g. wages and performance bonuses), working conditions (e.g. training facilities, travel and living arrangements) and workplace policies (e.g. maternity and motherhood, safeguarding) that place players at the centre of policy decisions. We recommend that player welfare and development policies be at the centre of strategic workforce development in women's football in a holistic approach that nurtures this talented and skilled playing workforce during this period of economic expansion, given the specific gendered experiences of women working within football.

References

Atkin, E., & Thomas-Humphrey, H. (2023, August 20). How much do women footballers get paid? *The Metro*. https://metro.co.uk/2022/08/01/how-much-do-women-footballers-get-paid-17104639/#:~:text=Women%27s%20Super%20League%20(WSL)%20is,bit%20more%20(£30%2C000)

Bø, K., & Backe-Hansen, K. L. (2007). Do elite athletes experience low back, pelvic girdle and pelvic floor complaints during and after pregnancy? *Scandinavian Journal of Medicine & Science in Sports, 17*(5), 480–487. https://doi.org/10.1111/j.1600-0838.2006.00599.x

Bowes, A., Culvin, A., & Carrick, S. (2023). Equal pay debates in international women's football. In A. Culvin & A. Bowes (Eds.), *Women's football in a global, professional era* (pp. 191–203). Emerald Publishing Limited. https://doi.org/10.1108/978-1-80071-052-820230013

Brackenridge, C., Bringer, J. D., Cockburn, C., Nutt, G., Pitchford, A., Russell, K., & Pawlaczek, Z. (2004). The Football Association's child protection in football research project 2002–2006: Rationale, design and first year results. *Managing Leisure, 9*(1), 30–46. https://doi.org/10.1080/1360671042000182943

Bryan, A., Pope, S., & Rankin-Wright, A. J. (2021). On the periphery: Examining women's exclusion from core leadership roles in the "extremely gendered" organization of men's club football in England. *Gender & Society, 35*(6), 940–970. https://doi.org/10.1177/08912432211046318

Carrick, S., Culvin, A., & Bowes, A. (2021). The butterfly effect? Title IX and the USWNT as catalysts for global equal pay. *Journal of Legal Aspects of Sport, 31*, 289–311. https://doi.org/10.18060/25604

Clarkson, B. G., Culvin, A., & Bowes, A. (2021, November 29). Women in sport are winning the fight for equal pay—slowly. *The Conversation*. https://theconversation.com/women-in-sport-are-winning-the-fight-for-equal-pay-slowly-167943

Clarkson, B. G., Plumley, D., Philippou, C., Wilson, R., & Webb, T. (2023). Money troubles and problems ahead? The financial health of professional women's football clubs in England. *Sport Business Management: An International Journal, 13*(5), 563–581. https://doi.org/10.1108/SBM-10-2022-0088

Culvin, A. (2023). Football as work: The lived realities of professional women footballers in England. *Managing Sport and Leisure, 28*(6), 684–697. https://doi.org/10.1080/23750472.2021.1959384

Culvin, A., & Bowes, A. (2021). The incompatibility of motherhood and professional women's football in England. *Frontiers in Sports and Active Living, 3*, 730151. https://doi.org/10.3389/fspor.2021.730151

Culvin, A., & Bowes, A. (2023). Introduction: Women's football in a global, professional era. In A. Culvin & A. Bowes (Eds.), *Women's football in a global, professional era* (pp. 1–13). Emerald Publishing Limited. https://doi.org/10.1108/978-1-80071-052-820230001

Culvin, A., Bowes, A., Carrick, S., & Pope, S. (2022). The price of success: Equal pay and the US Women's National Soccer Team. *Soccer & Society, 23*(8), 920–931. https://doi.org/10.1080/14660970.2021.1977280

Deloitte. (2023). *A balancing act: Annual review of football finance 2023*. https://www2.deloitte.com/uk/en/pages/sports-business-group/articles/annual-review-of-football-finance-womens-super-league.html

Engh, M. H., & Agergaard, S. (2015). Producing mobility through locality and visibility: Developing a transnational perspective on sports labour migration. *International Review for the Sociology of Sport, 50*(8), 974–992. https://doi.org/10.1177/1012690213509994

FIFA. (2019, June). *FIFA 2019 women's football convention report*. https://digitalhub.fifa.com/m/58527e8c8377de4e/original/m7ocddzbwyocx56tcall-pdf.pdf

FIFA. (2020, November). *Women's football: Minimum labour conditions*. https://digitalhub.fifa.com/m/033101649cc3c480/original/f9cc8eex7qligvxfznbf-pdf.pdf

FIFPro. (2017). 2017 *FIFPro global employment report: Working conditions in professional women's football*. https://fifpro.org/media/3eols2ok/2017-fifpro-women-football l-global-employment-report-final.pdf

FIFPro. (2020). *Player pregnancy & parental management: FIFPro policy guide*. https://fifpro.org/media/z4npufvw/2020-fifpro-parental-policy-guide.pdf

FIFPro. (2023). *Qualifying conditions report: Women's World Cup, Australia and New Zealand*. https://fifpro.org/media/iv2cvxt5/2023-qualifying-conditions-report_en_web.pdf

The Football Association. (2023, April 28). *FA professional game academy licenses awarded to twenty clubs as part of revamped player pathway*. https://www.england-football.com/articles/2023/Apr/28/FA-Professional-Game-Academy-licenses-awarded-to-twenty-clubs-as-part-of-revamped-player-pathway

Geertsema, C., Geertsema, L., Farooq, A., Harøy, J., Oester, C., Weber, A., & Bahr, R. (2021). Injury prevention knowledge, beliefs and strategies in elite female footballers at the FIFA Women's World Cup France 2019. *British Journal of Sports Medicine, 55*(14), 801–806. https://doi.org/10.1136/bjsports-2020-103131

Lewis, C. J., Sawiuk, R., & Grimes, S. M. (2023). "It looks like he cares, but he doesn't": Athletes' experiences of "good" and "bad" care in women's football. *Sports Coaching Review, 12*(1), 108–123. https://doi.org/10.1080/21640629.2022.2045137

MacInnes, P. (2023, July 13). Karen Carney review demands overhaul of women's football to transform future. *The Guardian*. https://www.theguardian.com/football/2023/jul/13/review-women-football-overhaul-future

McElwee, M. (2021, March 31). Sport must acknowledge its duty to address the issue of violence against women. *The Telegraph*. https://www.telegraph.co.uk/football/2021/03/31/sport-must-acknowledge-duty-address-issue-violence-against-women/

Michollek, N. (2023, July 18). Africa's World Cup women raise unfair pay and sexual abuse. *DW*. https://www.dw.com/en/africas-world-cup-women-raise-unfair-pay-and-sexual-abuse/a-66265367

Moore, G. (2017, April 21). Notts County demise places cloud over women's game. *Training Ground Guru*. https://trainingground.guru/articles/notts-county-demise-casts-doubt-on-future-of-womens-game

Notts County ladies "jobless and homeless" as club folds on eve of season. (2017, April 21). *The Guardian*. https://www.theguardian.com/football/2017/apr/21/notts-county-ladies-fold-two-days-before-season

Philippou, C. (2022, August 4). How women's football can avoid being corrupted when more money comes its way. *The Conversation*. https://theconversation.com/how-womens-football-can-avoid-being-corrupted-when-more-money-comes-its-way-188185

Philippou, C. (2023, July 18). How English women's football could become a billion pound industry—and where the money comes from to make it happen. *The Conversation*. https://theconversation.com/how-english-womens-football-could-become-a-billion-pound-industry-and-where-the-money-comes-from-to-make-it-happen-209754

Platts, C., & Smith, A. (2009). The education, rights and welfare of young people in professional football in England: Some implications of the white paper on sport. *International Journal of Sport Policy, 1*(3), 323–339. https://doi.org/10.1080/19406940903265590

Read, S. (2022, August 1). How much do women footballers get paid? *The BBC*. https://www.bbc.co.uk/news/business-62378095

Reavis, C., Springer, S., & Shields, B. (2022). *The national women's soccer league (B): Navigating a crisis, repairing a culture*. https://mitsloan.mit.edu/sites/default/files/2022-05/National%20Women%27s%20Soccer%20League%20%28B%29IC._2.pdf

Roberts, C.-M., & Kenttä, G. (2018). Motherhood in the exercising female. In J. Forsyth & C.-M. Roberts (Eds.), *The exercising female: Science and its application* (pp. 224–235). Routledge. https://doi.org/10.4324/9781351200271-17

Sanders, E., & Magowan, A. (2022, January 28). Why player-coach relationships are an issue in women's football. *The BBC*. https://www.bbc.co.uk/sport/football/59294074

Sport England. (2022, December). *Active lives children and young people survey academic year 2021–22 report.* https://sportengland-production-files.s3.eu-west-2.amazonaws.com/s3fs-public/2022-12/Active%20Lives%20Children%20and%20Young%20People%20Survey%20Academic%20Year%202021-22%20Report.pdf?

Tiesler, N. C. (2016). Three types of transnational players: Differing women's football mobility projects in core and developing countries. *Revista Brasileira de Ciências do Esporte*, *38*(2), 201–210. https://doi.org/10.1016/j.rbce.2016.02.015

UEFA. (2022, August 16). *The business case for women's football.* https://www.uefa.com/insideuefa/news/0278-15e1359d73bf-0abdd5cc60ba-1000-the-business-case-for-women-s-football/

UK Government. (2023). *Raising the bar: Reframing the opportunity in women's football.* https://assets.publishing.service.gov.uk/government/uploads/system/uploads/attachment_data/file/1169802/Raising_the_bar_-_reframing_the_opportunity_in_women_s_football.pdf

Whyatt, K. (2023, October 20). Unemployment, isolation, no insurance—the real impact of ACL injuries in women's football. *The Athletic*. https://theathletic.com/4915085/2023/10/20/acl-injury-crisis-impact-women-female/#

Williams, J. (2011). *Women's football, Europe and professionalization 1971–2011: Global gendered labor markets.* https://uefaacademy.com/wp-content/uploads/sites/2/2019/05/20110622_Williams-Jean_Final-Report.pdf

Wilson, R., & Plumley, D. (2018). Finance and accounting in football. In S. Chadwick, D. Parnell, P. Widdop, & C. Anagnostopoulos (Eds.), *Routledge handbook of football business and management* (pp. 186–198). Routledge. https://doi.org/10.4324/9781351262804

Wrack, S. (2020, November 19). "Only a first step": Mixed reactions as FIFA announces new maternity regulations. *The Guardian*. https://www.theguardian.com/football/2020/nov/19/fifa-announces-new-maternity-regulations-mixed-reaction

Wrack, S. (2023a, July 20). "Very hurtful": Mary Earps angry that fans cannot buy her England shirt. *The Guardian*. https://www.theguardian.com/football/2023/jul/20/mary-earps-angry-england-goalkeeper-shirt-womens-world-cup

Wrack, S. (2023b, March 24). "Collective action works": Is football closing in on equal pay for men and women? *The Guardian*. https://www.theguardian.com/football/2023/mar/24/fifpro-is-football-closing-in-equal-pay-for-men-and-women

3

MATCH DEMANDS AND PHYSIOLOGICAL DETERMINANTS

Naomi Datson, Ross Julian and Barry Drust

Introduction

Performance in football is a function of a combination of different factors that impact overall game performance. An individual's technical and tactical abilities, and their inherent understanding of the "when and where" of these skills, enable players to perform actions and take part in events that ultimately determine the outcome of games. Approaches to determine the physical demands of football can broadly be categorised into observations of match-activity profiles or descriptions of the physical capabilities of players using physical performance tests. While the initial data published in the area may be useful to create a platform to develop understanding, there is clearly a need for more specific, detailed data that create and develop more relevant ways to measure, characterise and ultimately translate information about the women's game. The aim of this chapter is, therefore, to provide useful reference information on the physical demands of women's football. This content will also be critically analysed to suggest current gaps in the available information and to consider the challenges that may make the available data more relevant to applied practice.

Physical match demands

The collection of physical match-performance data is common practice within football environments. The objective data gathered are often used by coaches and practitioners as they attempt to maximise player performance and/or minimise susceptibility to injury or illness. Time-motion analysis is the primary method for collecting physical match-performance data and global positioning systems (GPS) are

DOI: 10.4324/9781003381914-3

likely the most-used method of time-motion analysis in women's football, as the system does not require a specific stadium installation.

Total distance covered during a game is perhaps the most-cited metric when considering player physical performance. Total distance is indicative of volume of activity completed and therefore provides a global representation of a player's overall match physical demands. High-level senior players cover approximately 10 km per match (Ramos et al., 2019), with junior players (under-14 and under-16) covering approximately 7 km (Harkness-Armstrong et al., 2022). However, differences in match duration between junior and senior players, as well as the current tendency for long periods of added time to be played, mean that expressing total distance relative to match duration, that is the intensity metric of metres per minute, may be useful to permit comparisons.

Whilst total distance is a popular metric with coaches, in part due to its intuitive nature, it is often considered more purposeful to examine the distance covered in different activity categories or zones. Determining an appropriate speed threshold for each activity category has long been a discussion point in the women's football literature (Bradley & Vescovi, 2015). There are well-established thresholds in the men's game (Bush et al., 2015); however, the use of these thresholds to quantify women's match-play demands has been criticised due to the known biological differences between the sexes (Bradley & Vescovi, 2015). As a result, authors have used an array of different lower thresholds, often providing little or no justification for the specific threshold selection. The wide range of thresholds used in the literature makes between-study comparisons challenging (Harkness-Armstrong et al., 2022). Practitioners and researchers are advised to reflect on the specific cohort being monitored when selecting suitable thresholds, and to be cautious when making comparisons to other studies/groups (Malone et al., 2017). Regardless of the specific thresholds adopted, players complete more low-speed activity, for example, walking and jogging, compared to high-speed running and sprinting during match-play. Sprints occur intermittently and are typically short in nature, with 95% of all sprints in international match-play being recorded as less than 10 m (Datson et al., 2017). That said, sprints and high-speed activities are often associated with crucial moments within the match and consequently their importance should not be underestimated (Faude et al., 2012).

Another important component that contributes to the overall physical match demand is the requirement for a player to start, stop and change direction. High-level women's football is characterised by changes of activity with ~850 accelerations/decelerations >2 m/s^{-2} reported per match (Mara et al., 2017). The specific pattern of such activities, that is, the volume and intensity of work and rest periods, plays an important role in determining the physiological cost of the activity (Randell et al., 2021). During match-play the average recovery duration is ~40 s; however, a recovery duration of <10 s occurred twice as often as did a recovery duration of more than 30 s (Datson, Drust, et al., 2019). Consequently, awareness of maximum–minimum demands as well as the average is crucial when considering the provision of appropriate training strategies.

Position-specific match demands

Physical match performance profiles vary distinctly between playing positions (Figure 3.1). The physical match profile of the goalkeeper is less well studied; however, clearly their tactical role signifies a different physical profile to that of outfield players.

Variations in performance

The physical requirements of each match are different, with Trewin et al. (2018) highlighting the variability between matches as being 6% for total distance, 33% for high-speed running distance and 53% for sprint efforts. This information highlights the need for practitioners to use objective match-play data to help inform post-match recovery and training strategies. There is also variability within matches, with researchers often illustrating a reduction in total and high-speed running distances within the last 15 min compared to the first 15 min of match-play (Panduro et al., 2022). These changes in a player's physical performance within a match are typically attributed to fatigue; however, full consideration of contextual factors (e.g. playing formation, score line, environmental conditions) is needed prior to forming such conclusions. It should also be considered that, during the

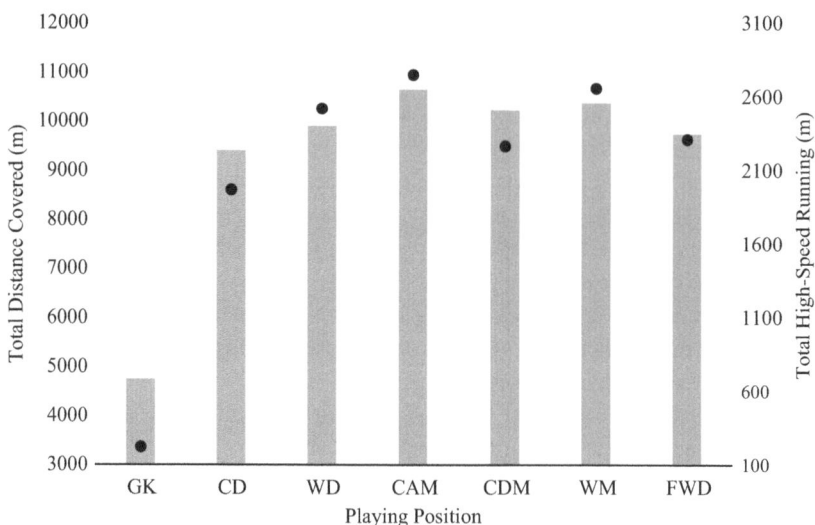

FIGURE 3.1   Physical match performance in elite women football players. Adapted from Scott et al. (2020).

initial stages of a match, teams often try to establish tactical superiority, which may lead to artificially increased values for high-intensity activities during the first 15 min (Weston et al., 2011). These findings challenge the practice of using the opening 15 min of match-play as a "baseline" for physical outputs.

In recent research, there has been a move away from considering the match in fixed epochs, that is, 0–15, 15–30 min, and focus instead has been on examining the peak demands of match-play to better understand the intermittent nature of the game. The most demanding 1-min period in elite women's match-play for total distance covered has been shown to be 168 m/min, and for high-speed running (>15 km/hr) 47 m/min (González-García et al., 2022). These peak periods have been promoted as a useful indicator for training session design; however, in reality, understanding the most challenging period of match-play is complex, as there will likely be large variability and a need to consider contextual factors and multiple variables concurrently (Novak et al., 2021).

Evolution of match demands

Recent data have shown that the physical demands of the women's game are evolving, with teams covering ~30% more distance in the highest speed zone (>23 km/hr) in the 2019 FIFA Women's World Cup compared to that in the 2015 edition (Bradley & Scott, 2020). This increase in physicality is likely due to the rise in the number of players and teams who are now employed on a full-time, professional basis. Regularly monitoring the match physical demands will help ensure the availability of contemporary data that reflect the progressing status of the women's game.

Linking physical match demands to tactical/technical characteristics

The physical demands of match-play have been studied in greater depth than the technical and tactical aspects of performance. However, it is important to remember that performance is largely tactical, with players completing co-ordinated behaviours on the field of play, whilst implementing technical skills (Randell et al., 2021). Research examining the tactical and technical aspects of performance is limited, but some promising recent work has considered the link between physical and tactical match performance in women players (Errekagorri et al., 2023).

Physiological profile of women footballers

Intertwined with the physical demands of football are the physical and physiological properties of each individual player. To optimise performance of the football players, a comprehensive understanding of their physiological profiles is often deemed necessary. To acquire this information, coaches and practitioners employ a range of techniques, including standardised fitness assessments, body composition measurements and wearable technology such as GPS or heart rate monitors. These tools provide objective data to help identify areas of strength and weakness in individual players as well as guide the formulation of targeted training strategies (Datson, Weston, et al., 2022). Furthermore, these data can be effectively employed throughout the process of fitness–fatigue monitoring. Continuous measurement of these metrics allows for the detection of deviations from previously achieved values, which can indicate factors such as fatigue or inadequate fitness levels. This information may be valuable for team selection, as it helps identify players who are adequately prepared for the demands of competition (Datson, Weston, et al., 2022). These data can also serve as benchmarks to gauge progress upon returning from an injury, enabling targeted interventions to regain optimal performance levels. However, it is pertinent to question whether extensive and continuous testing yields sufficient benefits to justify the investment of time and effort. The implementation of rigorous testing requires multiple resources (e.g. time availability, financial constraints, an adequate number of personnel for data collection, processing and analysis) to ensure effective data collection and utilisation. The availability of these resources may vary within the women's football domain, depending on the professional status of the club/league. Moreover, it is essential to note that the mere collection of these variables does not guarantee success on the field, meaning that the allocation of efforts towards exhaustive testing may be more effectively utilised in other areas of performance. For optimal testing, practitioners must thoughtfully incorporate a strong rationale, clear methodology and a strategic use of the information to enhance performance. Nonetheless, both in research and in practice settings, a range of measures, encompassing aerobic and anaerobic capacity, speed, strength (absolute and lower limb) and anthropometric characteristics, are collected (Datson et al., 2014).

Anthropometry and body composition

Within elite sports, the measurement of anthropometric profiles and body composition in football is widespread (Randell et al., 2021), due to its correlation with numerous aspects of athletic performance (Collins et al., 2021), whilst also being utilised to monitor the efficacy of training, nutritional and rehabilitation interventions (Randell et al., 2021). The anthropometric profiles of football players are highly heterogeneous, with variations having been found among playing positions (Datson et al., 2014). However, the anthropometric profiles of players have remained relatively stable over time, albeit professionalism in football has evolved (Datson et al., 2014). Some data exist regarding basic anthropometric descriptors (Table 3.1); however, they are limited in compositional evidence, such as lean mass and body fat, restricting the interpretation of nutritional needs and energy requirements. As such, more comprehensive measures of body composition should be performed to provide greater information and context.

TABLE 3.1 Overview of the physiological profile of the senior woman footballer.

Anthropometry and composition

Age (years)	Height (cm)	Body mass (kg)	Body fat (%)	Lean mass (kg)	Fat mass (kg)	Bone density (g cm^{-2})
21 (16–41)	167.1 (148.0–187.0)	60.7 (46.0–88.0)	20.7 (14.5–22.0)	56.8 (44.5–73.8)	14.5 (11.5–15.3)	1.13 (1.02–1.30)

Aerobic performance

$\dot{V}O_2$max (ml kg^{-1} min^{-1})	Yo-Yo IE 1 (m)	Yo-Yo IE 2 (m)	Yo-Yo IR 1 (m)
50 7 (34.1–57.6)	2424 (1680–3288)	1346 (994–1774)	936 (677.8–1666.7)

Anaerobic performance

10-m sprint (s)	20-m sprint (s)	30-m sprint (s)	RSA* total time (s)	CMJ (cm)
1.98 (2.31–1.87)	3.41 (3.85–3.17)	4.86 (5.21–4.70)	21.95 (22.3–21.6)	31.1 (51.0–23.7)

Data are presented as means (minimum and maximal ranges) from literature.
* All RSA results are based on the studies using the protocol of Gabbett (2010).
CMJ, Countermovement Jump; RSA, Repeated Sprint Ability; $\dot{V}O_2$max, maximal oxygen consumption; Yo-Yo IE, Yo-Yo Intermittent Endurance test; Yo-Yo IR, Yo-Yo Intermittent Recovery test.

While various methods for assessing body composition of football players are available, the most common method for estimating body fat is skinfold measurements. This is primarily due to its cost-effectiveness and practicality (Collins et al., 2021). Data suggest that players' body fat is on average 20.7% (Table 3.1) (Datson et al., 2014; Randell et al., 2021). More precise measurements can be obtained using dual-energy X-ray absorptiometry (DXA), which has been employed to study the body composition of women footballers (Randell et al., 2021) (Table 3.1). The use of DXA has shown that players have, on average, 56.8 kg of lean mass, 14.5 kg of fat mass and a total bone mineral density of 1.13 g cm^{-2} (Bellver et al., 2019; Minett et al., 2017; Moss et al., 2021). Nonetheless, the implementation of body composition assessments should be undertaken with caution. Their application ought to be restricted to inform metabolic and nutritional requirements, all the while safeguarding the positive body image of female football players. Integrating a multidisciplinary team that includes sport scientists, nutritionists and psychologists is necessary to mitigate the chances of players developing disordered eating patterns and the risk of low energy availability (Godoy-Izquierdo & Díaz, 2021; see also Chapters 9 and 10).

Aerobic qualities

As highlighted in the "physical match demands" section, there is a large aerobic component, with players operating at near maximal oxygen consumption ($\dot{V}O_2$max) during match-play (Krustrup et al., 2005). The gold-standard method to assess aerobic capacity is treadmill-based $\dot{V}O_2$max measurements, conducted using breath-by-breath information during a specific protocol (ramp or step). However, $\dot{V}O_2$max testing is expensive, requiring technical expertise for data collection and interpretation. Additionally, the protocols are considered non-sport specific due to the requirement for players to run continuously until exhaustion (Bok & Foster, 2021). Thus, researchers have attempted to design more practically applicable measurements, such as the Yo-Yo Intermittent Endurance tests and Recovery tests (Bradley et al., 2014; Bangsbo et al., 2008), to assess the aerobic fitness of footballers. However, such tests have been shown to lack validity in the prediction of $\dot{V}O_2$max in women footballers (Martínez-Lagunas et al., 2014). The Yo-Yo Intermittent Endurance test level 2 (Yo-Yo IE 2) has been the most utilised within the research and has been identified to relate closely to the physical match running demands (Bradley et al., 2014).

The Yo-Yo Intermittent Recovery (IR) tests 1 and 2 require players to perform at the aerobic/anaerobic transition (Bangsbo et al., 2008); average distances covered by elite players are shown in Table 3.1. Due to the more intense and physically demanding nature of the Yo-Yo IR 1, results significantly differ depending on the age group and level of competition (Datson, Lolli, et al., 2022; Emmonds et al., 2018); for example players in the under-20s age group have been observed to cover greater distances (860 ± 240 m) than players in the under-15s (710 ± 210 m) and under-17s (720 ± 230 m) (Ramos et al., 2021). Yo-Yo IR test 2 data are very scarce in women football players.

Although the various Yo-Yo intermittent tests have been shown (in some instances) to relate to physical match-play (Bradley et al., 2014), it can be questioned as to what important information can be derived from these tests. There are, of course, certain benefits for using field tests. For example they require minimal equipment, multiple players can be measured simultaneously, they have good reliability regardless of the participants' prior familiarisation and results can be determined almost immediately. However, unlike traditional $\dot{V}O_2$max testing, it is difficult to derive training prescriptions from the data. Moreover, it is also important to consider when to use the tests and why to use them, considering the burden of fatigue, motivation and issues with determining worthwhile change.

Anaerobic qualities

As highlighted in the "physical match demands" section, sprints and high-speed activities have been described to be the most frequent activity that precedes goal-based actions, including scoring and assisting (Faude et al., 2012). Therefore, practitioners often assess maximal and repeated sprinting capacities.

Despite much research on the running speed of women football players, there is still a lack of consistency in the protocols and split times used for measurement, making it challenging to describe benchmarks and average running capacities (Datson et al., 2014). That being said, current data on 10-m, 20-m, and 30-m sprint times can be observed in Table 3.1. Sprint performance has been shown to be a discriminant factor during talent-identification processes (Hoare & Warr, 2000).

Although sprinting profiles vary between playing positions (refer to position-specific match demands), there has been no significant difference observed in research in sprinting times between playing positions (Datson et al., 2014). However, trends indicate that defenders are generally slower (Vescovi, 2012). This finding could be due to the isolated single-sprint testing, which may not be sensitive enough to determine differences between playing positions. Therefore, other metrics, such as force velocity (the relationship between the strength and speed of a player), should also be considered when determining sprint development (Buchheit et al., 2014).

While single sprints can give insight into maximum sprinting speed, it is important to note that football players need to perform multiple high-intensity actions during matches (Datson, Drust, et al., 2019). Therefore, repeated-sprint ability (RSA) has been suggested to be an important aspect of football performance (Datson et al., 2019). Similar to sprinting, RSA protocols largely differ. Gabbett (2010) designed a reliable repeated-sprint test to reflect the demands of international women's football, with an error of measurement of only 1.5%. The test involves six sprints of 20 m on a 15-s cycle. The findings across two studies can be found in Table 3.1 (Gabbett, 2010; Lockie et al., 2020). However, it has been previously noted that RSA, in the fashion that it has been designed, is not indicative of match-play (Datson, Weston, et al., 2020; Schimpchen et al., 2016). Consequently, the practical application and implementation of RSA testing continue to be questioned within research (Schimpchen et al., 2016).

As well as sprinting, lower-limb power is a crucial component of sport-specific, physical performance (Guthrie et al., 2021). Jumping is a widely used method for measuring lower-limb power, and the countermovement jump (CMJ) is the most commonly used approach for lower-limb power assessment (Table 3.1) (Datson, Weston, et al., 2022). A benchmark height of over 34.4 cm for CMJ has been suggested as an indicator of superior performance (Castagna & Castellini, 2013). Although recommended thresholds for superior performance have been proposed, differences have yet to be observed between elite and sub-elite players (Sedano Campo et al., 2009). Jumping performance has, however, been shown to discriminate between different levels of competition and age groups (Datson et al., 2014).

Various techniques can be used to measure jumping performance but comparing data between studies is challenging due to the different protocols and equipment researchers use. Data on techniques, such as drop jump, squat jump and CMJ using arms, have been provided, but more information is needed to draw conclusive findings about women's performance. In practice, focusing on CMJ performance may be useful for monitoring, talent identification and athlete development, as a wide range of information is available on CMJ performance in elite women's and girls' football.

Practitioners' perspectives

One of the major challenges in any area of football research is the translation of the available information into the practice of those who routinely work with players. Better translation of the available information will lead to a better understanding of the limitations around performance and, therefore, will provide valuable target areas for strategies to support improvements in performance. There should be an awareness that context is always important in the translation of science and that, while we have data in an area on women players, this information may not relate to every specific population. Groups of players will not be the same, as there will be/is considerable variability in what is required of individuals across games and periods of matches and hence how these individuals may be described. It is probably fair to say that the ability to contextualise and optimise basic information to those specific individuals involved is probably a key skill needed by those involved at the frontline working with players.

Important considerations for the practical application of the data included in this chapter could include better use of match physical performance data. The developments in modern technology have enabled high amounts of data to be available on the physical performance of players in matches in quick timescales. There is little use in having good-quality data without understanding how these data can inform both the coaching process and the actions of those associated with player management at both a group and individual level. Engaging with coaches and other important stakeholders on what information is important for match-play models and training outcomes may be important areas to consider as the women's game develops.

Consideration of mechanical load

The traditional metabolic view of the demands of the sport remains important, though it is also important to evaluate other aspects of load that may be more *mechanical* in nature. These loads may be reflected in tissues and joints and be a function of the non-linear movements needed in the game. These types of demands are less well understood currently. The development of our understanding of these stresses is a key development area in the coming phases for the sport.

Understanding high-cost actions

The mechanical-load concept discussed earlier is an important concept in football, as such loads are probably of a *high cost* to the player. High physiological costs are probably also associated with movements such as sprinting and running at high speed. This will be the case when these movements are performed as isolated bouts; however, when these activities are completed in close proximity to each other (i.e. repeated bouts), they may be especially demanding. Though sprinting and high-speed running are well described in the literature (in terms of the total distance covered), there has been less frequent attempts to describe these types of movements in other ways that could help to more accurately reflect the physical challenges that they place on players. More detailed approaches may include more specific descriptions of the types of sprints/runs, analysis of the temporal organisation of such bouts or how the overall demands of these movements can be more physiologically determined and then represented.

Contextual references

It is clear that the physical outputs completed by players in games/training are a function of many contextual factors. While there are more frequent attempts to relate physical data to other available data streams (e.g. tactical/technical information), there are still large methodological and conceptual challenges in understanding how these relationships can be both determined and then presented in a meaningful way.

Appropriate physical assessments

The relative importance of assessments to any practitioner is probably a result of their philosophical stance on the balance between the ecological validity of tests and the need to reduce the influence of extraneous variables on test outcome. While such tests may be a quantitatively small part of any applied programme to support players, there is a requirement for any tests used to be valid and reliable. The lack of specific detailed knowledge in the specific nature and understanding of a number of tests (including appropriately robustly approaches to collect data) frequently prevents practitioners from having easy test solutions to implement. Better knowledge around the advantages and disadvantages of tests related to areas, such as test appropriateness for football, ease of delivery and robustness of data, would seem to be a way to help those working with players to understand the physical strengths and weaknesses of players and subsequently better impact their programme design.

Appropriate use of physical assessments

Effective strategies for the planning and implementation for optimising the use of tests in football are still an area for debate amongst practitioners. Even if tests that are used are quick and simple to deliver to groups of players, they still inevitably impact the available time to train and hence aspects of the programme that are needed for holistic player development. Understanding the influence of the timing of tests, both in terms of acute test delivery and for those time periods more associated with evaluating adaptive responses, would facilitate better decision-making on the practical delivery of tests.

Summary

In this chapter, we provided an overview of the published data illustrating both general and position-specific physical match demands, variations across and between matches and the interplay of tactical/technical factors with physical performance. We highlighted the evolution in the physicality of the women's game and the consequent need to ensure that players have the necessary fitness qualities to cope with increasing demands. Reference data for physical fitness tests have been presented alongside key considerations for practitioners regarding data interpretation and engagement with coaches and key stakeholders.

References

Bangsbo, J., Iaia, F. M., & Krustrup, P. (2008). The yo-yo intermittent recovery test. *Sports Medicine, 38*(1), 37–51. https://doi.org/10.2165/00007256-200838010-00004

Bellver, M., Del Rio, L., Jovell, E., Drobnic, F., & Trilla, A. (2019). Bone mineral density and bone mineral content among female elite athletes. *Bone, 127*, 393–400. https://doi.org/10.1016/j.bone.2019.06.030

Bok, D., & Foster, C. (2021). Applicability of field aerobic fitness tests in soccer: Which one to choose? *Journal of Functional Morphology and Kinesiology, 6*(3), 69. https://doi.org/10.3390/jfmk6030069

Bradley, P. S., & Scott, D. (2020). *Physical analysis of FIFA Women's World Cup France 2019TM*. FIFA.

Bradley, P. S., & Vescovi, J. D. (2015). Velocity thresholds for women's soccer matches: Sex specificity dictates high-speed-running and sprinting thresholds-female athletes in motion (FAiM). *International Journal of Sports Physiology and Performance*, *10*(1), 112–116. https://doi.org/10.1123/ijspp.2014-0212

Buchheit, M., Samozino, P., Glynn, J. A., Simpson, B. M., Al Haddad, H., & Mendez-Villanueva, A. (2014). Mechanical determinants of acceleration and maximal sprinting speed. *Journal of Sports Sciences*, *32*(20), 1906–1913. https://doi.org/10.1080/02640414.2014.965191

Bush, M., Barnes, C., Archer, D. T., Hogg, B., & Bradley, P. S. (2015). Evolution of match performance parameters for various playing positions in the English Premier League. *Human Movement Science*, *39*, 1–11. https://doi.org/10.1016/j.humov.2014.10.003

Castagna, C., & Castellini, E. (2013). Vertical jump performance in Italian male and female national team soccer players. *Journal of Strength and Conditioning Research*, *27*(4), 1156–1161. https://doi.org/10.1519/JSC.0b013e3182610999

Collins, J., Maughan, R. J., Gleeson, M., Bilsborough, J., Jeukendrup, A., Morton, J. P., Phillips, S. M., Armstrong, L., Burke, L. M., Close, G. L., Duffield, R., Larson-Meyer, E., Louis, J., Medina, D., Meyer, F., Rollo, I., Sundgot-Borgen, J., Wall, B. T., Boullosa, B.,. . . McCall, A. (2021). UEFA expert group statement on nutrition in elite football: Current evidence to inform practical recommendations and guide future research. *British Journal of Sports Medicine*, *55*(8), 416. https://doi.org/10.1136/bjsports-2019-101961

Datson, N., Drust, B., Weston, M., & Gregson, W. (2019). Repeated high-speed running in elite female soccer players during international competition. *Science and Medicine in Football*, *3*(2), 150–156. https://doi.org/10.1080/24733938.2018.1508880

Datson, N., Drust, B., Weston, M., Jarman, I. H., Lisboa, P. J., & Gregson, W. (2017). Match physical performance of elite female soccer players during international competition. *Journal of Strength and Conditioning Research*, *31*(9), 2379–2387. https://doi.org/10.1519/JSC.0000000000001575

Datson, N., Hulton, A., Andersson, H., Lewis, T., Weston, M., Drust, B., & Gregson, W. (2014). Applied physiology of female soccer: An update. *Sports Medicine*, *44*(9), 1225–1240. https://doi.org/10.1007/s40279-014-0199-1

Datson, N., Lolli, L., Drust, B., Atkinson, G., Weston, M., & Gregson, W. (2022). Inter-methodological quantification of the target change for performance test outcomes relevant to elite female soccer players. *Science and Medicine in Football*, *6*(2), 248–261. https://doi.org/10.1080/24733938.2021.1942538

Datson, N., Weston, M., Drust, B., Atkinson, G., Lolli, L., & Gregson, W. (2022). Reference values for performance test outcomes relevant to English female soccer players. *Science and Medicine in Football*, *6*(5), 589–596. https://doi.org/10.1080/24733938.2022.2037156

Datson, N., Weston, M., Drust, B., Gregson, W., & Lolli, L. (2020). High-intensity endurance capacity assessment as a tool for talent identification in elite youth female soccer. *Journal of Sports Sciences*, *38*(11–12), 1313–1319. https://doi.org/10.1080/02640414.2019.1656323

Emmonds, S., Till, K., Redgrave, J., Murray, E., Turner, L., Robinson, C., & Jones, B. (2018). Influence of age on the anthropometric and performance characteristics of high-level youth female soccer players. *International Journal of Sports Science and Coaching*, *13*(5), 779–786. https://doi.org/10.1177/1747954118757437

Errekagorri, I., Echeazarra, I., Olaizola, A., & Castellano, J. (2023). Evaluating physical and tactical performance and their connection during female soccer matches using global positioning systems. *Sensors*, *23*(1), 69. https://doi.org/10.3390/s23010069

Faude, O., Koch, T., & Meyer, T. (2012). Straight sprinting is the most frequent action in goal situations in professional football. *Journal of Sports Sciences*, *30*(7), 625–631. https://doi.org/10.1080/02640414.2012.665940

Gabbett, T. J. (2010). The development of a test of repeated-sprint ability for elite women's soccer players. *Journal of Strength and Conditioning Research*, *24*(5), 1191–1194. https://doi.org/10.1519/JSC.0b013e3181d1568c

Godoy-Izquierdo, D., & Díaz, I. (2021). Inhabiting the body(ies) in female soccer players: The protective role of positive body image. *Frontiers in Psychology, 12,* 718836. https://doi.org/10.3389/fpsyg.2021.718836

González-García, J., Giráldez-Costas, V., Ramirez-Campillo, R., Drust, B., & Romero-Moraleda, B. (2022). Assessment of peak physical demands in elite women soccer players: Can contextual variables play a role? *Research Quarterly for Exercise and Sport, 94*(2), 435–443. https://doi.org/10.1080/02701367.2021.2004297

Guthrie, B., Fields, J. B., Thompson, B., & Jones, M. T. (2021). Physical performance assessments of strength and power in women collegiate athletes. *International Journal of Exercise Science, 14*(6), 984–993.

Harkness-Armstrong, A., Till, K., Datson, N., Myhill, N., & Emmonds, S. (2022). A systematic review of match-play characteristics in women's soccer. *PLoS One, 17*(6). https://doi.org/10.1371/journal.pone.0268334

Hoare, D. G., & Warr, C. R. (2000). Talent identification and women's soccer: An Australian experience. *Journal of Sports Sciences, 18*(9), 751–758. https://doi.org/10.1080/02640410050120122

Krustrup, P., Mohr, M., Ellingsgaard, H., & Bangsbo, J. (2005). Physical demands during an elite female soccer game: Importance of training status. *Medicine and Science in Sports and Exercise, 37*(7), 1242–1248. https://doi.org/10.1249/01.mss.0000170062.73981.94

Lockie, R. G., Liu, T. M., Stage, A. A., Lazar, A., Giuliano, D. V., Hurley, J. M., Torne, I. A., Beiley, M. D., Birmingham-Babauta, S. A., Stokes, J. J., Risso, F. G., Davis, D. L., Moreno, M. R., & Orjalo, A. J. (2020). Assessing repeated-sprint ability in division I collegiate women soccer players. *Journal of Strength and Conditioning Research, 34*(7), 2015–2023. https://doi.org/10.1519

Malone, J. J., Lovell, R., Varley, M. C., & Coutts, A. J. (2017). Unpacking the black box: Applications and considerations for using GPS devices in sport. *International Journal of Sports Physiology and Performance, 12*(s2), S18–S26. https://doi.org/10.1123/ijspp.2016-0236

Mara, J. K., Thompson, K. G., Pumpa, K. L., & Morgan, S. (2017). The acceleration and deceleration profiles of elite female soccer players during competitive matches. *Journal of Science and Medicine in Sport, 20*(9), 867–872. https://doi.org/10.1016/j.jsams.2016.12.078

Martínez-Lagunas, V., Niessen, M., & Hartmann, U. (2014). Women's football: Player characteristics and demands of the game. *Journal of Sport and Health Science, 3*(4), 258–272. https://doi.org/10.1016/j.jshs.2014.10.001

Minett, M. M., Binkley, T. B., Weidauer, L. A., & Specker, B. L. (2017). Changes in body composition and bone of female collegiate soccer players through the competitive season and off-season. *Journal of Musculoskeletal Neuronal Interactions, 17*(1), 386–398.

Moss, S. L., Randell, R. K., Burgess, D., Ridley, S., Ócairealláin, C., Allison, R., & Rollo, I. (2021). Assessment of energy availability and associated risk factors in professional female soccer players. *European Journal of Sport Science, 21*(6), 861–870. https://doi.org/10.1080/17461391.2020.1788647

Novak, A. R., Impellizzeri, F. M., Trivedi, A., Coutts, A. J., & McCall, A. (2021). Analysis of the worst-case scenarios in an elite football team: Towards a better understanding and application. *Journal of Sports Sciences, 39*(16), 1850–1859. https://doi.org/10.1080/02640414.2021.1902138

Panduro, J., Ermidis, G., Røddik, L., Vigh-Larsen, J. F., Madsen, E. E., Larsen, M. N., Pettersen, S. A., Krustrup, P., & Randers, M. B. (2022). Physical performance and loading for six playing positions in elite female football: Full-game, end-game, and peak periods. *Scandinavian Journal of Medicine and Science in Sports, 32*(S1), 115–126. https://doi.org/10.1111/sms.13877

Ramos, G. P., Nakamura, F. Y., Penna, E. M., Mendes, T. T., Mahseredjian, F., Lima, A. M., Garcia, E. S., Prado, L. S., & Coimbra, C. C. (2021). Comparison of physical fitness and anthropometrical profiles among Brazilian female soccer national teams from U15 to senior categories. *Journal of Strength and Conditioning Research, 35*(8), 2302–2308. https://doi.org/10.1519/JSC.0000000000003140

Ramos, G. P., Nakamura, F. Y., Penna, E. M., Wilke, C. F., Pereira, L. A., Loturco, I., Capelli, L., Mahseredjian, F., Silami-Garcia, E., & Coimbra, C. C. (2019). Activity profiles in U17, U20, and senior women's Brazilian national soccer teams during international competitions: Are there meaningful differences? *Journal of Strength and Conditioning Research, 33*(12), 3414–3422. https://doi.org/10.1519/JSC.0000000000002170

Randell, R. K., Clifford, T., Drust, B., Moss, S. L., Unnithan, V. B., De Ste Croix, M. B. A., Datson, N., Martin, D., Mayho, H., Carter, J. M., & Rollo, I. (2021). Physiological characteristics of female soccer players and health and performance considerations: A narrative review. *Sports Medicine, 51*(7), 1377–1399. https://doi.org/10.1007/s40279-021-01458-1

Schimpchen, J., Skorski, S., Nopp, S., & Meyer, T. (2016). Are "classical" tests of repeated-sprint ability in football externally valid? A new approach to determine in-game sprinting behaviour in elite football players. *Journal of Sports Sciences, 34*(6), 519–526. https://doi.org/10.1080/02640414.2015.1112023

Scott, D., Haigh, J., & Lovell, R. (2020). Physical characteristics and match performances in women's international versus domestic-level football players: A 2-year, league-wide study. *Science and Medicine in Football, 4*(3), 211–215. https://doi.org/10.1080/24733938.2020.1745265

Sedano Campo, S., Vaeyens, R., Philippaerts, R. M., Redondo, J. C., De Benito, A. M., & Cuadrado, G. (2009). Effects of lower-limb plyometric training on body composition, explosive strength, and kicking speed in female soccer players. *Journal of Strength and Conditioning Research, 23*(6), 1714–1722. https://doi.org/10.1519/JSC.0b013e3181b3f537

Trewin, J., Meylan, C., Varley, M. C., & Cronin, J. (2018). The match-to-match variation of match-running in elite female soccer. *Journal of Science and Medicine in Sport, 21*(2), 196–201. https://doi.org/10.1016/j.jsams.2017.05.009

Vescovi, J. D. (2012). Sprint profile of professional female soccer players during competitive matches: Female athletes in motion (FAiM) study. *Journal of Sports Sciences, 30*(12), 1259–1265. https://doi.org/10.1080/02640414.2012.701760

Weston, M., Drust, B., & Gregson, W. (2011). Intensities of exercise during match-play in FA premier league referees and players. *Journal of Sports Sciences, 29*(5), 527–532. https://doi.org/10.1080/02640414.2010.543914

4

TALENT IDENTIFICATION

Stacey Emmonds, Adam Gledhill, Matthew Wright and Kevin Till

Introduction

Women's football has seen a substantial rise in participation, as well as increased financial support from governing bodies over the last decade. Financial support from the Union of European Football Associations (UEFA) has trebled (UEFA, 2019), and participation rates over the last 10 years have grown (the Fédération Internationale de Football Association [FIFA], 2019). Worldwide, FIFA is committed to increasing the number of players from approximately 13.3 million (2019) to 60 million by 2026 (FIFA, 2019). This increased growth and professionalism of the game have led to an increased investment in talent identification (ID) and development of players from a young age.

The identification and development processes in modern-day football are illustrated in Figure 4.1.

1. ***Identification***: Involves recognising players participating in the sport who have the potential to progress into a high-performance development programme consisting of a relatively systematic combination of coaching, support, training and match play designed to progress players (development is also known as talent promotion [Vaeyens et al., 2009]).
2. ***Detection***: Involves identifying players from outside the game who have the potential to progress into development programmes in football (Williams & Reilly, 2000).
3. ***Participation***: Involves playing at a recreational level and/or informal, playful settings. Selection refers to the ongoing process of choosing players within the development programme, who demonstrate attributes suitable for progression

DOI: 10.4324/9781003381914-4

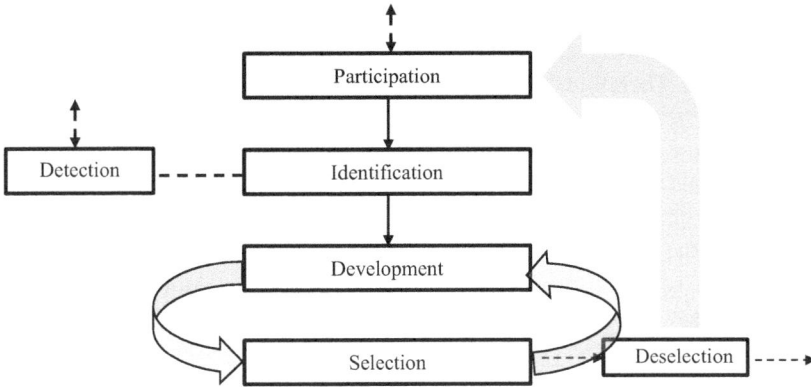

FIGURE 4.1   Key parts of the identification, selection and development process in football. Adapted from Williams & Reilly (2000).

to a future squad or team, such as next age-group team in a youth academy or nation (Williams & Reilly, 2000).

4. ***Deselection***: Is the process of removing players from the development programme, who no longer demonstrate the attributes to participate in, or to be selected for, future squads or teams.

Football-governing bodies and leagues around the world are now investing in talent development environments such as academies for players who are starting as young as 10 years. These academies align with similar academy structures that are in place in boys' football, although the funding and resources available in the women's game are still limited in comparison (e.g. sport science provision). Talent ID in women's football has traditionally been based on viewing players in a trial game or training environment, whereby the players aim to impress coaches. This approach to talent ID is not informed by scientific evidence, but rather coaches' subjective preconceived notion of the ideal player, which, when used in isolation, may result in repetitive misjudgements and limited consistency. However, in recent years there has been an increased amount of research exploring talent ID and development in the girls' and women's pathways (Andrew et al., 2022; Datson et al., 2020).

The early identification of individuals who will be successful at senior level is a complex and highly challenging process. Traditional talent-ID research has often focused on identifying characteristics that distinguish between elite and sub-elite youth performers (i.e. physical characteristics). This methodology assumes that the most talented youth players will become the most talented senior players (i.e. that talent is fixed). Researchers have shown differences in physical performance characteristics based upon competitive playing standard (Datson et al., 2020), player selection and age (Wright & Atkinson, 2019). However, the relative importance and influence that these characteristics have on future career progression has not been identified. Therefore, the aims of this chapter are to do the following:

1 Explore how biopsychosocial development of girls may have implications for talent ID and how this may differ from that of boys.
2 Consider challenges for talent ID and development.
3 Consider the practical applications for talent ID and development, how to implement scientific principles and provide practical solutions for talent ID/ development.

Growth, maturation and physical development

There is an abundance of research in the boys' football pathway demonstrating the impact that growth and maturation may have on talent ID and development (Kelly & Williams, 2020; Towlson et al., 2021). Researchers have shown that maturity status may have an impact on physical capabilities and, as such, talent ID and development, with boys of advanced maturity displaying better athleticism and more identification and selection opportunities (Morris et al., 2018; Towlson et al., 2021). However, findings from studies including those on boys may not be transferable to girls, given the differences in the timing and tempo of maturation between the sexes, alongside the differences in physical and physiological characteristics from the onset of puberty. In contrast to boys, whereby hormonal and morphological changes associated with maturation are advantageous to athletic development, girls experience different hormonal changes, such as an increase in oestrogen and progesterone, which may be associated with a widening of the hips and an increase in non-functional mass (Bland et al., 2021). Such hormonal and morphological changes may not be advantageous to athletic performance and, therefore, may have implications for talent ID and development (Figure 4.2).

When compared to boys, a clear plateau in the ability to apply force is observed around the age of peak height velocity (PHV), which occurs between 11 and 13 years of age (as determined via measures such as the standing broad jump, 10×5-m change-of-direction speed and handgrip strength) (Tomkinson et al., 2018). Furthermore, cross-sectional and longitudinal research in girls has shown progression in sprinting-related physical qualities after PHV (Emmonds et al., 2017; Wright & Atkinson, 2019); however, rapid (100 ms), lower body force application relative to body mass has shown marked reductions in players after PHV (Emmonds et al., 2017). This finding may be explained by a potential increase in fat mass associated with peak weight velocity that occurs in girls, 3.5 to 10.5 months after PHV. This finding is important for both performance and injury prevention. For example serious knee injuries, such as anterior-cruciate ligament ruptures, tend to occur within the first 50 ms of ground contact (Krosshaug et al., 2007). Improving the ability to apply force quickly to stabilise the knee is proven to reduce injury incidence and

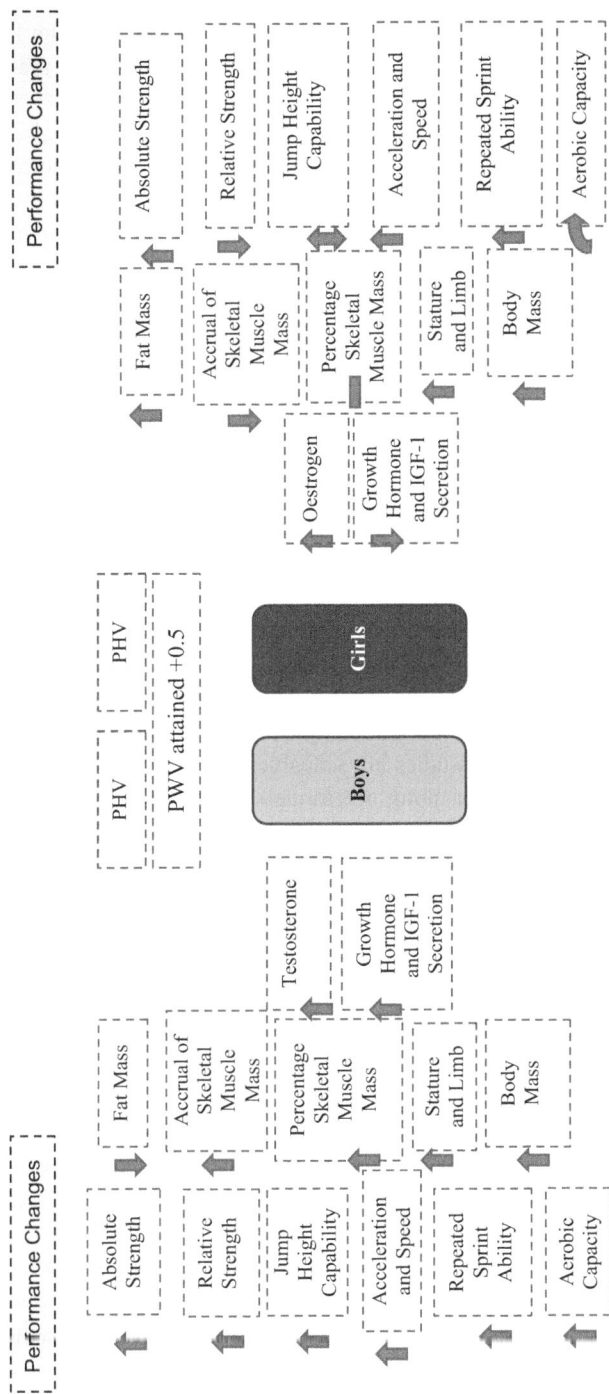

FIGURE 4.2 Summary of hormonal, morphological and performance change during the adolescent growth spurt for boys and girls. Arrows indicate the direction of change in the measure.

IGF-1, insulin-like growth factor-1; PHV, peak height velocity; PWV, peak weight velocity.

is a recommended strategy before PHV (Petushek et al., 2019). It is also important to recognise the potential decrement in strength relative to body mass after PHV in girls who have not had access to appropriate training interventions, and the potential impact for both talent ID and development.

The quantity and quality of research supporting talent development in girls' football is limited often to single-centre, non-controlled trials and often to analysis of observational rather than longitudinal data. However, alongside the increased resources and professionalism of women's football, there has been an increase in the scientific knowledge underpinning talent development over recent years (Table 4.1). High-intensity endurance capacity appears to have some prognostic power in identifying young players who have reached the elite level (Datson et al., 2020). For example Datson et al. (2020) reported that high-intensity aerobic power (assessed via the Yo-Yo intermittent recovery test level 1 [Yo-Yo IR 1]) at youth level is a predictor of progression into international squads at under-17 to under-20 (U17–U20). However, limited changes in high-intensity aerobic capacity of youth players between the age groups of U14 and U16 have been observed (Emmonds et al., 2018) or post-PHV (Emmonds et al., 2020). Indeed, when tracked longitudinally, players have shown no improvements in high-intensity aerobic capacity (Yo-Yo IR 1) during typical in-season football training (Wright & Innerd, 2019). Therefore, the development of high-intensity running capabilities should be a key component of talent-development training strategies. In addition, the slalom-dribbling test (Höner et al., 2019) has been reported to have the capability to differentiate between players who reached youth national team versus those at regional academy level. These studies are valuable, as they provide some initial insight into primarily physical or motor determinants required for success using a single time point of analysis. The major limitation of this methodological approach is that cross-sectional studies are limited in their capacity to provide a prediction of future success as adult players (Williams & Reilly, 2000). Talent development is a nonlinear, dynamic construct, so serial measurements of performance are needed over time to truly understand the trajectory of the elite youth players' development (Randell et al., 2021). Incorporating an array of potential performance determinants into a longitudinal evaluation of the player appears to be the optimal approach to understand talent ID and development in a woman's environment.

Talent development research rarely considers the potential effect of hormonal fluctuation (oestrogen and progesterone) throughout the menstrual cycle on performance measures (refer to Chapters 5 and 6 for further information). Currently, quantitative physiological evidence is inconclusive as to the effects of menstrual cycle phase on exercise performance (McNulty et al., 2020). However, in one study, 57% of athletes perceived that their performance was negatively affected in some menstrual cycle phases (Armour et al., 2020), and women reported negative symptoms related to their menstrual cycle that led to them missing or changing training (Bruinvels et al., 2021). O'Brien et al. (2011) reported psychological and

TABLE 4.1 Physiological and motor determinants of future playing success in elite girl football players.

Reference	n	Age	Playing Level	Determinants of Performance	Major Findings
Datson et al. (2020)	228	12.7–15.3	Elite performance camps (the English Football Association)	CMJ, 30-m linear sprint, Yo-Yo IR 1	Higher Yo-Yo IR 1 (2040 m) score more likely (47–82%) to be selected into Under 17–Under-20 international squads
Höner et al. (2019)	499	11.4	German Football Talent Programme	Sprint time, agility, dribbling, ball control and shooting	Dribbling was the most relevant motor predictor for German Youth National Team selection
Vescovi et al. (2011)	414	12–21	High club-level juniors and NCAA, Division 1 US College Players	CMJ, Illinois Agility Test (modified) and 36-m RST	No evidence of mean linear sprint speed (9.1 m) differences across all age groups
Mujika et al. (2009)	34	17–24	Elite senior players from the Spanish Super Liga and junior players from the Spanish 2nd Division	CMJ, Yo-Yo IR 1, 15-m linear sprint, 15-m ball dribbling	Elite players (1224 m) superior to junior (826 m) in Yo-Yo IR 1. No difference in 15-m sprint time between senior and junior players
Hoare and Warr (2000)	59	15–19	Individual sport and non-football team sport players recruited into a football training camp	VJ, 20-m PST, 20-m linear sprint, 505 Agility Test	17 selected players from the 59 demonstrated VJ height in the 80th percentile and maximal aerobic power in the 90th percentile compared to the Australian population values for 15-year-olds. 20-m sprint time faster (3.47 s) than the population average (3.64 s) at 15 years of age

Key: CMJ, countermovement jump; NCAA, National Collegiate Athletic Association; PST, progressive shuttle test; RST, repeated sprint test; VJ, vertical jump; Yo-Yo IR 1, Yo-Yo intermittent recovery test level 1.
Adapted from Randell et al. (2021).

behavioural symptoms such as fatigue, lethargy and poor coordination and concentration, which could clearly impact the talent ID or assessment of talent. Differences in the age at which girls start their menstrual cycle (median age of 12.4 years, 10th–90th percentile of 11.1 to 13.8 years [Harber, 2011]) and the start of regular, eumenorrhoeic cycles further complicate matters when considering potential effects on talent ID and development. Therefore, there is a need for high-quality research to better inform practitioners, but it is clear that repeated and serial measurements are required. Furthermore, it has been suggested that tracking menarche and menstrual status of young players should be integrated into athletic development systems (Harber, 2011).

An attempt to conduct a longitudinal study into talent development has been made by the German Football Federation (Leyhr et al., 2020). The researchers aimed to explore players' skill level (i.e. dribbling, passing, shooting) and physical fitness (i.e. 20-m sprints and a slalom agility run without the ball) over a four-year period. It was reported that players who were affiliated with professional clubs were ~1 s faster on the sprint, passing and agility drills than their peers who played at non-professional levels. These differences were apparent from U12–U15 age groups. However, it was found that the rate of improvement for these measures in both groups over time was non-linear. Furthermore, on their own, individual assessments did not have sufficient predictive power to determine success in senior football, suggesting there is a need for holistic profiling when exploring talent development. Additionally, no consideration was given to the maturity status of the players, and consequently it was not possible to differentiate between the influence of growth and maturation or training on the changes in talent development.

The combination of cross-sectional and longitudinal studies currently available in women's football provides a foundation for talent ID and development, but more work is required. For example evaluating the influence of the maturation-selection phenomenon across all age groups using a longitudinal study design is required and the application of constructs to investigate key psychological traits for future success such as resilience and perseverance is warranted.

Psychosocial considerations

The term *psychosocial* considers the interrelation of individual psychological characteristics with social influences and the ways in which these shape and guide behaviour (Gledhill et al., 2017). Most of the research in girls' and women's football, to date, has been focused on talent development, with significantly less work examining talent ID. With girls and women significantly under-represented in research, we will consider some of the available evidence from the women's/girls' football context as well as other evidence from systematic reviews and meta-analyses, where the extent to which psychosocial factors influence future football performance have been considered (e.g. Pettersen et al., 2023).

The majority of studies, in which psychosocial factors have been examined, are relatively small scale in nature and conflicting findings are presented (see Pettersen et al., 2023). For example whilst factors such as "grit", self-regulated learning (planning, evaluating and reflection) and mental toughness have previously been considered as important in this context, more recently in a small-scale study from Norway, these factors were not found to be significantly related to football performance (Pettersen et al., 2023).

The importance of self-control has recently been reinforced in small-scale research from German football (Wolff et al., 2019), using a sample of both men and women players. It was noted that youth players selected for talent development programmes displayed higher levels of self-control than their non-selected peers and these self-control differences were evident from an early age. Intuitively, it is likely that the increased self-control will allow young players to take part effectively, volitionally engage with appropriate amounts of deliberate practice and maintain appropriate general lifestyle behaviours (e.g. nutritional habits, sleep), all of which can influence talent ID and development (Wolff et al., 2019). Extraversion is a personality trait that has recently been associated with higher levels of performance in women's football (Pettersen et al., 2023). This finding is perhaps understandable given that individuals with higher levels of extraversion can often have better coping strategies specifically in high-pressure situations and can also demonstrate better communication skills, both of which would be important in navigating challenging football careers.

One of the key challenges within this domain has been *how* we best identify some of these important psychosocial considerations. Despite improved investment in the women's game with recent years, it is still not mandated by many governing bodies for sport psychology support to be provided. Therefore, we should consider the role of coaches in talent ID from a psychosocial perspective. Educating and supporting coaches with identifying behaviours indicative of psychosocial characteristics could be fruitful, as this can be integrated with standard talent-ID practices.

Challenges for talent ID and development

In the previous sections, we reviewed the physical and psychosocial characteristics related to talent ID and development in youth football. Whilst there are specific findings and considerations for implementing talent ID and development, Till and Baker (2020) listed three main challenges for talent ID and development. These challenges include the following:

1 What are we looking for (what is talent?)?
2 How do we identify and develop talent?
3 Are talent systems appropriate and healthy?

These challenges are important to consider, to understand how stakeholders think about talent, how they manage the resources within talent ID and development programmes and how they optimise opportunities to develop young players holistically.

What is talent?

The word *talent* is commonly used across all levels of sport. However, its use can be inconsistent and unclear, resulting in contradictions and inaccuracies in athlete identification and selection. For example coaches may state a young player has a "talent for football" but what does this really mean and what are we looking for? This question is not trivial and while coaches' definitions may differ, researchers and scientists may not have the answer either. In most talent ID research to date (e.g. Barraclough et al., 2022) cross-sectional designs have been used that compare athlete characteristics between playing levels (e.g. selected vs. non-selected) with the assumption that the differences in characteristics between playing standards reflect differences in talent or some other relevant predictor of long-term success. Importantly, approaches that only measure performance at "one-off" time points assume talent is a "fixed capacity", which is reflected in performance at that specific time in an athlete's development. This assumption can miss critical information about how such characteristics relate to future performance and development outcomes. Moreover, this view is inconsistent with more recent definitions of talent as being dynamic, emergent, multidisciplinary and nonlinear (Baker et al., 2018). Furthermore, talent ID involves identifying "potential" for future versions of the sport. The recent professionalisation of women's football has no doubt resulted in significant changes to the game (i.e. 30% increase in high-intensity running in match play [FIFA, 2019]), which will only evolve and change in the future. Therefore, practitioners identifying talent need to understand the current and future versions of the game to make valid decisions on the future success of a young player.

Whilst overcoming the above challenges is not straightforward, practitioners may want to consider the following solutions to support understanding "what we are looking for":

1 Position talent as (a) emergent (i.e. the process of becoming), (b) influenced by a host of factors within an environment (e.g. parents, coaches, peers and opportunities) and (c) individual (e.g. athletes with different abilities and skills require different developmental programmes).
2 Establish and apply a clear philosophy that values long-term development (i.e. player improvement) over short-term outcomes (e.g. winning and current performance).
3 Consider, assess and measure (where possible) both current performance and future potential.
4 Strongly consider how women's football may evolve over time in the future.

How do we identify and develop talent?

Studies in boys' and men's football demonstrate a lack of effective decisions about talent ID, particularly at younger ages (Güllich, 2014). This evidence indicates that early talent-ID approaches and the data available to inform such approaches are problematic, suggesting that making decisions about future adult and sports performance in childhood is very difficult. As discussed earlier, these decisions are more difficult due to the biopsychosocial factors affecting engagement, performance and development in youth sport (e.g. growth and maturation), which can be compounded by the policy structures of youth sport (i.e. annual age grouping). However, early talent-ID decisions are often a result of the amount and allocation of resources to support talent ID and development. An important question is, Are resources being used in the right place? Players need to be appropriately nurtured to maximise any investment in their development. However, this notion assumes that we know the factors related to optimal skill acquisition and development in players. In addition, effective system resourcing requires planning for other elements of the sport system related to long-term success, such as effectively educating and training coaches to be able to adequately implement the processes of talent ID and development and/or identifying emergent areas of research that might have value for future coaching and athlete development practice.

Practitioners may want to consider the following solutions to support identifying and developing talent:

1 Consider when talent ID should commence and why (i.e. what is the reason behind trying to identify talent at this point?).
2 Delay and widen talent ID opportunities and create pathways that allow athletes to enter and exit a talent programme seamlessly.
3 Develop multidisciplinary talent ID tools using subjective and objective data that consider biopsychosocial development (e.g. maturation).
4 Consider alternative grouping strategies (e.g. playing up and down age groups, bio-banding) to allow individuals to experience a range of developmental competition experiences.
5 Manage and deploy resources to allow the above to occur alongside appropriate investment in coach education, development and research.
6 Consider the importance of diversity of scouts/coaches involved in the talent ID process to ensure that a multitude of views are represented.

Practitioners' perspective

It is challenging to create an environment that enables talent to develop without increasing the risk of injury or burnout. At younger age groups, below PHV (e.g. U10s–U12s), the focus should be on engaging with a wide range of players and providing a broad scope of development opportunities; these could include technical and tactical coaching combined with a games programme that creates different learning opportunities. For example coaches could consider varying between girls or mixed football and varying the type of game, such as 3 v 3, Futsal, 5 v 5. It may also be advantageous to enable players to vary between playing grassroots football with their friends, as well as individual developmental programmes to develop players' sense of community. To encourage variety without simply adding to workloads (both for the player and for the parent/carers), it is important to provide flexibility.

At younger ages it is important to engage players in strength and movement skill development activities, which could be part of dedicated physical development coaching, structured warm-ups or encouraging girls to explore other sports such as gymnastics or martial arts. Encouraging success in other sports or in academic achievement provides opportunities for players to develop a broader sense of identity, which could be important for long-term mental health.

As players transition through PHV, there is a need for more focused support. For example from a physical perspective, specific support may be needed to address potential maturation-related decrements or plateaus in relative strength and aerobic capacity that are important for performance and injury risk. Talent development programmes are about balancing the need for comprehensive programmes with more specific and focused support, whilst still maintaining as wide a talent pool as possible. In our experience, the demands on players' time can increase substantially. Girls identified as "talented" are in demand for school and regional teams; hence, training/match load can often be chaotic (Taylor et al., 2015). Practitioners should consider how they can support and educate players to manage time and get appropriate rest and recovery, as well as ensuring that academic studies are completed. Ideally, there would be effective communication between practitioners leading the talent development programmes, schools, parents and players to ensure appropriate loading, but this is often challenging to achieve.

High-intensity aerobic capacity is a physical quality that has been shown to be potentially predictive of progression to international U17–U20 squads (Datson et al., 2020). However, post-PHV, this quality is likely to be reflective of a player's training status as well as physiological talent. Therefore, from a talent-ID perspective, it may be important to consider if players have had the opportunity to develop high-intensity aerobic capacity post-PHV, and from a talent-development perspective, programmes should provide the opportunity for players to develop these qualities beyond football-specific training (Wright & Innerd, 2019).

Developing players' ability to generate force quickly in relation to body mass is particularly important for both performance and injury prevention. Long-term injuries negatively affect talent development given the time lost to training, the difficult nature of rehabilitation and the potential risk of re-injury, as well as the psychological impact of return to play. Structured warm-ups, which include neuromuscular training such as strengthening exercises and landing stabilisation and/or appropriately coached and progressed plyometric exercise, can reduce injury risk and should be an integral part of talent development programmes (Nuhu et al., 2021). Moreover, we would argue that talent development programmes in women's football should invest in qualified strength and conditioning support, including access to coached resistance training, movement skill development and aerobic conditioning.

Summary

Talent ID and development is challenging in women's football. Practitioners and coaches working with youth players should be aware of the biopsychosocial factors as well as the context of the women's game that may influence talent ID and development. Coaches should be aware that growth and maturation may impact athletic development and talent ID/development differently between boys and girls and, therefore, there is a need for further research specific to the women's game.

Creating a strong talent development programme that is able to support players flexibly throughout maturation, ensuring they exit the programme as well-rounded individuals, having enjoyed their experience, is clearly challenging. There is a disparity in funding between boys' and girls' talent development programmes. To enhance the development of talent, national federations need to consider how best to manage and deploy current resources as well as how to grow future funding. Practitioners can use the research summarised in this chapter and the practical guidance to implement such knowledge and practices into their specific contexts.

References

Andrew, M., Finnegan, L., Datson, N., & Dugdale, J. H. (2022). Men are from quartile one, women are from? relative age effect in European soccer and the influence of age, success, and playing status. *Children*, *9*(11), 1747. https://doi.org/10.3390/children9111747

Armour, M., Parry, K. A., Steel, K., & Smith, C. A. (2020). Australian female athlete perceptions of the challenges associated with training and competing when menstrual symptoms are present. *International Journal of Sports Science & Coaching*, *15*(3), 316–323. https://doi.org/10.1177/1747954120916073

Baker, J., Wattie, N., & Schorer, J. (2018). A proposed conceptualization of talent in sport: The first step in a long and winding road. *Psychology of Sport and Exercise*, *43*, 27–33. https://doi.org/10.1016/j.psychsport.2018.12.016

Barraclough, S., Till, K., Kerr, A., & Emmonds, S. (2022). Methodological approaches to talent identification in team sports: A narrative review. *Sports*, *10*(6), 81. https://doi.org/10.3390/sports10060081

Bland, V. L., Bea, J. W., Blew, R. M., Roe, D. J., Lee, V. R., Funk, J. L., & Going, S. B. (2021). Influence of changes in soft tissue composition on changes in bone strength in peripubertal girls: The STAR longitudinal study. *Journal of Bone and Mineral Research*, *36*(1), 123–132. https://doi.org/10.1002/jbmr.4168

Bruinvels, G., Goldsmith, E., Blagrove, R., Simpkin, A., Lewis, N., Morton, K., Suppiah, A., Rogers, J. P., Ackerman, K. E., Newell, J., & Pedlar, C. (2021). Prevalence and frequency of menstrual cycle symptoms are associated with availability to train and compete: A study of 6812 exercising women recruited using the Strava exercise app. *British Journal of Sports Medicine*, *55*(8), 438–443. https://doi.org/10.1136/bjsports-2020-102792

Datson, N., Weston, M., Drust, B., Gregson, W., & Lolli, L. (2020). High-intensity endurance capacity assessment as a tool for talent identification in elite youth female soccer. *Journal of Sports Sciences, 38*(11–12), 1313–1319. https://doi.org/10.1080/02640414.2019.1656323

Emmonds, S., Morris, R., Murray, E., Robinson, C., Turner, L., & Jones, B. (2017). The influence of age and maturity status on the maximum and explosive strength characteristics of elite youth female soccer players. *Science and Medicine in Football, 1*(3), 209–215. https://doi.org/10.1080/24733938.2017.1363908

Emmonds, S., Scantlebury, S., Murray, E., Turner, L., Robinson, C., & Jones, B. (2020). Physical characteristics of elite youth female soccer players characterized by maturity status. *The Journal of Strength & Conditioning Research, 34*(8), 2321–2328. https://doi.org/10.1519/JSC.0000000000002795

Emmonds, S., Till, K., Redgrave, J., Murray, E., Turner, L., Robinson, C., & Jones, B. (2018). Influence of age on the anthropometric and performance characteristics of high-level youth female soccer players. *International Journal of Sports Science & Coaching, 13*(5), 779–786. https://doi.org/10.1177/1747954118757437

FIFA. (2019). *Women's football member associations survey report.* https://digitalhub.fifa.com/m/231330ded0bf3120/original/nq3ensohyxpuxovcovj0-pdf

Gledhill, A., Harwood, C., & Forsdyke, D. (2017). Psychosocial factors associated with talent development in football: A systematic review. *Psychology of Sport and Exercise, 31*, 93–112. https://doi.org/10.1016/j.psychsport.2017.04.002

Güllich, A. (2014). Selection, de-selection and progression in German football talent promotion. *European Journal of Sport Science, 14*(6), 530–537. https://doi.org/10.1080/17461391.2013.858371

Harber, V. (2011). The young female athlete: Using the menstrual cycle as a navigational beacon for healthy development. *Canadian Journal for Women in Coaching, 11*(3), 1–11.

Hoare, D., & Warr, C. R. (2000). Talent identification and women's soccer: An Australian experience. *Journal of Sports Sciences, 18*(9), 751–758. https://doi.org/10.1080/02640410050120122

Höner, O., Raabe, J., Murr, D., & Leyhr, D. (2019). Prognostic relevance of motor tests in elite girls' soccer: A five-year prospective cohort study within the German talent promotion program. *Science and Medicine in Football, 3*(4), 287–296. https://doi.org/10.1080/24733938.2019.1609069

Kelly, A. L., & Williams, C. A. (2020). Physical characteristics and the talent identification and development processes in male youth soccer: A narrative review. *Strength & Conditioning Journal, 42*(6), 15–34. https://doi.org/10.1519/SSC.0000000000000576

Krosshaug, T., Nakamae, A., Boden, B. P., Engebretsen, L., Smith, G., Slauterbeck, J. R., Hewett, T. E., & Bahr, R. (2007). Mechanisms of anterior cruciate ligament injury in basketball: Video analysis of 39 cases. *The American Journal of Sports Medicine, 35*(3), 359–367. https://doi.org/10.1177/0363546506293899

Leyhr, D., Raabe, J., Schultz, F., Kelava, A., & Höner, O. (2020). The adolescent motor performance development of elite female soccer players: A study of prognostic relevance for future success in adulthood using multilevel modelling. *Journal of Sports Sciences, 38*(11–12), 1342–1351. https://doi.org/10.1080/02640414.2019.1686940

McNulty, K. L., Elliott-Sale, K. J., Dolan, E., Swinton, P. A., Ansdell, P., Goodall, S., Thomas, K., & Hicks, K. M. (2020). The effects of menstrual cycle phase on exercise performance in eumenorrheic women: A systematic review and meta-analysis. *Sports Medicine, 50*, 1813–1827. https://doi.org/10.1007/s40279-020-01319-3

Morris, R., Emmonds, S., Jones, B., Myers, T. D., Clarke, N. D., Lake, J., Ellis, M., Singleton, D., Roe, G., & Till, K. (2018). Seasonal changes in physical qualities of elite youth soccer players according to maturity status: Comparisons with aged matched controls. *Science and Medicine in Football, 2*(4), 272–280. https://doi.org/10.1080/24733938.2018.1454599

Mujika, I., Santisteban, J., & Castagna, C. (2009). In-season effect of short-term sprint and power training programs on elite junior soccer players. *The Journal of Strength & Conditioning Research*, *23*(9), 2581–2587.

Nuhu, A., Jelsma, J., Dunleavy, K., & Burgess, T. (2021). Effect of the FIFA 11+ soccer specific warm up programme on the incidence of injuries: A cluster-randomised controlled trial. *PLoS One*, *16*(5), e0251839. https://doi.org/10.1371/journal.pone.0251839

O'Brien, S., Rapkin, A., Dennerstein, L., & Nevatte, T. (2011). Diagnosis and management of premenstrual disorders. *British Medical Journal*, *342*(7810), 1297–1303. https://doi.org/10.1136/bmj.d2994

Pettersen, S. D., Martinussen, M., Handegård, B. H., Rasmussen, L. M. P., Koposov, R., & Adolfsen, F. (2023). Beyond physical ability—predicting women's football performance from psychological factors. *Frontiers in Psychology*, *14*, 1146372. https://doi.org/10.3389/fpsyg.2023.1146372

Petushek, E. J., Sugimoto, D., Stoolmiller, M., Smith, G., & Myer, G. D. (2019). Evidence-based best-practice guidelines for preventing anterior cruciate ligament injuries in young female athletes: A systematic review and meta-analysis. *The American Journal of Sports Medicine*, *47*(7), 1744–1753. https://doi.org/10.1177/0363546518782460

Randell, R. K., Clifford, T., Drust, B., Moss, S. L., Unnithan, V. B., Croix, M. B. D. S., Datson, N., Martin, D., Mayho, H., Carter, J. M., & Rollo, I. (2021). Physiological characteristics of female soccer players and health and performance considerations: A narrative review. *Sports Medicine*, *51*, 1377–1399. https://doi.org/10.1007/s40279-021-01458-1

Taylor, J. M., Wright, M. D., Hurst, C., & Best, R. (2015, May). *Contribution of planned and unplanned training to overall load in elite youth female football players*. World Congress of Science in Soccer, Copenhagen, Denmark.

Till, K., & Baker, J. (2020). Challenges and [possible] solutions to optimizing talent identification and development in sport. *Frontiers in Psychology*, *11*, 664. https://doi.org/10.3389/fpsyg.2020.00664

Tomkinson, G. R., Carver, K. D., Atkinson, F., Daniell, N. D., Lewis, L. K., Fitzgerald, J. S., Lang, J. J., & Ortega, F. B. (2018). European normative values for physical fitness in children and adolescents aged 9–17 years: Results from 2 779 165 Eurofit performances representing 30 countries. *British Journal of Sports Medicine*, *52*(22), 1445–1456. https://doi.org/10.1016/j.jped.2022.02.004

Towlson, C., MacMaster, C., Gonçalves, B., Sampaio, J., Toner, J., MacFarlane, N., Barrett, S., Hamilton, A., Jack, R., Hunter, F., & Myers, T. (2021). The effect of bio-banding on physical and psychological indicators of talent identification in academy soccer players. *Science and Medicine in Football*, *5*(4), 280–292. https://doi.org/10.1080/24733938.2020.1862419

UEFA. (2019). *Time for action: Women's football strategy 2019–2024*. https://www.uefa.com/MultimediaFiles/Download/uefaorg/Womensfootball/02/60/51/38/2605138_DOWNLOAD.pdf

Vaeyens, R., Güllich, A., Warr, C. R., & Philippaerts, R. (2009). Talent identification and promotion programmes of Olympic athletes. *Journal of Sports Sciences*, *27*(13), 1367–1380. https://doi.org/10.1080/02640410903110974

Vescovi, J. D., Rupf, R., Brown, T. D., & Marques, M. C. (2011). Physical performance characteristics of high-level female soccer players 12–21 years of age. *Scandinavian Journal of Medicine & Science in Sports*, *21*(5), 670–678. https://doi.org/10.1111/j.1600-0838.2009.01081.x

Williams, A. M., & Reilly, T. (2000). Talent identification and development in soccer. *Journal of Sports Sciences*, *18*(9), 657–667. https://doi.org/10.1080/02640410050120041

Wolff, W., Bertrams, A., & Schüler, J. (2019). Trait self-control discriminates between youth football players selected and not selected for the German talent program: A Bayesian analysis. *Frontiers in Psychology*, *10*, 2203. https://doi.org/10.3389/fpsyg.2019.02203

Wright, M. D., & Atkinson, G. (2019). Changes in sprint-related outcomes during a period of systematic training in a girls' soccer academy. *The Journal of Strength & Conditioning Research, 33*(3), 793–800. http://doi.org/10.1519/JSC.0000000000002055

Wright, M. D., & Innerd, A. (2019). Application and interpretation of the yo-yo intermittent recovery test to the long-term physical development of girl's association football players. *Science and Medicine in Football, 3*(4), 297–306. https://doi.org/10.1080/24733938.2019.1609071

5

THE MENSTRUAL CYCLE AND HORMONE-BASED CONTRACEPTION

Kelly Lee McNulty, Paul Ansdell, Amal Hassan and Kirsty Marie Hicks

Introduction

It is well recognised that women remain under-represented in sport and exercise science literature (Cowley et al., 2021). Thus, at present, performance-, training- and recovery-based research in women footballers is lacking (Okholm et al., 2022; Randell et al., 2021). Consequently, it is not uncommon for the understanding and prescription of performance, training and recovery to be based on data from men (Emmonds et al., 2019). However, given the anatomical, physiological and endocrinological differences between the sexes (Ansdell et al., 2020), greater scrutiny is now being placed on whether using research conducted on men is fit for purpose in women's football (Okholm et al., 2022). Indeed, one unique consideration for women footballers is the potential influence of endogenous and exogenous sex hormones (i.e. the menstrual cycle and hormonal contraceptive use) on exercise performance, training and recovery.

The following are the aims of the chapter:

1 To describe the fluctuations in sex hormones that underpin the eumenorrhoeic menstrual cycle.
2 To discuss the literature that has investigated the effect of the menstrual cycle on football performance, training and recovery.
3 To describe the different types of hormonal contraception and how they work.
4 To summarise the literature regarding the impact of the oral contraceptive pill on football performance, training and recovery.

DOI: 10.4324/9781003381914-5

The eumenorrhoeic menstrual cycle

The menstrual cycle is the name given to the cyclic fluctuations in endogenous sex hormones and structural changes to the endometrial lining that occur roughly every month in women of reproductive age (from menarche to menopause) with the primary purpose of allowing reproduction (Davis & Hackney, 2017). The length of the menstrual cycle refers to the number of days from the first day of bleeding in the current cycle to the day before the onset of bleeding in the following cycle. Typically, this length has been described as 28 days, with most cycle lengths varying between 21 and 35 days (Davis & Hackney, 2017). The menstrual cycle is regulated by hormones released by the hypothalamus (gonadotropin releasing hormone, [GnRH]), pituitary gland (luteinising hormone [LH] and follicle stimulating hormone [FSH]) and the ovaries (oestrogen and progesterone) (Davis & Hackney, 2017). The changes in these hormone concentrations across the menstrual cycle are often used to differentiate between menstrual cycle phases. Indeed, in recent research it has been proposed that there are four distinctly different sex-hormone profiles across the menstrual cycle that represent the significant changes in both oestrogen and progesterone concentrations (Elliott-Sale et al., 2021): (1) phase one (early follicular phase), indicted by the onset of bleeding (commonly referred to as the period) until approximately day five of the cycle, categorised by the lowest oestrogen and progesterone concentrations; (2) phase two (the late follicular phase), occurring at approximately 14 to 16 hr prior to ovulation, classified by peaking oestrogen and low progesterone concentrations; (3) phase three (the ovulatory phase), indicated by a positive urinary ovulation test and lasting approximately 24 to 36 hr, categorised by medium oestrogen concentration and low progesterone concentrations; and (4) phase four (the mid-luteal phase), occurring at approximately seven days after ovulation, classified by high oestrogen and the highest progesterone concentrations. Whilst this four-phase definition allows the impact of key hormone ratios on performance, training and recovery outcomes to be examined, it is important to note that other time points outside these four phases, such as the late luteal (premenstrual) phase, are also important to consider for footballers (Bruinvels et al., 2022).

The menstrual cycle and football performance, training and recovery

Whilst the primary role of the menstrual cycle is to support reproductive function, it is well established that the cyclical changes in oestrogen and progesterone across the menstrual cycle can also affect biological tissues and systems containing the respective hormone receptor(s) (Constantini et al., 2005). For instance, these sex hormones have been shown to affect physiological processes within the cardiopulmonary, metabolic, musculoskeletal and nervous systems (Constantini et al., 2005), the integration of which determines many outcomes in football (see Chapter 3 for details pertaining to the physiological determinants of women's football). As such, the changes in sex hormones across the menstrual cycle have the potential to affect football performance as well as responses to training and recovery.

The menstrual cycle and performance

There are a range of suggested mechanisms by which the cyclical fluctuations in oestrogen and progesterone across the menstrual cycle might affect performance. For example oestrogen is thought to have an anabolic effect on skeletal muscle (Alexander et al., 2022; Chidi-Ogbolu & Baar, 2019; Lowe et al., 2010), and has been shown to play a role in substrate metabolism changes through increased muscle glycogen storage and increased fat utilisation (Boisseau & Isacco, 2022; Hackney, 2021). Additionally, when concentrations are high, progesterone has been shown to have an anti-oestrogenic effect, such as catabolic and neuro-inhibitory effects (Frankovich & Lebrun, 2000). Whilst these plausible mechanisms have the potential to exert either positive or negative effects on football performance, whether these translate to changes in actual football performance across the menstrual cycle are not well understood. For example within the literature, in which the effect of the menstrual cycle on indices of football performance has been investigated (Table 5.1), several researchers have reported reductions in some performance outcomes during the early follicular (Igonin et al., 2022) and mid-luteal (Julian et al., 2017) phases, whereas other researchers have shown no changes in performance outcomes across menstrual cycle phases (Campa et al., 2021; Julian et al., 2021; Sánchez et al., 2022; Tounsi et al., 2018). However, it is important to note that the effect of menstrual cycle phase on football-specific performance has not been extensively explored. Looking at broader data from a recent systematic review with meta-analysis in which the effect of menstrual cycle phase on exercise performance (strength and endurance) was identified, evaluated and summarised, the authors concluded that, on average, exercise performance might be reduced by a trivial amount during the early follicular phase compared with all other phases of the menstrual cycle (McNulty et al., 2020). However, alongside the trivial to small effect size, it was highlighted that the current quality of evidence in this area is low, and that large between-study variance exists; thus, from a practical perspective, based on the current evidence, general guidance on modulating exercise to achieve optimal performance across the menstrual cycle is not warranted (McNulty et al., 2020). As such, until further high-quality research is available (specific to footballers), we recommend that footballers, and those who work with them, should be aware of the menstrual cycle and its potential effects on performance, but this approach should be tailored to and informed by the individual player on a case-by-case basis (i.e. regular cyclical tracking of relevant performance metrics).

Whilst it is plausible that exercise performance across the menstrual cycle might be altered via hormonally mediated changes, other possible reasons for any effects include the influence of cycle-related symptoms, athlete perceptions (such as the perceived effects of the menstrual cycle on performance), lived experiences (such

TABLE 5.1 The effect of menstrual cycle phase on football-specific indices of performance.

Study (date)	Population (n)	Menstrual cycle phases investigated	Performance test	Study findings
Campa et al. (2021)	Elite players (n = 20)	Early follicular and ovulatory phase	Countermovement jump and 20-m sprint	No change in jumping and sprinting capacity was observed across the menstrual cycle.
Igonin et al. (2022)	Sub-elite players (n = 8)	Early follicular phase, late follicular phase and mid-luteal phase	Movement patterns during a game (i.e. total distance covered, velocity ranges and number of sprints)	The early follicular phase might negatively affect performance during competitive matches by decreasing the distances covered at different velocities and the number of sprints.
Julian et al. (2017)	Sub-elite players (n = 9)	Early follicular phase and mid-luteal phase	Yo-Yo Intermittent endurance test, countermovement jump and 3 × 30-m sprints	A reduction in maximal endurance performance was shown during the mid-luteal phase of the menstrual cycle but no differences were observed for jumping and sprint performance.
Julian et al. (2021)	Elite players (n = 15)	Early follicular phase and mid-luteal phase	Physical match performance assessed via global positioning systems	Menstrual cycle phase does not influence match physical performance of players to a significant degree.
Sánchez et al. (2022)	Youth players (n = 12)	Early follicular phase, the ovulatory phase and mid-luteal phase	Maximum speed in 40 m, ability to change direction, explosive strength of the lower limbs and vertical jump height	No differences between menstrual phases were obtained in any performance outcome.
Tounsi et al. (2018)	Tunisian high-level players (n = 11)	Early follicular phase, late follicular phase and mid-luteal phase	Five-jump test, repeated shuttle-sprint ability test and Yo-Yo intermittent recovery test	Football-specific endurance as well as jumping and repeated sprinting ability were not affected due to menstrual cycle phase.

as menstrual cycle stigma, access to period products) and changes in behaviour (such as training habits, clothing) associated with the menstrual cycle, as well as additional lifestyle factors that have a bidirectional relationship with sex hormones such as sleep, nutritional intake and stress. Firstly, the cyclical fluctuations in endogenous sex hormones across the menstrual cycle have been associated with a variety of physical (e.g. period pain, breast pain and bloating) and psychological (e.g. mood changes, anxiety and irritability) symptoms (Dickerson et al., 2003; Ferries-Rowe et al., 2020; Yonkers et al., 2008), which are likely incompatible with optimal performance. In footballers, it appears that cycle-related symptoms are prevalent; for example Read et al. (2022) reported that 93% and 100% of elite footballers, competing in the Women's Super League in England, experienced negative symptoms (such as abdominal pain) during the premenstrual and menstrual phases, respectively. Similarly, Parker et al. (2022) reported that negative menstrual-cycle-related symptoms were reported by 74% of elite footballers from the Women's Super League ($n = 75$) and were mainly experienced in the initial days of menstruation. Moreover, it appears that many footballers perceive the menstrual cycle to influence their ability to perform. For example Read et al. (2022) also reported that all players perceived their menstrual cycle to negatively impact physical (i.e. power and fatigue) and psychological (i.e. confidence and focus) performance particularly during the premenstrual and menstrual stages. Likewise, Pinel et al. (2022) highlighted that the players perceived their performance to be negatively impacted, both physically and mentally, during menstruation. In a study of Brazilian elite futsal players, the authors reported a perceived improvement in performance during the late follicular phase of the menstrual cycle in 73% of participants, compared to their performance in the early follicular and mid-luteal phases (Queiroga et al., 2021). From a practical perspective, these findings demonstrate the need for individual symptom and readiness-to-perform monitoring in footballers across the menstrual cycle, as symptoms and perceived effects might impact performance outcomes. Furthermore, in a study of elite football players, most participants frequently described the menstrual cycle as a taboo topic of conversation and players reported receiving inadequate menstrual health support (McHaffie et al., 2022). Additionally, factors such as uniform (i.e. white shorts), access to toilets, period products and disposable bins have the potential to influence performance (Mkumbuzi et al., 2021; Pinel et al., 2022). Collectively, these findings highlight the importance of understanding the impact of all facets of the menstrual cycle, rather than the potential effects of endogenous hormones on physiological and physical function in isolation when it comes to optimising football-specific performance, and also highlight the importance of working on an individual basis to overcome any challenges.

The menstrual cycle and training

Both oestrogen and progesterone have numerous physiological effects outside of the reproductive system by acting on receptor sites in target tissues. For example the anabolic effect of oestrogen is important to consider when it comes to strength training, as it might influence skeletal muscle strength and size, hypertrophy and protein synthesis (Knowles et al., 2019). In contrast, progesterone is thought to inhibit the effects of oestrogen, with some researchers reporting a catabolic effect of progesterone (Frankovich & Lebrun, 2000), although more research is needed to understand the effects of progesterone on muscle. Given these potential effects, variations in sex hormones across the menstrual cycle might influence strength training outcomes in women (Kissow et al., 2022). Specifically, in some studies it has been shown that women could gain muscle strength and size more efficiently by training during the follicular phase compared to luteal phase-based training (Reis et al., 1995; Sung et al., 2014; Vargas-Molina et al., 2022; Wikström-Frisén et al., 2017), with only one study reporting no effect (Sakamaki-Sunaga et al., 2016). However, it is important to note that only these five studies have investigated menstrual cycle phase-based strength training to date (and none has included footballers within their population), which makes it difficult to draw clear conclusions. In addition, several methodological shortcomings, such as differing study designs, small participant numbers, no measurement of oestrogen and progesterone to confirm menstrual cycle phase and grouping together of hormonal contraceptive users with naturally menstruating women, further bring into question the validity of the results. Furthermore, it is important to note that footballers require a complex blend of multiple training qualities that are trained concurrently; however, at present, menstrual-cycle, phase-based research has investigated only one component of training for footballers (i.e. strength) (Julian & Sargent, 2020). As such, little is known regarding the influence of menstrual-cycle, phase-based endurance and/or concurrent training responses specific to footballers. Overall, in the absence of high-quality evidence, it is premature to suggest a blanket approach to menstrual-cycle, phase-based training; instead we recommend that footballers, and those who work with them, should focus on individual training prescription (Colenso-Semple et al., 2023).

The menstrual cycle and recovery

The scientific principle behind training is that an improvement in exercise performance results from an adequate balance between stress and the appropriate response and recovery post- exercise (Kellmann et al., 2018). Specifically, many aspects of the effect of exercise on adaptation occur during the post-exercise recovery times, which are critical time points relative to the adaptation process associated with training (Bishop et al., 2008). Whilst several variables influence the recovery from exercise (such as the intensity and duration of exercise and the type of activity), what remains to be determined is how endogenous sex hormones affect these outcomes. For instance, oestrogen is reported to upregulate intracellular signalling pathways that stimulate skeletal muscle protein synthesis (Knowles et al., 2019). Thus, a strengthened anabolic response to exercise might help increase skeletal muscle repair and adaptation (Knowles et al., 2019). Additionally, over the last two decades, evidence has accumulated, primarily from animal models, in which it has been suggested that oestrogen might play a key role in the protection of skeletal muscle against exercise-induced muscle damage, as well as in muscle repair and regeneration (Enns & Tiidus, 2010; Tiidus, 2003, 2005). Whilst at a mechanistic level, endogenous sex hormones have the potential to directly and indirectly affect the recovery response post-exercise (Oosthuyse et al., 2023), whether the fluctuations in these hormones across the menstrual cycle can create optimal/suboptimal hormonal environments to maximise/minimise the recovery from exercise is unclear, with researchers reporting conflicting results (Hackney et al., 2019; Minahan et al., 2015; Romero-Parra, Alfaro-Magallanes, et al., 2020; Romero-Parra, Barba-Moreno, et al., 2020); to our knowledge no studies have been conducted on a football-specific population. To provide some guidance, a recent systematic review with meta-analysis was performed to identify, evaluate and summarise the available empirical evidence (Romero-Parra, Cupeiro, et al., 2021). Based on this meta-analysis, it was suggested that fluctuations in endogenous sex hormones across the menstrual cycle might affect exercise-induced muscle damage, particularly in terms of muscle soreness. Therefore, the authors highlighted that, practically, lower training loads or longer recovery periods could be considered during the early follicular phase, when sex hormone concentrations are at their lowest. However, it is evident from this review that further high-quality research is required. Overall, whilst oestrogen might play an important role in the recovery process, the significance of this role on the potential for reduced or enhanced recovery post-exercise in footballers across menstrual cycle phases is not yet fully known. As such, it is difficult to draw evidenced-based guidelines for footballers, and instead we suggest that any adjustments should be based on individual data.

Hormonal contraception

It is important to consider that not all footballers have a natural menstrual cycle (Parker et al., 2022). The cyclical fluctuations in sex hormones across the menstrual cycle described here might be altered by internal factors, such as amenorrhoea, oligomenorrhoea, anovulation and luteal phase defects (Elliott-Sale et al., 2021). Whilst an understanding of these internal dysfunctions is necessary for individuals working with footballers, how these internal disturbances affect health and performance in players is beyond the scope of this chapter (see instead Chapters 9 and 10). The menstrual cycle can also be manipulated through external ways, namely via hormonal contraceptive use (Elliott-Sale & Hicks, 2018). Indeed, hormonal contraceptives contain exogenous hormones that work by altering the natural menstrual cycle by changing the internal reproductive hormonal milieu (Davis & Hackney, 2017). Hormonal contraceptives are primarily designed to reduce the chances of an unplanned pregnancy, but are commonly used by many sportswomen for secondary reasons, such as (1) alleviating the symptoms of menorrhagia (heavy menstrual bleeding); (2) reducing the occurrence of cycle-related symptoms, such as dysmenorrhoea; (3) treating androgenisation symptoms, such as acne; (4) helping with various clinical conditions, such as symptomatic fibroids, functional ovarian cysts, benign breast disease, endometriosis and adenomyosis; and (5) decreasing the risk of ovarian and endometrial cancer and pelvic inflammatory disease (Elliott-Sale & Hicks, 2018). Additionally, many sportswomen use hormonal contraception to predict, alter and control (or omit entirely) bleeding, particularly around important sporting events and competitions (Schaumberg et al., 2018). Thus, hormonal contraceptives are a desirable option for many sportswomen. Specifically, in an audit of 75 elite players from the Women's Super League, it was shown that 28% of players reported current hormonal contraceptive use, with 43% having used hormonal contraception previously (Parker et al., 2022).

The term *hormonal contraceptive* has come to define a wide range of preparation types (combined, progestin-only and mono- bi- tri-phasic), delivery methods (pill, patch, vaginal ring, implant, injection and intrauterine system) and brands (Elliott-Sale & Hicks, 2018). A summary of hormonal contraceptive options available is provided in Table 5.2. Despite the expansion in preparation types and delivery methods, the combined, monophasic oral contraceptive pill is the most used option in elite footballers in England (Parker et al., 2022). Combined, monophasic oral contraceptive pills work via negative feedback on the gonadotropic hormones, preventing pituitary secretion of FSH and LH and ultimately resulting in a downregulation of endogenous oestrogen and progesterone. Specifically, combined, monophasic oral contraceptive pill use results in four distinct hormonal environments: (1) a downregulated endogenous oestradiol profile of approximately 60 pmol L^{-1} for 21 days that rises during the 7 pill-free days to approximately 140 pmol L^{-1}; (2) a chronically downregulated endogenous progesterone profile of approximately 5 nmol L^{-1}; (3) a daily surge of ethinyloestradiol and progestogen, which peaks within 1 hr after ingestion (from approximately 2 pg mL^{-1} to approximately 6 pg mL^{-1}), with baseline values accumulating slightly from approximately 2 pg mL^{-1} to approximately 3 pg mL^{-1} over the 21 pill-taking days; and (4) 7 exogenous, sex-hormone-free days (Rechichi et al., 2009). Additionally, it is important to consider that the type, amount, potency and androgenicity of synthetic hormones in various combined, monophasic oral contraceptive pills differ between brands. Overall, given the different sex hormone profiles experienced by pill users compared with naturally menstruating women and the changing sex hormone profile across the pill "cycle", it could be theorised that exercise performance, training and recovery responses might also differ.

The combined, monophasic oral contraceptive pill and football performance, training and recovery

The combined, monophasic oral contraceptive pill and performance

Despite the prevalence of the combined, monophasic oral contraceptive pill use among certain footballers, the potential effects of this hormonal contraceptive on

TABLE 5.2 Summary of hormonal contraceptive options.

Option	Preparation type	Delivery method	Brand examples
Oral contraceptive pill	Combined (i.e. ethinylestradiol and progestogen). Available in monophasic, biphasic and triphasic formulations	Self-administered, taken orally daily for 21 days followed by 7-day pill-free break or taken daily for 28 days (21 active pills and seven inactive pills)	Microgynon®, Rigevidon®
Oral contraceptive pill	Progestogen-only	Self-administered, taken orally daily for 28 days	Cerazette®, Norgeston®
Contraceptive patch	Combined (i.e. ethinylestradiol and progestogen)	Self-administered, releases hormones through the skin. Replaced every 7 days for 21 days followed by 7-day break	Evra®
Vaginal ring	Combined (i.e. ethinylestradiol and progestogen)	Self-administered, inserted into the vagina. Each ring lasts 21 days followed by 7-day break	NuvaRing®
Contraceptive injection	Progestogen-only	Medically administered, intramuscular injection. Lasts between 8 and 13 weeks	Depo-Provera®, Noristerat®
Contraceptive implant	Progestogen only	Medically administered, implanted under skin of the upper arm. Lasts up to 3 years	Nexplanon®
Intrauterine system	Progestogen only	Medically administered, inserted into uterus. Lasts between three to five years	Jaydess®, Kyleena®, Mirena®

football performance remain unclear. To provide some guidance, Elliott-Sale et al. (2020), on the basis of a systematic review and meta-analysis, indicated that oral contraceptive users had slightly inferior exercise performance (strength and endurance) in comparison to that of naturally menstruating women. However, from a practical perspective, it is important to note that, as effects tended to be trivial and variable across studies, the current evidence does not warrant general guidance on oral contraceptive use compared with non-use. Instead, these findings support consideration of an individual's response to oral contraceptives, as some players might experience no performance-related side effects, whereas others might experience substantial performance-related side effects. Additionally, it is important to consider that an individual's rationale for using contraceptives might be different. For example some players might experience substantial cycle-related symptoms (such as period pain, breast pain and bloating) and conditions (such as menorrhagia), and for these individuals the benefits of hormonal contraceptive use might outweigh the trivial negative detriment to performance. Indeed, Parker et al. (2022) highlighted that most elite players, who were using hormonal contraception, reported benefits of hormonal contraceptive use, such as reduced period pain and the ability to omit and control bleeding. It is important to note that 38% of players have still been found to experience negative symptoms, such as mood changes, although interestingly, negative symptoms were found to be greater in progestogen-only users compared to symptoms of combined users (Parker et al., 2022). Thus, these findings demonstrate the importance of considering and, where necessary, tracking symptoms related to hormonal contraceptive use in footballers, as these might impact perceived and actual performance outcomes. Data from the above review, in which exercise performance between pill-taking and pill-free days was also compared, show that exercise performance was consistent across the oral contraceptive cycle (Elliott-Sale et al., 2020). The authors suggested that different performance-related guidance was not warranted for pill-taking versus pill-free days. Overall, in the case of footballers who are focusing on performance, we recommend that an individualised approach is sought, based on each player's response to and requirement for oral contraceptive pill use.

The combined, monophasic oral contraceptive pill and training

There is currently a paucity of information in which the effect of oral contraceptives on adaptations to training has been investigated, and to our knowledge no studies have been carried out on a football population. To provide some guidance, Nolan et al. (2023) systematically reviewed the effect of oral contraceptive pill use on skeletal muscle hypertrophy, power and strength adaptations in response to resistance training. The authors concluded that oral contraceptive use had no effect on these adaptations in response to resistance training, and suggested that, practically, the focus should move away from blanket recommendations for all sportswomen to a focus on the individual's response to oral contraceptive pill use in a training context, as well as their reasons for use. Furthermore, adaptations to sprint interval training between oral contraceptive pill users and naturally menstruating women have been investigated; it was demonstrated that physiological adaptations might be dampened by oral contraceptive pill use (Schaumberg et al., 2016). In another study, the effect of a 10-week period of combined strength and endurance training between hormonal contraceptive users and those who had never used hormonal contraception was investigated (Myllyaho et al., 2021). The authors concluded that there was no difference in strength, endurance or body composition adaptations between the groups. Overall, there is a lack of clear evidence on the influence of exogenous sex hormones on training adaptation specific to footballers. Practically, it appears that there is no evidence-based rationale to advocate for or against the use of oral contraceptive pill use in footballers when it comes solely to training adaptation. Instead, we recommend considering each player's response to hormonal contraception in a training context and their reasons for use.

The combined, monophasic, oral contraceptive pill and recovery

The different sex-hormone profile experienced by oral contraceptive users, compared to those of naturally menstruating women, might have different implications for the recovery from exercise. Indeed, researchers have shown a reduced recovery after eccentric exercise in oral contraceptive pill users compared to the recovery in naturally menstruating women (Hicks et al., 2017; Mackay et al., 2019; Minahan et al., 2015; Roth et al., 2001). In contrast, other researchers have shown an improved recovery response in oral contraceptive pill users (Hayward et al., 1998; Thompson et al., 1997), as well as no differences between the groups (Savage & Clarkson, 2002). In a recent systematic review by Glenner-Frandsen et al. (2023), it was concluded that recovery might be slightly impaired in oral contraceptive users compared with the recovery in naturally menstruating women, with a potential for greater declines in muscle strength, elevated markers of exercise-induced muscle damage and greater perceived muscle soreness, particularly during the pill-free days compared to the early follicular phase. In one study, stress, inflammatory and metabolic biomarkers between oral contraceptive pill users and naturally menstruating women were investigated throughout a competitive season in footballers (Bozzini et al., 2021). In agreement with the review by Glenner-Frandsen et al. (2023), Bozzini et al. found an elevated exposure to stress, inflammatory and metabolic biomarkers over the competitive season in oral contraceptive pill users, which might have implications for recovery in footballers. Furthermore, given the changing hormonal profile between pill-taking and pill-free days, it could be theorised that the recovery response to exercise might differ across the pill cycle. For example Romero-Parra, Rael, et al. (2021) found that there was a greater creatine kinase response during the recovery period following an eccentric squat-based exercise during the pill-free days and suggested that a longer recovery period was needed at this time, although no difference in jump performance and perceived muscle soreness was reported. Despite these initial findings, relatively few studies have addressed the potential influence of oral contraceptive use versus naturally menstruating women and the different sex hormone environments across the pill cycle on the recovery responses following exercise, and further research is required specifically within a football population. Practically, we think these findings further emphasise the importance of considering the individual player, and any decision to use (or not use) hormonal contraception should be based on all relevant factors, such as personal, physical, emotional, practical, financial and health-related factors.

Summary

The current evidence does not provide blanket recommendations for performance, training and recovery across the menstrual cycle and with hormonal contraceptive use in footballers. Instead, we suggest that the focus should be on the individual player and their experience of the menstrual cycle and hormonal contraceptive use. This individualisation can be achieved through regular sex-hormone screening and, as a minimum, consistent, real-time, cycle tracking (such as cycle length, period duration, blood flow and the type, frequency and severity of symptoms, as well as perceptual and/or objective noteworthy changes in exercise performance, training and recovery), irrespective of the reproductive hormonal milieu (i.e. whether they are naturally menstruating or using hormone-based contraception), for at least 3 months. Indeed, these approaches would allow footballers and their support staff to identify temporal trends in individual player symptomology and performance, training and recovery responses and for them to begin to consider countermeasures to enhance health and performance. For more in-depth, practical recommendations for footballers, and for those who work with them, see Chapter 6. Overall, it is imperative that high-quality research on women is used to inform practice, but football is one example of where the current evidence base cannot support blanket menstrual cycle-based performance, training and recovery recommendations; instead application of evidence should be shaped (if required) to the individual player and their own experiences of the menstrual cycle and hormonal contraceptive use. Ultimately, this approach will help to optimise performance, training and recovery outcomes on any given day in a footballer's schedule.

References

Alexander, S. E., Pollock, A. C., & Lamon, S. (2022). The effect of sex hormones on skeletal muscle adaptation in females. *European Journal of Sport Science*, *22*(7), 1035–1045. https://doi.org/10.1080/17461391.2021.1921854

Ansdell, P., Thomas, K., Hicks, K. M., Hunter, S. K., Howatson, G., & Goodall, S. (2020). Physiological sex differences affect the integrative response to exercise: Acute and chronic implications. *Experimental Physiology*, *105*(12), 2007–2021. https://doi.org/10.1113/EP088548

Bishop, P. A., Jones, E., & Woods, A. K. (2008). Recovery from training: A brief review. *The Journal of Strength & Conditioning Research*, *22*(3), 1015–1024. https://doi.org/10.1519/JSC.0b013e31816eb518

Boisseau, N., & Isacco, L. (2022). Substrate metabolism during exercise: Sexual dimorphism and women's specificities. *European Journal of Sport Science, 22*(5), 672–683. https://doi.org/10.1080/17461391.2021.1943713

Bozzini, B. N., McFadden, B. A., Elliott-Sale, K. J., Swinton, P. A., & Arent, S. M. (2021). Evaluating the effects of oral contraceptive use on biomarkers and body composition during a competitive season in collegiate female soccer players. *Journal of Applied Physiology, 130*(6), 1971–1982. https://doi.org/10.1152/japplphysiol.00818.2020

Bruinvels, G., Hackney, A. C., & Pedlar, C. R. (2022). Menstrual cycle: The importance of both the phases and the transitions between phases on training and performance. *Sports Medicine, 52*(7), 1457–1460. https://doi.org/10.1007/s40279–022–01691–2

Campa, F., Micheli, M. L., Pompignoli, M., Cannataro, R., Gulisano, M., Toselli, S., Greco, G., & Coratella, G. (2021). The influence of menstrual cycle on bioimpedance vector patterns, performance, and flexibility in elite soccer players. *International Journal of Sports Physiology and Performance, 17*(1), 58–66. https://doi.org/10.1123/ijspp.2021-0135

Chidi-Ogbolu, N., & Baar, K. (2019). Effect of estrogen on musculoskeletal performance and injury risk. *Frontiers in Physiology, 9*, 1834. https://doi.org/10.3389/fphys.2018.01834

Colenso-Semple, L. M., D'Souza, A. C., Elliott-Sale, K. J., & Phillips, S. M. (2023). Current evidence shows no influence of women's menstrual cycle phase on acute strength performance or adaptations to resistance exercise training. *Frontiers in Sports and Active Living, 5*, 1054542. https://doi.org/10.3389/fspor.2023.1054542

Constantini, N. W., Dubnov, G., & Lebrun, C. M. (2005). The menstrual cycle and sport performance. *Clinics in Sports Medicine, 24*(2), e51–e82. https://doi.org/10.1016/j.csm.2005.01.003

Cowley, E. S., Olenick, A. A., McNulty, K. L., & Ross, E. Z. (2021). "Invisible sportswomen": The sex data gap in sport and exercise science research. *Women in Sport and Physical Activity Journal, 29*(2), 146–151. https://doi.org/10.1123/wspaj.2021-0028

Davis, H. C., & Hackney, A. C. (2017). The hypothalamic-pituitary-ovarian axis and oral contraceptives: Regulation and function. In A. Hackney (Ed.), *Sex hormones, exercise & women* (pp. 1–17). Springer. https://doi.org/10.1007/978-3-319-44558-8_1

Dickerson, L. M., Mazyck, P. J., & Hunter, M. H. (2003). Premenstrual syndrome. *American Family Physician, 67*(8), 1743–1752.

Elliott-Sale, K. J., & Hicks, K. M. (2018). Hormonal-based contraception and the exercising female. In J. Forsyth & C.-M. Roberts (Eds.), *The exercising female* (pp. 30–43). Routledge.

Elliott-Sale, K. J., McNulty, K. L., Ansdell, P., Goodall, S., Hicks, K. M., Thomas, K., Swinton, P. A., & Dolan, E. (2020). The effects of oral contraceptives on exercise performance in women: A systematic review and meta-analysis. *Sports Medicine, 50*(10), 1785–1812. https://doi.org/10.1007/s40279-020-01317-5

Elliott-Sale, K. J., Minahan, C. L., de Jonge, X. A. J., Ackerman, K. E., Sipilä, S., Constantini, N. W., Lebrun, C. M., & Hackney, A. C. (2021). Methodological considerations for studies in sport and exercise science with women as participants: A working guide for standards of practice for research on women. *Sports Medicine, 51*(5), 843–861. https://doi.org/10.1007/s40279-021-01435-8

Emmonds, S., Heyward, O., & Jones, B. (2019). The challenge of applying and undertaking research in female sport. *Sports Medicine-Open, 5*, 51. https://doi.org/10.1186/s40798-019-0224-x

Enns, D. L., & Tiidus, P. M. (2010). The influence of estrogen on skeletal muscle: Sex matters. *Sports Medicine, 40*, 41–58.

Ferries-Rowe, E., Corey, E., & Archer, J. S. (2020). Primary dysmenorrhea: Diagnosis and therapy. *Obstetrics & Gynecology, 136*(5), 1047–1058. https://doi.org/10.1097/AOG.0000000000004096

Frankovich, R. J., & Lebrun, C. M. (2000). Menstrual cycle, contraception and performance. *Clinics in Sports Medicine, 19*(2), 251–271. https://doi.org/10.1016/S0278-5919(05)70202-7

Glenner-Frandsen, A., With, C., Gunnarsson, T. P., & Hostrup, M. (2023). The effect of monophasic oral contraceptives on muscle strength and markers of recovery after exercise-induced muscle damage: A systematic review. *Sports Health, 15*(3), 318–327. https://doi.org/10.1177/19417381221121653

Hackney, A. C. (2021). Menstrual cycle hormonal changes and energy substrate metabolism in exercising women: A perspective. *International Journal of Environmental Research and Public Health, 18*(19), 10024. https://doi.org/10.3390/ijerph181910024

Hackney, A. C., Kallman, A. L., & Ağğön, E. (2019). Female sex hormones and the recovery from exercise: Menstrual cycle phase affects responses. *Biomedical Human Kinetics, 11*(1), 87–89. https://doi.org/10.2478/bhk-2019-0011

Hayward, R., Dennehy, C. A., Rodearmel, S. J., & Schneider, C. M. (1998). Serum creatine kinase, CK-MB and perceived soreness following eccentric exercise in oral contraceptive users. *Research in Sports Medicine: An International Journal, 8*(2), 193–207. https://doi.org/10.1080/15438629809512527

Hicks, K. M., Onambele-Pearson, G., Winwood, K., & Morse, C. I. (2017). Oral contraceptive pill use and the susceptibility to markers of exercise-induced muscle damage. *European Journal of Applied Physiology, 117*, 1393–1402. https://doi.org/10.1007/s00421-017-3629-6

Igonin, P. H., Rogowski, I., Boisseau, N., & Martin, C. (2022). Impact of the menstrual cycle phases on the movement patterns of sub-elite women soccer players during competitive matches. *International Journal of Environmental Research and Public Health, 19*(8), 4465. https://doi.org/10.3390/ijerph19084465

Julian, R., Hecksteden, A., Fullagar, H. H., & Meyer, T. (2017). The effects of menstrual cycle phase on physical performance in female soccer players. *PLoS One, 12*(3), e0173951. https://doi.org/10.1371/journal.pone.0173951

Julian, R., & Sargent, D. (2020). Periodisation: Tailoring training based on the menstrual cycle may work in theory but can they be used in practice? *Science and Medicine in Football, 4*(4), 253–254. https://doi.org/10.1080/24733938.2020.1828615

Julian, R., Skorski, S., Hecksteden, A., Pfeifer, C., Bradley, P. S., Schulze, E., & Meyer, T. (2021). Menstrual cycle phase and elite female soccer match-play: Influence on various physical performance outputs. *Science and Medicine in Football, 5*(2), 97–104. https://doi.org/10.1080/24733938.2020.1802057

Kellmann, M., Bertollo, M., Bosquet, L., Brink, M., Coutts, A. J., Duffield, R., Erlacher, D., Halson, S. L., Hecksteden, A., Heidari, J., & Beckmann, J. (2018). Recovery and performance in sport: Consensus statement. *International Journal of Sports Physiology and Performance, 13*(2), 240–245. https://doi.org/10.1123/ijspp.2017-0759

Kissow, J., Jacobsen, K. J., Gunnarsson, T. P., Jessen, S., & Hostrup, M. (2022). Effects of follicular and luteal phase-based menstrual cycle resistance training on muscle strength and mass. *Sports Medicine, 52*(12), 2813–2819. https://doi.org/10.1007/s40279-022-01679-y

Knowles, O. E., Aisbett, B., Main, L. C., Drinkwater, E. J., Orellana, L., & Lamon, S. (2019). Resistance training and skeletal muscle protein metabolism in eumenorrheic females: Implications for researchers and practitioners. *Sports Medicine, 49*, 1637–1650. https://doi.org/10.1007/s40279-019-01132-7

Lowe, D. A., Baltgalvis, K. A., & Greising, S. M. (2010). Mechanisms behind estrogens' beneficial effect on muscle strength in females. *Exercise and Sport Sciences Reviews, 38*(2), 61–67. https://doi.org/10.1097/JES.0b013e3181d496bc

Mackay, K., González, C., Zbinden-Foncea, H., & Peñailillo, L. (2019). Effects of oral contraceptive use on female sexual salivary hormones and indirect markers of muscle damage following eccentric cycling in women. *European Journal of Applied Physiology, 119*, 2733–2744. https://doi.org/10.1007/s00421-019-04254-y

McHaffie, S. J., Langan-Evans, C., Morehen, J. C., Strauss, J. A., Areta, J. L., Rosimus, C., Evans, M., Elliott-Sale, K. J., Cronin, C. J., & Morton, J. P. (2022). Normalising the conversation: A qualitative analysis of player and stakeholder perceptions of menstrual health support within elite female soccer. *Science and Medicine in Football, 6*(5), 633–642. https://doi.org/10.1080/24733938.2022.2145349

McNulty, K. L., Elliott-Sale, K. J., Dolan, E., Swinton, P. A., Ansdell, P., Goodall, S., Thomas, K., & Hicks, K. M. (2020). The effects of menstrual cycle phase on exercise performance in eumenorrheic women: A systematic review and meta-analysis. *Sports Medicine, 50*, 1813–1827. https://doi.org/10.1007/s40279-020-01319-3

Minahan, C., Joyce, S., Bulmer, A. C., Cronin, N., & Sabapathy, S. (2015). The influence of estradiol on muscle damage and leg strength after intense eccentric exercise. *European Journal of Applied Physiology, 115*, 1493–1500. https://doi.org/10.1007/s00421-015-3133-9

Mkumbuzi, N. S., Dlamini, S. B., Chibhabha, F., Govere, F. M., & Manda-Taylor, L. (2021). The menstrual cycle and football: The experiences of female African football players. *Science and Medicine in Football, 6*(5), 626–632. https://doi.org/10.1080/24733938.2021.2005252

Myllyaho, M. M., Ihalainen, J. K., Hackney, A. C., Valtonen, M., Nummela, A., Vaara, E., Hakkinen, K., Kyrolainen, H., & Taipale, R. S. (2021). Hormonal contraceptive use does not affect strength, endurance, or body composition adaptations to combined strength and endurance training in women. *The Journal of Strength & Conditioning Research, 35*(2), 449–457. https://doi.org/10.1519/JSC.0000000000002713

Nolan, D., McNulty, K. L., Manninen, M., & Egan, B. (2023). The effect of hormonal contraceptive use on skeletal muscle hypertrophy, power and strength adaptations to resistance exercise training: A systematic review and multilevel meta-analysis. *Sports Medicine, 54*(1), 105–125. https://doi.org/10.1007/s40279-023-01911-3

Okholm Kryger, K., Wang, A., Mehta, R., Impellizzeri, F. M., Massey, A., & McCall, A. (2022). Research on women's football: A scoping review. *Science and Medicine in Football, 6*(5), 549–558. https://doi.org/10.1080/24733938.2020.1868560

Oosthuyse, T., Strauss, J. A., & Hackney, A. C. (2023). Understanding the female athlete: Molecular mechanisms underpinning menstrual phase differences in exercise metabolism. *European Journal of Applied Physiology, 123*(3), 423–450. https://doi.org/10.1007/s00421-022-05090-3

Parker, L. J., Elliott-Sale, K. J., Hannon, M. P., Morton, J. P., & Close, G. L. (2022). An audit of hormonal contraceptive use in Women's Super League soccer players; implications on symptomology. *Science and Medicine in Football, 6*(2), 153–158. https://doi.org/10.1080/24733938.2021.1921248

Pinel, C. J., Mehta, R., & Okholm Kryger, K. (2022). The impact and experienced barriers menstruation present to football participation in amateur female footballers. *Journal of Sports Sciences, 40*(17), 950–1963. https://doi.org/10.1080/02640414.2022.2122328

Queiroga, M. R., da Silva, D. F., Ferreira, S. A., Weber, V. M. R., Fernandes, D. Z., Cavazzotto, T. G., Portela, B. S., Trataruga, M. P., & Vieira, E. R. (2021). Characterization of reproductive and morphological variables in female elite futsal players. *Frontiers in Psychology, 12*, 1436. https://doi.org/10.3389/fpsyg.2021.625354

Randell, R. K., Clifford, T., Drust, B., Moss, S. L., Unnithan, V. B., De Ste Croix, M. B., Datson, N., Martin, D., Mayho, H., Carter, J. M., & Rollo, I. (2021). Physiological characteristics of female soccer players and health and performance considerations: A narrative review. *Sports Medicine, 51*, 1377–1399. https://doi.org/10.1007/s40279-021-01458-1

Read, P., Mehta, R., Rosenbloom, C., Jobson, E., & Okholm Kryger, K. (2022). Elite female football players' perception of the impact of their menstrual cycle stages on their football performance. A semi-structured interview-based study. *Science and Medicine in Football, 6*(5), 616–625. https://doi.org/10.1080/24733938.2021.2020330

Rechichi, C., Dawson, B., & Goodman, C. (2009). Athletic performance and the oral contraceptive. *International Journal of Sports Physiology and Performance, 4*(2), 151–162. https://doi.org/10.1123/ijspp.4.2.151

Reis, F., Frick, U., & Schmidtbleicher, D. (1995). Frequency variations of strength training sessions triggered by the phases of the menstrual cycle. *International Journal of Sports Medicine, 16*(8), 545–550. https://doi.org/10.1055/s-2007-973052

Romero-Parra, N., Alfaro-Magallanes, V. M., Rael, B., Cupeiro, R., Rojo-Tirado, M. A., Benito, P. J., & Peinado, A. B. (2020). Indirect markers of muscle damage throughout the menstrual cycle. *International Journal of Sports Physiology and Performance*, *16*(2), 190–198. https://doi.org/10.1123/ijspp.2019-0727

Romero-Parra, N., Barba-Moreno, L., Rael, B., Alfaro-Magallanes, V. M., Cupeiro, R., Díaz, Á. E., Calderon, F. J., & Peinado, A. B. (2020). Influence of the menstrual cycle on blood markers of muscle damage and inflammation following eccentric exercise. *International Journal of Environmental Research and Public Health*, *17*(5), 1618. https://doi.org/10.3390/ijerph17051618

Romero-Parra, N., Cupeiro, R., Alfaro-Magallanes, V. M., Rael, B., Rubio-Arias, J. Á., Peinado, A. B., & Benito, P. J. (2021). Exercise-induced muscle damage during the menstrual cycle: A systematic review and meta-analysis. *The Journal of Strength & Conditioning Research*, *35*(2), 549–561. https://doi.org/10.1519/JSC.0000000000003878

Romero-Parra, N., Rael, B., Alfaro-Magallanes, V. M., de Jonge, X. J., Cupeiro, R., & Peinado, A. B. (2021). The effect of the oral contraceptive cycle phase on exercise-induced muscle damage after eccentric exercise in resistance-trained women. *The Journal of Strength & Conditioning Research*, *35*(2), 353–359. https://doi.org/10.1519/JSC.0000000000003897

Roth, S. M., Gajdosik, R., & Ruby, B. C. (2001). Effects of circulating estradiol on exercise-induced creatine kinase activity. *Journal of Exercise Physiology Online*, *4*(2), 10–17.

Sakamaki-Sunaga, M., Min, S., Kamemoto, K., & Okamoto, T. (2016). Effects of menstrual phase–dependent resistance training frequency on muscular hypertrophy and strength. *Journal of Strength and Conditioning Research*, *30*(6), 1727–1734. https://doi.org/10.1519/JSC.0000000000001250

Sánchez, M., Rodríguez-Fernández, A., Bosque, V. D., Bermejo-Martín, L., Sánchez-Sánchez, J., Ramírez-Campillo, R., & Villa-Vicente, J. (2022). Effects of the menstrual phase on the performance and well-being of female youth soccer players. *Cultura, Ciencia y Deporte*, *17*(51), 113–129. https://doi.org/10.12800/ccd.v17i51.1610

Savage, K. J., & Clarkson, P. M. (2002). Oral contraceptive use and exercise-induced muscle damage and recovery. *Contraception*, *66*(1), 67–71. https://doi.org/10.1016/S0010-7824(02)00320-7

Schaumberg, M. A., Emmerton, L. M., Jenkins, D. G., Burton, N. W., de Jonge, X. A. J., & Skinner, T. L. (2018). Use of oral contraceptives to manipulate menstruation in young, physically active women. *International Journal of Sports Physiology and Performance*, *13*(1), 82–87. https://doi.org/10.1123/ijspp.2016-0689

Schaumberg, M. A., Jenkins, D., Janse de Jonge, X., Emmerton, L., & Skinner, T. I. N. A. (2016). Oral contraceptive use dampens physiological adaptations to sprint interval training. *Medicine and Science in Sports and Exercise*, *49*(4), 717–727. https://doi.org/10.1249/MSS.0000000000001171

Sung, E., Han, A., Hinrichs, T., Vorgerd, M., Manchado, C., & Platen, P. (2014). Effects of follicular versus luteal phase-based strength training in young women. *Springerplus*, *3*(1), 668. https://doi.org/10.1186/2193-1801-3-668

Thompson, H. S., Hyatt, J. P., De Souza, M. J., & Clarkson, P. M. (1997). The effects of oral contraceptives on delayed onset muscle soreness following exercise. *Contraception*, *56*(2), 59–65. https://doi.org/10.1016/S0010-7824(97)00093-0

Tiidus, P. M. (2003). Influence of estrogen on skeletal muscle damage, inflammation and repair. *Exercise and Sport Sciences Reviews*, *31*(1), 40–44.

Tiidus, P. M. (2005). Can oestrogen influence skeletal muscle damage, inflammation and repair? *British Journal of Sports Medicine*, *39*(5), 251–253. https://doi.org/10.1136/bjsm.2005.016881

Tounsi, M., Jaafar, H., Aloui, A., & Souissi, N. (2018). Soccer-related performance in eumenorrheic Tunisian high-level soccer players: Effects of menstrual cycle phase and moment of day. *The Journal of Sports Medicine and Physical Fitness*, *58*(4), 497–502. https://doi.org/10.23736/s0022-4707.17.06958-4

Vargas-Molina, S., Petro, J. L., Romance, R., Bonilla, D. A., Schoenfeld, B. J., Kreider, R. B., & Benítez-Porres, J. (2022). Menstrual cycle-based undulating periodized program effects on body composition and strength in trained women: A pilot study. *Science & Sports*, *37*(8), 753–761. https://doi.org/10.1016/j.scispo.2021.11.003

Wikström-Frisén, L., Boraxbekk, C. J., & Henriksson-Larsen, K. (2017). Effects on power, strength and lean body mass of menstrual/oral contraceptive cycle based resistance training. *Journal of Sports Medicine and Physical Fitness*, *57*(1–2), 43–52. https://doi.org/10.23736/S0022-4707.16.05848-5

Yonkers, K. A., O'Brien, P. S., & Eriksson, E. (2008). Premenstrual syndrome. *The Lancet*, *371*(9619), 1200–1210. https://doi.org/10.1016/S0140-6736(08)60527-9

6

MENSTRUAL CYCLE MONITORING, APPLICATION AND IMPLEMENTATION

Ross Julian, Jonathan Hughes and Debby Sargent

Introduction

Understanding female biology's impact on football performance is crucial, but research often has methodological limitations (see Chapter 5; Elliott-Sale et al., 2021; McNulty et al., 2020). Although anecdotal reports suggest benefits from menstrual cycle monitoring and tailored training, these practices have yet to be widely adopted (Pender, 2019). Convincing stakeholders to invest in menstrual cycle monitoring alongside other practices is challenging, due to additional time, costs and resources to cycle monitoring, as well as considering its overlap with other evidence-based practices, particularly given the prevalence of contraceptive use and the variable effects of the menstrual cycle on individuals. Overcoming challenges in incorporating menstrual cycle monitoring into practice, even for clubs seeking marginal performance improvements, is important, given the roadblocks in monitoring processes, interpreting findings and translating knowledge into actionable strategies. Progress in this field hinges on interim actions driven by the limited available information, allowing coaches and support practitioners to assist footballers better while awaiting more comprehensive research. Accordingly, the main aims of the current chapter are to raise awareness of the menstrual cycle's effects on football performance and provide practical monitoring guidance for integrating the menstrual cycle into training programmes. Moreover, we aim to address barriers, encourage self-awareness and offer coaches a structured framework to optimise training, considering menstrual cycle variations.

Menstrual cycle and training

As inferred in Chapter 5, physiological fluctuations during the menstrual cycle suggest the concept of "windows of adaptation", where hormonal conditions may

DOI: 10.4324/9781003381914-6

accelerate training adaptations. However, designing exercise prescriptions around these windows is considered premature across current research (Carmichael et al., 2021; Colenso-Semple et al., 2023; Kissow et al., 2022; Knowles et al., 2019; McNulty et al., 2020; Meignie et al., 2021; Thompson et al., 2020). However, when considering implementing menstrual cycle-based training, practitioners should be mindful of the following:

1 Training programmes should be supervised to achieve the desired dose and adaptations.
2 Oestrogen levels vary significantly during the follicular phase, challenging the idea of a continuous anabolic environment throughout a phase-based regimen (Chidi-Ogbolu & Baar, 2019).
3 Motor tasks depend on various physical qualities that are affected differently by oestrogen and progesterone, making the impact on specific training attributes complex (Meignie et al., 2021).
4 Coaches should stay informed about evolving research to determine the applicability of phase-based training for different training modalities.

It's not all about the physiological effects of the menstrual cycle!

While the exact impact of menstrual cycle hormones on sports performance remains unclear, other menstrual cycle factors, such as menstrual cycle-associated symptoms, could affect footballers' training and competition (for more information on menstrual cycle symptomology, please refer to Chapter 5). The reported unpleasant psychological and physiological symptoms may affect players' actual and perceived capacity to train and compete (Bruinvels et al., 2021; Findlay et al., 2020), and training adaptations may only be made if players attend and adhere to training.

Adherence

Training adherence describes the capacity of an athlete to stick to the exercise programme prescribed for them, which is important to achieve the dose of training required to drive the desired training objectives/adaptations. Both questionnaire (Bruinvels et al., 2021; Findlay et al., 2020; Pinel et al., 2022) and interview-based (Brown et al., 2021; Findlay et al., 2020; McHaffie et al., 2022; Read et al., 2022) research provides consistent evidence that athletes perceive performance to be relatively worse during the early follicular and late luteal phases, especially in those individuals who report a more significant number and severity of symptoms (Bruinvels et al., 2021). Training performance is often more negatively affected than competition performance (Findlay et al., 2020). Competition may improve focus and distract from menstrual pain (Findlay et al., 2020; Read et al., 2022).

Competitive pressure and limited control over menstruation can worsen these effects for some players (Brown et al., 2021; McHaffie et al., 2022). Menstrual cycle symptoms, including appetite changes, low energy, pain and mood changes, can significantly impact high-performing players (Read et al., 2022). Footballers who continue despite these challenges may need help maintaining commitment and intensity (Read et al., 2022).

Ratings of perceived exertion are higher in the early and mid-follicular phases than they are in the mid-luteal phase (Mattu et al., 2020; Paludo et al., 2022). This finding may explain reductions in high-intensity exercise, technical training and internal training load during the follicular phase (Cristina-Souza et al., 2019; Pinel et al., 2022). Minor objective performance reductions also support these perceived effects (McNulty et al., 2020). In football-specific studies, it has been shown that premenstrual syndrome (PMS) and premenstrual dysphoric disorder (PMDD) symptoms worsen aerobic capacity, powerful movements, reaction times and speed during the premenstrual and menstrual phases, all of which are essential for football performance (Pinel et al., 2022; Read et al., 2022). Mood disturbances further affect exercise adherence, with depressed mood, reduced motivation and decreased desire to compete contributing to training challenges (Bruinvels et al., 2021; Garcia-Pinillos et al., 2021; McHaffie et al., 2022; Oxfeldt et al., 2020; Paludo et al., 2022).

Attendance

Menstrual-related disorders (e.g. PMS) have been shown to have a considerable impact on the quality of life for physically active women, frequently resulting in absences from work, school and social activities (Bruinvels et al., 2021). Similarly, menstruation has been identified as a barrier to sports participation in both recreational (Pinel et al., 2022) and elite footballers (Read et al., 2022). Of 127 amateur players, 24% and 3% reported that menstruation explained why they missed football training for 1–3 or 4–8 days per month, respectively (Pinel et al., 2022). Elite footballers have been found to miss between 4.1% (Martin et al., 2018) and 13.3% (Read et al., 2022) of training/competition due to the severity of symptoms/pain.

Exacerbated symptoms of PMS/PMDD affect training attendance, with more severe symptoms leading athletes to adjust their schedules, including avoiding tough sessions or missing training entirely (Kolic et al., 2023; Prado et al., 2023). The extent of disruption varies, with non-elite athletes often reorganising training (Prado et al., 2023). In contrast, elite athletes are less likely to miss events due to PMS symptoms, with 4–32% adjusting training (Ekenros et al., 2017; Majumder et al., 2022). Coaches should be aware of these adjustments to avoid misinterpreting commitment (Oxfeldt et al., 2020). Adjustments are more common when training in front of others, possibly due to concerns about how menstruation is perceived, especially in team sports (Kolic et al., 2023).

In summary, optimising football player training involves considering menstrual cycle and adapting training accordingly. Periodised programmes can utilise symptom-free periods for intense workouts and focus on lower-intensity exercises during PMS/PMDD symptoms. Coaches should also be sensitive to psychological effects. Neglecting players' needs can lead to dissatisfaction, reduced motivation and subpar performance, potentially causing deselection or reduced attrition. Integrating menstrual cycle awareness into coaching is essential for effective player management.

Menstrual cycle monitoring and application

In high-level team sports, the systematic collection and analysis of athlete-monitoring data are widely practiced to assess fatigue levels, adaptation and performance potential and to minimise injury or illness risks (Thornton et al., 2019). Recognising the considerable influence of the menstrual cycle on these monitoring goals, integrating menstrual cycle tracking into daily protocols and considering menstrual cycle phases during testing offer significant benefits for optimising footballers' performance and wellbeing.

Determination of menstrual cycle hormone profile

Understanding each footballer's menstrual cycle phase is crucial for effective phase-based training, integrating the menstrual cycle into athlete monitoring systems (AMS) and conducting precise physical testing (Julian et al., 2017). While various methods exist for determining menstrual cycle phases, most are impractical for assessing large squads due to invasiveness, cost and time constraints (Julian & Sargent, 2020; Thornton et al., 2019), as depicted in Figure 6.1. Though less accurate, training diaries and wellness tracking offer practical alternatives that can become the cornerstone of menstrual cycle inclusion into AMS (Julian & Sargent, 2020).

Continuous monitoring of menstrual cycle profiles is essential due to significant variations among individuals in hormone production and release (Hampson, 2020). Only a small percentage of females have a classic 28-day cycle, with elite athletes often experiencing irregular cycles, including anovulatory ones (Bruinvels et al., 2016; Gimunova et al., 2022; Solli et al., 2020). Moreover, high-volume training in footballers can lead to relative energy deficiency in sport, impacting performance and health, including menstrual dysfunction (Oxfeldt et al., 2020; Solli et al., 2020). Menstrual-cycle-related disorders, including PMS and PMDD, may worsen with increased menstrual flow and intense training, particularly with age or a history of weight loss (Bruinvels et al., 2016; Czajkowska et al., 2020; Shi et al., 2023). Ongoing menstrual cycle monitoring is essential for optimising performance, wellbeing and player health.

While the direct impact of the menstrual cycle on objective sports-performance measures lacks strong scientific evidence, it can serve as a valuable tool for explaining changes in wellbeing metrics and optimising training strategies (Carmichael et al., 2021). Coaches can use the menstrual cycle as an adjunctive tool to enhance overall player wellbeing and performance outcomes.

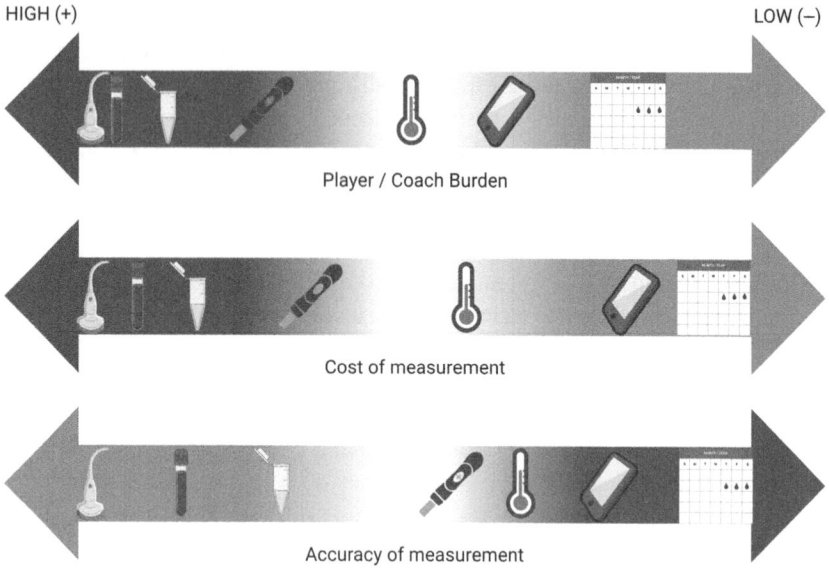

FIGURE 6.1 Overview of methods to determine the menstrual cycle phase concerning the burden of the coach and athlete, the cost and accuracy of that measurement.

Physical testing

Physical tests are routinely administered during the preseason and throughout the season to gauge the efficacy of training, load and adaptation (Datson et al., 2020, 2022). These evaluations are often controlled by maintaining uniformity in test parameters, such as consistent time of day and test sequence, to reduce extraneous influences and optimise the precision of findings. However, the menstrual cycle needs to be more frequently noticed and factored into the planning and execution of such assessments (Julian et al., 2017). Though McNulty and colleagues (2020) contend that the menstrual cycle may exert only trivial effects on performance, it is important to recognise that even minor effects can lead to implications for determining whether a change in physical performance is practically relevant (Datson et al., 2022). Moreover, symptoms such as pain, fatigue and mood can influence performance (Findlay et al., 2020), particularly during maximal test protocols. In pursuit of methodological rigour and reduction of confounding noise, it is important to acknowledge and integrate aspects of the menstrual cycle when conducting assessments, even if achieving simultaneous cycle synchronisation during testing proves unfeasible due to interindividual variability. As such, it is recommended that practitioners document the menstrual cycle phase and related symptomology (Julian et al., 2017; Julian & Sargent, 2020) to complement their interpretation of practically meaningful changes.

Player monitoring: who, what, where

Football players compete throughout their menstrual cycle, but its impact on performance varies significantly (Armour et al., 2020; Bruinvels et al., 2022). While some players believe their performance is affected during menstruation, others peak at this time (Brown et al., 2021). This variability underscores the importance of identifying those most influenced by the menstrual cycle.

Conventional tracking based on a *normal* menstrual cycle excludes individuals with irregular cycles, hormonal contraceptive users (about 30% of players in the English Women's Super League [Parker et al., 2022]) and those with menstrual dysfunction (approximately 20% [Gimunova et al., 2022]). Despite the use of hormonal contraception to alleviate symptoms, complaints and side effects persist (Oxfeldt et al., 2020). Supplementing established AMS with symptom tracking, cycle length and symptom clusters supports the entire team, guiding decisions on training adjustments, symptom management and overall wellbeing.

Existing AMS already include regular readiness questionnaires, encompassing factors like sleep disturbances and muscle soreness, such as the Hooper Index (Rabbani et al., 2019). Connections have been established between these factors and menstrual cycle phase, particularly the premenstrual phase, as well as their relation to progesterone withdrawal and acute-phase inflammatory responses (Armour et al., 2020; King & Critchley, 2010; Romero-Parra et al., 2021). Furthermore, observed and perceived recovery rates and significant components of AMS exhibit variations throughout the menstrual cycle (Hackney et al., 2019). By tracking readiness to perform, recovery rates and perceptions during vulnerable phases, coaches and sports scientists can enhance athlete preparedness and minimise issues related to menstrual symptoms. Integrating these approaches into AMS provides better support for players and leads to improved performance.

Coach and player considerations

Normalising menstrual cycle discussions among players, coaches and staff is crucial (Brown et al., 2021; Findlay et al., 2020; McGawley et al., 2023). Barriers, like athlete–coach relationships and a lack of awareness, hinder open communication (Höök et al., 2021; Laske et al., 2022; McGawley et al., 2023). Many athletes and coaches avoid these discussions, believing coaches cannot help, viewing the menstrual cycle as private, fearing differential treatment or feeling unsure about advice (Clarke et al., 2021; Findlay et al., 2020; Kolic et al., 2023; Marais et al., 2022). Educating coaches and players, addressing privacy concerns and fostering confidence in discussing the menstrual cycle are essential to improve interactions (Figure 6.2).

In a team, player and coach confidence in discussing and adapting training, based on menstrual cycle monitoring, varies. Barriers include a more significant understanding of the menstrual cycle's impact and when to initiate conversations

High coach confidence

Coach's philosophy:
High coach confidence, low player confidence.

- Robust menstrual monitoring programming likely in place.
- Low player compliance.
- Player probably uncomfortable having conversations with the coach and may seek avoidance strategies to prevent discussion.
- Depending on player compliance to other aspects of the monitoring system, the coach perceptions of the athlete could be negatively affected.
- Player unlikely to reach full potential.

Real 3 pointer:
High coach and player confidence.

- Robust menstrual monitoring programming likely in place.
- High player compliance, offering consistency and richness of information. Conversations are comfortable and happen on a formal and informal basis.
- Programmes are evolved over time to accommodate menstrual cycle symptomology.
- Positive impact on coach-player relationship – highly motivated partnership.
- Increased chance of player reaching their full potential.

Low player confidence

High player confidence

Own goal:
Low coach and player confidence.

- Menstrual monitoring and communication possibly non-existent.
- Failure of player to reach full potential - may be frustrating for both parties.
- Demotivated player and coach – dropout potential.

Captain's choice:
Low coach confidence, high player confidence.

- Formal menstrual monitoring programme and follow-up may be limited.
- Player likely to self-monitor, regulate and adapt their training programme accordingly, without coach knowledge.
- Player may feel awkward approaching the coach and could resort to confiding in others.
- May tarnish the coach-player relationship – athlete feels their needs are not being catered for.
- Player unlikely to reach full potential, wellbeing may be affected.

Low coach confidence

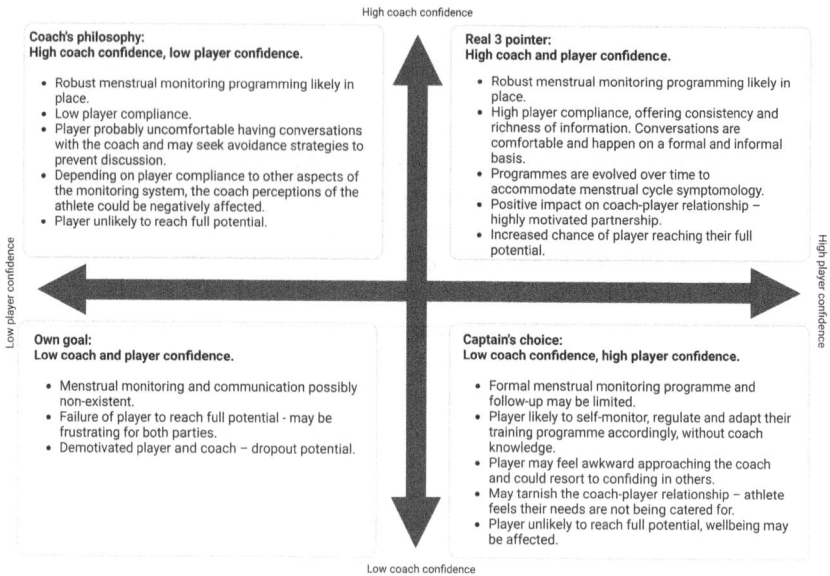

FIGURE 6.2   Four typical coach–athlete interactions that could happen within any group of players.

(Bruinvels et al., 2022; McGawley et al., 2023). Clubs may need menstrual-cycle policies due to limited research on phase-based training. Coaches should learn about their players' menstrual cycle and tailor training, considering emotional, physical and physiological factors. Assessing comfort levels can guide communication techniques. Enhancing menstrual-cycle education and awareness is crucial for effective monitoring and coaching practice.

Do more practical aspects of menstrual management offer more significant performance gains?

Improved management by footballers and the interdisciplinary team can significantly alleviate the negative menstrual experiences described by the players, allowing them to focus more on performance goals and to be less distracted. Several actionable areas have been identified to address these challenges:

1 Fear of leaking: Athletes may stress over menstrual leaking, especially when wearing light-coloured or tight-fitting uniforms. Offering the option to change into less visible uniform colours and providing extra clothing can help alleviate this concern (Bruinvels et al., 2016; Findlay et al., 2020; Pinel et al., 2022).
2 Access to facilities: Exercising in outdoor or unfamiliar settings, as occurs with away fixtures, can limit access to facilities for changing and managing menstrual

products. Addressing this issue involves informing players about available facilities during away training or competitions. Providing period products without requiring players to ask, and choosing training locations with nearby changing rooms, can also help (Pinel et al., 2022).

3   Travel challenges: Managing menstrual symptoms during extensive travel can be challenging. Support teams can improve logistical planning for frequent access to quality changing and restroom facilities during travel. Additionally, minimising match-day travel and arranging overnight stays can enhance comfort and symptom management, although this may be financially challenging (Read et al., 2022).

4   Symptom management: Managing dysmenorrhoea and associated symptoms (PMS/PMDD) can significantly affect players' wellbeing and performance. Offering players access to various therapeutic approaches like heat treatments, rest, mindful exercises (e.g. yoga, stretching) and pain-relief measures can help relieve discomfort. Providing designated "time-out" periods and necessary resources for symptom management can positively impact wellbeing, potentially improving training programme adherence and recovery rates (Read et al., 2022).

As remarked by some athletes, "sometimes it's not actually the period that's affecting performance[;] it can be just that extra thing to think about" (Brown & Knight, 2022, p. 238). Implementing simple and practical procedures can enhance the player's menstrual experiences, enabling them to concentrate better on their performance and reduce distractions. By focusing on these practical measures, coaches and support teams can potentially impact players' wellbeing and performance more than creating a phase-dependent environment. Enhancing menstrual experiences through these interventions may improve overall athletic performance and wellbeing.

Summary and practitioners' perspective

Professionals working with football players should consider physiological and psychological menstrual symptoms in contraceptive and non-contraceptive users. These symptoms can significantly affect training attendance, adherence and adaptation, ultimately impacting performance. Players with a regular menstrual cycle, who are experiencing significant hormonal fluctuations, may require adjustments to their training regimen to optimise outcomes. However, organising training can be challenging due to the complex interplay of psychological and physiological factors. In Figure 6.3, a framework is provided for coaches, presenting a hormonal profile of a typical 28-day menstrual cycle divided into six phases, including ovulation. The framework categorises information into psychological effects related to PMS symptoms (tension-anxiety, depression, anger-hostility, vigour-activity, fatigue-inertia, confusion), general training considerations (volume, intensity, perceived effort, co-ordination/drill challenge) and specific training qualities suitable

	Early Follicular (Menses)	Mid Follicular	Late Follicular	Ovulation	Early Luteal	Mid Luteal	Late Luteal
Menstrual Cycle — Hormones: Oestrogen, Progesterone, Luteinising Hormone, Follicle Stimulating Hormone; Body Temperature 37°C / 36°C							
Menstrual Phase	Follicular			Ovulation	Luteal		
Mood States							
Tension-Anxiety	Tension	Tension	Tension				Tension
Depression	Depression	Depression		Depression			Depression
Anger-Hostility	Anger	Anger		Anger			Anger
Vigour-Activity	Vigour	Vigour		Vigour			Vigour
Anger-Hostility	Fatigue	Fatigue		Fatigue			Fatigue
Confusion	Confusion	Confusion		Confusion			Confusion
Training Prescription							
Volume	Low	Low-Moderate	Moderate-High	Low	Low-Moderate	High	Low
Intensity	Low-Moderate	Moderate	Moderate-High	Very High	Very High	Moderate	Low
Perceived Effort	Very High	Low-Moderate	Low	Low	Moderate	Moderate-High	Very High
Co-ordination/Drill Challenge	Simple	Complex	Difficult	Simple	Complex	Difficult	Simple
Physical Quality Suitability							
Mobility	Mobility						Mobility
Strength & Power	Strength & Power	Strength & Power	Strength & Power	Strength & Power	Strength & Power	Strength & power	Strength & power
Speed/Plyometric (Plyo)/Change of Direction (COD)		Speed/Plyo COD	Increased Injury Potential	Increased Injury Potential	Speed/Plyo/COD		
Recovery	Recovery						Recovery
Conditioning	Anaerobic	High Intensity Anaerobic	High Volume Aerobic	High Intensity Anaerobic	Anaerobic	High Volume Aerobic	Low Volume Anaerobic

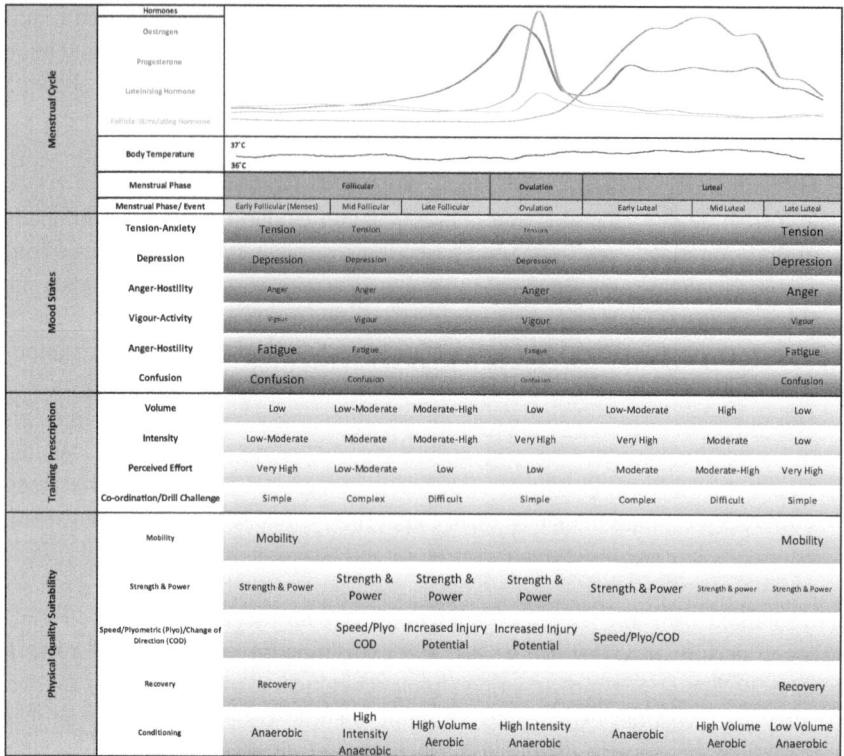

FIGURE 6.3 Coach, athlete and support practitioner decision-making framework to accommodate menstrual cycle symptomology into daily practice.

for different cycle stages (mobility, strength and power, speed/plyometric/change of direction, recovery, conditioning), indicating windows of adaptation. The text size reflects mood state intensity or training focus. Empty cells indicate that there are insufficient data to make a definite conclusion. This framework applies to players with negative symptomology. Those unaffected can follow a more conventional training approach without specific consideration of menstrual cycle psychophysiology. Players may fall into three categories:

- Players with psychological impact (PMS symptoms and general training considerations apply).
- Players with more physiological impact (general training considerations and specific training qualities areas are essential).
- Players with psychological and physiological effects (all sections apply).

The monitoring and testing system can classify players and determine which framework components apply to each player, and physiological and perceived impacts can be assessed. Long-term compliance from players and support staff may pose challenges, including resource requirements like time, cost and human resources. Teams should efficiently identify affected players who would benefit from phase-dependent training regimens, focusing on rescheduling rather than reducing training loads to ensure adequate overload. The monitoring system should also be used to evaluate the effects of phase-dependent training.

Figure 6.3 should be read both horizontally and vertically. By following the figure horizontally, how training can vary during a four-week mesocycle can be seen. Following the figure vertically reveals potential windows of adaptation influenced by psychological and physiological factors. For instance, strength-based exercises may be emphasised during the follicular phase, when the anabolic effects of oestrogen are high. However, negative psychological impacts may affect these windows. Despite inconclusive evidence, custom programmes tailored to menstrual-cycle symptom characteristics could yield small training improvements in affected players, potentially impacting team performance and morale. Practitioners and footballers should gain knowledge and awareness to apply theory to practice and benefit from the insights of this review.

References

Armour, M., Parry, K. A., Steel, K., & Smith, C. A. (2020). Australian female athletes perceive the challenges associated with training and competing when menstrual symptoms are present. *International Journal of Sports Science & Coaching, 15*(3), 316–323. https://doi.org/10.1177/1747954120916073

Brown, N., & Knight, C. J. (2022). Understanding female coaches' and practitioners' experience and support provision in relation to the menstrual cycle. *International Journal of Sports Science & Coaching, 17*(2), 235–243. https://doi.org/10.1177/17479541211058579

Brown, N., Knight, C. J., & Forrest, L. J. (2021). Elite female athletes' experiences and perceptions of the menstrual cycle on training and sport performance. *Scandinavian Journal of Medicine & Science in Sports, 31*(1), 52–69. https://doi.org/10.1111/sms.13818

Bruinvels, G., Burden, R., Brown, N., Richards, T., & Pedlar, C. (2016). The prevalence and impact of heavy menstrual bleeding (menorrhagia) in elite and non-elite athletes. *PLoS One, 11*(2), e0149881. https://doi.org/10.1371/journal.pone.0149881

Bruinvels, G., Goldsmith, E., Blagrove, R., Simpkin, A., Lewis, N., Morton, K., Suppiah, A., Rogers, J. P., Ackerman, K. E., Newell, J., & Pedlar, C. (2021). Prevalence and frequency of menstrual cycle symptoms are associated with availability to train and compete: A study of 6812 exercising women recruited using the Strava exercise app. *British Journal of Sports Medicine, 55*(8), 438–443. https://doi.org/10.1136/bjsports-2020-102792

Bruinvels, G., Hackney, A. C., & Pedlar, C. R. (2022). Menstrual cycle: The importance of both the phases and the transitions between phases on training and performance. *Sports Medicine, 52*(7), 1457–1460. https://doi.org/10.1007/s40279-022-01691-2

Carmichael, M. A., Thomson, R. L., Moran, L. J., & Wycherley, T. P. (2021). The impact of menstrual cycle phase on athletes' performance: A narrative review. *International Journal of Environmental Research and Public Health, 18*(4), 1667. https://doi.org/10.3390/ijerph18041667

Chidi-Ogbolu, N., & Baar, K. (2019). Effect of estrogen on musculoskeletal performance and injury risk. *Frontiers in Physiology, 9*, 1834. https://doi.org/10.3389/fphys.2018.01834

Clarke, A., Govus, A., & Donaldson, A. (2021). What male coaches want to know about the menstrual cycle in women's team sports: Performance, health and communication. *International Journal of Sports Science & Coaching, 16*(3), 544–553. https://doi.org/10.1177/1747954121989237

Colenso-Semple, L. M., D'Souza, A. C., Elliott-Sale, K. J., & Phillips, S. M. (2023). Current evidence shows no influence of women's menstrual cycle phase on acute strength performance or adaptations to resistance exercise training. *Frontiers in Sports and Active Living*, *5*, 1054542. https://doi.org/10.3389/fspor.2023.1054542

Cristina-Souza, G., Santos-Mariano, A. C., Souza-Rodrigues, C. C., Osiecki, R., Silva, S. F., Lima-Silva, A. E., & De Oliveira, F. R. (2019). Menstrual cycle alters training strain, monotony and technical training length in young. *Journal of Sports Sciences*, *37*(16), 1824–1830. https://doi.org/10.1080/02640414.2019.1597826

Czajkowska, M., Drosdzol-Cop, A., Naworska, B., Galazka, I., Gogola, C., Rutkowska, M., & Skrzypulec-Plinta, V. (2020). The impact of competitive sports on menstrual cycle and menstrual disorders, including premenstrual syndrome, premenstrual dysphoric disorder and hormonal imbalances. *Ginekologia Polska*, *91*(9), 503–512. https://doi.org/10.5603/Gp.2020.0097

Datson, N., Lolli, L., Drust, B., Atkinson, G., Weston, M., & Gregson, W. (2022). Inter-methodological quantification of the target change for performance test outcomes relevant to elite female soccer players. *Science and Medicine in Football*, *6*(2), 248–261. https://doi.org/10.1080/24733938.2021.1942538

Datson, N., Weston, M., Drust, B., Gregson, W., & Lolli, L. (2020). High-intensity endurance capacity assessment as a tool for talent identification in elite youth female soccer. *Journal of Sports Sciences*, *38*(11–12), 1313–1319. https://doi.org/10.1080/02640414.2019.1656323

Ekenros, L., Papoutsi, Z., Friden, C., Wright, K. D., & Hirschberg, A. L. (2017). Expression of sex steroid hormone receptors in human skeletal muscle during the menstrual cycle. *Acta Physiologica*, *219*(2), 486–493. https://doi.org/10.1111/apha.12757

Elliott-Sale, K. J., Minahan, C. L., de Jonge, X. A. K. J., Ackerman, K. E., Sipila, S., Constantini, N. W., Lebrun, C. M., & Hackney, A. C. (2021). Methodological considerations for studies in sport and exercise science with women as participants: A working guide for standards of practice for research on women. *Sports Medicine*, *51*(5), 843–861. https://doi.org/10.1007/s40279-021-01435-8

Findlay, R. J., Macrae, E. H. R., Whyte, I. Y., Easton, C., & Forrest, L. J. (2020). How the menstrual cycle and menstruation affect sporting performance: Experiences and perceptions of elite female rugby players. *British Journal of Sports Medicine*, *54*(18), 1108–1113. https://doi.org/10.1136/bjsports-2019-101486

Garcia-Pinillos, F., Bujalance-Moreno, P., Jerez-Mayorga, D., Velarde-Sotres, A., Anaya-Moix, V., Pueyo-Villa, S., & Lago-Fuentes, C. (2021). Training habits of eumenorrheic active women during the different phases of their menstrual cycle: A descriptive study. *International Journal of Environmental Research and Public Health*, *18*(7), 3662. https://doi.org/10.3390/ijerph18073662

Gimunova, M., Paulinyova, A., Bernacikova, M., & Paludo, A. C. (2022). The prevalence of menstrual cycle disorders in female athletes from different sports disciplines: A rapid review. *International Journal of Environmental Research and Public Health*, *19*(21), 14243. https://doi.org/10.3390/ijerph192114243

Hackney, A. C., Kallman, A. L., & Aggon, E. (2019). Female sex hormones and the recovery from exercise: Menstrual cycle phase affects responses. *Biomedical Human Kinetics*, *11*(1), 87–89. https://doi.org/10.2478/bhk-2019-0011

Hampson, E. (2020). A brief guide to the menstrual cycle and oral contraceptive use for researchers in behavioral endocrinology. *Hormones and Behavior*, *119*, 104655. https://doi.org/10.1016/j.yhbeh.2019.104655

Höök, M., Bergström, M., Sæther, S. A.-O., & McGawley, K. A.-O. (2021). "Do elite sport first, get your period back later": Are barriers to communication hindering female athletes? *International Journal of Environmental Research and Public Health*, *18*(22), 12075. https://doi.org/10.1371/journal.pone.0173951

Julian, R., Hecksteden, A., Fullagar, H. H. K., & Meyer, T. (2017). The effects of menstrual cycle phase on physical performance in female soccer players. *PLoS One*, *12*(3), e0173951. https://doi.org/10.1371/journal.pone.0173951

Julian, R., & Sargent, D. (2020). Periodisation: Tailoring training based on the menstrual cycle may work in theory but can they be used in practice? *Science and Medicine in Football*, *4*(4), 253–254. https://doi.org/10.1080/24733938.2020.1828615

King, A. E., & Critchley, H. O. D. (2010). Oestrogen and progesterone regulation of inflammatory processes in the human endometrium. *Journal of Steroid Biochemistry and Molecular Biology*, *120*(2–3), 116–126. https://doi.org/10.1016/j.jsbmb.2010.01.003

Kissow, J., Jacobsen, K. J., Gunnarsson, T. P., Jessen, S., & Hostrup, M. (2022). Effects of follicular and luteal phase-based menstrual cycle resistance training on muscle strength and mass. *Sports Medicine*, *52*(12), 2813–2819. https://doi.org/10.1007/s40279-022-01679-y

Knowles, O. E., Aisbett, B., Main, L. C., Drinkwater, E. J., Orellana, L., & Lamon, S. (2019). Resistance training and skeletal muscle protein metabolism in eumenorrheic females: Implications for researchers and practitioners. *Sports Medicine*, *49*(11), 1637–1650. https://doi.org/10.1007/s40279-019-01132-7

Kolic, P., Thomas, L., Morse, C. I., & Hicks, K. M. (2023). Presentation of self, impression management and the period: A qualitative investigation of physically active women's experiences in sport and exercise. *Journal of Applied Sport Psychology*, *35*(3), 478–497. https://doi.org/10.1080/10413200.2022.2032479

Laske, H., Konjer, M., & Meier, H. E. (2022). Menstruation and training—a quantitative study of (non-)communication about the menstrual cycle in German sports clubs. *International Journal of Sports Science & Coaching*, *19*(1), 129–140. https://doi.org/10.1177/17479541221143061

Majumder, T., Topranin, V. D., Sandbakk, O., & Noordhof, D. A. (2022). Indian endurance athletes' menstrual cycle: Practices, knowledge, communication, health and changes in perceptions across the phases. *International Journal of Sports Physiology and Performance*, *17*(12), 1706–1715. https://doi.org/10.1123/ijspp.2022-0131

Marais, N. A.-O., Morris-Eyton, H. A.-O., & Janse van Rensburg, N. A.-O. (2022). The perceived knowledge of the menstruation cycle and adjustment of swimming sets by swimming coaches based on menstrual-related issues. *South African Journal of Sports Medicine*, *34*(1). https://doi.org/10.17159/2078-516X/2022/v34i1a13851

Martin, D., Sale, C., Cooper, S. B., & Elliott-Sale, K. J. (2018). Period prevalence and perceived side effects of hormonal contraceptive use and the menstrual cycle in elite athletes. *International Journal of Sports Physiology and Performance*, *13*(7), 926–932. https://doi.org/10.1123/ijspp.2017-0330

Mattu, A. A.-O. X., Iannetta, D. A.-O. X., MacInnis, M. J., Doyle-Baker, P. K., & Murias, J. M. (2020). Menstrual and oral contraceptive cycle phases do not affect submaximal and maximal exercise responses. *Scandinavian Journal of Medicine & Science in Sports*, *30*(3), 472–484. https://doi.org/10.1111/sms.13590

McGawley, K., Sargent, D., Noordhof, D., Badenhorst, C. E., Julian, R., & Govus, A. D. (2023). Improving menstrual health literacy in sport. *Journal of Science and Medicine in Sport*, *26*(7), 351–357. https://doi.org/10.1016/j.jsams.2023.06.007

McHaffie, S. J., Langan-Evans, C., Morehen, J. C., Strauss, J. A., Areta, J. L., Rosimus, C., Evans, M., Elliott-Sale, K. J., Cronin, C. J., & Morton, J. P. (2022). Normalising the conversation: A qualitative analysis of player and stakeholder perceptions of menstrual health support within elite female soccer. *Science and Medicine in Football*, *6*(5), 633–642. https://doi.org/10.1080/24733938.2022.2145349

McNulty, K. L., Elliott-Sale, K. J., Dolan, E., Swinton, P. A., Ansdell, P., Goodall, S., Thomas, K., & Hicks, K. M. (2020). The effects of menstrual cycle phase on exercise performance in eumenorrheic women: A systematic review and meta-analysis. *Sports Medicine*, *50*(10), 1813–1827. https://doi.org/10.1007/s40279-020-01319-3

Meignie, A., Duclos, M., Carling, C., Orhant, E., Provost, P., Toussaint, J. F., & Antero, J. (2021). The effects of menstrual cycle phase on elite athlete performance: A critical and systematic review. *Frontiers in Physiology*, *12*, 654585. https://doi.org/10.3389/fphys.2021.654585

Oxfeldt, M., Dalgaard, L. B., Jorgensen, A. A., & Hansen, M. (2020). Hormonal contraceptive use, menstrual dysfunctions and self-reported side effects in elite athletes in Denmark. *International Journal of Sports Physiology and Performance*, *15*(10), 1377–1384. https://doi.org/10.1123/ijspp.2019-0636

Paludo, A. C., Paravlic, A., Dvorakova, K., & Gimunova, M. (2022). The effect of menstrual cycle on perceptual responses in athletes: A systematic review with meta-analysis. *Frontiers in Psychology*, *13*, 926854. https://doi.org/10.3389/fpsyg.2022.926854

Parker, L. J., Elliott-Sale, K. J., Hannon, M. P., Morton, J. P., & Close, G. L. (2022). An audit of hormonal contraceptive use in Women's Super League soccer players; implications on symptomology. *Science and Medicine in Football*, *6*(2), 153–158. https://doi.org/10.108 0/24733938.2021.1921248

Pender, K. (2019, July). Ending period "taboo" gave USA marginal gain at World Cup. *The Telegraph*. https://www.telegraph.co.uk/world-cup/2019/07/13/revealed-next-frontier-sports-science-usas-secret-weapon-womens/

Pinel, C. J. J., Mehta, R., & Kryger, K. O. (2022). The impact and experienced barriers menstruation present to football participation in amateur female footballers. *Journal of Sports Sciences*, *40*(17), 1950–1963. https://doi.org/10.1080/02640414.2022.2122328

Prado, R. C. R., Willett, H. N., Takito, M. Y., & Hackney, A. C. (2023). Impact of premenstrual syndrome symptoms on sport routines in nonelite athlete participants of summer Olympic sports. *International Journal of Sports Physiology and Performance*, *18*(2), 142–147. https://doi.org/10.1123/ijspp.2022-0218

Rabbani, A., Clemente, F. M., Kargarfard, M., & Chamari, K. (2019). Match fatigue time-course assessment over four days: Usefulness of the Hooper index and heart rate variability in professional soccer players. *Frontiers in Physiology*, *10*, 109. https://doi.org/10.3389/fphys.2019.00109

Read, P., Mehta, R., Rosenbloom, C. A.-O. X., Jobson, E., & Okholm Kryger, K. A. O. (2022). Elite female football players' perception of the impact of their menstrual cycle stages on their football performance. A semi-structured interview-based study. *Science & Medicine in Football*, *6*(5), 616–625. https://doi.org/10.1080/24733938.2021.2020330

Romero-Parra, N., Cupeiro, R., Alfaro-Magallanes, V. M., Rael, B., Rubio-Arias, J. A., Peinado, A. B., Benito, P. J., & Grp, I. S. (2021). Exercise-induced muscle damage during the menstrual cycle: A systematic review and meta-analysis. *Journal of Strength and Conditioning Research*, *35*(2), 549–561. https://doi.org/10.1519/Jsc.0000000000003878

Shi, Y. Q., Shi, M. Y., Liu, C., Sui, L., Zhao, Y., & Fan, X. (2023). Associations with physical activity, sedentary behavior and premenstrual syndrome among Chinese female college students. *BMC Women's Health*, *23*(1), 173. https://doi.org/10.1186/s12905-023-02262-x

Solli, G. S., Sandbakk, S. B., Noordhof, D. A., Ihalainen, J. K., & Sandbakk, O. (2020). Changes in self-reported physical fitness, performance and side effects across the phases of the menstrual cycle among competitive endurance athletes. *International Journal of Sports Physiology and Performance*, *15*(9), 1324–1333. https://doi.org/10.1123/ijspp.2019-0616

Thompson, B., Almarjawi, A., Sculley, D., & de Jonge, X. J. (2020). The effect of the menstrual cycle and oral contraceptives on acute responses and chronic adaptations to resistance training: A systematic review of the literature. *Sports Medicine*, *50*(1), 171–185. https://doi.org/10.1007/s40279-019-01219-1

Thornton, H. R., Delaney, J. A., Duthie, G. M., & Dascombe, B. J. (2019). Developing athlete monitoring systems in team sports: Data analysis and visualization. *International Journal of Sports Physiology and Performance*, *14*(6), 698–705. https://doi.org/10.1123/ijspp.2018-0169

7

PREGNANCY AND MOTHERHOOD

Amal Hassan, Emma Brockwell, Sinead Dufour,
Rosalyn Cooke, Monica Rho, and Margie Davenport

Introduction

With the average age of women footballers participating at international level increasing (Lewis, 2021; the Fédération Internationale de Football Association [FIFA], 2023) and following the publication of FIFA's global minimum maternity standards in 2020 (FIFA, 2020), it is perhaps unsurprising that the 2023 FIFA Women's World Cup showcased an impressive number of athlete-mothers. As investment and support for women's football grows, it is possible that we will see motherhood becoming even more commonplace amongst women footballers as the age of peak performance and the window of peak fertility continue to converge.

Despite this recent increased visibility of footballer-mothers, there are limited data specific to perinatal footballers that can assist players, coaches and clinicians in facilitating optimal decision-making related to training and play. As football-specific guidelines and recommendations begin to evolve, it remains important to recognise the uniqueness of each pregnancy, birth and player (including their uniqueness as individuals, their playing career aspirations and their motivations to continue play). Thus, the key considerations presented herein must be individualised.

The aims of the chapter are as follows:

1 To describe the key maternal physiological adaptations throughout the perinatal period.
2 To summarise the benefits of physical activity during pregnancy and the post-partum period.
3 To present contemporary evidence underpinning the evolving guidance for athletic training during pregnancy and for those returning to sport after birth.
4 To provide basic practical guidance for those supporting the perinatal footballer.

DOI: 10.4324/9781003381914-7

Pregnancy

Physiological adaptations and important considerations for footballers

Pregnancy comprises a 40-week period of profound physiological adaptation, supporting foetal growth and development. Given the complexity and speed of adaptations from the maternal endocrine system and placenta, sport-specific considerations for the footballer are needed. With increasing gestation, maternal and placental hormones rise and affect nearly every maternal organ system. Key adaptations include a 50% increase in blood volume, a 30% increase in cardiac output and approximately a 15-beats/min increase in heart rate. The increase in blood volume is primarily due to an increase in plasma, resulting in haemodilution. Therefore, more than a third of women will experience physiological anaemia during pregnancy (Stevens et al., 2013). For the footballer, already at greater risk of developing iron deficiency (Landahl et al., 2005), ensuring adequate nutrition and hydration is essential. To counter increases in cardiac output and heart rate, systemic vasodilation occurs early in pregnancy and serves to prioritise maternal-foetal and maternal-renal circulation. One of the most notable changes to the respiratory system is the 30–50% increase in resting ventilation that may contribute to a sensation of breathlessness (Knuttgen & Emerson, 1974; Pernoll et al., 1975). Educating the pregnant footballer of this possibility is important as they continue to train during pregnancy.

During pregnancy, resting energy expenditure increases by ~30% (Bader et al., 1955; Davenport et al., 2016; Jaque-Fortunato et al., 1996; Pernoll et al., 1975; Ueland et al., 1973). Maternal adaptations, including an increase in insulin secretion of up to 250% combined with a ~40% reduction in muscle glucose uptake ensure adequate glucose supply to the developing foetus (Davenport et al., 2016; Friedman et al., 1999). Nutritional intake during pregnancy needs to be sufficient for appropriate gestational weight gain, exercise performance and prevention strategies for hypoglycaemia. This intake is vital for pregnant players who are training due to the high-intensity, intermittent nature of football (O'Connor et al., 2016).

As pregnancy progresses, biomechanical adaptations occur to accommodate the growing uterus. Centre of mass shifts forward, degree of lumbar lordosis increases, trunk stability reduces, stride length and hip extension during ambulation reduce, whilst step width and knee flexion increase (Conder et al., 2019). It is recommended that fitness coaches and clinicians be aware of these adaptations and the potential impact on kinematics, and direct pregnant players to consider adjusting and individualising their movement strategies, and when tailoring exercise rehabilitation.

During pregnancy, maternal bone mineral density (BMD) declines by ~6% (To et al., 2003). Although women footballers are generally reported to have supranormal bone density (Alfredson et al., 1996; Ferry et al., 2011), it is possible that some may not. For example some footballers may have experienced late-onset menarche, have had poor energy availability and have been diagnosed with or are at risk of the female athlete triad or relative energy deficiency in sport. These players could enter pregnancy with lower regional bone density than expected. Multiple factors in pregnancy can impact bone physiology, presenting as transient osteoporosis, which can progress to an insufficiency fracture (Maliha et al., 2012). Transient osteoporosis of pregnancy (TOP) often declares itself with the presence of pain from an insufficiency fracture. True incidence of TOP is unknown because it is likely that more women have TOP without progression to an insufficiency fracture. If a pregnant player has TOP, they are more likely to present with symptoms, since they are likely more active than the average pregnant woman. Awareness of TOP is important, but it should not deter pregnant footballers from training during pregnancy. It is important to protect bone health during and following pregnancy through adequate nutritional intake, particularly of calcium and Vitamin D (Lappe et al., 2008), as well as continued weight-bearing, football-specific exercise to support bone health (Milanović et al., 2022).

In light of these impactful multi-system adaptations due to pregnancy, an important consideration is the wellbeing and mental health of the pregnant player. Although prevalence is unknown in footballers, mental health problems affect nearly one-fifth of pregnant women during the perinatal period and can last up to a year (Austin et al., 2008). Understanding how this unique phase of life can impact a pregnant player should enable performance-medical staff to support the player's safe and continued participation in football.

Physical activity guidelines and the benefits for mother and baby

Global guidelines recommend at least 150 min of moderate-intensity physical activity spread over three or more days of the week during pregnancy (Bull et al., 2020; Mottola et al., 2018; UK Chief Medical Officers' Physical Activity Guidelines, 2019). Fulfilling the recommendation reduces risk of developing major pregnancy complications such as pre-eclampsia, gestational hypertension, gestational diabetes (40% reduction), prenatal depression (70% reduction) and macrosomia by 39% (Davenport, McCurdy, et al., 2018; Davenport, Meah, et al., 2018; Davenport, Ruchat, et al., 2018). Being physically active prior to and throughout pregnancy is associated with a decreased risk of lumbopelvic pain, medical and surgical interventions in birth and diastasis of the rectus abdominis (Barakat et al., 2012; Domenjoz et al., 2014; Shiri et al., 2018; Sperstad et al., 2016; Watkins et al., 2021). Carrying out pelvic-floor muscle training during pregnancy may contribute to shortening of the second stage of labour and to reducing severe perineal trauma, which could prolong a player's return to sport (Sobhgol et al., 2020). Physical activity during pregnancy is positively associated with improved sleep (Cannon et al., 2023). It has been suggested that engagement in high-intensity interval training (HIIT) has a greater impact on sleep duration than moderate-intensity continuous training during healthy pregnancy (Wowdzia et al., 2022). Some physical activity, particularly during the first trimester, may also contribute to the management of nausea and fatigue (Sytsma et al., 2018).

While physical activity and exercise is health promoting for the vast majority of the obstetric population, there are *relative* and *absolute* contraindications where physical activity may not be recommended. While these guidelines vary, and the evidence base underpinning the classification of medical and pregnancy-related contraindications to exercise in pregnancy is being challenged (Meah et al., 2020), it is recommended that players and clinicians consult their obstetrician with any concerns, to guide appropriate participation. Use of the *Get Active Questionnaire for Pregnancy* may be helpful in these cases. The questionnaire is a self-administered, pre-participation screening tool that is designed to identify individuals who may have a contraindication that would require additional screening with their healthcare provider (Canadian Society for Exercise Physiology [CSEP], 2021; Davenport, Neil-Sztramko, et al., 2022). Key considerations for activities to avoid are given in country-specific guidelines, such as the Canadian guidelines for physical activity throughout pregnancy, which also provide recommendations on reasons for urgent termination of exercise and consultation with a medical care provider (Mottola et al., 2018); such guidelines should be understood by all players.

Training considerations for pregnant footballers

Current pregnancy physical activity guidelines are too conservative for athletes and players who regularly engage in high intensity, duration and/or volumes of training that substantially exceed the global recommendations (FIFA, 2020; Ponorac et al., 2020; Stevens et al., 2013). In 2015/2016 the International Olympic Committee (IOC) led a panel of research and clinical perinatal exercise experts through an extensive review of available literature, resulting in five documents regarding pregnant and postpartum athletes (Alfredson et al., 1996; Conder et al., 2019; Friedman et al., 1999; O'Connor et al., 2016; To et al., 2003). However, based on limited empirical evidence, the IOC panel was unable to provide concrete recommendations about the safety limits of exercise or practical recommendations for training and performance optimisation for pregnant athletes. In the last eight years, in new research it has been suggested that elite sport participation during pregnancy is not associated with adverse events during pregnancy, labour or delivery (Kimber et al., 2021; Wowdzia et al., 2021).

Most public health guidelines recommend avoiding Olympic lifting, heavy lifting and high-intensity exercise. However, this caution is based on scant empirical evidence. In 2016, the IOC cautioned exceeding 90% maximal heart rate (HR_{max}) during pregnancy due to small laboratory-based studies, in which it was demonstrated that there was potential for transient foetal bradycardia following graded exercise to maximal effort. However, the absolute recommendation to avoid all high-intensity activity has been challenged. In a recent meta-analysis, it was demonstrated that vigorous-intensity physical activity had a small reduction in the risk of prematurity, a short lengthening of gestation (0.21 weeks) and no impact on other maternal or foetal health (Beetham et al., 2019). Wowdzia et al. (2022) determined no adverse maternal or foetal responses to a session of HIIT involving 10 × 1-min intervals ≥90% HR_{max}, and potential for an increase in the duration of sleep post-exercise (Wowdzia et al., 2022, 2023). In 2020, the updated World Health Organization guidelines suggested that those already engaging in high-intensity physical activities before pregnancy can continue during pregnancy (Bull et al., 2020). These data demonstrate an alternative for players to engage in high-intensity exercise, without adverse effects.

Currently, there is no conclusive evidence to support avoiding heavy weightlifting during pregnancy in a recreational (non-elite) setting. In a 2023 self-report survey of 679 athletes engaged in resistance exercise of >80% one-repetition maximum before and during pregnancy, it was found that most athletes experienced no pregnancy complications while continuing to engage in activities discouraged by many prenatal physical activity guidelines (Olympic lifting, Valsalva, supine exercise). Those who continued to train until delivery experienced a 51% reduction in the odds of having pregnancy and delivery complications compared to those who followed current guidelines and reduced their training level prior to delivery (OR 0.49, 95% confidence interval 0.29–0.81) (Prevett et al., 2023). Modification can be achieved through exercise selection, equipment and prescription whilst ensuring physiological stimulus is maintained throughout pregnancy.

Pregnancy, childbirth and participation in high-impact and strenuous exercise are established risk factors for symptoms of pelvic floor dysfunction, including stress urinary incontinence. Thus, athletes are at high risk for pelvic floor dysfunction during the perinatal care period. Pelvic floor dysfunction has been shown to negatively impact the physical and mental health of athletes, often serving as a barrier to exercise participation, whilst also having a detrimental impact on performance (Dakic et al., 2023; National Institute for Health and Care Excellence [NICE], 2021). Reassuringly, pelvic-floor muscle training has been shown to be both preventive and curative (Dufour & Wu, 2020; NICE, 2021), and it is recommended that, where possible, pregnant players are screened and referred to a pelvic health physiotherapist, who can support them throughout the perinatal period (Donnelly, 2023).

The IOC guideline recommends that players avoid full contact football after the first trimester due to theoretical concerns over the safety of the foetus during these activities, since risk of direct trauma, or placental abruption are considered possible (The Football Association, 2009a, 2009b). Research is ongoing examining the appropriateness of this recommendation; however, until empirical evidence is available, this cut-off is appropriate. It is important for the pregnant players to be fully informed of the risks of participating in the contact aspect of the sport while pregnant. If the player chooses to participate in the contact nature of the sport, it should be their decision with the support of their obstetrician. Those who wish to continue non-contact training with their team should be encouraged to do so; however, some modifications to the training may be needed as pregnancy progresses. Previous studies in male athletes have demonstrated that ceasing all training for just eight weeks required more than double the time to rehabilitate and return to peak performance (Godfrey et al., 2005). Continuing some level of training and neurocognitive patterning may facilitate return to sport and performance following childbirth (Bø et al., 2016). However, it is essential that the duration and approach to training be individually tailored by the medical and coaching staff, with input from the player also.

Pregnancy frameworks in the football environment

When considering pregnancy and postpartum return-to-play in footballers, it is advisable to take a proactive approach, so that programming occurs well ahead of each distinct phase. These approaches might be trimester-specific and further broken down if preferred. Identifying the key multidisciplinary team members (including the obstetrician), seeking external expertise (i.e. pelvic health physiotherapist) and providing clear documentation of protocols, conversations and meetings are strongly recommended. Above all, it is vital these processes are player centred and that the wishes of the player are considered as the central theme.

For optimal outcomes, it is recommended that the footballer and the performance-medical multidisciplinary team have a clear idea of key phase-specific objectives (e.g. physical, psychological, medical and football related), which should be facilitated by medical, physical and psychosocial regression and progression criteria, rather than simply being dictated by time. Medical teams will need to consider their level of experience in managing pregnancy-related medical symptoms, illness, emergency and trauma, and concordant emergency action plans should be developed. If a player wishes to train or participate in activities beyond the guidance of medical staff, the use of an athlete contract can be considered (Mountjoy et al., 2023).

Postpartum

Physiological adaptations and important considerations for footballers

Following childbirth, the body gradually returns to the non-pregnant state. While many physiological adaptations reverse quickly after childbirth, others remain transiently or permanently altered, such as cardiovascular adaptations, which appear to persist beyond the first year postpartum and which may create a cardiovascular advantage for the postpartum athlete (Clapp & Capeless, 1997; Hart et al., 1986).

Levels of oestrogen and progesterone decrease rapidly in the days after birth in order to stimulate milk production (Alex et al., 2020), and for those who go on to breastfeed or pump breast milk, lactation becomes a highly energetic process requiring roughly 450–500 kcal/day (Lambrinou et al., 2019). This hormonally driven process also leads to changes in bone metabolism (demineralisation) to support the supply of adequate calcium and other nutrients necessary for producing breast milk (Canul-Medina & Fernandez-Mejia, 2019). This physiological shift favours bone resorption over bone formation, and poses an additional risk, particularly to athletes returning to sport early postpartum. Following pregnancy, BMD remains depressed until the resumption of menses, after which it is generally accepted to recover within six months (To et al., 2003). In a recent systematic review, it was identified that there was a higher-than-expected risk of stress fractures in those returning to sport before six weeks postpartum (Kimber et al., 2021). These data strongly suggest that protecting bone health in athletes returning from pregnancy is essential. Screening for additional risk factors that can negatively impact BMD, ensuring appropriate load, progression and continuing to encourage adequate intake of calcium and vitamin D through diet and supplementation should be considered as key preventive measures against lactation-associated bone loss and stress fracture (Lappe et al., 2008).

Following childbirth, breast tissue continues to remodel to support lactation in those breastfeeding, or pumping, increasing in size and impacting biomechanics (McGhee & Steele, 2020). Ensuring adequate support of the breast by selecting a bra with appropriate compression and encapsulation, ideally bespoke, is essential for both comfort and breast health (refer to Chapter 13). Breastfeeding or expressing milk before exercise is encouraged to reduce breast weight and make exercise more comfortable but the player's preference should be respected. Considering frequent and complete removal of milk from the breast is best, to the risk of developing engorgement or mastitis (Australian Institute of Sport, n.d.). Fluid and nutrition intake to support the hydration and energy needs of both exercise and lactation are essential to maintaining milk supply and optimal health.

Pelvic floor dysfunction is common in the postpartum period, with urinary incontinence and pelvic organ prolapse being the two most common dysfunctions. Medical and operative birth procedures increase the likelihood of a perineal injury and increase the likelihood of pelvic floor dysfunction (Cardozo et al., 2023). Although stress urinary incontinence is common and often accepted as inevitable by women postpartum, conservative management focusing on individualised lifestyle interventions and pelvic-floor muscle training have been shown to be highly effective at reducing or resolving symptoms (Dufour & Wu, 2020; NICE, 2021). A physiotherapist with specialised training in pelvic health can effectively address pelvic floor dysfunction, which is important, as this issue often stands in the way of athletic training and performance.

Following pregnancy, diastasis of the rectus abdominis may occur if the inter-rectus distance remains large or the function of the abdominal wall is compromised (Berg-Poppe et al., 2022). This condition is characterised by the thinning and widening of the *linea alba* and a tendency for midline bowing as a consequence of increased intra-abdominal pressure (Lambrinou et al., 2019). Conservative treatments such as exercise therapy alone or in addition to other modalities effectively improves diastasis of the rectus abdominis (Berg-Poppe et al., 2022). Key considerations for players will relate to football and position-specific performance demands and injury risk; hence, key objectives of rehabilitation should be focused on developing adequate capacity and movement strategies to eventually manage high and repetitive loading of the deep core and abdominal wall (Berg-Poppe et al., 2022).

Sleep and mental health are important factors to consider during the postpartum period. Both present challenges to return-to-play timelines and to performance. To ensure the wellbeing of postpartum players, continued use of comprehensive wellness reporting and active screening for significant mental health issues, for example using the Edinburgh Postnatal Depression Scale is recommended (Cox & Holden, 2003). Mental health screening should be delivered by the team physician to supplement a mental state assessment, with onward emergency referral pathways identified in advance of the early postpartum phase. Sleep can be challenging to manage in the postpartum period, and modification of activities to match-reported levels of readiness and recovery is encouraged.

Return to sport in the postpartum period

There remains very limited guidance for athletes returning to sport postpartum. Most medical advice recommends a gradual resumption of physical activity once bleeding (lochia) has stopped after a vaginal delivery, or after approximately six weeks following a caesarean delivery. However, each recovery timeline can vary depending on factors including mode of delivery, degree of perineal trauma during childbirth, complications during pregnancy or delivery and overall physical and mental health. Many athletes return to training prior to six weeks postpartum and while many will return to or exceed their pre-pregnancy level of performance, these athletes are also potentially at risk for developing injuries (Kimber et al., 2021). Thus, the need for sufficient time for healing and the development of sport-specific fitness prior to return to activity is important.

Fear of losing their position on a team or not being able to qualify for major competition may drive many athletes to return to sport too soon (Davenport, Nesdoly, et al., 2022). Athletes have advocated for a flexible return-to-sport timeline to allow a gradual return to training and competition that allows them to be prepared emotionally and physically (Davenport et al., 2023). Having a supportive and knowledgeable team of coaches, trainers and medical professionals, who can work together to develop an individualised plan for each athlete, is essential (Davenport et al., 2023). Pregnancy provides a unique opportunity for footballers and their teams to plan ahead for postpartum recovery. A number of frameworks have been developed that provide guidance on rehabilitation following childbirth, which critically consider the unique physiological and psychological changes that are commonly experienced, whilst providing athletes, coaches and medical professionals with guidance on how and when an athlete can return safely and successfully.

The 2019 Postpartum Return-to-Running Guideline was the first to re-imagine postpartum return to activity by utilising a rehabilitation lens (Goom et al., 2019). This, and other frameworks developed since its release, require that athletes reach specific healing and functional milestones before returning to high-impact activities, and are placed in the context of common postpartum complaints including musculoskeletal pain and urinary incontinence, whilst also considering the mental health of new mothers (Deering et al., 2020; Donnelly, Brockwell, et al., 2022; Donnelly, Moore, et al., 2022; Goom et al., 2019).

The 6Rs framework follows the principles of return-to-sport-rehabilitation frameworks but was contextualised to meet the unique considerations of the postpartum period (Donnelly, Moore, et al., 2022). Importantly, the 6Rs emphasise a flexible, whole-systems, biopsychosocial approach to suit individual healing and readiness, where planning for return to sport can begin during pregnancy. "Ready" (the first of the "Rs") seeks to prepare the athlete for motherhood and plan for postpartum recovery (pregnancy). "Review" evaluates the athlete's overall wellbeing and identifies areas that require rehabilitation. "Restore" emphasises rehabilitation of physical and psychological wellbeing in the early postpartum period. "Recondition" marks the transition of the athlete to sport-specific conditioning and skills. "Return" marks the transition to a structured training environment with "Refine" representing continued evaluation and provision of strategies to maintain availability to train and perform (Donnelly, Moore, et al., 2022).

Return-to-play considerations for the postpartum footballer

While there is an absence of football-specific return-to-play guidelines, following the general framework of the 6Rs in an athlete-centred manner can facilitate optimal care and shared decision-making. The multidisciplinary team should be similar to the makeup of the team during pregnancy, with plans for early phase recovery having ideally been completed towards the end of pregnancy. This strategy allows the player to take some time after birth to adjust, whilst also having some pre-programmed, early-phase rehabilitation to undertake if appropriate.

The continued involvement of a pelvic health physiotherapist is highly recommended as they are invaluable to preparing the player to withstand increasing training loads through the return-to-sport continuum (Donnelly & Moore, 2023). As the player progresses through the return-to-sport protocol, continued assessment of key postpartum objectives (e.g. physical function, recovery, psychological readiness and energy balance) should guide decision-making, rather than the number of weeks post-birth (Ardern et al., 2016; Donnelly, Moore, et al., 2022) (67, 70).

Conclusion

As support for the women's game and players continues to grow, opportunities to remain in football through the perinatal period will increase the number of athlete-mothers engaged in both grassroots and elite-level football. Continuing to advance research and support for footballers in the perinatal period and beyond is essential to inspire and support future generations of players, ensuring their safe and successful continued participation in training through pregnancy and return to play postpartum.

References

Alex, A., Bhandary, E., & McGuire, K. P. (2020). Anatomy and physiology of the breast during pregnancy and lactation. In S. Alipour & R. Omranipour (Eds.), *Diseases of the breast during pregnancy and lactation. Advances in experimental medicine and biology* (vol. 1252). Springer International Publishing. https://doi.org/10.1007/978-3-030-41596-9_1

Alfredson, H., Nordström, P., & Lorentzon, R. (1996). Total and regional bone mass in female soccer players. *Calcified Tissue International, 59*(6), 438–442. https://doi.org/10.1007/BF00369207

Ardern, C. L., Bizzini, M., & Bahr, R. (2016). It is time for consensus on return to play after injury: Five key questions. *British Journal of Sports Medicine, 50*(9), 506–508. https://doi.org/10.1136/bjsports-2015-095475

Austin, M.-P., Priest, S. R., & Sullivan, E. A. (2008). Antenatal psychosocial assessment for reducing perinatal mental health morbidity. *Cochrane Database of Systematic Reviews, 4*, CD005124. https://doi.org/10.1002/14651858.CD005124.pub2

Australian Institute of Sport (AIS). (n.d.). *Breastfeeding as an athlete*. https://www.ais.gov.au/__data/assets/pdf_file/0018/1021554/Breastfeeding-athlete-infographic.pdf

Bader, R. A., Bader, M. E., Rose, D. J., & Braunwald, E. (1955). Hemodynamics at rest and during exercise in normal pregnancy as studied by cardiac catheterization. *The Journal of Clinical Investigation, 34*(10), 1524–1536. https://doi.org/10.1172/JCI103205

Barakat, R., Pelaez, M., Lopez, C., Montejo, R., & Coteron, J. (2012). Exercise during pregnancy reduces the rate of cesarean and instrumental deliveries: Results of a randomized controlled trial. *The Journal of Maternal-Fetal & Neonatal Medicine, 25*(11), 2372–2376. https://doi.org/10.3109/14767058.2012.696165

Beetham, K. S., Giles, C., Noetel, M., Clifton, V., Jones, J. C., & Naughton, G. (2019). The effects of vigorous intensity exercise in the third trimester of pregnancy: A systematic review and meta-analysis. *BMC Pregnancy and Childbirth, 19*(1), 281–281. https://doi.org/10.1186/s12884-019-2441-1

Berg-Poppe, P., Hauer, M., Jones, C., Munger, M., & Wethor, C. (2022). Use of exercise in the management of postpartum diastasis recti: A systematic review. *Journal of Women's Health Physical Therapy, 46*(1), 35–47. https://doi.org/10.1097/JWH.0000000000000231

Bø, K., Artal, R., Barakat, R., Brown, W., Davies, G. A. L., Dooley, M., Evenson, K. R., Haakstad, L. A. H., Henriksson-Larsen, K., Kayser, B., Kinnunen, T. I., Mottola, M. F., Nygaard, I., van Poppel, M., Stuge, B., & Khan, K. M. (2016). Exercise and pregnancy in recreational and elite athletes: 2016 evidence summary from the IOC expert group meeting, Lausanne. Part 1—exercise in women planning pregnancy and those who are pregnant. *British Journal of Sports Medicine, 50*(10), 571–589. https://doi.org/10.1136/bjsports-2016-096218

Bull, F. C., Al-Ansari, S. S., Biddle, S., Borodulin, K., Buman, M. P., Cardon, G., Carty, C., Chaput, J.-P., Chastin, S., Chou, R., Dempsey, P. C., DiPietro, L., Ekelund, U., Firth, J., Friedenreich, C. M., Garcia, L., Gichu, M., Jago, R., Katzmarzyk, P. T., . . . Willumsen, J. F. (2020). World Health Organization 2020 guidelines on physical activity and sedentary behaviour. *British Journal of Sports Medicine, 54*(24), 1451–1462. https://doi.org/10.1136/bjsports-2020-102955

Canadian Society for Exercise Physiology. (2021). *CSEP get active questionnaire for pregnancy*. CSEP. https://csep.ca/2021/05/27/get-active-questionnaire-for-pregnancy/

Cannon, S. S., Lastella, M., Evenson, K. R., & Hayman, M. J. (2023). The association between physical activity and sleep during pregnancy: A systematic review. *Behavioral Sleep Medicine, 21*(4), 513–528. https://doi.org/10.1080/15402002.2022.2124258

Canul-Medina, G., & Fernandez-Mejia, C. (2019). Morphological, hormonal, and molecular changes in different maternal tissues during lactation and post-lactation. *The Journal of Physiological Sciences, 69*(6), 825–835. https://doi.org/10.1007/s12576-019-00714-4

Cardozo, L., Rovner, E., Wagg, A., Wein, A., & Abrams, P. (Eds.). (2023). *Incontinence* (7th ed.). ICI-ICS, International Continence Society.

Clapp, J. F., & Capeless, E. (1997). Cardiovascular function before, during, and after the first and subsequent pregnancies. *The American Journal of Cardiology, 80*(11), 1469–1473. https://doi.org/10.1016/S0002-9149(97)00738-8

Conder, R., Zamani, R., & Akrami, M. (2019). The biomechanics of pregnancy: A systematic review. *Journal of Functional Morphology and Kinesiology, 4*(4), 72. https://doi.org/10.3390/jfmk4040072

Cox, J., & Holden, J. (2003). *Perinatal mental health: A guide to the Edinburgh postnatal depression scale*. The Royal College of Psychiatrists.

Dakic, J. G., Hay-Smith, J., Lin, K.-Y., Cook, J., & Frawley, H. C. (2023). Experience of playing sport or exercising for women with pelvic floor symptoms: A qualitative study. *Sports Medicine—Open, 9*(1), 25–25. https://doi.org/10.1186/s40798-023-00565-9

Davenport, M. H., McCurdy, A. P., Mottola, M. F., Skow, R. J., Meah, V. L., Poitras, V. J., Jaramillo Garcia, A., Gray, C. E., Barrowman, N., Riske, L., Sobierajski, F., James, M., Nagpal, T., Marchand, A.-A., Nuspl, M., Slater, L. G., Barakat, R., Adamo, K. B., Davies, G. A., & Ruchat, S.-M. (2018). Impact of prenatal exercise on both prenatal and postnatal anxiety and depressive symptoms: A systematic review and meta-analysis. *British Journal of Sports Medicine, 52*(21), 1376–1385. https://doi.org/10.1136/bjsports-2018-099697

Davenport, M. H., Meah, V. L., Ruchat, S.-M., Davies, G. A., Skow, R. J., Barrowman, N., Adamo, K. B., Poitras, V. J., Gray, C. E., Jaramillo Garcia, A., Sobierajski, F., Riske, L., James, M., Kathol, A. J., Nuspl, M., Marchand, A.-A., Nagpal, T. S., Slater, L. G., Weeks, A., . . . Mottola, M. F. (2018). Impact of prenatal exercise on neonatal and childhood outcomes: A systematic review and meta-analysis. *British Journal of Sports Medicine, 52*(21), 1386–1396. https://doi.org/10.1136/bjsports-2018-099836

Davenport, M. H., Neil-Sztramko, S. E., Lett, B., Duggan, M., Mottola, M. F., Ruchat, S.-M., Adamo, K. B., Andrews, K., Artal, R., Beamish, N. F., Chari, R., Forte, M., Lane, K. N., May, L. E., Maclaren, K., & Zahavich, A. (2022). Development of the get active questionnaire for pregnancy: Breaking down barriers to prenatal exercise. *Applied Physiology, Nutrition, and Metabolism, 47*(7), 787–803. https://doi.org/10.1139/apnm-2021-0655

Davenport, M. H., Nesdoly, A., Ray, L., Thornton, J. S., Khurana, R., & McHugh, T.-L. F. (2022). Pushing for change: A qualitative study of the experiences of elite athletes during pregnancy. *British Journal of Sports Medicine, 56*(8), 452–457. https://doi.org/10.1136/bjsports-2021-104755

Davenport, M. H., Ray, L., Nesdoly, A., Thornton, J., Khurana, R., & McHugh, T.-L. F. (2023). We're not superhuman, we're human: A qualitative description of elite athletes' experiences of return to sport after childbirth. *Sports Medicine, 53*(1), 269–279. https://doi.org/10.1007/s40279-022-01730-y

Davenport, M. H., Ruchat, S.-M., Poitras, V. J., Jaramillo Garcia, A., Gray, C. E., Barrowman, N., Skow, R. J., Meah, V. L., Riske, L., Sobierajski, F., James, M., Kathol, A. J., Nuspl, M., Marchand, A.-A., Nagpal, T. S., Slater, L. G., Weeks, A., Adamo, K. B., Davies, G. A., . . . Mottola, M. F. (2018). Prenatal exercise for the prevention of gestational diabetes mellitus and hypertensive disorders of pregnancy: A systematic review and meta-analysis. *British Journal of Sports Medicine, 52*(21), 1367–1375. https://doi.org/10.1136/bjsports-2018-099355

Davenport, M. H., Skow, R. J., & Steinback, C. D. (2016). Maternal responses to aerobic exercise in pregnancy. *Clinical Obstetrics and Gynecology, 59*(3), 541–551. https://doi.org/10.1097/GRF.0000000000000201

Deering, R. E., Christopher, S. M., & Heiderscheit, B. C. (2020). From childbirth to the starting blocks: Are we providing the best care to our postpartum athletes? *The Journal of Orthopaedic and Sports Physical Therapy, 50*(6), 281–284. https://doi.org/10.2519/jospt.2020.0607

Domenjoz, I., Kayser, B., & Boulvain, M. (2014). Effect of physical activity during pregnancy on mode of delivery. *American Journal of Obstetrics and Gynecology, 211*(4), 401.e1–401.e11. https://doi.org/10.1016/j.ajog.2014.03.030

Donnelly, G. M., Brockwell, E., Rankin, A., & Moore, I. S. (2022). Beyond the musculoskeletal system: Considering whole-systems readiness for running postpartum. *Journal of Women's Health Physical Therapy, 46*(1), 48–56. https://doi.org/10.1097/JWH.0000000000000218

Donnelly, G. M., & Moore, I. S. (2023). Sports medicine and the pelvic floor. *Current Sports Medicine Reports, 22*(3), 82–90. https://doi.org/10.1249/JSR.0000000000001045

Donnelly, G. M., Moore, I. S., Brockwell, E., Rankin, A., & Cooke, R. (2022). Reframing return-to-sport postpartum: The 6 Rs framework. *British Journal of Sports Medicine, 56*(5), 244–245. https://doi.org/10.1136/bjsports-2021-104877

Dufour, S., & Wu, M. (2020). No. 397—conservative care of urinary incontinence in women. *Journal of Obstetrics and Gynaecology Canada, 42*(4), 510–522. https://doi.org/10.1016/j.jogc.2019.04.009

Ferry, B., Duclos, M., Burt, L., Therre, P., Le Gall, F., Jaffré, C., & Courteix, D. (2011). Bone geometry and strength adaptations to physical constraints inherent in different sports: Comparison between elite female soccer players and swimmers. *Journal of Bone and Mineral Metabolism, 29*(3), 342–351. https://doi.org/10.1007/s00774-010-0226-8

FIFA. (2020, December). *Women's football: Minimum labour conditions for players.* https://digitalhub.fifa.com/m/033101649cc3c480/original/f9cc8eex7qligvxfznbf-pdf.pdf

FIFA. (2023, August 22). *FIFA Women's World Cup player analysis.* FIFA High Performance & CIES Football Observatory. https://www.fifatrainingcentre.com/en/community/fifa-research/fifa-womens-world-cup-player-analysis.php

The Football Association. (2009a). *Pregnancy and football—guidelines for officials.* https://resources.thefa.com/images/ftimages/data/league479698/36661.doc

The Football Association. (2009b). *Pregnancy and football—guidelines for players 2009.* https://resources.thefa.com/images/ftimages/data/league479698/21470.doc

Friedman, J. E., Ishizuka, T., Shao, J., Huston, L., Highman, T., & Catalano, P. (1999). Impaired glucose transport and insulin receptor tyrosine phosphorylation in skeletal muscle from obese women with gestational diabetes. *Diabetes, 48*(9), 1807–1814. https://doi.org/10.2337/diabetes.48.9.1807

Godfrey, R. J., Ingham, S. A., Pedlar, C. R., & Whyte, G. P. (2005). The detraining and retraining of an elite rower: A case study. *Journal of Science and Medicine in Sport, 8*(3), 314–320. https://doi.org/10.1016/S1440-2440(05)80042-8

Goom, T., Donnelly, G., & Brockwell, E. (2019, March). *Returning to running postnatal—guidelines for medical, health and fitness professionals managing this population.* https://www.absolute.physio/wp-content/uploads/2019/09/returning-to-running-postnatal-guidelines.pdf

Hart, M. V., Morton, M. J., Hosenpud, J. D., & Metcalfe, J. (1986). Aortic function during normal human pregnancy. *American Journal of Obstetrics and Gynecology, 154*(4), 887–891. https://doi.org/10.1016/0002-9378(86)90477-1

Jaque-Fortunato, S. V/, Wiswell, R. A., Khodiguian, N., & Artal, R. (1996). A comparison of the ventilatory responses to exercise in pregnant, postpartum, and nonpregnant women. *Seminars in Perinatology, 20*(4), 263–276. https://doi.org/10.1016/S0146-0005(96)80019-X

Kimber, M. L., Meyer, S., Mchugh, T.-L., Thornton, J., Khurana, R., Sivak, A., & Davenport, M. H. (2021). Health outcomes after pregnancy in elite athletes: A systematic review and meta-analysis. *Medicine and Science in Sports and Exercise*, *53*(8), 1739–1747. https:// doi.org/10.1249/MSS.0000000000002617

Knuttgen, H. G., & Emerson, K. (1974). Physiological response to pregnancy at rest and during exercise. *Journal of Applied Physiology*, *36*(5), 549–553. https://doi.org/10.1152/ jappl.1974.36.5.549

Lambrinou, C. P., Karaglani, E., & Manios, Y. (2019). Breastfeeding and postpartum weight loss. *Current Opinion in Clinical Nutrition and Metabolic Care*, *22*(6), 413–417. https:// doi.org/10.1097/MCO.0000000000000597

Landahl, G., Adolfsson, P., Börjesson, M., Mannheimer, C., & Rödjer, S. (2005). Iron deficiency and anemia: A common problem in female elite soccer players. *International Journal of Sport Nutrition and Exercise Metabolism*, *15*(6), 689–694. https://doi. org/10.1123/ijsnem.15.6.689

Lappe, J., Cullen, D., Haynatzki, G., Recker, R., Ahlf, R., & Thompson, K. (2008). Calcium and vitamin D supplementation decreases incidence of stress fractures in female navy recruits. *Journal of Bone and Mineral Research*, *23*(5), 741–749. https://doi.org/10.1359/ jbmr.080102

Lewis, M. (2021, April 28). *World cup qualifying memories from 1991*. U.S. Soccer. https:// www.ussoccer.com/stories/2021/04/world-cup-qualifying-memories-from-1991

Maliha, G., Morgan, J., & Vrahas, M. (2012). Transient osteoporosis of pregnancy. *Injury*, *43*(8), 1237–1241. https://doi.org/10.1016/j.injury.2012.03.009

McGhee, D. E., & Steele, J. R. (2020). Biomechanics of breast support for active women. *Exercise and Sport Sciences Reviews*, *48*(3), 99–109. https://doi.org/10.1249/ JES.0000000000000221

Meah, V. L., Davies, G. A., & Davenport, M. H. (2020). Why can't I exercise during pregnancy? Time to revisit medical "absolute" and "relative" contraindications: Systematic review of evidence of harm and a call to action. *British Journal of Sports Medicine*, *54*(23), 1395–1404. https://doi.org/10.1136/bjsports-2020-102042

Milanović, Z., Čović, N., Helge, E. W., Krustrup, P., & Mohr, M. (2022). Recreational football and bone health: A systematic review and meta-analysis. *Sports Medicine*, *52*(12), 3021–3037. https://doi.org/10.1007/s40279-022-01726-8

Mottola, M. F., Davenport, M. H., Ruchat, S.-M., Davies, G. A., Poitras, V. J., Gray, C. E., Jaramillo Garcia, A., Barrowman, N., Adamo, K. B., Duggan, M., Barakat, R., Chilibeck, P., Fleming, K., Forte, M., Korolnek, J., Nagpal, T., Slater, L. G., Stirling, D., & Zehr, L. (2018). 2019 Canadian guideline for physical activity throughout pregnancy. *British Journal of Sports Medicine*, *52*(21), 1339–1346. https://doi.org/10.1136/bjsports-2018-100056

Mountjoy, M., Ackerman, K. E., Bailey, D. M., Burke, L. M., Constantini, N., Hackney, A. C., Heikura, I. A., Melin, A., Pensgaard, A. M., Stellingwerff, T., Sundgot-Borgen, J. K., Torstveit, M. K., Jacobsen, A. U., Verhagen, E., Budgett, R., Engebretsen, L., & Erdener, U. (2023). 2023 International Olympic committee's (IOC) consensus statement on Relative energy deficiency in sport (REDs). *British Journal of Sports Medicine*, *57*(17), 1073–1098. https://doi.org/10.1136/bjsports-2023-106994

National Institute for Health and Care Excellence. (2021). *Pelvic floor dysfunction: Prevention and non-surgical management*. https://www.nice.org.uk/guidance/ng210/chapter/ Recommendations

O'Connor, D. L., Blake, J., Bell, R., Bowen, A., Callum, J., Fenton, S., Gray-Donald, K., Rossiter, M., Adamo, K., Brett, K., Khatri, N., Robinson, N., Tumback, L., & Cheung, A. (2016). Canadian consensus on female nutrition: Adolescence, reproduction, menopause, and beyond. *Journal of Obstetrics and Gynaecology Canada*, *38*(6), 508. https:// doi.org/10.1016/j.jogc.2016.01.001

Pernoll, M. L., Metcalfe, J., Schlenker, T. L., Welch, J. E., & Matsumoto, J. A. (1975). Oxygen consumption at rest and during exercise in pregnancy. *Respiration Physiology*, *25*(3), 285–293. https://doi.org/10.1016/0034-5687(75)90004-3

Ponorac, N., Popović, M., Karaba-Jakovljević, D., Bajić, Z., Scanlan, A., Stojanović, E., & Radovanović, D. (2020). Professional female athletes are at a heightened risk of iron-deficient erythropoiesis compared with nonathletes. *International Journal of Sport Nutrition and Exercise Metabolism, 30*(1), 48–53. https://doi.org/10.1123/ijsnem.2019-0193

Prevett, C., Kimber, M. L., Forner, L., de Vivo, M., & Davenport, M. H. (2023). Impact of heavy resistance training on pregnancy and postpartum health outcomes. *International Urogynecology Journal, 34*(2), 405–411. https://doi.org/10.1007/s00192-022-05393-1

Shiri, R., Coggon, D., & Falah-Hassani, K. (2018). Exercise for the prevention of low back and pelvic girdle pain in pregnancy: A meta-analysis of randomized controlled trials. *European Journal of Pain, 22*(1), 19–27. https://doi.org/10.1002/ejp.1096

Sobhgol, S. S., Smith, C. A., & Dahlen, H. G. (2020). The effect of antenatal pelvic floor muscle exercises on labour and birth outcomes: A systematic review and meta-analysis. *International Urogynecology Journal, 31*(11), 2189–2203. https://doi.org/10.1007/s00192-020-04298-1

Sperstad, J. B., Tennfjord, M. K., Hilde, G., Ellström-Engh, M., & Bø, K. (2016). Diastasis recti abdominis during pregnancy and 12 months after childbirth: Prevalence, risk factors, and report of lumbopelvic pain. *British Journal of Sports Medicine, 50*(17), 1092–1096. https://doi.org/10.1136/bjsports-2016-096065

Stevens, G. A., Finucane, M. M., De-Regil, L. M., Paciorek, C. J., Flaxman, S. R., Branca, F., Peña-Rosas, J. P., Bhutta, Z. A., & Ezzati, M. (2013). Global, regional, and national trends in haemoglobin concentration and prevalence of total and severe anaemia in children and pregnant and non-pregnant women for 1995–2011: A systematic analysis of population-representative data. *The Lancet Global Health, 1*(1), e16–e25. https://doi.org/10.1016/S2214-109X(13)70001-9

Sytsma, T. T., Zimmerman, K. P., Manning, J. B., Jenkins, S. M., Nelson, N. C., Clark, M. M., Boldt, K., & Borowski, K. S. (2018). Perceived barriers to exercise in the first trimester of pregnancy. *The Journal of Perinatal Education, 27*(4), 198–206. https://doi.org/10.1891/1058-1243.27.4.198

To, W. W. K., Wong, M. W. N., & Leung, T.-W. (2003). Relationship between bone mineral density changes in pregnancy and maternal and pregnancy characteristics: A longitudinal study. *Acta Obstetricia et Gynecologica Scandinavica, 82*(9), 820–827. https://doi.org/10.1034/j.1600-0412.2003.00227.x

Ueland, K., Novy, M. J., & Metcalfe, J. (1973). Cardiorespiratory responses to pregnancy and exercise in normal women and patients with heart disease. *American Journal of Obstetrics and Gynecology, 115*(1), 4–10. https://doi.org/10.1016/0002-9378(73)90081-1

UK Chief Medical Officers' Physical Activity Guidelines. (2019). *Physical activity for pregnant women.* https://assets.publishing.service.gov.uk/media/620a28288fa8f54916f45dfc/physical-activity-for-pregnant-women.pdf

Watkins, V. Y., O'Donnell, C. M., Perez, M., Zhao, P., England, S., Carter, E. B., Kelly, J. C., Frolova, A., & Raghuraman, N. (2021). The impact of physical activity during pregnancy on labor and delivery. *American Journal of Obstetrics and Gynecology, 225*(4), 437.e1–437.e8. https://doi.org/10.1016/j.ajog.2021.05.036

Wowdzia, J. B., Hazell, T. J., Berg, E. R. V., Labrecque, L., Brassard, P., & Davenport, M. H. (2023). Maternal and fetal cardiovascular responses to acute high-intensity interval and moderate-intensity continuous training exercise during pregnancy: A randomized crossover trial. *Sports Medicine, 53*(9), 1819–1833. https://doi.org/10.1007/s40279-023-01858-5

Wowdzia, J. B., Hazell, T. J., & Davenport, M. H. (2022). Glycemic response to acute high-intensity interval versus moderate-intensity continuous exercise during pregnancy. *Physiological Reports, 10*(18), e15454. https://doi.org/10.14814/phy2.15454

Wowdzia, J. B., McHugh, T.-L., Thornton, J., Sivak, A., Mottola, M. F., & Davenport, M. H. (2021). Elite athletes and pregnancy outcomes: A systematic review and meta-analysis. *Medicine and Science in Sports and Exercise, 53*(3), 534–542. https://doi.org/10.1249/MSS.0000000000002510

8

SPORTS NUTRITION NEEDS

*Rebecca K. Randell, Ian Rollo, Samantha L. Moss
and Tom Clifford*

Introduction

Historically, science in women's football has failed to keep pace with its popularity. However, research has shown that elite players are required to complete higher match and training volumes than ever before (Nassis et al., 2020). During the season, elite teams complete between five to seven training sessions, in addition to one to two competitive matches per week. The physical demands of elite women's matches are now well documented, with outfield players covering average total distances of ~10.5 km, of which 1.5–2.0 km are completed as high-intensity running (Mohr et al., 2008). Further information on match demands and physiological determinants are discussed in Chapter 3.

Considering the exercise volume and physical and mental demands that players are exposed to, the role diet plays in optimising performance has increased in importance (Randell et al., 2021), and sex should be taken into account when considering the nutritional needs of players (Collins et al., 2021). However, unless clear distinctions were made, many of the key recommendations in the article by Collins et al. were applied to both sexes.

The foremost objective for an elite player is to ensure their dietary intake is well balanced and meets the recommended macro- and micronutrient intakes. In addition, the diet should supply the nutrients needed to cover the energy demands of training and match-play, and enable them to optimise physiological adaptations and

Rebecca K. Randell and Ian Rollo are employed by PepsiCo R&D. Samantha L. Moss has received consulting fees from PepsiCo R&D. The views expressed are those of the authors and do not necessarily reflect the position or policy of PepsiCo, Inc.

DOI: 10.4324/9781003381914-8

accelerate recovery between matches (de Sousa et al., 2022). Maintaining energy balance is of particular importance as data indicate that some elite players experience periods of an energy deficit during the season (Moss et al., 2021), and if not addressed, chronic energy deficiency can lead to low energy availability and deleterious health and performance effects (Ackerman et al., 2019). The aim of this chapter is to review the latest studies on sports nutrition specific to women's football and establish clear nutritional guidelines (where possible) for elite-level players.

Carbohydrate

Carbohydrate is a primary fuel source that should be ingested prior, during and after matches or training sessions. After competitive matches, 80% of Type 1 and 69% of Type 2 muscle fibres have been found to be glycogen depleted, which likely contributes to declines in repeated sprint performance (Krustrup et al., 2022). Therefore, appropriate fuelling strategies will ensure glycogen does not limit performance (Kerksick et al., 2018).

Daily carbohydrate intakes

It is recommended that players consume 3 to 8 g per kg of body mass per day (hereafter written as g kg body-mass^{-1} day^{-1}) of carbohydrates depending on exercise demands (Collins et al., 2021). Higher intakes (6–8 g kg body-mass^{-1} day^{-1}) are suggested for congested fixture periods (i.e. matches every 3 to 4 days) compared with single-match weeks (3–8 g kg body-mass^{-1} day^{-1}), preseason training (4–8 g kg body-mass^{-1} day^{-1}) and off-season training (<4 g kg body-mass^{-1} day^{-1}) (Collins et al., 2021). Although proposed as suitable for both men and women (Collins et al., 2021), these guidelines were informed by data collected almost entirely on men. Therefore, current recommendations do not account for women-specific differences that might warrant altered guidelines, such as different muscle fibre composition (Haizlip et al., 2015) and hormonal-related alterations in substrate use during exercise (Campbell & Febbraio, 2001). Further research is required to address whether specific carbohydrate guidelines for women are necessary.

Based on the current guidelines, women football players do not normally achieve sufficient carbohydrate intakes during the season. Typical daily carbohydrate intakes in elite players range from ~3–5.5 g kg body-mass^{-1} day^{-1} (Moss et al., 2021), and are therefore below or at the lower end of recommendations for a two-match week and a single-match week, respectively (Collins et al., 2021). Moreover, players typically do not periodise carbohydrate intake according to the changing exercise demands (Moss et al., 2021). A substantial number of top-division players reported carbohydrate intakes of <3 g kg body-mass^{-1} day^{-1} on a double-training session day (62%) and matchday (39%) (Moss et al., 2021), which are likely to result in impaired training and match performance due to insufficient glycogen availability.

The reasons for inappropriate fuelling practices are likely multifaceted (e.g. limited provision of food and qualified personnel, lack of feeding opportunities and limited education). In one qualitative study, many players reported a fear of carbohydrates, due to misunderstandings about how carbohydrates might impact body composition, alongside external pressure from social media, key stakeholders and regular skinfold testing (McHaffie et al., 2022). Accounts of "over-testing" body composition have been reported to alter eating habits of players, specifically via avoidance of carbohydrates (Culvin, 2019) (see also Chapter 10, on disordered eating). Therefore, it is pertinent for organisations to create and maintain healthy cultures around carbohydrate and body composition, alongside providing the necessary infrastructure (e.g. staff, food availability, education) to bring about change.

Carbohydrate intake before training and matches

On the day before high-intensity training and matches, ingesting 6–8 g kg body-mass^{-1} day^{-1} is recommended, as higher pre-exercise glycogen stores enhance the capacity for repeated bouts of exercise to be completed (Bangsbo et al., 1992). Although studies in women footballers are needed, the capacity to load muscle glycogen is not sex dependent, provided that high carbohydrate intakes (i.e. >9 g kg body-mass^{-1} day^{-1}) are ingested (Tarnopolsky et al., 2001). For menstruating women (i.e. those not on hormonal contraception), high carbohydrate intakes might be beneficial during the mid-follicular phase of the cycle, as resting muscle glycogen may be lower (Hackney, 1990; McLay et al., 2007). However, there are some reservations about whether high carbohydrate intakes are feasible for many women athletes (Moss & Randell, 2022). For example for a woman consuming 2,000 kcal day^{-1}, a carbohydrate intake of 8–10 g kg body-mass^{-1} day^{-1} would equate to approximately 93–120% of habitual energy intake (assuming a body mass of 60 kg). Consequently, implementation of a successful nutrition strategy requires a co-ordinated effort between players and nutritionists/dieticians.

The 3–4-hr-before-match or high-intensity training session provides an opportunity to "top up" glycogen stores by ingesting a further 1–3 g kg^{-1} of carbohydrate. This top up might be particularly important for morning or early afternoon exercise, considering that an overnight fast depletes liver glycogen (an important energy source) (Rothman et al., 1991). When considering the type of carbohydrate selected for the pre-exercise meal, high glycaemic index (GI) carbohydrates enable fast absorption and delivery, and are therefore preferred to low GI carbohydrates (Williams & Rollo, 2015).

Carbohydrate intake during training and matches

During matches, players should take advantage of the available opportunities (e.g. at half-time, extra-time and during stoppages such as injuries) to consume carbohydrates, in order to limit performance decrements during the later stages of a match (Krustrup et al., 2022). One solution is to ingest a 30-g carbohydrate beverage before each half, which has been found to improve high-intensity running capacity and retain passing performance during a simulated football match in men (Rodriguez-Giustiniani et al., 2019); however, more research is needed in women players.

Carbohydrate intake post-training and matches

Replenishing glycogen stores after high-intensity training and matches is essential. The recovery time available between exercise bouts will dictate the necessary refuelling strategy. In cases where exercise bouts are taking place in quick succession (e.g. 4–8 hr recovery time), immediate replenishment is suggested, via ingesting ~1 g kg^{-1} body-mass hr^{-1} for 4 hr (Thomas et al., 2016). For such instances, specially formulated nutrition products are convenient options for rapid refuelling, with a carbohydrate-rich meal recommended as soon as is logistically possible. However, when recovery times are longer (e.g. >8 hr), daily carbohydrate recommendations can be followed (see the section earlier). The amount of carbohydrate consumed is regarded as more crucial than the specific type, format or timing of intake for optimising glycogen resynthesis (Burke et al., 2006).

Protein

Dietary protein can augment resistance-training-induced gains in lean muscle mass and endurance-training-induced gains in mitochondrial mass (Moore et al., 2014; Morton et al., 2018). Dietary protein also supports immune function (Witard et al., 2014) and skeletal muscle remodelling after exercise (Moore et al., 2014; Morton et al., 2018), enabling players to train and recover more efficiently. In this section, we summarise the recommendations for optimal protein intakes in football players; note that the recommendations are derived from research in both men and women from a variety of training backgrounds, as there is limited research available in elite women football players.

Daily intakes

Irrespective of sex, athletes have greater daily protein requirements than do non-athletes. Indeed, athletes are recommended to consume 1.2–2.0 g kg body-mass^{-1} day^{-1} of dietary protein, compared to 0.8 g kg body-mass^{-1} day^{-1} for most non-athlete individuals (Thomas et al., 2016). Specific to football players, protein intakes of 1.6–2.2 g kg body-mass^{-1} day^{-1} are recommended to optimise training adaptations (Collins et al., 2021). This is a broad range, with no consideration to potential differences in male and female requirements. To derive specific protein-intake recommendations for women's team-sport athletes, Wooding et al. (2017) used the amino acid oxidation method to estimate whole body protein synthesis over a day (Wooding et al., 2017). They estimated that, following a bout of intermittent exercise, women's team-sport athletes had an average protein requirement of ~1.4 g kg body-mass^{-1} day^{-1} and a recommended daily allowance of ~1.7 g kg body-mass^{-1} day^{-1} (Wooding et al., 2017). As amino acid oxidation is greater if carbohydrate availability is low—as has been reported in female football players (Moss et al., 2021)—and there is uncertainty on how protein requirements may vary across the menstrual cycle, it would seem prudent to recommend protein intakes of ≥1.7 g kg body-mass^{-1} day^{-1} for football players (Moore et al., 2022).

While total protein intake is the main determinant of muscle protein synthesis (MPS), it has been shown that rates are maximised when protein intake is evenly distributed throughout the day. For example in healthy men and women, consuming 90 g day^{-1} of protein as 3 × ~30-g boluses (breakfast, lunch and dinner) stimulated 24-hr MPS to a greater extent than skewing protein intakes towards higher intakes at dinner (65 g) (Mamerow et al., 2014). Therefore, to optimise adaptive remodelling, players should consume three to five protein-rich meals/snacks every 3–4 hr (Areta et al., 2013). Each feed should contain ~0.40 g kg^{-1} of protein, as this is likely sufficient to maximally stimulate MPS in healthy women after football activity (Moore et al., 2022). In addition, players should choose leucine-rich sources, as this amino acid maximises the anabolic response to exercise, at least when isolated sources such as whey or casein protein are consumed (Burd et al., 2019). Lastly, it has been suggested that consuming a large bolus (45 g) of milk protein after evening exercise, 30 min before bedtime, increases overnight rates of myofibrillar and mitochondrial MPS (Trommelen et al., 2023). This finding suggests that, at least after night matches, consuming a whey or casein-protein supplement before bed could augment muscle repair and adaptations.

Protein type

In most studies, it has been suggested that animal protein sources, such as milk, better stimulate MPS than do plant protein sources such as soy (Tang et al., 2009) and wheat (Gorissen et al., 2016), probably due to the quicker absorption rate and the higher essential amino acid content of animal proteins (Morgan et al., 2021). One way to stimulate analogous increases in MPS is to increase the dose of plant protein relative to animal protein (Dunlop et al., 2017). Nonetheless, protein type may have little impact on longer-term skeletal muscle adaptation as body composition, muscle hypertrophy and strength were found to be comparable when diets were supplemented with equal amounts of animal or plant proteins following >eight weeks of resistance training (Babault et al., 2015). This finding suggests that players should choose protein sources based on personal preference, while focusing on total daily intakes and distribution. It is also important to note that isolated protein supplements (e.g. whey or soy protein powders) are not necessarily more effective than food sources; indeed, several protein-rich foods such as mycoprotein (Dunlop et al., 2017), quark (Hermans et al., 2023) and cheese (Hermans et al., 2022) have all been shown to stimulate MPS to comparable levels.

Protein intake post-training and matches

Football training and matches can evoke symptoms of muscle damage, such as muscle soreness and decrements in muscle function, which can persist for 72 hr post-exercise (Goulart et al., 2022). As recovery time between training and matches is limited (in some instances <48 hr), these deleterious symptoms may affect subsequent performance (Julian et al., 2021). One proposed strategy to alleviate these symptoms is to consume a high-quality source of protein immediately (or <1 hr) following exercise (Ranchordas et al., 2017). Although this practice is widespread, especially on match-day (Field et al., 2021), evidence to support protein's role in attenuating acute increases in muscle soreness and deficits in muscle function is equivocal. While some researchers have shown that consuming whey (Lollo et al., 2014), milk (Rankin et al., 2019) or casein (Abbott et al., 2019) protein <1 hr post-exercise may alleviate symptoms of muscle damage, others do not (Apweiler et al., 2018; Eddens et al., 2017). Nonetheless, in men football players, the decline in lower-limb muscle strength ≤3 days after a match was found to be lower when daily protein intakes were 2.4 g kg^{-1} body-mass day^{-1} compared to 1.3 g kg^{-1} body-mass day^{-1} (Poulios et al., 2018). Similarly, in women dancers, Brown and colleagues (Brown et al., 2018) found that declines in reactive strength index after repeated sprint exercise were attenuated when daily protein intakes were 1.8 versus 1.2 g kg^{-1} body-mass day^{-1} for two days post-exercise. On the basis of these studies, we suggest that, to minimise unwanted symptoms of muscle damage, players should focus on consuming sufficiently high total daily protein intakes rather than what they consume in single post-exercise meals.

Fluid

Body water plays a vital role during exercise by regulating the body's core temperature. The primary method for dissipating heat, generated by the contracting muscles during exercise, is through sweating and the subsequent evaporation of sweat from the skin's surface. Whether in cool or hot conditions, football players commonly experience significant fluid loss (via sweating) during football-type activity (Broad et al., 1996; Tarnowski et al., 2022). Insufficient fluid intake without compensating for body sweat losses can lead to hypohydration (Sawka et al., 2007). In elite players, body mass losses of ~2% have been found to increase heart rate, blood lactate and ratings of perceived exertion (Ali et al., 2011). Impairments in cognition and technical skill may also arise at higher levels of body mass loss (3–4%), and when exercise is performed in the heat (Nuccio et al., 2017), although more research is needed in women. Thus, from a practical perspective, preventing dehydration (at a level of >2% body mass loss) may reduce the physiological strain as well as any potential performance decrements.

Thermoregulation and hydration responses may be influenced by hormonal changes; however, data are limited, and therefore insufficient evidence is available to support sex-specific hydration guidelines (Giersch et al., 2020). Yet, given that most hydration guidelines are based on body mass or individual sweat rates, and because women typically have smaller body sizes on average compared to men, adopting a personalised approach can enhance the feasibility of women meeting these recommendations. Furthermore, individual hydration recommendations for training and matches depend on factors like sweat rate, initial hydration, heat acclimatisation, exercise intensity and the environment (Sawka et al., 2007).

Fluid intake before training and matches

To maintain performance and reduce cardiovascular and thermoregulatory strain from dehydration, players should begin training and matches in a well-hydrated state (Nuccio et al., 2017). In a systematic review, ~47% of football players were reported to be in a hypohydrated state prior to matches and training; therefore, pre-exercise fluid intake is an area of improvement for many players (Chapelle et al., 2020). Daily monitoring of body mass (Cheuvront et al., 2010), thirst levels (Armstrong et al., 2014), urine colour (Armstrong et al., 2010), osmolality and urine-specific gravity (Armstrong et al., 1998) offer valuable insights into an individual's hydration status. Urine osmolality below 700 mOsmol kg^{-1} or a specific gravity lower than 1.020 typically indicate a state of proper hydration (euhydration), while readings exceeding 900 mOsmol kg^{-1} are indicative of dehydration (hypohydration) (Kenefick & Cheuvront, 2012). Consuming 5–10 mL kg^{-1} of fluid 2–4 hr before training or matches can achieve adequate hydration (Thomas et al., 2016). Following these guidelines becomes more important when players face hot and humid conditions, or when they have had limited time to ingest sufficient fluids (e.g. early morning training sessions).

Fluid intake during training and matches

During exercise, the aim is to prevent significant dehydration. Assessing body mass change during training and matches, using pre- and post-exercise weigh-ins, while accounting for any fluid/food intake, is a simple method for analysing sweat rate, and, in turn, providing individualised fluid-intake recommendations (Armstrong et al., 2007). Compared to training, match play leads to more substantial body mass losses (>0.83%), sweat rates (0.36 L hr^{-1}) and sodium losses in players (Tarnowski et al., 2022). Furthermore, greater body mass losses and sweat rates are observed in hot (25.0°C) versus temperate conditions (14.8°C) (Broad et al., 1996; Tarnowski et al., 2022). Sweat rates vary greatly between women football players and are also largely dependent on exercise intensity and environmental conditions; therefore, a personalised hydration strategy is strongly recommended.

When considering the sweat rate response across the menstrual cycle, a higher core temperature threshold for regional sweat initiation occurs in the luteal phase compared to the follicular phase (Kuwahara et al., 2005); however, whole-body sweat rate does not appear to differ between the phases of the menstrual cycle (Freemas et al., 2023; Giersch et al., 2020). Although evidence is limited, we suggest that hydration strategies do not need to be tailored to menstrual cycle phase. Offering clear guidelines with personalised fluid amounts and timings (e.g. after warm-up, half-time, before extra time) can help players better manage their hydration. In the latter stages of matches (>70 min) or if the match goes into extra time, when dehydration may be present and fuel stores are at their lowest, consuming a 6–8% carbohydrate-electrolyte solution (30–60 g hr^{-1}) before each half can help sustain performance (Kerksick et al., 2018) (see the carbohydrate section).

Fluid intake post-training and matches

Following training and matches, a focus for football players is physical recovery. From a nutritional standpoint, ingestion of carbohydrate (see the carbohydrate section), protein (see the protein section) and fluid is crucial, with players aiming to replace any fluid and electrolyte losses soon after exercise cessation. This fluid deficit can usually be achieved by drinking water alongside a meal or a snack containing sodium. If sufficient time between exercise bouts is available, fluid restoration and electrolyte balance can be achieved through normal drinking/eating habits. However, targeted post-exercise fluid recommendations may be necessary if training/matches are being completed in quick succession (<24 hr) or following a late training session/match. Fluid replacement recommendations should range from 1 to ~1.5 L for each kilogram of body mass lost (Thomas et al., 2016).

Practitioners' perspective

- Implementing an appropriate sports nutrition strategy, alongside a well-balanced diet, can influence performance, recovery, growth, maturation, illness risk and general health in football players. It is important for sports nutritionists to be aware of the secondary symptoms of low energy availability to identify players who may be at risk.
- Daily carbohydrate recommendations should be adjusted day to day and meal to meal depending on daily and upcoming physical activity demands. When high carbohydrate amounts are needed, practitioners should work closely with their players and find practical solutions that ensure recommended amounts are achievable.
- A pre-match nutrition and hydration plan will ensure that players begin well fuelled and hydrated. This plan should begin ~3–4 hr prior to kick-off and include sources of high GI carbohydrates. Hydration recommendations are based on body mass, but players should be encouraged to pay attention to their urine colour and volume.
- The nutritional aims during activity are to prevent significant dehydration and provide fast-absorbing fuel (carbohydrate). When natural stops in match-play occur, practitioners should ensure drinking bottles (containing both water and

sports drinks) are available to players. Sources of carbohydrate (gel, gummies, bananas) and fluid (water and sports drinks containing carbohydrate and electrolytes) should also be provided to players at half time.

- Beverage palatability can significantly impact voluntary fluid ingestion. Fluid that is cool (~15°C) with flavouring, electrolytes and light sweetening is preferred by athletes (Baker & Jeukendrup, 2014).
- Post-training/matches, the role of the practitioner is to ensure that players recover from the exercise and focus on the ingestion of protein for muscle repair, carbohydrate for glycogen replenishment and fluids for rehydration. The recovery period is of particular importance if training/matches are completed in the same day or in <24 hr.
- Sports nutritionists/dieticians working in football should recognise the additional challenges that might arise working in team sports environments and plan accordingly. These challenges include the following:

  - Late kick-off times, reducing the amount of time for players to get nutrients in post-match.
  - Food availability and options in the changing rooms pre-, during and post-matches.
  - Peer influence when selecting foods.
  - Appetite suppression post-match/training.
  - Playing in different environments that is hot/cold or at high altitude.
  - Matches going into extra time require increased exercise duration.
  - Player being sent off requires increased exercise demands from remaining players on the pitch.
  - Travel/different cuisines/accessibility of foods in hotels.
  - Sports nutrition differences for starting players versus substitutes.
  Cultural and religious dietary needs.
  - Food intolerances/allergies/preferences.

Summary

Nutrition plays an important role in the health and performance of football players. Provision of individualised sports nutrition strategies, focusing on carbohydrate intake, protein intake and hydration, could enhance physical performance and help maintain health throughout the season.

References

Abbott, W., Brett, A., Cockburn, E., & Clifford, T. (2019). Pre-sleep casein protein ingestion: Acceleration of functional recovery in professional soccer players. *International Journal of Sports Physiology and Performance*, *14*(3), 385–391. https://doi.org/10.1123/ijspp.2018-0385

Ackerman, K. E., Holtzman, B., Cooper, K. M., Flynn, E. F., Bruinvels, G., Tenforde, A. S., Popp, K. L., Simpkin, A. J., & Parziale, A. L. (2019). Low energy availability surrogates correlate with health and performance consequences of relative energy deficiency in sport. *British Journal of Sports Medicine, 53*(10), 628–633. https://doi.org/10.1136/bjsports-2017-098958

Ali, A., Gardiner, R., Foskett, A., & Gant, N. (2011). Fluid balance, thermoregulation and sprint and passing skill performance in female soccer players. *Scandinavian Journal of Medicine & Science in Sports, 21*(3), 437–445. https://doi.org/10.1111/j.1600-0838.2009.01055.x

Apweiler, E., Wallace, D., Stansfield, S., Allerton, D., Brown, M., Stevenson, E., & Clifford, T. (2018). Pre-bed casein protein supplementation does not enhance acute functional recovery in physically active males and females when exercise is performed in the morning. *Sports, 7*(1), 5. https://doi.org/10.3390/sports7010005

Areta, J. L., Burke, L. M., Ross, M. L., Camera, D. M., West, D. W. D., Broad, E. M., Jeacocke, N. A., Moore, D. R., Stellingwerff, T., Phillips, S. M., Hawley, J. A., & Coffey, V. G. (2013). Timing and distribution of protein ingestion during prolonged recovery from resistance exercise alters myofibrillar protein synthesis. *The Journal of Physiology, 591*(9), 2319–2331. https://doi.org/10.1113/jphysiol.2012.244897

Armstrong, L. E., Casa, D. J., Millard-Stafford, M., Moran, D. S., Pyne, S. W., & Roberts, W. O. (2007). American college of sports medicine position stand: Exertional heat illness during training and competition. *Medicine and Science in Sports and Exercise, 39*(3), 556–572. https://doi.org/10.1249/MSS.0b013e31802fa199

Armstrong, L. E., Ganio, M. S., Klau, J. F., Johnson, E. C., Casa, D. J., & Maresh, C. M. (2014). Novel hydration assessment techniques employing thirst and a water intake challenge in healthy men. *Applied Physiology, Nutrition, and Metabolism, 39*(2), 138–144. https://doi.org/10.1139/apnm-2012-0369

Armstrong, L. E., Herrera Soto, J. A., Hacker, F. T., Casa, D. J., Kavouras, S. A., & Maresh, C. M. (1998). Urinary indices during dehydration, exercise, and rehydration. *International Journal of Sport Nutrition, 8*(4), 345–355. https://doi.org/10.1123/ijsn.8.4.345

Armstrong, L. E., Pumerantz, A. C., Fiala, K. A., Roti, M. W., Kavouras, S. A., Casa, D. J., & Maresh, C. M. (2010). Human hydration indices: Acute and longitudinal reference values. *International Journal of Sport Nutrition and Exercise Metabolism, 20*(2), 145–153. https://doi.org/10.1123/ijsnem.20.2.145

Babault, N., Païzis, C., Deley, G., Guérin-Deremaux, L., Saniez, M.-H., Lefranc-Millot, C., & Allaert, F. A. (2015). Pea proteins oral supplementation promotes muscle thickness gains during resistance training: A double-blind, randomized, placebo-controlled clinical trial vs. whey protein. *Journal of the International Society of Sports Nutrition, 12*(1), 3. https://doi.org/10.1186/s12970-014-0064-5

Baker, L. B., & Jeukendrup, A. E. (2014). Optimal composition of fluid-replacement beverages. In *Comprehensive physiology* (1st ed., pp. 575–620). Wiley. https://doi.org/10.1002/cphy.c130014

Bangsbo, J., Nørregaard, L., & Thorsøe, F. (1992). The effect of carbohydrate diet on intermittent exercise performance. *International Journal of Sports Medicine, 13*(2), 152–157. https://doi.org/10.1055/s-2007-1021247

Broad, E. M., Burke, L. M., Cox, G. R., Heeley, P., & Riley, M. (1996). Body weight changes and voluntary fluid intakes during training and competition sessions in team sports. *International Journal of Sport Nutrition, 6*(3), 307–320. https://doi.org/10.1123/ijsn.6.3.307

Brown, M. A., Stevenson, E. J., & Howatson, G. (2018). Whey protein hydrolysate supplementation accelerates recovery from exercise-induced muscle damage in females. *Applied Physiology, Nutrition, and Metabolism, 43*(4), 324–330. https://doi.org/10.1139/apnm-2017-0412

Burd, N. A., Beals, J. W., Martinez, I. G., Salvador, A. F., & Skinner, S. K. (2019). Food-first approach to enhance the regulation of post-exercise skeletal muscle protein synthesis and remodeling. *Sports Medicine, 49*(1), 59–68. https://doi.org/10.1007/s40279-018-1009-y

Burke, L. M., Loucks, A. B., & Broad, N. (2006). Energy and carbohydrate for training and recovery. *Journal of Sports Sciences*, *24*(7), 675–685. https://doi.org/10.1080/02640410500482602

Campbell, S. E., & Febbraio, M. A. (2001). Effects of ovarian hormones on exercise metabolism: *Current Opinion in Clinical Nutrition and Metabolic Care*, *4*(6), 515–520. https://doi.org/10.1097/00075197-200111000-00009

Chapelle, L., Tassignon, B., Rommers, N., Mertens, E., Mullie, P., & Clarys, P. (2020). Pre-exercise hypohydration prevalence in soccer players: A quantitative systematic review. *European Journal of Sport Science*, *20*(6), 744–755. https://doi.org/10.1080/17461391.2019.1669716

Cheuvront, S. N., Ely, B. R., Kenefick, R. W., & Sawka, M. N. (2010). Biological variation and diagnostic accuracy of dehydration assessment markers. *The American Journal of Clinical Nutrition*, *92*(3), 565–573. https://doi.org/10.3945/ajcn.2010.29490

Collins, J., Maughan, R. J., Gleeson, M., Bilsborough, J., Jeukendrup, A., Morton, J. P., Phillips, S. M., Armstrong, L., Burke, L. M., Close, G. L., Duffield, R., Larson-Meyer, E., Louis, J., Medina, D., Meyer, F., Rollo, I., Sundgot-Borgen, J., Wall, B. T., Boullosa, B., . . . McCall, A. (2021). UEFA expert group statement on nutrition in elite football. Current evidence to inform practical recommendations and guide future research. *British Journal of Sports Medicine*, *55*(8), 416. https://doi.org/10.1136/bjsports-2019-101961

Culvin, A. (2019). *Football as work: The new realities of professional women footballers in England* [PhD thesis, University of Central Lancashire].

de Sousa, M. V., Lundsgaard, A.-M., Christensen, P. M., Christensen, L., Randers, M. B., Mohr, M., Nybo, L., Kiens, B., & Fritzen, A. M. (2022). Nutritional optimization for female elite football players-topical review. *Scandinavian Journal of Medicine & Science in Sports*, *32*(Suppl 1), 81–104. https://doi.org/10.1111/sms.14102

Dunlop, M. V., Kilroe, S. P., Bowtell, J. L., Finnigan, T. J. A., Salmon, D. L., & Wall, B. T. (2017). Mycoprotein represents a bioavailable and insulinotropic non-animal-derived dietary protein source: A dose-response study. *British Journal of Nutrition*, *118*(9), 673–685. https://doi.org/10.1017/S0007114517002409

Eddens, L., Browne, S., Stevenson, E. J., Sanderson, B., Van Someren, K., & Howatson, G. (2017). The efficacy of protein supplementation during recovery from muscle-damaging concurrent exercise. *Applied Physiology, Nutrition, and Metabolism*, *42*(7), 716–724. https://doi.org/10.1139/apnm-2016-0626

Field, A., Harper, L. D., Chrismas, B. C. R., Fowler, P. M., McCall, A., Paul, D. J., Chamari, K., & Taylor, L. (2021). The use of recovery strategies in professional soccer: A worldwide survey. *International Journal of Sports Physiology and Performance*, *16*(12), 1804–1815. https://doi.org/10.1123/ijspp.2020-0799

Freemas, J. A., Goss, C. S., Ables, R., Baker, T. B., Bruinvels, G., Mündel, T., Martin, B. J., Carter, S. J., Chapman, R. F., & Schlader, Z. J. (2023). Fluid balance during physical work in the heat is not modified by the menstrual cycle when fluids are freely available. *Journal of Applied Physiology*, *134*(6), 1376–1389. https://doi.org/10.1152/japplphysiol.00580.2022

Giersch, G. E. W., Morrissey, M. C., Katch, R. K., Colburn, A. T., Sims, S. T., Stachenfeld, N. S., & Casa, D. J. (2020). Menstrual cycle and thermoregulation during exercise in the heat: A systematic review and meta-analysis. *Journal of Science and Medicine in Sport*, *23*(12), 1134–1140. https://doi.org/10.1016/j.jsams.2020.05.014

Gorissen, S. H., Horstman, A. M., Franssen, R., Crombag, J. J., Langer, H., Bierau, J., Respondek, F., & van Loon, L. J. (2016). Ingestion of wheat protein increases in vivo muscle protein synthesis rates in healthy older men in a randomized trial. *The Journal of Nutrition*, *146*(9), 1651–1659. https://doi.org/10.3945/jn.116.231340

Goulart, K. N. O., Coimbra, C. C., Campos, H. O., Drummond, L. R., Ogando, P. H. M., Brown, G., Couto, B. P., Duffield, R., & Wanner, S. P. (2022). Fatigue and recovery time course after female soccer matches: A systematic review and meta-analysis. *Sports Medicine—Open*, *8*(1), 72. https://doi.org/10.1186/s40798-022-00466-3

Hackney, A. (1990). Effects of the menstrual cycle on resting muscle glycogen content. *Hormone and Metabolic Research*, *22*(12), 647. https://doi.org/10.1055/s-2007-1004994

Haizlip, K. M., Harrison, B. C., & Leinwand, L. A. (2015). Sex-based differences in skeletal muscle kinetics and fiber-type composition. *Physiology*, *30*(1), 30–39. https://doi.org/10.1152/physiol.00024.2014

Hermans, W. J. H., Fuchs, C. J., Hendriks, F. K., Houben, L. H. P., Senden, J. M., Verdijk, L. B., & van Loon, L. J. C. (2022). Cheese ingestion increases muscle protein synthesis rates both at rest and during recovery from exercise in healthy, young males: A randomized parallel-group trial. *The Journal of Nutrition*, *152*(4), 1022–1030. https://doi.org/10.1093/jn/nxac007

Hermans, W. J. H., Fuchs, C. J., Nyakayiru, J., Hendriks, F. K., Houben, L. H. P., Senden, J. M., Van Loon, L. J. C., & Verdijk, L. B. (2023). Acute quark ingestion increases muscle protein synthesis rates at rest with a further increase after exercise in young and older adult males in a parallel group intervention trial. *The Journal of Nutrition*, *153*(1), 66–75. https://doi.org/10.1016/j.tjnut.2022.10.003

Julian, R., Page, R. M., & Harper, L. D. (2021). The effect of fixture congestion on performance during professional male soccer match-play: A systematic critical review with meta-analysis. *Sports Medicine*, *51*(2), 255–273. https://doi.org/10.1007/s40279-020-01359-9

Kenefick, R. W., & Cheuvront, S. N. (2012). Hydration for recreational sport and physical activity. *Nutrition Reviews*, *70*, S137–S142. https://doi.org/10.1111/j.1753-4887.2012.00523.x

Kerksick, C. M., Wilborn, C. D., Roberts, M. D., Smith-Ryan, A., Kleiner, S. M., Jäger, R., Collins, R., Cooke, M., Davis, J. N., Galvan, E., Greenwood, M., Lowery, L. M., Wildman, R., Antonio, J., & Kreider, R. B. (2018). ISSN exercise & sports nutrition review update: Research & recommendations. *Journal of the International Society of Sports Nutrition*, *15*(1), 38. https://doi.org/10.1186/s12970-018-0242-y

Kilding, A., Tunstall, H., Wraith, E., Good, M., Gammon, C., & Smith, C. (2009). Sweat rate and sweat electrolyte composition in international female soccer players during game specific training. *International Journal of Sports Medicine*, *30*(6), 443–447. https://doi.org/10.1055/s-0028-1105945

Krustrup, P., Mohr, M., Nybo, L., Draganidis, D., Randers, M. B., Ermidis, G., Ørntoft, C., Røddik, L., Batsilas, D., Poulios, A., Ørtenblad, N., Loules, G., Deli, C. K., Batrakoulis, A., Nielsen, J. L., Jamurtas, A. Z., & Fatouros, I. G. (2022). Muscle metabolism and impaired sprint performance in an elite women's football game. *Scandinavian Journal of Medicine & Science in Sports*, *32*(S1), 27–38. https://doi.org/10.1111/sms.13970

Kuwahara, T., Inoue, Y., Abe, M., Sato, Y., & Kondo, N. (2005). Effects of menstrual cycle and physical training on heat loss responses during dynamic exercise at moderate intensity in a temperate environment. *American Journal of Physiology. Regulatory, Integrative and Comparative Physiology*, *288*(5), R1347–R1353. https://doi.org/10.1152/ajpregu.00547.2004

Lollo, P. C. B., Amaya-Farfan, J., Faria, I. C., Salgado, J. V. V., Chacon-Mikahil, M. P. T., Cruz, A. G., Oliveira, C. A. F., Montagner, P. C., & Arruda, M. (2014). Hydrolysed whey protein reduces muscle damage markers in Brazilian elite soccer players compared with whey protein and maltodextrin: A twelve-week in-championship intervention. *International Dairy Journal*, *34*(1), 19–24. https://doi.org/10.1016/j.idairyj.2013.07.001

Mamerow, M. M., Mettler, J. A., English, K. L., Casperson, S. L., Arentson-Lantz, E., Sheffield-Moore, M., Layman, D. K., & Paddon-Jones, D. (2014). Dietary protein distribution positively influences 24-h muscle protein synthesis in healthy adults. *The Journal of Nutrition*, *144*(6), 876–880. https://doi.org/10.3945/jn.113.185280

McHaffie, S. J., Langan-Evans, C., Morehen, J. C., Strauss, J. A., Areta, J. L., Rosimus, C., Evans, M., Elliott-Sale, K. J., Cronin, C. J., & Morton, J. P. (2022). Carbohydrate fear, skinfold targets and body image issues: A qualitative analysis of player and stakeholder perceptions of the nutrition culture within elite female soccer. *Science & Medicine in Football, 6*(5), 675–685. https://doi.org/10.1080/24733938.2022.2101143

McLay, R. T., Thomson, C. D., Williams, S. M., & Rehrer, N. J. (2007). Carbohydrate loading and female endurance athletes: Effect of menstrual-cycle phase. *International Journal of Sport Nutrition and Exercise Metabolism, 17*(2), 189–205. https://doi.org/10.1123/ijsnem.17.2.189

Mohr, M., Krustrup, P., Andersson, H., Kirkendal, D., & Bangsbo, J. (2008). Match activities of elite women soccer players at different performance levels. *Journal of Strength and Conditioning Research, 22*(2), 341–349. https://doi.org/10.1519/JSC.0b013e318165fef6

Moore, D. R., Camera, D. M., Areta, J. L., & Hawley, J. A. (2014). Beyond muscle hypertrophy: Why dietary protein is important for endurance athletes. *Applied Physiology, Nutrition, and Metabolism, 39*(9), 987–997. https://doi.org/10.1139/apnm-2013-0591

Moore, D. R., Sygo, J., & Morton, J. P. (2022). Fuelling the female athlete: Carbohydrate and protein recommendations. *European Journal of Sport Science, 22*(5), 684–696. https://doi.org/10.1080/17461391.2021.1922508

Morehen, J. C., Rosimus, C., Cavanagh, B. P., Hambly, C., Speakman, J. R., Elliott-Sale, K. J., Hannon, M. P., & Morton, J. P. (2022). Energy expenditure of female international standard soccer players: A doubly labeled water investigation. *Medicine & Science in Sports & Exercise, 54*(5), 769–779. https://doi.org/10.1249/MSS.0000000000002850

Morgan, P. T., Harris, D. O., Marshall, R. N., Quinlan, J. I., Edwards, S. J., Allen, S. L., & Breen, L. (2021). Protein source and quality for skeletal muscle anabolism in young and older adults: A systematic review and meta-analysis. *The Journal of Nutrition, 151*(7), 1901–1920. https://doi.org/10.1093/jn/nxab055

Morton, R. W., Murphy, K. T., McKellar, S. R., Schoenfeld, B. J., Henselmans, M., Helms, E., Aragon, A. A., Devries, M. C., Banfield, L., Krieger, J. W., & Phillips, S. M. (2018). A systematic review, meta-analysis and meta-regression of the effect of protein supplementation on resistance training-induced gains in muscle mass and strength in healthy adults. *British Journal of Sports Medicine, 52*(6), 376–384. https://doi.org/10.1136/bjsports-2017-097608

Moss, S. L., & Randell, R. K. (2022, July). *Sports nutrition recommendations for elite female soccer players*. Sports Science Exchange #227. https://www.ssiweb.org/sports-science-exchange/article/sports-nutrition-recommendations-for-elite-female-soccer-players

Moss, S. L., Randell, R. K., Burgess, D., Ridley, S., ÓCaireallláin, C., Allison, R., & Rollo, I. (2021). Assessment of energy availability and associated risk factors in professional female soccer players. *European Journal of Sport Science, 21*(6), 861–870. https://doi.org/10.1080/17461391.2020.1788647

Nassis, G. P., Massey, A., Jacobsen, P., Brito, J., Randers, M. B., Castagna, C., Mohr, M., & Krustrup, P. (2020). Elite football of 2030 will not be the same as that of 2020: Preparing players, coaches, and support staff for the evolution. *Scandinavian Journal of Medicine & Science in Sports, 30*(6), 962–964. https://doi.org/10.1111/sms.13681

Nuccio, R. P., Barnes, K. A., Carter, J. M., & Baker, L. B. (2017). Fluid balance in team sport athletes and the effect of hypohydration on cognitive, technical, and physical performance. *Sports Medicine, 47*(10), 1951–1982. https://doi.org/10.1007/s40279-017-0738-7

Poulios, A., Fatouros, I. G., Mohr, M., Draganidis, D. K., Deli, C., Papanikolaou, K., Sovatzidis, A., Nakopoulou, T., Ermidis, G., Tzatzakis, T., Laschou, V. C., Georgakouli, K., Koulouris, A., Tsimeas, P., Chatzinikolaou, A., Karagounis, L. G., Batsilas, D., Krustrup, P., & Jamurtas, A. Z. (2018). Post-game high protein intake may improve recovery of football-specific performance during a congested game fixture: Results from the PRO-FOOTBALL study. *Nutrients, 10*(4), 494. https://doi.org/10.3390/nu10040494

Ranchordas, M. K., Dawson, J. T., & Russell, M. (2017). Practical nutritional recovery strategies for elite soccer players when limited time separates repeated matches. *Journal of the International Society of Sports Nutrition, 14*(1), 35. https://doi.org/10.1186/s12970-017-0193-8

Randell, R. K., Clifford, T., Drust, B., Moss, S. L., Unnithan, V. B., De Ste Croix, M. B. A., Datson, N., Martin, D., Mayho, H., Carter, J. M., & Rollo, I. (2021). Physiological characteristics of female soccer players and health and performance considerations: A narrative review. *Sports Medicine (Auckland, N.Z.)*, *51*(7), 1377–1399. https://doi.org/10.1007/s40279-021-01458-1

Rankin, P., Callanan, D., O'Brien, K., Davison, G., Stevenson, E. J., & Cockburn, E. (2019). Can milk affect recovery from simulated team-sport match play? *Nutrients*, *12*(1), 112. https://doi.org/10.3390/nu12010112

Rodriguez-Giustiniani, P., Rollo, I., Witard, O. C., & Galloway, S. D. R. (2019). Ingesting a 12% carbohydrate-electrolyte beverage before each half of a soccer match simulation facilitates retention of passing performance and improves high-intensity running capacity in academy players. *International Journal of Sport Nutrition and Exercise Metabolism*, *29*(4), 397–405. https://doi.org/10.1123/ijsnem.2018-0214

Rothman, D. L., Magnusson, I., Katz, L. D., Shulman, R. G., & Shulman, G. I. (1991). Quantitation of hepatic glycogenolysis and gluconeogenesis in fasting humans with 13C NMR. *Science*, *254*(5031), 573–576. https://doi.org/10.1126/science.1948033

Sawka, M. N., Burke, L. M., Eichner, E. R., Maughan, R. J., Montain, S. J., & Stachenfeld, N. S. (2007). American college of sports medicine position stand: Exercise and fluid replacement. *Medicine and Science in Sports and Exercise*, *39*(2), 377–390. https://doi.org/10.1249/mss.0b013e31802ca597

Tang, J. E., Moore, D. R., Kujbida, G. W., Tarnopolsky, M. A., & Phillips, S. M. (2009). Ingestion of whey hydrolysate, casein, or soy protein isolate: Effects on mixed muscle protein synthesis at rest and following resistance exercise in young men. *Journal of Applied Physiology*, *107*(3), 987–992. https://doi.org/10.1152/japplphysiol.00076.2009

Tarnopolsky, M. A., Zawada, C., Richmond, L. B., Carter, S., Shearer, J., Graham, T., & Phillips, S. M. (2001). Gender differences in carbohydrate loading are related to energy intake. *Journal of Applied Physiology*, *91*(1), 225–230. https://doi.org/10.1152/jappl.2001.91.1.225

Tarnowski, C. A., Rollo, I., Carter, J. M., Lizarraga-Dallo, M. A., Oliva, M. P., Clifford, T., James, L. J., & Randell, R. K. (2022). Fluid balance and carbohydrate intake of elite female soccer players during training and competition. *Nutrients*, *14*(15), 3188. https://doi.org/10.3390/nu14153188

Thomas, D. T., Erdman, K. A., & Burke, L. M. (2016). Position of the academy of nutrition and dietetics, dietitians of Canada, and the American college of sports medicine: Nutrition and athletic performance. *Journal of the Academy of Nutrition and Dietetics*, *116*(3), 501–528. https://doi.org/10.1016/j.jand.2015.12.006

Trommelen, J., Van Lieshout, G. A. A., Pabla, P., Nyakayiru, J., Hendriks, F. K., Senden, J. M., Goessens, J. P. B., Van Kranenburg, J. M. X., Gijsen, A. P., Verdijk, L. B., De Groot, L. C. P. G. M., & Van Loon, L. J. C. (2023). Pre-sleep protein ingestion increases mitochondrial protein synthesis rates during overnight recovery from endurance exercise: A randomized controlled trial. *Sports Medicine*, *53*(7), 1445–1455. https://doi.org/10.1007/s40279-023-01822-3

Williams, C., & Rollo, I. (2015). Carbohydrate nutrition and team sport performance. *Sports Medicine*, *45*(S1), 13–22. https://doi.org/10.1007/s40279-015-0399-3

Witard, O. C., Turner, J. E., Jackman, S. R., Kies, A. K., Jeukendrup, A. E., Bosch, J. A., & Tipton, K. D. (2014). High dietary protein restores overreaching induced impairments in leukocyte trafficking and reduces the incidence of upper respiratory tract infection in elite cyclists. *Brain, Behavior, and Immunity*, *39*, 211–219. https://doi.org/10.1016/j.bbi.2013.10.002

Wooding, D. J., Packer, J. E., Kato, H., West, D. W. D., Courtney-Martin, G., Pencharz, P. B., & Moore, D. R. (2017). Increased protein requirements in female athletes after variable-intensity exercise. *Medicine & Science in Sports & Exercise*, *49*(11), 2297. https://doi.org/10.1249/MSS.0000000000001366

9

EATING DISORDERS AND ELITE WOMEN'S FOOTBALL

Carly Perry, Maria Luisa Fernanda Pereira Vargas, Alex Culvin and Ali Bowes

Introduction

Eating disorders (EDs), such as anorexia nervosa, bulimia nervosa and binge eating, are clinical mental illnesses characterised by severe and persistent disturbances in eating behaviours and associated distressing thoughts and emotions (American Psychiatric Association, 2016). In the general population, prevalence rates range from 0.1% to 2.3% depending on country, gender, age and the type of eating disorder (Qian et al., 2021). Amongst women athletes, rates are higher, with 6% to 45% of this population believed to experience an eating disorder in their lifetime (Bratland-Sanda & Sundgot-Borgen, 2013). However, prevalence rates are difficult to determine due to definition issues, a lack of awareness and inconsistent measures. Amongst athletes, prevalence rates are especially difficult to establish due to increased stigma and a lack of recognition due to the normalisation of certain food and weight behaviours in the sporting environment (Lichtenstein et al., 2022).

Given the difficulty in establishing eating-disorder diagnoses for athletes, researchers and practitioners often utilise the term *disordered eating* (DE) to account for and provide a perspective for non-clinical populations (Currie, 2010). Compared to EDs, DE does not have an official definition; however, it is most often understood as subclinical issues related to eating psychopathology (Howard et al., 2020). Disordered eating can include a spectrum of maladaptive thoughts, attitudes and behaviours related to food (Wells et al., 2020). This spectrum can range from major disturbances surrounding eating and the body (such as starvation, purging and bingeing) that meet the clinical diagnosis of anorexia nervosa, bulimia nervosa or binge eating, to more mild patterns of atypical eating and body attitudes (such as calorie restriction, body checking and excessive energy expenditure)

DOI: 10.4324/9781003381914-9

(Wells et al., 2020). Throughout this chapter both EDs and DE are used. We use *EDs* when discussing research and/or media reports whereby clinical diagnosis was sought or explored using validated eating-disorder questionnaires and *DE* to describe non-clinical reports, findings and experiences. We most readily use the terms together, which allows for the population who have received a clinical diagnosis as well as those who may not have received a clinical diagnosis to be included in this discussion.

To date, researchers who have investigated EDs and DE amongst women athletes have primarily focused on gathering prevalence rates for eating-disorder symptoms and on exploring associated risk factors, such as personality traits (such as perfectionism), transitions (such as selection/de-selection and retirement), competitive stressors (such as injury and team culture) and sports type (lean vs. contact sport) (Perry et al., 2021). In the majority of research, the focus has been on women athletes who compete in "appearance-based" or "lean-physique" sports, where a certain physique and/or particular weight is needed for success (such as gymnastics and running). Such women are considered to be at an increased risk for EDs or DE, compared to women in team and/or contact sports (such as football and rugby), where more muscular bodies are needed for sport performance (Mancine et al., 2020; Perry et al., 2021).

To obtain a deeper insight into the cultural norms embedded within sport that can contribute to DE, sport scholars have drawn heavily on sociological literature such as Hughes and Coakley's (1991) work on *sport ethic*. In their work, the authors highlight how an athlete's adherence to socially constructed value systems in sporting subcultures are central to being identified as a "real athlete" and how this can then perpetuate eating disorder and DE attitudes and behaviours in sport. Building on Hughes and Coakley's theoretical ideas, Williams (2012) argues for a "discourse of excellence" that informs athletic identity and is influential in the construction of supranormal sporting nutritional habits, concluding that this discourse can impact (sub-elite/elite) athletes' eating decisions and cause them to eat for excellence. To date, however, the focus of this research has rarely been on women competing in contact and team sports, which limits our understanding.

There has been rapid acceleration of professionalisation in women's football across some countries across the world (Culvin & Bowes, 2023). This professionalisation means that in some areas of the world, women are now able to earn a full-time living from playing football. A career as a professional footballer is one imbued with specific pressures and increased expectations; thus, in this chapter, we will focus specifically on professional (i.e. elite) women's football.

Given the obvious workplace pressures on semi-professional and professional women footballers (Culvin, 2021), it becomes critical to better understand how EDs and DE can occur and present, so that this population can be better supported. This understanding is important as the development of EDs and DE can pose harmful short- and long-term effects, not only for sports performance but also for long-term health. For example EDs and DE can pose a risk for injury and other psychopathology such as depression and anxiety, as well as a risk of relative energy deficiency in sport (discussed in Chapter 10) (Mancine et al., 2020; Walter et al., 2022). The presence of daily performance pressures that accompany being an elite footballer (such as injury, transitions and body-related pressures) are well-known risk factors for eating disorder and DE onset and maintenance (Wells et al., 2020). As such, it is important that practitioners understand EDs/DE and how EDs may occur and present within this population, as well as understanding specific subcultures that may exacerbate EDs and DE.

The aims of this chapter are as follows:

1 To provide a critical evaluation of the evidence on EDs and DE within elite women's football.
2 To consider the unique risk factors for EDs and DE in elite women's footballers.
3 To propose practical applications and offer suggestions for policy change.

Accordingly, our aim is to encourage meaningful conversations amongst practitioners, academics and others wishing to support this population.

Disordered eating and elite women's football

During the aforementioned period of increasing professionalisation, professional women footballers, such as Chelsea Blissett (Australia) (Lewis, 2023), Molly Bartrip (England) (Bartrip, 2022) and Clare Rafferty (England) (Heath, 2022), have discussed struggles with body image, EDs and DE in the mainstream media. Relatedly, prominent players, such as Fara Williams (England) (Thomas, 2022), Lindsey Horan and Megan Rapinoe (both the United States) (Coleman, 2022), have shared their concerns regarding the occurrence of body shaming and unhealthy body-management practices (e.g. fat testing and "fat-club"), which they have experienced in professional women's football environments. Such concerns warrant further discussion, as body-management practices have been shown to negatively impact athletes' relationship with food, weight and body image and have potential to lead to the onset of EDs (McGannon & McMahon, 2019).

There are four studies in which EDs and DE have been explored among elite footballers. These studies involved professional footballers in the United States (Prather et al., 2016), semi-professional and professional footballers in the UK (Abbott et al., 2021, Perry et al., 2022) and professional footballers in Australia (Kilic et al., 2021). Across these studies, prevalence rates for clinical eating-disorder symptoms ranged from 0% to 43%. The large disparity in prevalence estimation is likely due to the different cut-off scores and questionnaires used. In the four studies, the relationship between eating disorder scores and risk factors (such as perfectionism, injury status and menstrual dysfunction) was explored. Perfectionism scores on the 12-item Clinical Perfectionism Questionnaire (Fairburn et al., 2003) was a significant predictor of eating disorder risk in all footballers (regardless of sex) and in the general population (Abbott et al., 2021), and severe injury in the previous six months was associated with higher eating disorder scores (Kilic et al., 2021). Perry et al. (2022) found that 35% of elite women footballers in England indicated they were currently trying to lose weight, and that 45% reported that they had attempted to lose weight in the previous four weeks. This latter finding requires further attention, given that these data were collected in-season, which may be explained by pressures around fitness and performance brought about by professionalisation.

Perry et al. (2022) suggested that higher DE scores were not associated with currently needing psychological support, yet higher depression and anxiety scores were associated with players currently wanting and/or needing psychological support. This finding could indicate that DE symptoms are not self-recognised and/or that DE behaviours are normalised in the footballers' sporting environment (Perry et al., 2022). While these current findings offer insight into an understudied population and topic, far more research is needed to better understand footballers' lived experiences with DE and EDs.

A unique population with unique needs: implications for practitioners

Drawing on the sport psychology and sociology literature, we will now discuss the stressors that elite women footballers can encounter that can influence EDs and DE. We will focus on the following three factors as they are the most relevant for specifically understanding how EDs/DE may develop and persist within this population: (1) the professionalisation of women's football, (2) conflicting body-image ideals and (3) severe injury.

Professionalisation of women's football

Women's football has been professionalised or semi-professionalised in many countries across the world, albeit in a fragmented way (Culvin & Bowes, 2023). Ambiguity exists, however, between the growing professionalisation of women's football and the precarious work conditions in which players operate (Culvin, 2021). The rapid professionalisation has, for instance, resulted in players experiencing inconsistent workplace environments, with short contracts, financial instability, a lack of support, inadequate working conditions and limited post-career options, which players expressed as negatively impacting their wellbeing (Culvin, 2019, 2021). One specific area of concern is body-image issues and DE behaviours.

In congruence with the changes to the game are increased performance pressures as well as media attention and visibility. Resultantly, professional women footballers in England have reported feeling that their bodies were under constant scrutiny and surveillance by both those within their club (from teammates and coaches) and those outside of their club (such as fans, sponsors and social media) (Culvin, 2019). For example footballers were found to feel constantly tasked with promoting/conforming to a brand image that emphasised femininity, which they reported to negatively impact their body image and eating behaviours (Culvin, 2019). Given that such performance and aesthetic pressures are not abating, it is critical that players are offered support in managing body image and eating concerns. Support should be offered to players through their club, federation and player union (or a variation of these) and could involve workshops with experts that cover different apparent "threats" to EDs/DE (such as social media, navigating sponsorship and club expectations). Additionally, it is critical that players are offered psychological support and are supported by technical staff who are proficient in nutrition and who are qualified (McHaffie et al., 2022).

Conflicting body-image ideals

Football is a sport which is not traditionally understood as being at risk for EDs (Sundgot-Borgen & Torstveit, 2007). Athletes who participate in sports in which lean and aesthetic bodies are required and evaluated by judges as part of performance success (such as figure skating and gymnastics) are said to have poor body image and engage in more maladaptive eating and body practices, and thus are considered more at risk for DE (Kong & Harris, 2015). However, women athletes competing in contact-based sports, such as football, also encounter objectification, social pressures and peer influence surrounding their bodies and food, which are not any less impacted by athletic and societal body ideals (Perry et al., 2021).

Body image is a social construct that assumes differences in a person's perception of their body in relation to their social context (Tiggemann & Lynch, 2001). As such, regardless of sport type, athletes possess both a social and an athletic body image. Whilst the former includes an evaluation of a female body in comparison to socially constructed definitions of a feminine body in line with neo-capitalistic culture that typically emphasises thinness (Choi, 2003), the latter includes an evaluation of a body in relation to its capacity to achieve athletic performance. For example women's football is a contact sport that can demand a physique that conflicts with an athlete's desired social self-presentation (George, 2005). Krane et al. (2004) coined the term *female athlete paradox* to describe the paradox whereby athletes attempt to meet both social and athletic ideals. Pereira Vargas et al. (2021) explored the paradox within a competitive powerlifting sample of women, finding that athletes grappled with meeting both body ideals required for optimal powerlifting performance (strength gain aided by gaining weight) versus what is typically required within a Western society (a lean physique). Ultimately, these athletes held onto the ideal of gaining muscle tone with minimal fat gain, which led to those with DE behaviours staying within lighter weight classes.

In the context of elite women's football, George (2005) highlighted how footballers viewed their physiques in conflicting ways. Whilst the players understood that muscle gain was a requirement to be successful at an elite level, they faced societal expectations regarding sexualisation and notions of femininity, which clashed with the increase in muscle mass. Footballers' bodies were consistently scrutinised by their coaches and fellow athletes in line with the standards required by the sport as well as those of society. In turn, many footballers felt dissatisfied with their bodies, which resulted in an enhanced preoccupation with body fat and muscularity. This extreme preoccupation led some athletes to experience EDs. There is still limited insight behind how elite women footballers negotiate their athletic and social body ideals, which requires further exploration so that more about EDs within specific subcultures can be understood and supported.

Severe injury

Elite women footballers encounter high rates of severe injury when compared to women competing in other sports and when compared to elite men footballers (Crossley et al., 2020). These elite footballers are specifically at risk for lower-limb injuries (Horan et al., 2023), such as anterior-cruciate ligament (ACL) rupture (Volpi et al., 2016). Lower-limb injuries result in significant time loss for individuals and are currently a significant area of concern amongst elite women's football clubs globally (Horan et al., 2023). Given the current concerns and severe injury rates, practitioners must be educated on the psychological consequences of injury (such as sadness, depression, feelings of isolation, fear of re-injury, lack of motivation, frustration, anger, alterations in appetite, sleep disturbance and feeling disengaged) as well as the physical consequences, so that footballers can be best supported (Putukian, 2016).

A potential psychological consequence of athletic injury may be the onset of DE attitudes and behaviours. Kilic et al. (2021) found that severe injury in the previous six months was associated with higher DE rates in professional men and women footballers. Using qualitative methods, similar conclusions have been drawn. Reel et al. (2018), for instance, found that many dancers engaged in DE behaviours during injury. The dancers reported restricting calories, emotional eating and finding new ways to exercise non-injured parts of their body in order to maintain their athletic identity, lean physique and self-presentation (Reel et al., 2018). Despite the limited research, education and intervention in this area are warranted, due to the potential short- and long-term consequences of an athlete experiencing EDs or DE during injury, such as delayed return to sport, inability to gain appropriate strength back and potential re-injury. We recommend that a proactive approach be taken, where possible. For example when a player encounters a severe injury (such as an ACL rupture), a nutritionist and psychologist should be involved as part of the player's recovery. In practice, an increased awareness of eating-disorder symptom presentation in this specific sample and its impact is needed, as well as a better understanding of how and where to signpost the footballer. We encourage organisations and clubs to integrate and mandate topics of eating-disorder awareness into coach education programmes and training conducted by appropriate medical professionals to help better support the players.

Practitioners' perspective

From a practitioner's perspective, several recommendations can be given, based on what works in practice, to help guide practitioners, organisations, researchers and athletes in how to work with and support elite women footballers. It is our hope that these holistic recommendations offer insight into DE prevalence and provide tools to challenge DE within the sport.

Empower players and staff through education

Players and staff should be made better aware of ED symptomology, problematic language and pathways for support and should be provided with tailored and specific nutritional needs. McHaffie et al. (2022) identified that footballers under-fuelled and restricted carbohydrates due to misunderstandings about the impact of carbohydrate intake on body composition, and also feared weight gain and the associated impacts on body image. Such understandings are not only detrimental to performance, but, based on research, women athletes who adhere to strict diets or restrict certain food groups are at a higher risk for an eating-disorder diagnosis (de Borja et al., 2021). Frequent individual and team educational sessions on nutrition should, therefore, be provided for players.

Staff, specifically coaches and the multidisciplinary team that support players, must be educated on the impact that language and body measurement practices can have on players' relationships with food, weight and body image. Footballers' body image issues and eating-disorder symptoms are influenced by key stakeholders such as coaches, as well as the skinfold culture surrounding measurement of body composition (McHaffie et al., 2022). Such issues are amplified by the lack of full-time, professionally accredited nutritionists overseeing the provision of nutrition support, which should be considered alongside increasing education.

Move away from "old-school" performance measures

Quantifiable performance measures, such as daily player weighing and skinfold analysis, are routine for footballers, yet it becomes pertinent for those involved in implementing such testing to consider at what point performance-orientated goals outweigh the cost of mental health concerns (McHaffie et al., 2022; Roderick et al., 2017). Often, to be considered a genuine professional footballer, players accept an intense approach to accountability, surveillance, measurement and quantification (Roderick et al., 2017). The drive for perfection in women's football appears to be a very real pressure faced by players, as they fear the reality of losing their professional status; consequently, players appear vulnerable and accept control from their coaches (Culvin, 2019). Increased exposure via social media and the growth of commercialisation in women's football have led to increased surveillance and the critique of athletic bodies, as well as the meanings players ascribe to their bodies (Kohe & Purdy, 2016). Relatedly, Culvin (2019) suggests that professional footballers in England value both physical capital and "looking athletic", and both were high on the agenda of players, which had implications on the physical as well as mental health of the players.

Constructive, collaborative solutions between players, stakeholders and researchers are needed to dispel the commonly held myth that "lean and light" equates to successful football performance. Indeed, through collaborative approaches, stakeholders should be encouraged to adapt policies and practices to challenge perceptions and identify high-performance approaches that move away from an out-dated "thin-to-win" ideology. Further, there is a need for enhanced nutritional and body composition literacy amongst players, coaches, technical staff and practitioners, which specifically promotes the inclusion of different body types as being capable of football performance success. Surveillance practices such as player weighing and body fat testing should be urgently reviewed to limit the impact on DE.

Provide clear pathways for help-seeking and disclosure

It is common for footballers to be exposed to and experience unsafe workplaces due to the inadequate working conditions and lack of strategic long-term objectives for clubs and players (Culvin, 2019). Players who describe surveillance, both inside and outside of work, are not cognisant that these conditions are unacceptable and should not be normalised. The development of educational practices on what constitutes a healthy working environment is needed to enable players to mitigate inadequate and unsafe work environments and to establish healthy high-performance cultures (Fédération Internationale des Associations de Footballeurs Professionnels [FIFPro, 2020]). However, educational tools are not a "silver-bullet"; policy that is developed and enforced should be prioritised by stakeholders and practitioners alike. Another essential component of a healthy environment at work, which allows players to perform at their peak, is one with a safe reporting mechanism in place. A safe reporting mechanism can take on various formats, such as anonymous hotlines to surveys and access to a person of trust. These mechanisms can be facilitated through a player union or association, football federations and external partners.

Policy is one way to establish a safe reporting mechanism at work (Culvin, 2019). Indeed, policy and regulation can protect the player, and importantly, their career. Protection of the health and integrity of the footballers should be prioritised when we consider EDs and the sensitivities that emerge alongside the disorder. Sensitivities are understood here as team selection, protected dialogue and fear of retaliation. As such, we recommend that when developing future policies to protect players, safe reporting and disclosure are considered at both the domestic and international levels. If players are in an environment that is safe and free from harmful practices or substandard conditions, they are more likely to feel safer disclosing. Team staff should also consider the value of respecting player autonomy by allowing players to see their own doctors in seeking help and treatment outside of football for an eating disorder. Considering the burden of forced disclosure within sport and its potential consequences such as lack of support, ridicule and stigma (Crawford et al., 2023; Wood et al., 2017), it is understandable why players may wish to receive support outside of the game and keep mental health separated from the gaze of football. Allowing players to seek guidance and help from their own trusted doctors outside of sport is already part of maternity and parental policy in football (FIFPro, 2021). A specific policy and guidance on athletes seeking help for EDs should be considered. At the same time, such policy must consider that player welfare and health are at the forefront. For example an under-fuelled player on the pitch is dangerous and important for club doctors to be aware of, which means that it might not always be possible to respect player autonomy in help-seeking.

Player voice should be central to policy development

Players are the central and most important component of professional football; without the players, football, in any sense, ceases to exist. Yet dominant narratives in public discourse, perpetuated by the media, centre on how players should just "shut up and play", which means that player-centric approaches are rare (Culvin, 2019). This rhetoric fails to adequately recognise professional footballers as human beings and, therefore, their welfare is often not considered as a priority.

Professional players make football the most impactful and popular sport across the world. Moreover, they have a distinct insight on the most important questions affecting national and international football, as well as their working environment. The development and implementation of policies that shape the conditions that players experience at work should be developed with the unique understanding and insight of professional footballers. To ensure a sustainable game that prioritises the health and safety of professional footballers, it is essential that players are provided with a role in the development, governance and growth of their game.

Summary

Despite what was thought about the types of sports that put athletes at risk of EDs and DE, women footballers can and do experience EDs. There is a need to further understand this population's experiences of EDs and DE, and a need for policy and guidance on how to support these athletes. In this chapter, we have highlighted the unique subculture of professional women's football that can perpetuate and legitimise unhealthy eating behaviours due to engrained beliefs of what type of body is needed for successful performance. Further, we have highlighted how conflicting body-image ideals between the physique required for football versus societal norms can pose a risk for eating disorder and DE development. From a practitioner's perspective, further guidance and policy are required that place a footballer's health at the forefront through the following: (1) education, (2) regulation or erasure of harmful surveillance practices, or, if these practices are deemed necessary (such as skinfold tests), information to players regarding the exact purpose of such testing and how those data are to be used (i.e. not for deselection purposes), (3) the creation of strategies for safe reporting and (4) centralising player voice and involving them in decision-making processes.

References

Abbott, W., Brett, A., Brownlee, T. E., Hammond, K. M., Harper, L. D., Naughton, R. J., Anderson, L., Munson, E. H., Sharkey, J. V., Randell, R. K., & Clifford, T. (2021). The prevalence of disordered eating in elite male and female soccer players. *Eating and Weight Disorders*, *26*(2), 491–498. https://doi.org/10.1007/s40519-020-00872-0

American Psychiatric Association. (2016). *Feeding and eating disorders: DSM-5® selections*. American Psychiatric Publishing.

Bartrip, M. (2022, February 10). Ana. *The Players' Tribune*. https://www.theplayerstribune.com/posts/molly-bartrip-tottenham-hotspur-soccer-mental-health

Bratland-Sanda, S., & Sundgot-Borgen, S. (2013). Eating disorders in athletes: Overview of prevalence, risk factors and recommendations for prevention and treatment. *European Journal of Sport Science*, *13*(5), 499–508. https://doi.org/10.1080/17461391.2012.740504

Choi, P. Y. L. (2003). Muscle matters: Maintaining visible differences between women and men. *Sexualities, Evolution & Gender*, *5*(2), 71–81. https://doi.org/10.1080/146166603 10001632554

Coleman, M. (2022, June 2). Megan Rapinoe says former OL reign coach made "fat-shaming" remarks. *Sports Illustrated*. https://www.si.com/soccer/2022/06/02/megan-rapinoe-says-former-ol-reign-coach-made-fat-shaming-remarks

Crawford, K. L., Wilson, B., Hurd, L., & Beauchamp, M. R. (2023). Reaching out: Help-seeking among professional male ice hockey athletes. *Qualitative Research in Sport, Exercise and Health*, *15*(3), 364–381. https://doi.org/10.1080/2159676X.2022.2111458

Crossley, K. M., Patterson, B. E., Culvenor, A. G., Bruder, A. M., Mosler, A. B., & Mentiplay, B. F. (2020). Making football safer for women: A systematic review and meta-analysis of injury prevention programmes in 11 773 female football (soccer) players. *British Journal of Sports Medicine*, *54*, 1089–1098. https://doi.org/10.1136/bjsports-2019-101587

Culvin, A. (2019). *Football as work: The new realities of professional women footballers in England.* [Doctoral dissertation, University of Central Lancashire]. https://clok.uclan.ac.uk/29714/1/29714%20Culvin%20Alexandra%20Final%20e-Thesis%20%28Master%20Copy%29.pdf

Culvin, A. (2021). Football as work: The lived realities of professional women footballers in England. *Managing Sport and Leisure*, *28*(6), 684–697. https://doi.org/10.1080/2375 0472.2021.1959384

Culvin, A., & Bowes, A. (2023). Introduction: Women's football in a global, professional era. In A. Culvin & A. Bowes (Eds.), *Women's football in a global, professional era* (pp. 1–13). Emerald Publishing Limited. https://doi.org/10.1108/978-1-80071-052-820230001

Currie, A. (2010). Sport and eating disorders—understanding and managing the risks. *Asian Journal of Sports Medicine*, *1*(2), 63–68. https://doi.org/10.5812/asjsm.34864

de Borja, C., Holtzman, B., McCall, L. M., Carson, T. L., Moretti, L. J., Farnsworth, N., & Ackerman, K. E. (2021). Specific dietary practices in female athletes and their association with positive screening for disordered eating. *Journal of Eating Disorders*, *9*(1), 50. https://doi.org/10.1186/s40337-021-00407-7

Fairburn, C. G., Cooper, Z., & Shafran, R. (2003). *Clinical perfectionism questionnaire (CPQ)* [Database record]. APA PsycTests. https://doi.org/10.1037/t59141-000

FIFPro. (2020). *Raising our game: 2020 Women's football report*. https://www.fifpro.org/media/vd1pbtbj/fifpro-womens-report_eng-lowres.pdf

FIFPro. (2021). *Pathway to maternity regulations for professional footballers*. https:// www.fifpro.org/media/avwggshx/pathway-to-maternity-regulations-for-professional-footballers-alexandra-gomez-bruinewoud.pdf

George, M. (2005). Making sense of muscle: The body experiences of collegiate women athletes. *Sociological Inquiry*, *75*(3), 317–345. https://doi.org/10.1111/j.1475-682X.2005.00125.x

Heath, G. (2022, October 15). *Guest feature: Claire Rafferty opens up about eating disorders for world mental health day*. Women in Football. https://www. womeninfootball.co.uk/news/2022/10/15/guest-feature-claire-rafferty-opens-up-about-eating-disorders-for-world-mental-health-day/#:~:text=Next-,GUEST%20 FEATURE%3A%20CLAIRE%20RAFFERTY%20OPENS%20UP%20 ABOUT%20EATING,FOR%20WORLD%20MENTAL%20HEALTH%20 DAY&text=%E2%80%9CWe%20were%20weighed%20every%20day,football%20 fuelled%20her%20disordered%20eating

Horan, D., Kelly, S., Büttner, F., Blake, C., Hägglund, M., & Delahunt, E. (2023). Injury incidence rates in women's football: A systematic review and meta-analysis of prospective injury surveillance studies. *British Journal of Sports Medicine*, *57*, 471–480. https:// doi.org/10.1136/bjsports-2021-105177

Howard, L. M., Heron, K. E., & Cramer, R. (2020). The deliberate denial of disordered eating behaviors scale: Development and initial validation in young women with subclinical disordered eating. *Journal of Psychopathology and Behavioural Assessment*, *42*, 774–786. https://doi.org/10.1007/s10862-020-09819-2

Hughes, R., & Coakley, J. (1991). Positive deviance among athletes: The implications of overconformity to the sport ethic. *Sociology of Sport Journal*, *8*(4), 307–325. https://doi. org/10.1123/ssj.8.4.307

Kohe, G. Z., & Purdy, L. G. (2016). In protection of whose "wellbeing?" Considerations of "clauses and a/effects" in athlete contracts. *Journal of Sport and Social Issues*, *40*(3), 218–236. https://doi.org/10.1177/0193723516633269

Kong, P., & Harris, L. (2015). The sporting body: Body image and eating disorder symptomatology among female athletes from leanness focused and nonleanness focused sports. *Journal of Psychology*, *149*(2), 141–160. https://doi.org/10.1080/00223980.2013.846291

Kilic, Ö., Carmody, S., Upmeijer, J., Kerkhoffs, G. M. M. J., Purcell, R., Rice, S., & Gouttebarge, V. (2021). Prevalence of mental health symptoms among male and female Australian professional footballers. *BMJ Open Sport & Exercise Medicine*, *7*(3), e001043. https://doi.org/10.1136/bmjsem-2021-001043

Krane, V., Choi, P., Baird, S. M., Aimar, C. M., & Kauer, K. J. (2004). Living the paradox: Female athletes negotiate femininity and muscularity. *Sex Roles*, *50*, 315–329. https:// doi.org/10.1023/B:SERS.0000018888.48437.4f

Lewis, S. (2023, February 10). *Melbourne city and Young Matildas player Chelsea Blissett wants to change how football talks about eating disorders*. ABC News. https://www.abc. net.au/news/2023-02-11/chelsea-blissett-eating- disorders/101897130

Lichtenstein, M. B., Johansen, K. K., Runge, E., Hansen, M. B., Holmberg, T. T., & Tarp, K. (2022). Behind the athletic body: A clinical interview study of identification of eating disorder symptoms and diagnoses in elite athletes. *BMJ Open Sport & Exercise Medicine*, *8*(2), e001265. https://doi.org/10.1136/bmjsem-2021-001265

Mancine, R. P., Gusfa, D. W., Moshrefi, A., & Kennedy, S. F. (2020). Prevalence of disordered eating in athletes categorized by emphasis on leanness and activity type—a systematic review. *Journal of Eating Disorders*, *8*(47), 1–9. https://doi.org/10.1186/s40337-020-00323-2

McGannon, K. R., & McMahon, J. (2019). Understanding female athlete disordered eating and recovery through narrative turning points in autobiographies. *Psychology of Sport and Exercise*, *40*, 42–50. https://doi.org/10.1016/j.psychsport.2018.09.003

McHaffie, S. J., Langan-Evans, C., Morehen, J. C., Strauss, J. A., Areta, J. L., Rosimus, C., Evans, M., Elliott-Sale, K. J., Cronin, C. J., & Morton, J. P. (2022). Carbohydrate fear, skinfold targets and body image issues: A qualitative analysis of player and stakeholder perceptions of the nutrition culture within elite female soccer. *Science and Medicine in Football, 6*(5), 675–685. https://doi.org/10.1080/24733938.2022.2101143

Pereira Vargas, L. M., & Winter, S. (2021). Weight on the bar vs. weight on the scale: A qualitative exploration of disordered eating in competitive female powerlifters. *Psychology of Sport & Exercise, 52*, 101822. https://doi.org/10.1016/j.psychsport.2020.101822

Perry, C., Champ, F., Macbeth, J., & Spandler, H. (2021). Mental health and elite female athletes: A scoping review. *Psychology of Sport and Exercise, 56*(2), 101961. https://doi.org/10.1016/j.psychsport.2021.101961

Perry, C., Chauntry, A., & Champ, F. (2022). Elite female footballers in England: An exploration of mental ill-health and help-seeking intentions. *Science and Medicine in Football, 6*(5), 650–659. https://doi.org/10.1080/24733938.2022.2084149

Prather, H., Hunt, D., McKeon, K., Simpson, S., Meyer, E. B., Yemm, T., & Brophy, R. (2016). Are elite female soccer athletes at risk for disordered eating attitudes, menstrual dysfunction, and stress fractures? *PM & R, 8*(3), 208–213. https://doi.org/10.1016/j.pmrj.2015.07.003

Putukian, M. (2016). The psychological response to injury in student athletes: A narrative review with a focus on mental health. *British Journal of Sports Medicine, 50*, 145–148. https://doi.org/10.1136/bjsports-2015-095586

Qian, J., Wu, Y., Liu, F., Zhu, Y., Jin, H., Zhang, H., Wan, Y., Li, C., & Yu, D. (2021). An update on the prevalence of eating disorders in the general population: A systematic review and meta-analysis. *Eating and Weight Disorders, 27*, 415–428. https://doi.org/10.1007/s40519-021-01162-z

Reel, J. J., Podlog, L., Hamilton, L., Greviskes, L., Voelker, D. K., & Gray, C. (2018). Injury and disordered eating behaviors: What is the connection for female professional dancers? *Journal of Clinical Sport Psychology, 12*(3), 365–381. https://doi.org/10.1123/jcsp.2017-0007

Roderick, M., Smith, A., & Potrac, P. (2017). The sociology of sports work, emotions and mental health: Scoping the field and future directions. *Sociology of Sport Journal, 34*(2), 99–107. https://doi.org/10.1123/ssj.2017-0082

Sundgot-Borgen, J., & Torstveit, M. K. (2007). The female football player, disordered eating, menstrual function and bone health. *British Journal of Sports Medicine, 41*(1), 68–72. https://doi.org/10.1136/bjsm.2007.038018

Thomas, F. (2022, June 10). Fara Williams interview: Women's football must address its "fat club" culture. *The Telegraph.* https://www.telegraph.co.uk/football/2022/06/10/fara-williams-interview-womens-football-must-address-fat-club/

Tiggemann, M., & Lynch, J. E. (2001). Body image across the life span in adult women: The role of self-objectification. *Developmental Psychology, 37*(2), 243–253. https://doi.org/10.1037/0012-1649.37.2.243

Volpi, P., Bisciotti, G. N., Chamari, K., Cena, E., Carimati, G., & Bragazzi, N. L. (2016). Risk factors of anterior cruciate ligament injury in football players: A systematic review of the literature. *Muscles, Ligaments and Tendons Journal, 6*(4), 480–485. https://doi.org/10.11138/mltj/2016.6.4.48

Walter, N., Heinen, T., & Elbe, A. (2022). Factors associated with disordered eating and eating disorder symptoms in adolescent elite athletes. *Sports Psychiatry, 1*(2), 47–56. https://doi.org/10.1024/2674-0052/a000012

Wells, K., Jeacocke, N. A., Appaneal, R., Smith, H. D., Vlahovich, N., Burke, L. M., & Hughes, D. (2020). The Australian institute of sport (AIS) and national eating disorders collaboration (NEDC) position statement on disordered eating in high performance sport. *British Journal of Sports Medicine, 54*, 1247–1258. https://doi.org/10.1136/bjsports-2019-101813

Williams, O. (2012). Eating for excellence: Eating disorders in elite sport—inevitability and "immunity". *European Journal for Sport and Society, 9*(1–2), 33–55. https://doi.org/10.1080/16138171.2012.11687888

Wood, S., Harrison, L. K., & Kucharska, J. (2017). Male professional footballers' experiences of mental health difficulties and help-seeking. *The Physician and Sports Medicine, 45*(2), 120–128. https://doi.org/10.1080/00913847.2017.1283209

10

DISORDERED EATING AND RELATIVE ENERGY DEFICIENCY IN SPORT

A case study

Melissa Streno and Rebecca McConville

Introduction

Providers in the field of sport nutrition and clinical sport psychology have noticed an increase in women football players seeking treatment for disordered eating and/or eating disorders in recent years (Perry et al., 2022). The physical and mental demands of football are associated with numerous risk factors for disordered eating and eating disorders (Abbott et al., 2021). The unique risk factors for disordered eating and eating disorders in elite women's footballers are explored in Chapter 9. The aim of this chapter is to share a case study, from a practitioner's perspective, to demonstrate the risk female footballers have in the development of an eating disorder and/or use of disordered eating behaviours. We are hopeful that sharing this case study will generate more focused research and illuminate the need for more specialised attention within women's football.

Background on relative energy deficiency in sport in women's football

Eating disorders and disordered eating are defined and discussed in Chapter 9 of this book. In this chapter, we discuss low energy availability, which is a state of mismatch between energy intake and energy expenditure, where the body does not have enough energy to support physiological function to maintain health (Magee et al., 2020). Mountjoy et al. (2014, p. 491) provide the following definition: "The syndrome of relative energy deficiency in sport refers to impaired physiological function including, but not limited to, metabolic rate, menstrual function, bone health, immunity, protein synthesis, cardiovascular health caused by relative energy deficiency." The aetiological factor of this syndrome is low energy availability

DOI: 10.4324/9781003381914-10

(Mountjoy et al., 2018). Despite the fact that football is estimated to have over 260 million people participating, there continues to be a lack of research or empirical evidence regarding incidences of low energy availability for both women and men. In the United States, specifically in the Division 1 soccer league, the prevalence rate of low energy availability was reported as being 26–33% (Reed et al., 2013) and for professional levels as being at 23% (Moss et al., 2021).

Case study

The following case study is one of many, which contributes to the urgent need for more research and attention in the area of relative energy deficiency in sport in women's football, as well as highly supported approaches to treatment.

It was as early as eight years old that Taylor (name has been changed to protect identity of individual) recalls the start of her disordered thoughts. This attentional shift aligned with growing awareness of her physical body. Amidst involvement in high-level football around the same time, she recalls asking her mom frequently if she was "fat", noting fears of weight gain as she became acutely aware of herself in comparison to others. She said that low self-esteem and dislike for her appearance contributed to a negative self-image as she endured challenges of puberty and battled comorbid anxiety and depressive symptoms into high school. Similar to certain factors that drive eating disorders, low self-esteem and a negative body-image perception stemming from comparison can lead to pressure to use disordered behaviours. As Arthur-Cameselle et al. (2017) point out, it is not just teammates who model particular disordered behaviours; it is also the sustained effort to stand out amongst a team or group of competitors that will drive an athlete to use behaviours more consistently and intensely, which can easily morph into a battle amongst a group of athletes. Similar to cultural norms for various sports, and even positions or roles within a particular sport, comparison and competition tendencies automatically become an excuse for disordered behaviours to be deemed acceptable in the player's mind.

Taylor's experience paralleled high-level competitive opportunities and expectations in football that led to her being recruited to play in college at age 17. While some habits and events associated with a sport might be considered benign, specific associations between certain eating disorder behaviours and norms within a sport can compound the belief that they are acceptable. This acceptance is particularly common at certain points in a season or when athletes see their teammates engaging in disordered behaviours. Perry and colleagues (2022) found serious mental health concerns when looking at elite football players from England, most notably symptoms related to an eating disorder. Interestingly, according to Perry, "higher disordered eating scores were not associated with currently needing psychological support" (Perry et al., 2022, p. 658). This finding supports the concern that some of these disordered behaviours have become normalised within a team and/or sport and are not seen as concerning or negatively impactful on health.

Increased time and rigid focus around what Taylor was eating, as well as how she was burning her fuel, continued during the in-season as well as during her off-season training. One particular season, which did not go as well as she hoped, led to a steep increase in the use of more consistent and detrimental eating disordered behaviours. These behaviours included, but were not limited to, counting calories, restricting the amounts and variety of her food intake, eliminating specific food groups and exercising outside the normal and prescribed training routine. During the off-season, this diet mentality was reinforced, as meals back at home were void of carbohydrates. Her desire for weight loss was more openly revealed, yet normalised, in a home environment focused on weight. Consequently, Taylor's weight dropped quickly, and she began experiencing expected physical and psychological consequences aligned with relative energy deficiency in sport. Not only was Taylor noticing a lower mood and isolative tendencies from her friends and team; she was also experiencing low energy, amenorrhoea, fatigue and cold intolerance. Taylor's mood disturbances were amplified when she began to experience difficulty sleeping, despite feeling exhausted. She was encouraged to go on sleep medication; however, she chose to focus on shifting nutritional choices and engage in more intentional recovery from training, to assess how these impacted her sleep quality.

Alongside more consistent sessions and interventions from an eating disorder outpatient team, Taylor slowly made more intentional shifts and built awareness around disordered thoughts and urges. Throughout her work towards recovery, eating-disorder thoughts remained loud and intense. This barrier made recovery-focused choices difficult to sustain, especially as she continued training and competing with her team. As expected, the more often she moved away from listening to and giving into the disordered urges or thoughts, the louder they became, especially the part of the disordered voice telling her she must look a particular way to be successful in her sport in the position of goalkeeper. Coupled with this challenge was Taylor's intense fear of weight gain due to belief that this equates to laziness and a lack of control. Many athletes have likely viewed their body through a lens solely influenced by their participation in sport, as well as for the purpose of sport.

Another challenge that presented was a lack of eating competence around nutritional needs for health, as well as those for sport. Despite the understanding that athletes have high energy needs and different nutritional goals, many athletes grow up in diet-centric households filled with lower calorie food options and a focus on maintenance of weight. Taylor often experienced this first-hand, not having carbohydrates at meals and observing her parents limit their own intake with the aim of losing weight. This modelling led her to believe that these same practices pertained to her. Consequently, she never learned how to listen to what her body authentically needed or wanted from a fuelling standpoint, and she rarely associated food with enjoyment. Her nutrition sessions with a sport dietician centred around the development of eating competence regarding food choices, the experience of eating according to pleasure and the development of hunger/fullness awareness and cues. Further, exploration of interoceptive awareness relating to situations that could impact her ability to sense physiological signals became a prioritised nutrition goal.

Psycho-education regarding the nutrition needs and challenges that women football players face was critical for Taylor. Football players have a unique nutritional demand, since some players are estimated to be running approximately 10 km during a game, with almost 25% of the game reaching high-intensity output (see Chapter 3 on match demands and physiological determinants). The unique energy needs of women football players require an endurance component due to the volume of running in a game; they also require repeated bouts of high intensity that demand power and explosion. Football players should consume sufficient carbohydrates to ensure glucose availability and adequate stores of glycogen (Dasa et al., 2023), recommended to be 3–8 kg body mass (BM) per day, depending on competitive and training demands (Collins et al., 2021) (see Chapter 8 on nutritional needs). The lack of awareness in regard to energy and nutrition demands of women football players may be a contributor to the incidence of low energy availability and development of relative energy deficiency in sport (Logue, 2018).

Energy availability is viewed as the energy left for the body to maintain physiological function. As the availability level lowers, there is increased risk of physiological dysfunction. One approach to evaluating the risk of energy deficiency in athletes involves examining the level of energy availability, expressed as kilocalories per kilogram fat-free mass (FFM) per day and calculated by subtracting the energy expended from total energy intake. The calculated energy availability is considered low if <30 kcal kg FFM^{-1} day^{-1}, moderate if 30–45 kcal kg FFM^{-1} day^{-1} and optimal if >45 kcal kg FFM^{-1} day^{-1} (Loucks et al., 2011; Magee et al., 2020; Mountjoy et al., 2018). Diagnosis of low energy availability contributing to relative energy deficiency in sport is associated with an increased risk of disordered eating and/or eating disorders (Abbott et al., 2021).

Upon initial assessment, it was found that Taylor consumed <3 g kg BM^{-1} of carbohydrate and had an energy availability of 25 kcal kg FFM^{-1} day^{-1}. Taylor experienced difficulty falling asleep and staying asleep, despite feeling exhausted and fatigued. She also noted that, as a result of her sleep disturbances, her anxiety had increased, which impacted her ability to stay focused with schoolwork and during training. It became clear that one of the multiple functions of her disordered eating was the sense of control felt when limiting her intake, specifically carbohydrates, as a means to numb and distract from uncomfortable emotional distress. Carbohydrates were feared growing up due to the perception of associated weight gain. With support, Taylor began to focus on carbohydrate availability by intentionally planning carbohydrate-rich choices at each meal and snack, as well as using the plate method with a visual portion guide to increase her energy availability and avoid a fixation around numbers. With time, she more routinely planned both her pre- and post-training fuel to combat the tendency to skip both.

Taylor reported a noticeable physical improvement in her reaction time, despite ongoing intrusive thoughts that posed cognitive obstacles daily. She also started to experience a remarkable difference in her ability to fall asleep sooner and to experience long periods of quality sleep. She began to spend more time at meals as a way to challenge her variety and food fears amongst teammates. She began to notice, as she spent more meals with teammates, how many of her food choices were driven by perfectionism and fear by labelling most foods as healthy versus unhealthy.

Her athletic trainer weighed her weekly and shared this trend with her outpatient providers to assess restoration progress into her natural set weight range. Throughout a gradual 6-month period, Taylor moved closer to being fully weight restored with a more regular menstruation pattern. Tracking menstrual patterns is important because it is a vital marker of health (see Chapters 5 and 6 on the menstrual cycle).

In a recent study, it was confirmed that the focus on controlling weight remains a current experience of elite football players (Perry et al., 2022). However, it has also been demonstrated that football players do not pose the risk for disordered eating compared to non-athlete controls (Abbott et al., 2021). Further, football does not have a specific weight-component factor as other sports might that are associated with higher prevalence of disordered eating and eating disorders. This element does not eliminate the chance of developing an eating disorder if an individual has participated in a sport outside the risk category, including football. In fact, preventive measures should be secured to ensure behaviours or patterns predisposing or influencing an individual to have an eating disorder are not ignored. Many of the reasons are relative to the athletic setting, but biological, psychological and social aspects can also influence the development of this illness (Dennis, 2023). It would be easy to assume these harmful behaviour patterns begin to take shape once a player has left football. However, because of the unique environment of competitive sports, players are at risk for body dissatisfaction and the development of an eating disorder well before their transition out of sport. As seen with Taylor, an eating disorder can develop at any point in a player's career. One of the most common precursors for using disordered eating as a means of control is change or transition points during one's athletic career. Transitions that occur mid-season as a result of things like injury or illness, variation in a line-up, change in positions, school transfer and interpersonal shifts with teammates must be considered. Many of these transitions are sudden and unanticipated, which may drive some individuals to attempt to regain a lost sense of control through manipulation of food and exercise.

One of Taylor's defining athletic transitions occurred when she experienced a coaching change mid-career. The coaching change illuminated the need for control as uncertainty around position security, teammate transfers and overall relation with her new coach surfaced. The pull to maintain some form of control during this transitional experience also triggered familiar disordered-eating tendencies such as weighing herself, avoiding eating out with the team, calorie counting after difficult conversations with her coach, engaging in additional workouts and exercising rigidity with her daily food choices. Taylor acknowledged that these changes led to more anxiety on the pitch, slower reaction time, strained relationship with teammates (as she felt she was constantly comparing) and overall performance decline.

The 2020 pandemic was another experience of unexpected and uncertain transition during Taylor's college football career. A halting stop to games, less contact with her team and an overall encouraged period of isolation all precipitated more engagement with disordered behaviours, when, yet again, specific life realms felt out of her control. One of the ironic components of an eating disorder is that when an individual uses behaviour with the intention of feeling in control, they are actually more out of control. Truly regaining control is aligning authentically to what one's physical and psychological needs are, as well as using the body and mind as guides to making healthful and balanced decisions that support energy and rest needs.

A lack of consistent and/or long-standing evidence and research around disordered eating in football players makes it crucial to be aware of, as the player prepares for their transition out of sport. Differences in ideal body composition can lead to internal conflict with society's expectation for physical appearance, weight, shape and size. As would be expected, de Bruin et al. (2011) revealed a more negative body-image view in the sport context compared to that in the social setting. Further, those engaging in disordered eating patterns also exemplified greater negative body-image thoughts or ideals (de Bruin et al., 2011). Ling and colleagues' (2023) research with retired football players highlighted participants' concern about their weight both during and after their career. Expectedly, Godoy-Izquierdo and Diaz's research team (2021) found that a positive body image was a protective factor for women football players against developing an eating disorder. This insight not only supports the long-standing relationship between negative body image and the development of disordered-eating habits but also suggests the unfortunate possibility of these behaviours continuing after sport. Based on research, the obstacles and challenges athletes face related to the transition out of college, as well as variables related to each individual's experience, have been revealed (Giannone, 2017; Park et al., 2013). This time period is filled with unknowns, as these former athletes begin their launch into a world that offers far less support, structure and certainty to which they have been accustomed.

In the midst of transitioning out of college football, Taylor considered and was selected for a semi-professional team the following year. Not only did this lead to the re-emergence of meeting new teammates and a shifting routine, but the pressure to perform in order to maintain a spot on the team, and possibly move up, was exacerbated. This period of uncertainty and unfamiliarity magnifies as a player attempts to carve out their path more autonomously and without as much structure as they have known. Taylor noticed a resurgence of disordered behaviours paralleling the increased expectations in her new competitive football setting.

While still few and far between, the evidence and studies that have been published closely predicted Taylor's experience transitioning out of sport. As many other athletes experience, Taylor has spent years battling dysmorphic and self-defeating thoughts about her body, her appearance and what this perception means about her. As athletes explore their evolving identity outside of sport, they require and benefit from guidance in exploring these adaptations in their body's functioning. One of the myths that Taylor fell victim to was the misinformed belief that her number on the scale dictated her athletic ability. She began to see this idea as fact, despite weight and appearance likely having minimal influence on her athletic greatness.

One of the few studies in which the impact of retirement or transition out of sport on body image has been examined was conducted by Stephan and Bilard in 2003. Focusing on transitioning Olympic athletes, they described various phases that these individuals endured while transitioning out of sport. Respondents did not report shifts in their body satisfaction scores immediately after the transition or during the period when they began replacing their training or competition time with professional responsibilities. In the study, it was suggested that this dismissal of body-image concerns could have been a form of identity protection due to the difficulties of coping with a changing body. Within five months post-termination, however, body satisfaction scores decreased, likely due to increased awareness of physical changes and abilities resulting from less time spent training. When the transitioning athletes experienced any pain or exhaustion while participating in activity again, their views of a "high performance body" shifted to one of "suffering" (Stephan & Bilard, 2003, p. 102). The athletes' speculation of a negative body image and overall dissatisfaction supports the need for social and psychological support for those transitioning out of sport, especially considering the likely influence this has on their self-worth and self-esteem.

In many cases like Taylor's, a negative self-view or negative body image can influence mood and other psychological experiences connected to body dysmorphia or disordered behaviours such as depression, isolation, anxiety and low self-esteem.

During this time of transition, Taylor and her treatment team began incorporating the key components of eating competence: positive eating attitudes, food acceptance skills, internal regulation skills and contextual skills. Taylor struggled most of her life to understand hunger and fullness signals due to eating around set training sessions and class schedules, as well as experiencing heightened anxiety before, during and after meals. Secondary to these issues was her inability to practice mindful eating, as fuelling was thought of as a chore instead of a pleasurable or satisfying experience. Taylor began to create her own hunger/fullness scale by also taking note of situations that impacted interoceptive awareness such as stress, poor sleep quality and distraction at work. She also began relying on friends and social experiences for more spontaneous challenges with restaurants or types of food, as well as holding her accountable to fuel well.

When Taylor transitioned into a relationship, she found it hard, but useful, to mirror her partner's ability to eat intuitively and try new foods. Taylor challenged herself to allow her partner to choose where they would go out to eat on dates, which limited time spent researching menus and planning her day accordingly. She often said that this was her first experience with someone she was close to who modelled a healthy relationship around food and body image. This relationship helped propel Taylor towards taking risks in building a support system with those not directly involved with football.

Summary

Many individuals, including Taylor, start their athletic career at a very early age. For Taylor, free time and school days revolved around her sport, shaping an identity that centred on coaches' expectations, personal expectations, demands on the body and a relationship with food and exercise that was fused with football. Support systems were composed of people connected to the sport routine, including caregivers, coaches, teammates and their families, athletic staff and, often, even media figures. As Taylor learned to leverage the same strengths that were part of her athletic identity during the transition away from football, she started to gain confidence in trusting that she was more than just her identity within the sport performance setting. This idea has been supported and maintained by trying new hobbies and interests, as well as meeting friends outside the football world. As recommended for sustainable and full eating-disorder recovery, consistent check-ins and support with her treatment team remain a priority. Many of the same skills and tools Taylor utilised throughout her recovery continue to help her navigate life changes and challenges not related to football.

References

Abbott, W., Brett, A., Brownlee, T. E., Hammond, K. M., Harper, L. D., Naughton, R. J., Anderson, L., Munson, E. H., Sharkey, J. V., Randell, R. K., & Clifford, T. (2021). The prevalence of disordered eating in elite male and female soccer players. *Eating and Weight Disorders*, *26*(2), 491–498. https://doi.org/10.1007/s40519-020-00872-0

Arthur-Cameselle, J., Sossin, K., & Quatromoni, P. (2017). A qualitative analysis of factors related to eating disorder onset in female collegiate athletes and non-athletes. *Eating Disorders*, *25*(3), 199–215. https://doi.org/10.1080/10640266.2016.1258940

Collins, J., Maughan, R. J., Gleeson, M., Bilsborough, J., Jeukendrup, A., Morton, J. P., Phillips, S. M., Armstrong, L., Burke, L. M., Close, G. L., Duffield, R., Larson-Meyer, E., Louis, J., Medina, D., Meyer, F., Rollo, I., Sundgot-Borgen, J., Wall, B. T., Boullosa, B., . . . McCall, A. (2021). UEFA expert group statement on nutrition in elite football: Current evidence to inform practical recommendations and guide future research. *British Journal of Sports Medicine*, *55*(8), 416. https://doi.org/10.1136/bjsports-2019-101961

Dasa, M. S., Friborg, O., Kristoffersen, M., Pettersen, G., Plasqui, G., Sundgot-Borgen, J. K., & Rosenvinge, J. H. (2023). Energy expenditure, dietary intake and energy availability in female professional football players. *BMJ Open Sport and Exercise Medicine*, *9*(1), e001553. https://doi.org/10.1136/bmjsem-2023-001553

de Bruin, A. P., Oudejans, R. R., Bakker, F. C., & Woertman, L. (2011). Contextual body image and athletes' disordered eating: The contribution of athletic body image to disordered eating in high performance women athletes. *European Eating Disorders Review*, *19*(3), 201–215. https://doi.org/10.1002/erv.1112

Dennis, A. B. (2023). *Risk factors*. National Eating Disorders Association. https://www.nationaleatingdisorders.org/risk-factors/#sources

Giannone, Z. A. (2017). *Sport career transition: Strengths, challenges and innovations over time*. Advancing Career Development in Canada. https://ceric.ca/2017/02/sport-career-transition-strengths-challenges-and-innovations-over-time/

Godoy-Izquierdo, D., & Diaz, I. (2021). Inhabiting the body(ies) in female soccer players: The protective role of positive body image. *Frontiers in Psychology*, *12*, 2011. https://doi.org/10.3389/fpsyg.2021.718836

Ling, D. I., Hannafin, J. A., Prather, H., Skolnik, H., Chiaia, T. A., de Mille, P., Lewis, C. L., & Casey, E. (2023). The women's soccer health study: From head to toe. *Sports Medicine*, *53*(10), 2001–2010. https://doi.org/10.1007/s40279-023-01860-x

Logue, D., Madigan, S. M., Delahunt, E., Heinen, M., McDonnell, S., & Cornish, C. A. (2018). Low energy availability in athletes: A review of prevalence, dietary patterns, physiological health, and sports performance. *Sports Medicine*, *48*, 73–96. https://doi.org/10.1007/s40279-017-0790-3

Loucks, A. B., Kiens, B., & Wright, H. H. (2011). Energy availability in athletes. *Journal of Sports Sciences*, *29*(Suppl 1), S7–S15. https://doi.org/10.1080/02640414.2011.588958

Magee, M. K., Lockard, B. L., Zabriskie, H. A., Schaefer, A. Q., Luedke, J. A., Erickson, J. L., Jones, M. T., & Jagim, A. R. (2020). Prevalence of low energy availability in collegiate women soccer athletes. *Journal of Functional Morphology Kinesiology*, *5*(4), 96. https://doi.org/10.3390/jfmk5040096

Moss, S. L., Randell, R. K., Burgess, D., Ridley, S., ÓCairealláin, C., Allison, R., & Rollo, I. (2021). Assessment of energy availability and associated risk factors in professional female soccer players. *European Journal of Sport Science*, *21*(6), 861–870. https://doi.org/10.1080/17461391.2020.1788647

Mountjoy, M., Sundgot-Borgen, J. K., Burke, L. M., Ackerman, K. E., Blauwet, C., Constantini, N., Lebrun, C., Lundy, B., Melin, A. K., Meyer, N. L., Sherman, R. T., Tenforde, A. S., Torstveit, M. K., & Budgett, R. (2018). IOC consensus statement on relative energy deficiency in sport (RED-S): 2018 update. *British Journal of Sports Medicine*, *52*(11), 687–697. https://doi.org/10.1136/bjsports-2018-099193

Mountjoy, M., Sundgot-Borgen, J. K., Burke, L. M., Carter, S., Constantini, N., Lebrun, C., Meyer, N., Sherman, R., Steffen, K., Budgett, R., & Ljungqvist, A. (2014). The IOC consensus statement: Beyond the female athlete triad—relative energy deficiency in sport (RED-S). *British Journal of Sports Medicine*, *48*(7), 491–497. https://doi.org/10.1136/bjsports-2014-093502

Park, S., Lavallee, D., & Tod, D. (2013). Athletes' career transition out of sport: A systematic review. *International Review of Sport and Exercise Psychology*, *6*(1), 22–53. https://doi.org/10.1080/1750984X.2012.687053

Perry, C., Chauntry, A. J., & Champ, F. M. (2022). Elite female footballers in England: An exploration of mental ill-health and help-seeking intentions. *Science and Medicine in Football*, *6*(5), 650–659. https://doi.org/10.1080/24733938.2022.2084149

Reed, J. L., De Souza, M. J., & Williams, N. I. (2013). Changes in energy availability across the season in division I female soccer players. *Journal of Sports Sciences*, *31*(3), 314–324. https://doi.org/10.1080/02640414.2012.733019

Stephan, Y., & Bilard, J. (2003). Repercussions of transition out of elite sport on body image. *Perceptual and Motor Skills*, *96*(1), 95–104. https://doi.org/10.2466/pms.2003.96.1.95

11

PSYCHOSOCIAL DEVELOPMENT AND TRANSITIONS

Alice Stratford and Francesca M. Champ

Introduction

Women's football has grown exponentially across the last decade. For example the game has seen league professionalisation and expansion both in the UK (e.g. introduction of the Women's Super League) and in the United States (e.g. introduction of National Women's Super League), development of competitions such as the Football Association (the FA) cup and Champions League (to follow similar structures as the men's game) and subsequently the opportunity for players to engage solely in football as a full-time occupation (Culvin & Bowes, 2023). With such substantial growth at senior levels of the game, governing bodies across the world are subsequently recognising the importance of facilitating the participation and development of younger players. To this end, strategies and development plans (such as those introduced by the English FA (The FA, 2017, 2019, 2021) are focusing upon the importance of facilitating the participation and development of younger players. Despite such work, in a major review published by Karen Carney MBE in July 2023, it was identified that wholesale changes were required to create a better and more sustainable future for all of those within the women's game across the world, from ensuring young girls have the right to play football at school to ensuring that "professionalisation" of the leagues goes beyond just that of demanding professional standards from players but provides environments and opportunities for players to develop and grow, giving them optimal opportunity to successfully transition into senior, professional environments. Within these development pathways, the chance to evolve and mature psychosocially is imperative, to allow youth footballers to develop their sense of identity, recognise their strengths to support their existence in a competitive, professional environment and navigate how they exist within a team of experienced athletes. In this chapter, we aim to

DOI: 10.4324/9781003381914-11

explore how such psychosocial developments and maturation can be impacted by the events and processes that surround the junior-to-senior transition.

Psychosocial development and transitions

A plethora of factors, encompassing biological, social, psychological and cultural factors, will influence how footballers experience and navigate their sporting journey. In this chapter, we critically explore the reciprocal relationship between psychosocial factors and an athlete's ability to cope with career transitions. We view psychosocial characteristics to be those that combine individual psychological behaviours and features, which, combined with social influence, will shape and guide how an athlete reacts, processes and performs (Stratford, 2023). For example researchers have identified that personal qualities (e.g. optimism, adaptive perfectionism) and psychological characteristics (e.g. resilience, a high level of emotional intelligence, a high level of self-awareness) (Gledhill et al., 2017) enable athletes to thrive at the highest level, help them to maintain perspective during periods of sporting challenge and protect them from poor psychological wellbeing. In additional to psychological factors, the important role that sociocultural influences play cannot be overlooked. For example the professional sports culture is often described as ruthless, highly competitive and volatile (Nesti, 2016). Moreover, the requirement to "conform" or be rejected can often leave athletes feeling that their identity is threatened (Champ et al., 2020). Subsequently, the environment that football organisations create is imperative in facilitating the development of psychosocial skills and an athlete's ability to cope with career transitions. We emphasise the importance of women's football organisations adopting a long-term approach to talent development, which looks beyond early performance success and encourages the holistic development of all players. Finally, clubs should strive to develop high-performance cultures that encourage autonomy, allow for the development of meaningful relationships and encourage each performer to be true to their identity.

It is inevitable that a number of transitions will be experienced across any sporting career. In this chapter, we adopt Schlossberg's (1981) definition of transitions as "an event or non-event, which results in a change in assumptions about oneself and the world and thus requires a corresponding change in one's behaviour and relationships" (p. 5). Examples of such transitions include injury, (de)selection, migration/moving club and the junior-to-senior transition. From our experiences of working with footballers, coaches and women's teams, we suggest that athletes' sporting careers are typically nonlinear and are shaped by a range of personal, social, cultural and political factors. A common thread, however, is the potential for these factors to influence psychosocial development and wellbeing positively or negatively. Based on current research, it has been suggested that there are a number of factors that are associated with successful transition outcomes, including (1) individual factors (personal goals, previous transition experience and personality traits), (2) sociocultural factors (managing social norms, feeling ready to be with older players) and (3) availability of support and resources (communication with staff and players, knowledge of staff expectations and requirements, individual development plans) (Stratford, 2023). However, to date, there has been very little published research in which the focus has exclusively been on supporting and facilitating the development of footballers, particularly during periods of career transition.

The junior-to-senior transition has most frequently been cited as the toughest transition that any player will face (Morris et al., 2017). For example Vanden Auweele et al. (2004) identified that only 17% of national junior athletic champions successfully transitioned to elite senior athletes, with the remainder dropping to a recreational level or dropping out of sport completely. In the context of women's football, this dropout generally occurs at around 20 years of age, when players move from the Under-20 (U20) age group to the senior team. These environments focus on exposing players to a range of different playing environments (e.g. different teams through a dual-registration process, a range of league and cup competitions) and readying players for the wide and diverse challenges of senior football, at both club and international levels. Using the English academy setup as an example, currently players who have progressed through the youth development pathway sit within a Professional Game Academy between the ages of 14 and 20 (composed of an Under-16 [U16s] and U20s team). These environments are dual career driven, with the focus of supporting players through both their education and their football development. In this chapter, *dual career* means balancing athletic commitments with education and/or work. More specifically, players under the age of 18 are required to be in education, and those over the age of 18 have to commit to a dual career either through higher/further education or through an education-based work programme such as an apprenticeship. Subsequently, the junior-to-senior transition often coincides with a period of educational transition (i.e. from further education to higher education or out of education completely), thus potentially heightening the stress and challenges faced by the athlete. Until recently, the vast majority of sports literature has overlooked the potential (positive and negative) impact that occupying a dual role might have on an athlete's performance and wellbeing. On the one hand, some researchers (e.g. Lally, 2007; Stambulova et al., 2015; Warriner & Lavallee, 2008) have highlighted the long-term benefits of being a dual-career athlete in facilitating the athletes to proceed with a "normal" life upon the termination of their sporting careers. For example being a dual-career athlete might have benefits in terms of a more balanced lifestyle (preventing identity foreclosure), positive socialisation effects, development of coping strategies and positive effects on self-regulation (Harrison et al., 2022). However, others have identified major psychosocial challenges such as an increased risk of injury and overtraining, burnout, reduced psychological wellbeing and premature dropout from sports and/or education (Drole et al., 2023).

The players who make it through the academy system, and successfully transition into a senior environment, have subsequently managed not only challenges related to their sporting development and success, but a plethora of changes within their individual, psychological, sociocultural and broader educational development (McGreary et al., 2021). These changes include competitive stressors (such as high expectations, competition and training schedule), family stressors (such as death, illness and relationship breakdown), organisational stressors (such as contractual issues, relationship with the coach/teammates) and career transitions (such as deselection, relocation and injury). The shift in environment from a nurturing- and development-focused setting to a sole emphasis on performance is often acknowledged as one of the most testing periods of an athlete's sporting career, requiring athletes to spend additional time training/competing and facing an increased pressure to perform.

The support staff, who are working with players through this journey, must have an understanding of the potential impact that the demands and shifts can have on the players, both on and off the pitch, in order to provide proactive and reactive player support. Without this support, players may be susceptible to both performance slumps and reduced wellbeing. More specifically, it has been suggested that young females are an at-risk population for mental ill health (Solmi et al., 2022). This finding is particularly concerning when we consider that footballers are likely to be transitioning from junior to senior football in pursuit of sporting excellence during a period when they are most vulnerable to the onset of common mental-disorder symptoms such as anxiety or depression.

Case study

In this final part of the chapter, we present an applied case study, detailing one player's journey as they move from the developmental academy to the first-team setting. Specific attention is given to key moments and events during the transition, and the subsequent behaviours and reactions of both the player and practitioners in the surrounding environments. We will build on this case study by offering a nuanced understanding of managing the junior-to-senior transition and how multidisciplinary teams can work together to support player psychosocial development.

Liv plays at the same club she first joined when she was 10 years old and has been there for her entire playing career. Liv's journey along the development pathway has coincided with some of the biggest growth and changes in the women's professional game. Whilst this undoubtedly brought additional challenges, such as managing the balance between being a teenage girl and using social media as a platform for self-representation and promotion, it has also meant that Liv has been fortunate enough to have a psychosocial support team (performance psychologist, lifestyle advisor, education officer and safeguarding officer) dedicated to supporting her through each stage of her development.

Liv, a dual-career athlete, balanced full-time education alongside her time in the U16s, and further education during her time within the U20's squad. After completing college (aged 18), Liv had originally planned to go to a local university and continue as a dual-career athlete, but the opportunity to train with the first team full time led her to defer this option for a year, while she endeavoured to secure a professional playing contract. Such decisions are becoming increasingly common within the women's game, and, to this end, the women's pathway is somewhat mirroring that of men's football. Liv and her family were supported by a club-based education officer during the time that she was faced with the decision to move away from education. She also became a member of a professional player's football union to ensure that she could attain support further down the line if she chose to return to her studies. Although Liv would speak about leaving education as a "weight off her shoulders", she also identified that "one day, I will have to go back to it as I'll need a 'proper job when I retire'". These snippets demonstrate that career transitions are often not black and white, smooth or short-term experiences; rather, they are complex, multifaceted decisions that have the potential to impact the performer in both the short term and the long term. Therefore, applied practitioners must adopt a highly personalised approach when working with athletes to help and support them when making important decisions.

Liv's planning for the junior-to-senior transition began long before it took place. Therefore, the transition was voluntary, expected and perceived in a positive light (e.g. the opportunity to reach her sporting potential). Each of these factors has been identified as protective against the negative impact of career transitions. Liv had prepared for the increased training and match demands/standards of practice by integrating with the first-team squad over a period of several weeks and had started to develop social connections with members of the first-team squad by attending home matches. Furthermore, her support network within the academy environment had started a "handover" in the weeks before Liv made the jump up to the first team. The increased communication ensured that support would be in place prior to, during and after transition and meant that Liv had access to emotional, psychological, tangible and esteemed support when she needed it. Her team of practitioners agreed that their primary purpose in working with Liv was to help her navigate the identity-related conflicts that she would experience during the transition and help her to act in a manner that was coherent with her identity even during uncomfortable experiences (Morris et al., 2017).

Throughout her journey, Liv has faced a number of different challenges, including balancing education and part-time work and navigating a number of identity and role-related conflicts both inside and outside of football. We have identified the transition pathway to demonstrate a three-phase process of transition, by which Liv follows a process from the first team of interest, involvement and investment from the first team, which forms the foundation of our knowledge. This pathway highlights the transition to be one of multiple stages, which often encompasses feelings of being pulled back and forth, confusion around belonging and the requirement to be patient and navigate the transition as part of a bigger career transition and subsequent investment.

During her academy career, Liv established herself as a dependable, hard-working character who showed equal measures of high standards and commitment, compassion and a sociable nature. Her consistent role as captain throughout her later seasons in the U16s and U20s was therefore no surprise to any of the academy staff. In her earlier playing years, Liv thrived in the nurturing and development environment of the academy, exhibiting traits such as high adaptability, being team orientated, determined and motivated. The psychosocial skills are indicative of an athlete likely to succeed at professional, senior level (Drew et al., 2019). Upon settling into her second year in the U20's squad (alongside her final year in college), Liv began to struggle to manage her education alongside her footballing commitments. Being a dual-career athlete comes with a number of demands including time management, physical presence at both college and training/games and developing psychosocial skills to succeed in both environments (Harrison et al., 2020). It was during this time in the season that support from both an education officer and a performance lifestyle advisor was crucial, to ensure that Liv felt she was in a position in which she could thrive and achieve in both environments. Reaching a balance between the two environments was almost impossible for Liv; if she wasn't focusing on performing well in exams, she was working to develop on the pitch, all whilst moving along the natural transition to officially reaching adulthood and managing the psychosocial and maturity developments that occur in line with this. It was here that wider multidisciplinary meetings became crucial, to allow the staffing team to align their understanding and priorities for development, and to ensure all support was coherent and united.

Liv began to voice her uncertainty around remaining in the U20's squad beyond this season if there was no interest or investment from the first-team environment. Her day-to-day existence at the academy began to become increasingly less enjoyable. Whilst she still loved to play and still wanted to secure a professional playing contract, Liv began to find the environment increasingly child-like, bereft of challenge or maturity and laden with mollycoddling. As her day-to-day existence at college offered almost too much in the way of challenge, her academy existence offered too little. It is here within men's football that players will enter an environment (often an U23's team or lower league senior team) that offers them the opportunity to transition from a development-focused phase to a post-academy, developing mastery phase (Richardson et al., 2012). This phase within the men's game sees players wrestle with isolation, lack of social support and insecurities. This phase also offers invaluable, vital opportunities to experience a competitive game structure, psychosocial maturity, different behavioural norms and demands and more professional, performance environments, all of which are seen to be key in the eyes of both players and coaches in making the transition to a senior playing level (Prendergast & Gibson, 2022). The setup of the development pathway within the women's game often does not afford such a clear developing mastery phase, and, as such, the opportunities that are offered for young, youth players in the men's game are not offered to Liv. This is something that both coaching and support staff were aware of, and, as a result, came together as a multidisciplinary team to work alongside one another to ensure that Liv's development, both on and off the pitch, was maximised during this period of her development. The team worked together to provide Liv with a physical and psychosocial development plan that aimed to prepare her for a senior environment. This plan included specific physical targets, discussions around the expectations and behaviours required at first-team level, consideration of psychological challenges that she may face in a first-team environment and development of psychosocial skills within her role as captain in the academy team. Throughout this time, the first-team captain began to take on more of a mentor role, giving the player the opportunity to interact with first-team players and to get an insight into what being a first-team player looked like day to day. It was during this phase, as a consequence of her consistent tactical, technical, physical and psychosocial development, that the first team began to show initial interest in Liv.

As initial interest in Liv grew, and the first team became more confident of her capabilities, she began to attend first-team training sessions. At first, she was invited to train up when players were injured, as a last-minute call up, but as she demonstrated her ability to fit in with the squad, to work hard and remain committed, she became a more regular figure in their weekly training schedule. Despite this interest bringing her hopes of a senior-team contract into slightly more focus, Liv found the transition difficult. In the initial few weeks, the excitement and apprehension outweighed the physical, emotional and time demands; however, as Liv became more settled, she began, like many other players who had made the transition before her, to feel the jump between the two environments (Andersson & Barker-Ruchti, 2019). Liv identified that, despite yearning for a more adult, grown-up environment, the social norms and behaviours of the senior team were very different to those of the academy. The pressures and expectations of the team became more player led, rather than reinforced solely by the coaches or other staff. The communication styles between players were harsher and more to the point, yet words were then easily forgotten once off the pitch. Players were expected to be the creators, the drivers and maintainers of the culture and values, something which Liv felt she had not yet earned the right to contribute to when players were calling one another out or discussing how better to apply and reinforce standards. Moreover, Liv felt uncomfortable with the increased level of autonomy due to her limited understanding of the unwritten rules and codes of conduct within the organisation. She was afraid that as the *newbie* (the newest and most inexperienced player), she would struggle to pick things up at the same speed as everyone else, leaving her with the label, "she's not ready yet". Liv explored her change in roles between the two teams and existential anxiety with her psychologist, starting to recognise adaptations to her identity as a player and the alternative roles that she had. At first, Liv was quite unsettled and unsure by this identity shift, but through discussions and reflections, she began to navigate and become more comfortable with this over time. Working to identify where future challenges, differences and areas for growth and adaptation might lie once in the first-team environment supported Liv through dealing with this period.

Liv's battle with belonging continued for much of her first full season with the first team. Despite this battle, coaching staff within the organisation would describe her as a well-integrated and valued member of the team. To Liv, this incongruence just further demonstrated that she was no longer seen or heard in the same way that she was when playing in the U20s.

On her first day back for preseason, the first-team manager sat down with Liv and made her aware that two European clubs (both overseas from her current club) had enquired about signing her on a season-long loan. The manager explained that, from a footballing perspective, the loan move would offer a level of exposure to first-team football that wouldn't be possible at her current club and would also provide a good opportunity for her to learn the workings of a different organisation. Liv's initial feelings were very different. She was now faced with the prospect of moving to an unfamiliar country, learning a new language, developing new social connections and reaching optimal levels of senior performance in an environment that was totally outside of her comfort zone, but ultimately, she would have little choice over whether the loan move would go ahead.

This case study highlights that career transitions are highly personal and despite being voluntary, planned and perceived in a positive light, they still have the potential to be an incredibly turbulent period in an athlete's life. Furthermore, when considering the practitioner approach, working on a case-by-case basis is vital. In order to navigate and optimise transition support, each individual's psychosocial characteristics, development and optimal environment should be carefully identified and considered (Stratford, 2023). We have purposely left Liv's story open as a metaphor to demonstrate the volatile and ever-changing nature of the first-team environment.

We hope to have highlighted that the shifting context of women's football is affording young players with opportunities that they only dreamed of 15–20 years ago; however, with this increased globalisation and professionalism comes a range of psychological, social and cultural challenges that players might not have experienced before. To this end, we stress the important need for women's football organisations to employ a team of practitioners responsible for supporting the psychological, social and educational development of players and to facilitate the creation of a culture where athletes are supported to develop holistically beyond performance measures and are encouraged to express their "true selves".

References

Andersson, R., & Barker-Ruchti, N. (2019). Career paths of Swedish top-level women soccer players. *Soccer & Society, 20*(6), 857–871. https://doi.org/10.1080/14660970.2018. 1431775

Champ, F. M., Ronkainen, N. J., Littlewood, M. A., & Eubank, M. (2020). Supporting identity development in talented youth athletes: Insights from existential and cultural psychological approaches. *Journal of Sport Psychology in Action, 11*(4), 219–232. https://doi. org/10.1080/21520704.2020.1825027

Culvin, A., & Bowes, A. (2023). Introduction: Women's football in a global, professional era. In A. Culvin & A. Bowes (Eds.), *Women's football in a global, professional era* (pp. 1–13). Emerald Publishing Limited. https://doi.org/10.1108/978-1-80071-052-820230001

Drew, K., Morris, R., Tod, D., & Eubank, M. (2019). A meta-study of qualitative research on the junior-to-senior transition in sport. *Psychology of Sport and Exercise, 45*, 101556. https://doi.org/10.1016/j.psychsport.2019.101556

Drole, K., Paravlic, A., Steffen, K., & Doupona, M. (2023). Effects of physical, psychosocial and dual-career loads on injuries and illnesses among elite handball players: Protocol of prospective cohort study. *BMJ Open, 13*(3), e069104. https://doi.org/10.1136/bmjopen-2022-069104

The Football Association. (2017). *The gameplan for growth the FA's strategy for women's and girls' football: 2017–2020.* https://www.thefa.com/-/media/thefacom-new/files/womens/fawomensstrategydocfinal-13317.ashx?la=en

The Football Association. (2019). *The gameplan for growth the FA's strategy for women's and girls' football: 2017–2020. Year one review and report.* https://www.thefa.com/-/media/thefacom-new/files/womens/2017-2018/the-gameplan-for-growth-year-one.ashx?la=en

The Football Association. (2021). *Inspiring positive change: The FA Strategy for Women's and Girls' Football: 2020–2024.* https://www.thefa.com/-/media/thefacom-new/files/about-the-fa/2020/inspiring-positive-change-womens-football-strategy-202024.ashx

Gledhill, A., Harwood, C., & Forsdyke, D. (2017). Psychosocial factors associated with talent development in football: A systematic review. *Psychology of Sport and Exercise, 31*, 93–112. https://doi.org/10.1016/j.psychsport.2017.04.002

Harrison, G. E., Vickers, E., Fletcher, D., & Taylor, G. (2020). Elite female soccer players' dual career plans and the demands they encounter. *Journal of Applied Sport Psychology, 34*(1), 133–154. https://doi.org/10.1080/10413200.2020.1716871

Harrison, G. E., Vickers, E., Fletcher, D., & Taylor, G. (2022). Elite female soccer players' dual career plans and the demands they encounter. *Journal of Applied Sport Psychology, 34*(1), 133–154. https://doi.org/10.1080/10413200.2020.1716871

Lally, P. (2007). Identity and athletic retirement: A prospective study. *Psychology of Sport and Exercise, 8*(1), 85–99. https://doi.org/10.1016/j.psychsport.2006.03.003

McGreary, M., Morris, R., & Eubank, M. (2021). Retrospective and concurrent perspectives of the transition into senior professional female football within the United Kingdom. *Psychology of Sport and Exercise, 53*, 101855. https://doi.org/10.1016/j.psychsport.2020.101855

Morris, R., Tod, D., & Eubank, M. (2017). From youth team to first team: An investigation into the transition experiences of young professional athletes in soccer. *International Journal of Sport and Exercise Psychology, 15*(5), 523–539. https://doi.org/10.1080/161 2197X.2016.1152992

Nesti, M. S. (2016). Working within professional football. In R. J. Schinke & D. Hackfort (Eds.), *Psychology in professional sports and the performing arts: Challenges and strategies* (pp. 206–218). Routledge.

Prendergast, G., & Gibson, L. (2022). A qualitative exploration of the use of player loans to supplement the talent development process of professional footballers in the under 23 age group of English football academies. *Journal of Sports Sciences*, *40*(4), 422–430. https://doi.org/10.1080/02640414.2021.1996985

Richardson, D., Littlewood, M., Nesti, M., & Benstead, L. (2012). An examination of the migratory transition of elite young European soccer players to the English Premier League. *Journal of Sports Sciences*, *30*(15), 1605–1618. https://doi.org/10.1080/0264 0414.2012.733017

Schlossberg, N. K. (1981). A model for analyzing human adaptation to transition. *The Counseling Psychologist*, *9*(2), 2–18. https://doi.org/10.1177/001100008100900202

Solmi, M., Radua, J., Olivola, M., Croce, E., Soardo, L., Salazar de Pablo, G., Il Shin, J., Kirkbride, J. B., Jones, P., Kim, J. H., Kim, J. Y., Carvalho, A. F., Seeman, M. V., Correll, C. U., & Fusar-Poli, P. (2022). Age at onset of mental disorders worldwide: Large-scale meta-analysis of 192 epidemiological studies. *Molecular Psychiatry*, *27*(1), 281–295. https://doi.org/10.1038/s41380-021-01161-7

Stambulova, N. B., Engström, C., Franck, A., Linnér, L., & Lindahl, K. (2015). Searching for an optimal balance: Dual career experiences of Swedish adolescent athletes. *Psychology of Sport and Exercise*, *21*, 4–14. https://doi.org/10.1016/j.psychsport.2014.08.009

Stratford, A. (2023). *Understanding the psycho-social and cultural aspects of professional women's football: An examination of the junior to senior transition* [PhD thesis, Liverpool John Moores University]. https://researchonline.ljmu.ac.uk/id/eprint/19606/

Vanden Auweele, Y. V., Boen, F., De Geest, A., & Feys, J. (2004). Judging bias in synchronized swimming: Open feedback leads to nonperformance-based conformity. *Journal of Sport and Exercise Psychology*, *26*(4), 561–571. https://doi.org/10.1123/jsep.26.4.561

Warriner, K., & Lavallee, D. (2008). The retirement experiences of elite female gymnasts: Self identity and the physical self. *Journal of Applied Sport Psychology*, *20*(3), 301–317. https://doi.org/10.1080/10413200801998564

12

MENTAL HEALTH IN PROFESSIONAL WOMEN'S FOOTBALL

Francesca M. Champ and Kristin McGinty-Minister

Aims of the chapter

In line with the overriding objectives of the book surrounding knowledge and application, this chapter has two primary aims:

1 To offer a critical presentation of current understandings of mental health in women's professional football.
2 To draw upon the authors' experiences of working within the game and prevalent scientific knowledge to offer practical guidance on how to design and implement culturally bespoke mental health strategies.

Introduction

There is no question that mental health and mental illness now lie at the top of the agenda for many sports organisations, clubs and researchers (Kuettel & Larsen, 2020). As a result, mental health position statements have been released by several sports organisations such as the International Olympic Committee (Reardon et al., 2019) in the last five years with the aim of providing better mental health support for athletes during and after their career. Such initiatives and the substantial increase in interest surrounding mental health in sport have occurred as a consequence of several top-level performers speaking out about their mental struggles. One of the first and most well-known figures to speak out in women's football was ex-England international Kelly Smith. Upon retiring, Kelly revealed experiencing suicidal thoughts, depression and alcoholism after struggling to cope with long-term injuries (Dickinson, 2017). The number of professional women footballers speaking about mental illness has continued to grow worldwide with a vast

DOI: 10.4324/9781003381914-12

array of contributing factors being cited, many of which will be presented in this chapter.

Despite the increased attention and focus on mental health in sport, there are still several competing bodies of thought around what the term *mental health* actually means. For example some definitions place a strong focus on the absence of mental illness, whereas others incorporate biological, psychological, emotional and social factors to focus on wellbeing more broadly. In this chapter, we adopt the World Health Organization's (2022) definition of mental health as "a state of well-being in which every individual realises his or her own potential, can cope with the normal stresses of life, can work productively and fruitfully, and is able to make a contribution to his or her community" (p. 231). In line with this conceptualisation, it is important to recognise that mental health is not the absence of mental illness but the presence of social, emotional and psychological wellbeing. Mental health and mental illness are separate but interrelated concepts, both of which contribute to a player's overall wellbeing (Keyes, 2014). Keyes suggests that mental health exists on a continuum from "mentally healthy" through to "mental illness" and stresses the important point that it is both plausible and entirely normal for an athlete to fluctuate across the dual continuum of mental health during their sporting careers. Subsequently, some players who are clinically diagnosed with mental disorders can, and do, recover to experience periods of optimal mental health. Likewise, some players may (for a short time) perform at their best in their sporting life even if they have a clinical mental disorder, as sport may serve as a coping mechanism.

Mental health in women's football

Across the elite athlete population, the prevalence of mental illness is in line with that of the general population, at 5–35% annually (Perry et al., 2021). While it has been suggested that, at any one time, a vast array of factors (e.g. personal, family, societal, economic, cultural) will influence mental health, there are undoubtedly characteristics which make certain populations more at risk. For example Bellis et al. (2012) recognised that age and sex are important risk factors. More specifically, young adults aged 16–24 and 25–44 are most at risk; additionally, women in these age categories are three times more likely than men to demonstrate symptoms of common mental disorders. Women footballers are likely to reach "peak" levels of performance at around 25 years of age (Barreira, 2016), meaning that they are likely to be striving for performance excellence at a time when they are most vulnerable to mental illness (Perry et al., 2021). Beable et al. (2017) supported this suggestion and identified that 21% of elite women athletes experience moderate depressive symptoms with individuals under the age of 25 years, with those pursuing a dual career being the most at risk. Women's football researchers have adopted quantitative methods to explore the prevalence of mental illness and help-seeking intentions. Generally, the prevalence of moderate and severe depressive symptoms is similar across studies that have been conducted with women players in the top leagues in England, Germany (e.g. Junge & Prinz, 2018) and Australia (Kilic et al., 2021). However, the prevalence of disordered-eating symptoms varied greatly depending on where the participants were playing. To date, not enough research exists to critically discuss potential causation factors.

Globally, women's football is currently in the midst of a huge shift in professionalisation (discussed in Chapter 1). The opportunity for senior players to move away from being dual-career athletes (a known risk factor for mental ill-health) and focus solely on their footballing careers, coupled with greater access to high-quality resources and facilities, has facilitated the potential for women footballers to flourish. However, Culvin (2023) recognised that the higher levels of professionalisation can actually have the reverse effect on mental health and mental illness if the increased pressure and expectations placed on players to perform at the top level are not matched with appropriate financial, psychosocial and physical support. More specifically, Culvin (2023) argued that women footballers are now experiencing more inconsistent workplaces, financial instability and a lack of support after their playing career, which have negatively influenced mental health.

In addition to the stressors mentioned earlier, players are likely to encounter a variety of personal, competitive, organisational and societal stressors coupled with negative stigmas and stereotypes surrounding help seeking. Each of the aforementioned stressors has the potential to negatively impact mental health or lead to the onset of common mental disorder symptomology (Kuettel & Larsen, 2020). In adopting a person-centred approach to understanding mental health, it is important that we recognise that elite footballers are first and foremost human beings, and, as such, experience many of the same day-to-day personal stressors (e.g. poor sleep, losing keys, stuck in traffic when running late) and major life events (e.g. bereavement, relationship breakdown) as do the rest of the population. However, players cope with such events and a range of other more nuanced stressors both in the public eye and while being heavily scrutinised. It is widely accepted that players often have a non-linear pathway to sporting success and, as such, will inevitably experience turbulent and challenging periods, which might result in the onset of mental illness or compromised mental health (Kuettel & Larsen, 2020). Some of the competitive (athlete-specific) risk factors for compromised mental health or mental illness include injury, performance failure, overtraining, meeting expectations of self and others and extended travel away from home (Kuettel & Larsen, 2020). At an organisational level, women footballers have spoken out about how the organisational culture within many professional women's clubs has been detrimental to their mental health. For example former England player Fara Williams described how a culture of "weight shaming" has contributed to players experiencing disordered eating and distorted perceptions of body image (BBC Sport, 2022) (see also Chapter 9 on eating disorders). Additional organisational risk factors include a "win-at-all-costs" approach, lack of role clarity, conflicting values and beliefs, ineffective communication/poor relationships, negative stigmas/stereotypes surrounding help seeking and isolation (Champ et al., 2019).

So far, we have placed a focus on negative contributing factors to compromised mental health and mental illness symptomology or disorder; however, it is important to recognise that there are several protective factors that are positively related to player mental health and that are protective against mental illness. It is important to note that this section is significantly shorter than the previous section; there is, therefore, a need for research on mental health in football to broaden its focus and place a greater emphasis on what contributes to footballers' functioning at the top end of the mental health spectrum (i.e. thriving). Kuettel and Larsen (2020) noted that a supportive and safe environment within which athletes feel trusted, valued and able to develop positive social relationships has been proven to facilitate positive mental health. Furthermore, at a personal level, several factors such as feeling competent, in control, happy and having access to appropriate support were all positively related to athletes' mental health (Kuettel & Larsen, 2020). Pascoe et al. (2022) postulate that proactively addressing gendered stressors might contribute positively to mental health outcomes for women athletes.

Designing a mental health strategy

In this section, we critically explore how professional football clubs can design culturally informed strategies to both promote thriving and prevent the onset of mental illness in players. Although the primary aim of any mental health strategy should be centred around wellbeing, it is important to recognise that, when done properly, the introduction of such initiatives should also facilitate the creation of a sustainable culture of performance excellence. We propose that mental health strategies should consist of three core components: (1) education and awareness, (2) identifying, supporting and referring individuals and (3) a multi-disciplinary team approach. Through each of the components, we aim to adopt an ecological systems model for athlete mental health (Purcell et al., 2019), in which the wider ecological factors that can contribute to mental health are acknowledged.

Before discussing each of the three components in more detail, we first present a quote from Brene Brown's famous TED Talk that resonates with both authors and has acted as a pillar for the creation of the components, "Vulnerability is the birthplace of courage, creativity and change" (Brown, 2012). Subsequently, psychological safety is an important first step to focus on when designing a mental health strategy. Put simply, psychological safety exists on a continuum (much like mental health) and is the belief that an environment is safe for interpersonal risk taking (Edmondson, 1999). Responsibility for the creation of a psychologically safe environment lies with all of its members; however, those in positions of perceived power should take responsibility to ensure that (1) all individuals feel free to take risks without fear of retribution, (2) there is no fear of psychological or physical threat or harm within the environment (e.g. embarrassment, rejection, punishment), (3) there are frequent opportunities for positive social interactions that help to create a sense of "family", (4) there is an active promotion of positive emotional states (e.g. through the encouragement of positive wellbeing) and (5) equality, diversity and inclusivity are placed at the forefront of the organisation's values, initiatives and behaviours (Vella et al., 2021). If each of these factors is in place, those within professional football clubs are more likely to have a genuine interest and investment in each other, have positive intentions for each other and demonstrate respect, even in the face of challenge. Moreover, these characteristics lie at the heart of creating a person-centred strategy to support mental health. While these concepts seem at odds with many environments that are central to men's football (e.g. Champ et al., 2019), many of these concepts reflect behaviours and ideas women have been socialised to express or internalise (e.g. sensitivity, empathy and openness).

Education and awareness

The education and awareness component of the mental health strategy relates to developing the knowledge and understanding of all stakeholders around mental health in women's football and ensuring that there is a coherent and aligned approach within clubs on how to support mental health. A first step to knowledge enhancement relates to the ways in which mental health is spoken about and understood at individual and cultural levels. However, in writing this section, it is important to recognise that very few professional football clubs will have the funding/resources to implement everything that we suggest. Subsequently, alternative sources of support are also noted.

Mental health literacy

Mental health literacy (MHL) is an integral component to psychological safety in sporting environments that often leverage performance and stigmatise discussions surrounding mental health (Vella et al., 2021). For the purpose of this chapter, we propose that MHL is knowledge and beliefs about the broad spectrum of mental health and mental illness that aids in the prevention, recognition and management of compromised mental health or mental illness (Jorm et al., 1997), as well as the promotion of the more positive aspects of mental health (e.g. wellbeing) in order to promote holistic, positive human functioning (McGinty-Minister et al., 2023). Mental health literacy is associated with better mental health outcomes (Breslin et al., 2017), increased resilience (Vella et al., 2021), improved recognition of mental illness symptomology (Breslin et al., 2017), improved help-seeking behaviours amongst athletes (Bu et al., 2020; Vella et al., 2021), better knowledge and understanding surrounding referrals (Breslin et al., 2017) and importantly reduced stigma surrounding mental health and mental illness (e.g. Gorczynski et al., 2019). On the other hand, organisations with low MHL limit help seeking and compromise the mental health of their athletes.

Mental health literacy is both a deeply personal and a culturally specific concept that must adapt to the needs of each organisation (Gorczynski et al., 2021). There are several ways organisations and stakeholders can improve their MHL, thereby improving mental health and mental illness outcomes. Importantly, researchers (e.g. McGinty-Minister et al., 2023; O'Gorman et al., 2020) have demonstrated that those with the most influence over athletes' mental health (such as stakeholders) often demonstrate the least MHL, regularly leading to poor mental health outcomes in athletes and contributing to organisational cultures grounded in stigma and suspicion. At a minimum, it is imperative that stakeholders engage in appropriate training by reputable organisations, so that they are aware of and are equipped to deal with a potential mental-illness crisis. Additionally, further education surrounding mental health and mental illness would aid in individual understanding and reducing stigma that might influence stakeholder practice. Individuals should make themselves aware of their club's referral process and engage with any relevant practitioners (e.g. psychologists, psychiatrists) within their organisation to learn more about how they can improve their own MHL. If a club does not have access to a referral pathway, conversations with the relevant in-house medical professional would be a good starting point. Similar to psychological safety, while there is an individual burden to improve their MHL, responsibility falls upon leaders and the organisation to ensure that MHL is an integral cultural component. Clubs should rely on (and trust) sport psychologists, sport psychiatrists and clinical psychiatrists to evaluate MHL and design and implement MHL interventions (Gorczynski et al., 2021); this might include cultural shifts, the addition of new staff, changes to referral practices and educational workshops for players, stakeholders and management. However, the introduction of guest sessions by relevant organisations/individuals and/or the use of free online resources to aid MHL would be a positive first step for organisations with fewer resources. Organisations should understand sex-specific factors that may influence mental health and mental illness (e.g. sexism, stressors surrounding motherhood) and ensure that these are accounted for in their MHL interventions. Importantly, stakeholders and organisations should be prepared to continuously evolve their MHL as they would other aspects of health and performance. Organisations should recognise that the mental health of each person within an organisation contributes to organisational MHL, culture and performance and prioritise the mental health of stakeholders as well as players.

To further raise awareness of mental health and develop MHL, guest sessions could be utilised for players and staff. Our suggestion would be that such sessions are delivered by a variety of individuals/organisations across a player's microsystem (e.g. fellow performers, sports medicine specialists), exosystem and macrosystem. These sessions may provide the opportunity for both story-sharing and the dissemination of relevant information.

Resources

The second aspect of the education and awareness strand relates to resources that are housed within clubs and will likely contribute to a favourable *early-intervention* approach, where clubs can work to optimise mental health and respond rapidly to mental illness. More specifically, we recommend that all professional football clubs invest in an online hub or portal, where appropriate mental health resources can be stored and accessed by players and staff. While the exact nature of these resources should be culturally bespoke to each club, they should aim to provide the initial building blocks for more informed and literate organisations. Some basic ideas that might be utilised include the following: What is mental health? How to start a conversation about mental health? Taking the first steps to getting help, How to spot the signs that someone is struggling, Mental health in professional women's football, Common mental disorders and Supporting your teammates. Additionally, professional players can access mental health support through bespoke companies (e.g. in England, Sporting Chance as part of the membership to the Players Football Association, https://www.thepfa.com/players/wellbeing). Clubs should ensure that they draw upon both internal and external resources so that the best support is available.

Identifying, supporting and referring individuals

As part of this component of the mental health strategy, it is important that all players (and staff) are made explicitly aware of who the mental health professionals are within the organisation and how to access them.

Mental health screening

It is our recommendation that formal and informal screening, to help players understand their mental health and allow for the early identification of those who need additional support, should be included routinely as part of the players' involvement with a professional football club. Informal mental health screening could consist of a wellbeing check-in with the club's sport psychologist or club doctor on a four- to six-weekly basis. However, more formal mental health screening should be utilised during appropriate breaks during the season (i.e. start of preseason, Christmas break) and should be designed to (1) help players develop a greater understanding of their own mental health and (2) allow for the early identification of any mental health challenges or mental illness symptomology or disorder. Any screening psychometric (e.g. Generalised Anxiety Disorder-7 Assessment, Patient Health Questionnaire-9) that is utilised should be validated with the athletic population and disseminated by an individual with the relevant credentials (e.g. accredited sport psychologist or club doctor). In addition to the aforementioned screening, we recommend that players be screened for mental illness during times when they may be classed as at "higher risk" for the onset of common mental disorder symptomology (e.g. exposure to career transitions) (Champ et al., 2019).

Triangulation

In adopting an ecological framework to support the design of a mental health strategy, we recognise that all individuals within a player's macrosystem (e.g. teammates, coaches, medical staff) are in a position to notice important "changes" in the way that a player may behave/present inside and outside of the football environment. More specifically, a coach may identify that a player is unusually late for training over a number of days, or the sport scientist might recognise that a player's scores have dipped on the daily wellness monitoring (e.g. low mood, higher fatigue and reduced sleep duration/quality). With the appropriate training and resources, we suggest that colleagues can have a crucial role in (1) identifying an individual who might be struggling, (2) starting a conversation about mental health and subsequently (3) linking them to the appropriate professional care. Data that are gathered and triangulated by those within an organisation who are responsible for mental health support should be critically discussed before deciding on which intervention is most appropriate. Importantly, a key factor to successful triangulation is MHL at a cultural level so stakeholders (1) know what to look for regarding compromised wellbeing or mental illness symptomology and (2) exhibit behaviours that encourage help seeking amongst their players (e.g. minimising stigma).

Referral pathway

We present a basic schematic for a referral pathway that might be adopted by professional football clubs to support those who are suffering from mild and moderate symptoms of mental illness (Figure 12.1). As a first port of call, and dependent on resources, support would ideally be provided in house by the club's team of mental health professionals and be monitored appropriately with the inclusion of the player. Sometimes, a multidisciplinary team approach to mental health support is most appropriate; for example if a player is presenting with disordered eating symptoms, the club doctor, nutritionist and sport psychologist might work together to support the player's presenting problem. However, when necessary, a mental health professional within the club (i.e. sport psychologist or doctor) should make a referral for specialist mental healthcare. In line with relevant codes of practice, this should be done when a player poses a risk to themselves and/or to others. Guidance should be in place for all referrals around the level of contact that is expected between the player and the club and the level/type of information that will be shared between the provider of the specialist mental healthcare and the in-house support team. However, if such resources are not available, clubs should ensure that players are aware of and understand how to seek support from reputable mental health charities (e.g. Mind UK, Mental Health America).

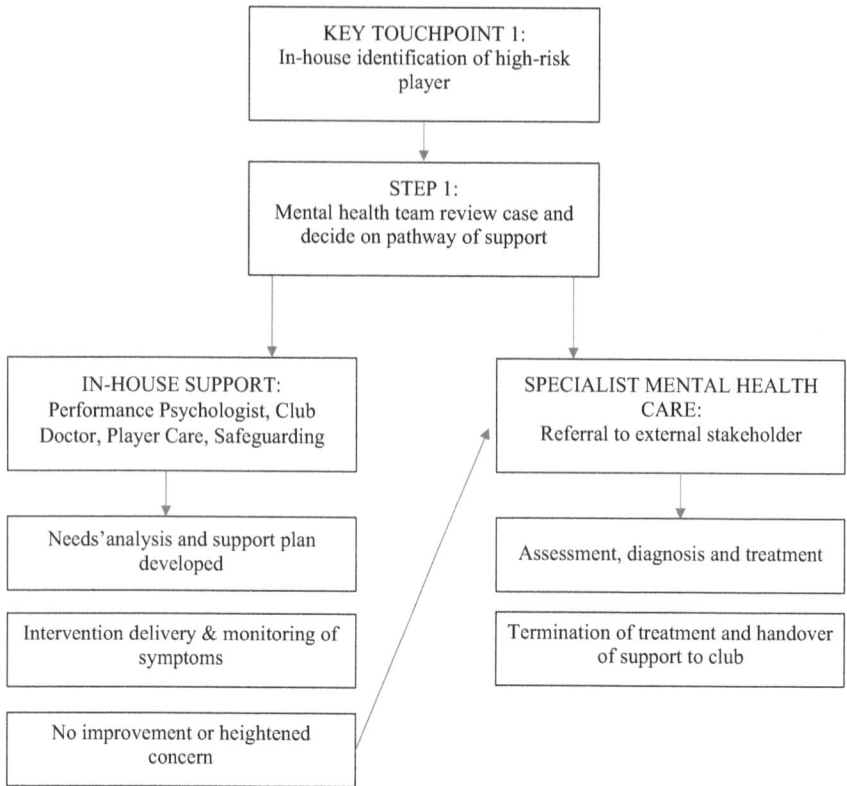

FIGURE 12.1   Template mental health referral pathway.

For any player who has been unable to train/play due to mental illness, a protocol should be in place to facilitate their return to the environment and training itself. The primary aim of this protocol is to ensure that the player has a successful return to sport without compromising their mental health or exacerbating mental illness.

A collaborative responsibility for supporting mental health

While an entire chapter (or a book) can be written about a collaborative approach to supporting mental health, we think it is important to present a brief outline of the concept, particularly due to its important links with MHL and psychological safety. Although it is important to emphasise that specific mental health support should only be provided by recognised professionals, we believe that all stakeholders within an organisation have an important role in facilitating positive mental health. For example in line with the principles of MHL and psychological safety, all individuals should take responsibility to actively challenge discriminatory behaviour, negative stigmas and stereotypes about mental health and women's football more broadly. It is generally accepted that there is a close connection between mental health and equality, diversity and inclusion (e.g. Mental Health Foundation). More specifically, individuals from minority backgrounds are more likely to experience compromised mental health or mental illness and less likely to engage in help seeking (Parra et al., 2023); this impact is likely to be minimised in mental-health-literate environments that prioritise help seeking. Importantly, informal or formal multidisciplinary teams are integral for triangulation and can provide valuable information about players' mental health, mental-illness symptomology and lives more broadly.

Finally, in adopting an ecological systems' approach to supporting mental health, it is important that we recognise the potential positive influence players can have on one another. For example new signings and younger players who have recently made the junior-to-senior transition may be introduced to a "buddy" system to orient them into the environment. The aim of assigning new players to a buddy is to facilitate the development of social connections, provide players with a point of contact for any questions that they might have and share experiences. Moreover, it is hoped that a buddy system would also facilitate an early intervention approach to mental health with a buddy being the first point of contact who can raise any potential concerns or changes in a player's behaviour.

Monitoring and evaluation

As with any intervention, it is imperative that any mental health strategy that is introduced/delivered by clubs is monitored and evaluated with the aim of determining effectiveness and efficiency. We would suggest that such evaluation occurs annually as part of the season review and that multistakeholder perceptions are attained using quantitative and qualitative measures.

Conclusion

In summary, mental health and mental illness in women's football are complex and highly personalised constructs, which must be understood in the context of the broader elite sports ecology and society. Women footballers are not immune to mental illness; rather, they face a number of gender, age and sport-specific stressors that might perpetuate compromised mental health and mental illness. Given the increased professionalisation of the game (and the challenges that this brings), we suggest that all professional women's clubs work with mental health practitioners to design a culturally bespoke mental health strategy that emphasises the prevention of mental illness as well as facilitates the promotion of optimal mental health.

References

Barreira, J. (2016). Age of peak performance of elite women's soccer players. *International Journal of Sports Science*, *6*(3), 121–124. https://doi.org/10.5923/j.sports.20160603.09

BBC Sport. (2022, June 1o). Williams says WSL sides put players in "fat club". *BBC Sport*. https://www.bbc.co.uk/sport/football/61760136

Beable, S., Fulcher, M., Lee, A. C., & Hamilton, B. (2017). SHARPSports mental health awareness research project: Prevalence and risk factors of depressive symptoms and life stress in elite athletes. *Journal of Science and Medicine in Sport*, *20*(12), 1047–1052. https://doi.org/10.1016/j.jsams.2017.04.018

Bellis, M. A., Lowery, Deacon, L., Stansfield, J., & Perkins, C. (2012). Variations in risk and protective factors for life satisfaction and mental wellbeing with deprivation: A cross-sectional study. *BMC Public Health*, *12*(1), 492. https://doi.org/10.1186/1471-2458-12-492

Breslin, G., Shannon, S., Haughey, T., Donnelly, P., & Leavey, G. (2017). A systematic review of interventions to increase awareness of mental health and well-being in athletes, coaches and officials. *Systematic Reviews*, *6*(1), 177–177. https://doi.org/10.1186/s13643-017-0568-6

Brown, B. (2012). *Daring greatly: How the courage to be vulnerable transforms the way we live, love, parent, and lead*. Gotham Books.

Bu, D., Chung, P. K., Zhang, C. Q., Liu, J., & Wang, X. (2020). Mental health literacy intervention on help-seeking in athletes: A systematic review. *International Journal of Environmental Research and Public Health*, *17*(19), 7263–7217. https://doi.org/10.3390/ijerph17197263

Champ, F. M., Nesti, M. S., Ronkainen, N. J., Tod, D. A., & Littlewood, M. A. (2019). An exploration of the experiences of elite youth footballers: The impact of organizational culture. *Journal of Applied Sport Psychology*, *32*(2), 146–167. https://doi.org/10.1080/10413200.2018.1514429

Culvin, A. (2023). Football as work: The lived realities of professional women footballers in England. *Managing Sport and Leisure*, *28*(6), 684–697. https://doi.org/10.1080/23750472.2021.1959384

Dickinson, M. (2017, January 11). Kelly Smith chasing the dream after nightmare years. *The Times*. https://www.thetimes.co.uk/article/kelly-smith-chasing-the-dream-again-after-nightmare-years-57wf96rg9

Edmondson, A. (1999). Psychological safety and learning behavior in work teams. *Administrative Science Quarterly*, *44*(2), 350–383. https://doi.org/10.2307/2666999

Gorczynski, P., Currie, A., Gibson, K., Gouttebarge, V., Hainline, B., Castaldelli-Maia, J. M., Mountjoy, M., Purcell, R., Reardon, C. L., Rice, S., & Swartz, L. (2021). Developing mental health literacy and cultural competence in elite sport. *Journal of Applied Sport Psychology*, *33*(4), 387–401. https://doi.org/10.1080/10413200.2020.1720045

Gorczynski, P., Gibson, K., Thelwell, R., Papathomas, A., Harwood, C., & Kinnafick, F. (2019). The BASES expert statement on mental health literacy in elite sport. *The Sport and Exercise Scientist*, *59*, 6–7. https://www.bases.org.uk/imgs/7879_bas_expert_statement__pages_735.pdf

Jorm, A. F., Korten, A. E., Jacomb, P. A., Christensen, H., Rodgers, B., & Pollitt, P. (1997). "Mental health literacy": A survey of the public's ability to recognise mental disorders and their beliefs about the effectiveness of treatment. *The Medical Journal of Australia*, *166*(4), 182–186. https://doi.org/10.5694/j.1326-5377.1997.tb140071.x

Junge, A., & Prinz, B. (2018). Depression and anxiety symptoms in 17 teams of female football players including 10 German first league teams. *British Journal of Sports Medicine*, *53*(8), 471–477. https://doi.org/10.1136/bjsports-2017-098033

Keyes, C. L. M. (2014). Mental health as a complete state: How the salutogenic perspective completes the picture. In G. F. Bauer & O. Hämmig (Eds.), *Bridging occupational, organizational and public health: A transdisciplinary approach* (pp. 179–192). Springer. https://doi.org/10.1007/978-94-007-5640-3_11

Kilic, Ö., Carmody, S., Upmeijer, J., Kerkhoffs, G. M. M. J., Purcell, R., Rice, S., & Gouttebarge, V. (2021). Prevalence of mental health symptoms among male and female Australian professional footballers. *BMJ Open Sport & Exercise Medicine, 7*(3), e001043. https://doi.org/10.1136/bmjsem-2021-001043

Kuettel, A., & Larsen, C. H. (2020). Risk and protective factors for mental health in elite athletes: A scoping review. *International Review of Sport and Exercise Psychology, 13*(1), 231–265. https://doi.org/10.1080/1750984x.2019.1689574

McGinty-Minister, K. L., Champ, F., Eubank, M., Littlewood, M., & Whitehead, A. (2023). Stakeholder conceptualizations of mental health and mental illness in English premier league football academies. *Managing Sport and Leisure*, 1–20. https://doi.org/10.1080/23750472.2023.2239259

O'Gorman, J., Partington, M., Potrac, P., & Nelson, L. (2020). Translation, intensification and fabrication: Professional football academy coaches' enactment of the elite player performance plan. *Sport Education and Society, 26*(3), 309–325. https://doi.org/10.1080/13573322.2020.1726313

Parra, L. A., Spahr, C. M., Goldbach, J. T., Bray, B. C., Kipke, M. D., & Slavich, G. M. (2023). Greater lifetime stressor exposure is associated with poorer mental health among sexual minority people of color. *Journal of Clinical Psychology, 79*(4), 1130–1155. https://doi.org/10.1002/jclp.23463

Pascoe, M., Pankowiak, A., Woessner, M. N., Brockett, C. L., Hanlon, C., Spaaij, R., Robertson, S., McLachlan, F., & Parker, A. (2022). Gender-specific psychosocial stressors influencing mental health among women elite and semielite athletes: A narrative review. *British Journal of Sports Medicine, 56*(23), 1381–31387. https://doi.org/10.1136/bjsports-2022-105540

Perry, C., Champ, F., Macbeth, J. L., & Spandler, H. (2021). Mental health and elite female athletes: A scoping review. *Psychology of Sport and Exercise, 56*, 101961. https://doi.org/10.1016/j.psychsport.2021.101961

Purcell, R., Gwyther, K., & Rice, S. (2019). Mental health in elite athletes: Increased awareness requires an early intervention framework to respond to athlete needs. *Sports Medicine—Open, 5*, 46. https://doi.org/10.1186/s40798-019-0220-1

Reardon, C. L., Hainline, B., Aron, C. M., Baron, D., Baum, A. L., Bindra, A., Budgett, R., Campriani, N., Castaldelli-Maia, J. M., Currie, A., Derevensky, J. L., Glick, I. D., Gorczynski, P., Gouttebarge, V., Grandner, M. A., Han, D. H., McDuff, D., Mountjoy, M., Polat, A., . . . Engebretsen, L. (2019). Mental health in elite athletes: International Olympic Committee consensus statement (2019). *British Journal of Sports Medicine, 53*(11), 667–699. https://doi.org/10.1136/bjsports-2019-100715

Vella, S. A., Swann, C., Batterham, M., Boydell, K. M., Eckermann, S., Ferguson, H., Fogarty, A., Hurley, D., Liddle, S. K., Lonsdale, C., Miller, A., Noetel, M., Okley, A. D., Sanders, T., Schweickle, M. J., Telenta, J., & Deane, F. P. (2021). An intervention for mental health literacy and resilience in organized sports. *Medicine & Science in Sports & Exercise, 53*(1), 139–149. https://doi.org/10.1249/MSS.0000000000002433

World Health Organization. (2022, June 17). *Mental health*. https://www.who.int/news-room/fact-sheets/detail/mental-health-strengthening-our-response

13

BREAST HEALTH

Nicola Brown, Melissa Jones and Joanna Wakefield-Scurr

Introduction

Research in breast biomechanics has progressed significantly over the past two decades, leading to a better understanding of breast movement during sports activities and improved breast-support options for women. Given the intermittent physical nature of football, requiring multiple and constant changes of direction, accelerations and decelerations, breast movement is an important consideration for footballers. However, there is still much to learn about breast biomechanics within football specifically. Furthermore, despite breasts being vulnerable to injury, research regarding sports-related breast injuries is in its infancy. The first sports bra was patented in 1977, designed to provide breast support and limit breast movement during sporting activities. The sports bra industry has since diversified, offering elite athletes and recreational exercisers many advancements in sports bra design. However, the selection of a well-fitting sports bra can be challenging, and it is estimated that up to 59% of athletes are reported to wear ill-fitting sports bras, which can compromise performance and comfort while wearing the bra (Brisbine et al., 2020b; Wakefield-Scurr, Sanchez, Jones, Hockley, et al., 2022). Additionally, despite the recognised benefits of appropriate breast support, there is wide variation across clubs and governing bodies (including the English Football Association, Union of European Football Associations and Fédération Internationale de Football Association) with regard to the provision of evidence-based guidelines on breast support for footballers.

In this chapter, we provide a summary of the negative consequences associated with breast movement and present evidence on the benefits of wearing appropriate breast support when exercising, with a specific focus on how the latter can influence participation and performance. We then present information on breast-support

DOI: 10.4324/9781003381914-13

options, highlighting specific sports bra considerations for footballers and how to obtain correct bra fit. Lastly, we consider the importance of breast education and awareness initiatives and provide practical recommendations to facilitate discussions between players and coaches/medical staff about breast-related issues.

Aims of the chapter

The aims of this chapter are as follows:

1 To describe the anatomy of the breast to aid understanding of why and how the breast moves during sports activities and why the breast is vulnerable to injury.
2 To present evidence of the health and performance benefits of wearing appropriate breast support during football.
3 To provide insight into the breast-support options available to footballers, with a focus on design features suitable for footballers and how to obtain optimal bra fit.
4 To highlight the importance of breast education and awareness initiatives.
5 To provide practical recommendations for those working within women's football to support footballers in managing breast-related issues.

Breast anatomy: what is the problem?

The location and anatomy of the female breast cause a number of challenges for sportswomen. Composed predominantly of fat and glandular tissue, the breast has limited connection to the pectoral muscles below it (McGhee & Steele, 2020). Anatomical support for the breast comes from the breast skin and the internal fascia tissue (McGhee & Steele, 2020), both of which lack mechanical strength, making the breast highly deformable. This limited natural breast support allows independent breast movement to occur during dynamic activities such as those that occur in football training and match-play, with the breast moving in multiple directions (Haake & Scurr, 2010). Movement of the breast during sports activities is associated with breast pain (Mason et al., 1999), potential breast tissue damage (Norris et al., 2020) and embarrassment (Scurr et al., 2016), all of which can deter women from participating in football. One in four adult women (Burnett et al., 2015) and half of adolescent girls (Scurr et al., 2016) report that their breasts negatively affect their participation in sport. Research also indicates that breast movement can cause alterations in physiological variables, such as breathing frequency (White et al., 2011), absolute and relative oxygen consumption (Fong & Powell, 2022) and biomechanical variables, such as upper body running profiles (Milligan et al., 2015), which can have potential performance implications in football.

In addition to limited anatomical support, breasts lack musculoskeletal protection, making them more susceptible to direct impact or compression from external sources such as contact with another player or objects during sports activities (Brisbine et al., 2019, 2020a; Wakefield-Scurr et al., 2023). The extensive superficial capillary network of the breast increases the risk of contusions and hae-matomas from such impacts (Holschen, 2004), and breast impacts can result in localised pain, swelling, discolouration and tenderness. Although yet to be considered in football, exposure to physical contacts and tackles in the game may place players at risk of breast injury.

Breast movement and benefits of external breast support

Despite the lack of specific research on breast movement in women's football, considerable breast movement is reported during other sports when the breast is not properly supported. Up to 15 cm of unsupported breast movement has been reported during running (Scurr et al., 2010) and 19 cm during jumping activities (Bridgman et al., 2010). Furthermore, it is estimated that breasts can bounce as many as 10,000 times during a 60-min slow run (McGhee & Steele, 2020) and that, if not properly supported, breasts can experience accelerations of up to ~25.9 m/s^{-2} (Norris et al., 2020). Given that during 90 min of match-play elite women footballers typically cover total distances of ~10,000 m and engage in up to 200 accelerations (>1 m s^{-2}) and 170 decelerations (<−1 m s^{-2}) (Griffin et al., 2020), external breast support (e.g. a sports bra) is required to reduce breast motion associated with playing football. Additionally, women officiating in football matches have been reported to cover total distances of ~1,000 m and reach maximal speeds of 25 km/hr (Sánchez et al., 2022); the importance of breast support for this group should also be considered.

Sports bras can be effective at reducing breast movement during running (Mason et al., 1999) and jumping (Mills et al., 2015), some of the main physical movements observed in football. This movement reduction can reduce movement-related breast pain (Scurr et al., 2010), which is reported to be experienced by 44–72% of active women (McGhee & Steele, 2020). Sports bras also reduce the level of breast skin strain experienced during sporting activities, thus reducing breast skin-damage risk and protecting the health of the tissue (Norris et al., 2020). Further health benefits of appropriate breast support include improved posture (Jones et al., 2021), reduced musculoskeletal pain symptoms (Schinkel-Ivy & Drake, 2016; Spencer & Briffa, 2013), reduced embarrassment and increased willingness to exercise (Risius et al., 2016). From a sports performance perspective, appropriate breast support has a positive effect on running mechanics (Milligan et al., 2015), upper body muscle activity (Milligan et al., 2014), gait parameters (White et al., 2009) and breathing frequency (White et al., 2011). Appropriate breast support may also play an important role from an injury-prevention perspective, with recent research establishing that lower levels of breast support are associated with knee joint and trunk biomechanical profiles, which are suggested to increase anterior-cruciate ligament injury risk (Fong et al., 2022).

Breast injuries

Sports injury surveillance systems have narrow injury definitions (Clarsen & Bahr, 2014), and currently there are no injury surveillance systems within women's football that incorporate breast injuries. Consequently, specific data on the prevalence and mechanisms of breast injuries within women's football are not currently available. In a retrospective study of 194 collegiate athletes that included footballers, 48% reported having experienced a breast injury, with 18% perceiving breast injuries to negatively affect their performance (Smith et al., 2018). Despite this finding, only 10% of these injuries were reported at the time and only 2% received treatment (Smith et al., 2018). Furthermore, in a study of 297 Australian athletes competing in contact football codes (Australian Football, Rugby League, Rugby Union [XVs)] and Rugby 7s), a high prevalence of breast issues was reported (58%), with players reporting to have modified their sporting activity (e.g. running and tackling) to prevent breast impacts; yet half of 242 coaches and medical professionals surveyed were unaware that breast issues were a problem, with three-quarters estimating that fewer than 5% of players would experience a breast injury (Brisbine et al., 2020a). Even with suitable reporting mechanisms, evidence indicates that athletes may be reluctant to report breast injuries sustained during sports, particularly to staff of the opposite sex (Drummond et al., 2007). During football, breast impacts may occur intentionally, when catching the ball on the chest, or unintentionally, during direct impacts from the ball, players or the ground. Additionally, frictional breast injuries may occur as a result of ill-fitting breast support, irritating the skin (Brown et al., 2014). Breast padding or protection has yet to be considered but has been recommended in contact football codes (Brisbine et al., 2020b).

Given the limited focus on women's football to date, research is needed to establish the prevalence, causes and performance effects of breast injuries within the game, in addition to exploring the perceptions of players, coaches and other staff towards breast injuries. Comprehensive, robust and consistent reporting of sports-related breast injuries is required to develop a full understanding of the issue and to make future recommendations for the management of breast injuries in football.

Types of sports bra and design features

The sports bra market has expanded to include various styles and designs to accommodate different activities, body types and personal preferences. Furthermore, technological advancements in construction techniques, fabric materials and design elements have enhanced the level of support offered by sports bras. There are currently three distinct sports bra designs on the market to choose from: compression, encapsulation and combination (Figure 13.1). Compression bras are normally constructed from one piece of strong elastic material designed to flatten the breasts against the chest wall (Page & Steele, 1999; Starr et al., 2005). Typically, they pull over the head and do not have cups. Encapsulation bras incorporate individual-moulded or structured cups to surround and support each breast separately, similar to "everyday" bras (Page & Steele, 1999; Starr et al., 2005). Combination sports bras both encapsulate and compress the breasts

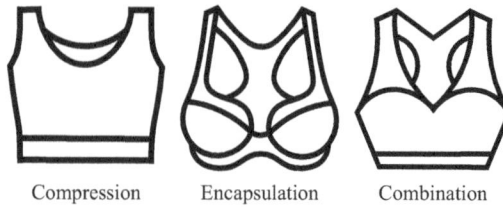

Compression   Encapsulation   Combination

FIGURE 13.1   Types of sports bra.

to varying degrees dependent on the specific design features. Some researchers have suggested that compression bras are more suitable for smaller-breasted women (<D cup), with larger-breasted women (≥D cup) recommended to select encapsulation-style sports bras (Lorentzen & Lawson, 1987; McGhee & Steele, 2010; Starr et al., 2005). However, there is a lack of consensus on whether one sports bra type is superior, and this is likely influenced by the wide variation in other sports bra features, which includes neck lines, cup styling, strap configurations, fabric elasticity and adjustability options (Page & Steele, 1999; Yu & Zhou, 2016; Zhou et al., 2013).

Football involves a significant amount of running, jumping and sudden changes in direction. Running and jumping activities require high levels of vertical breast support, whereas agility and cutting manoeuvres require greater mediolateral breast support (Risius et al., 2015). Sports bras with higher necklines (those that reach the upper boundary of the breast tissue) are considered more supportive in restricting the upward movement of the breast (Bowles et al., 2012); thus they may be a useful feature for footballers to consider when selecting sports bras. Additionally, opting for sports bras with side panels or high side seams incorporated into the side of the cups may be advantageous, as these can limit mediolateral movement (McGhee & Steele, 2010; Zhou et al., 2012).

When it comes to shoulder straps, vertical, wide (4.5 cm), padded straps are considered to improve comfort and bra-strap pressure on the shoulders, particularly for larger-breasted women (Coltman et al., 2015). Various shoulder-strap configurations are available (e.g. vertical, crossover, racer back), although these appear to have little impact on support levels (Bowles & Steele, 2013). However, shoulder straps slipping or cutting into the shoulder are one of the most disliked features of sports bras (Bowles et al., 2012), and non-vertically aligned straps can help prevent strap slippage (Bowles & Steele, 2013), particularly during vigorous and dynamic movements in football. Adjustability of shoulder straps and underbands has also been identified to be features of higher-performing sports bras (Norris et al., 2021), and should be considered to accommodate for varying torso sizes and improve support and comfort (Coltman et al., 2015; Norris et al., 2021).

Football is a physically demanding sport that can lead to sweating, particularly when competing in hot and humid environments. The extra layer of a sports bra can negatively affect the cooling ability of the skin on the breast, inhibiting heat dissipation and resulting in thermal discomfort (Ayres et al., 2013; Yick et al., 2022). To help maintain a comfortable breast temperature and avoid skin irritation, a bra made from material that can wick sweat away from the body may be advantageous (Ayres et al., 2013; Lin et al., 2015). Avoiding moulded or padded cups is also recommended as these can increase heat and sweating (Zhou et al., 2012), although it is acknowledged that moulded or padded cups can enhance breast shape, which has been linked to increased confidence (Risius et al., 2014), so personal preference should be considered. The influence of wearing breast protective padding on breast and body temperature has yet to be considered in any sport.

Performance and comfort can be compounded at the elite level, where footballers may be required to wear branded sports bras by sponsors, limiting their sports bra choices. Visibility of competing logos can result in fines, so it is common for players to wear two bras or perform in predefined sponsors' bras that provide inadequate support (Okholm Kryger et al., 2022). Sponsors need to be educated on the negative health and performance implications of inappropriate breast support and allow athletes the freedom to make their own intimate apparel choices or provide a wider range of breast-support options that suit their athletes' needs. Clubs and key football stakeholders may play a critical role in consulting with sponsors and influencing them to address the breast-support needs of footballers. Within a cohort of 60 Olympic athletes, 23% reported that clothing regulations affected their sports bra choice, and conflicts between sports bras and heart rate monitors or global positioning system (GPS) trackers were also reported (Wakefield-Scurr, Sanchez, & Jones, 2022). With increased investment in data analytics within women's football, attention should be given to the interaction between sports bras and data-capturing devices to maximise comfort and avoid compromising the function of the sports bra (Okholm Kryger et al., 2022). Furthermore, within the sports bra market, it is common to see brands marketing their products as low-, medium- or high-impact support and/or suitable for specific sports. However, there has been limited research exploring breast motions in specific sports to support these categorisations, and as yet no evidence-based standards have been established to determine the level of support a sports bra may provide during certain activities (Burbage et al., 2018). In an analysis of 98 sports bras, breast movement reduction ranged from 36% to 74%, indicating the variability of products on the market (Norris et al., 2021). The development of any football-specific breast support should be underpinned by research that has established the three-dimensional torso and breast motion of footballers during training and match environments, in order to inform the design of optimal football-specific breast support (Okholm Kryger et al., 2022).

Sports bra fit

The characteristics of an effective sports bra are highly individual, affected by the position, shape and composition of the breast, the shape of the torso, the activity type, history of bra use, wearer comfort and environmental conditions. This complicated interaction of variables means there is no such thing as the ultimate sports bra. An effective sports bra for one woman may not be effective for another and may not work for the same woman in a different environment or for a different activity. Furthermore, it is suggested that a sports bra should fit appropriately in order to function appropriately. However, the selection of a well-fitting sports bra can be challenging. There is a wide choice of brands, styles and sizes on the market, and there is a lack of standardisation of bra sizing by bra manufacturers (White et al., 2012). Additionally, breasts can change size, shape and position throughout the menstrual cycle and at different life stages, and most women are not trained in bra sizing and fitting (Wood et al., 2008). It is therefore unsurprising that 85–90% of active women have been reported to be wearing ill-fitting everyday bras (Coltman et al., 2017; McGhee & Steele, 2010), and 52–59% of athletes have been reported to be wearing ill-fitting sports bras (Brisbine et al., 2020b; Wakefield-Scurr, Sanchez, Jones, Hockley, et al., 2022). In a bra-fit evaluation of 45 women, White and Scurr (2012) found that the traditional method of tape measurement to be unreliable, overestimating the underband size 76% of the time and underestimating the cup size 84% of the time. Furthermore, the majority of women have reported wanting to independently fit and purchase their own bras (McGhee & Steele, 2010; White & Scurr, 2012). It is recommended that women are educated on professional bra-fitting criteria to improve their ability to independently choose a well-fitted bra. A summary of key sports bra components to consider when establishing correct bra fit is summarised in Figure 13.2.

Breast education and awareness

Breast and bra knowledge in the general population has been shown to be poor with the majority of women (77%) reporting average or below average knowledge (Burnett et al., 2015) and subsequently wearing an ill-fitting bra. Similar numbers have been reported in athletic populations, with 83% of 111 elite athletes in the UK High Performance System (Wakefield-Scurr, Sanchez, Jones, Hockley, et al., 2022) and 72% of 1,285 marathon runners (Brown et al., 2014) reporting average or below average breast and bra knowledge. Specific knowledge gaps among athletes include knowledge about sports bra styles and bra fit (Wakefield-Scurr, Sanchez, & Jones, 2022). Athletes have, however, expressed a desire to know more about bra styles and fitting (Wakefield-Scurr, Sanchez, & Jones, 2022). In a small number of studies, education programmes have been implemented in order to assess whether athletes' bra knowledge can be improved and if this, in turn, leads them to make better choices regarding bra selection and bra fit (McGhee et al., 2010; Wakefield-Scurr, Sanchez, & Jones, 2022). While not focused on football, these studies have included athletes from similarly dynamic sports such as netball and hockey. Information on breasts and bras provided through educational materials and individual bra assessments have improved athletes' knowledge of bra fit, bra styles and the importance of appropriate breast support (McGhee et al., 2010; Wakefield-Scurr,

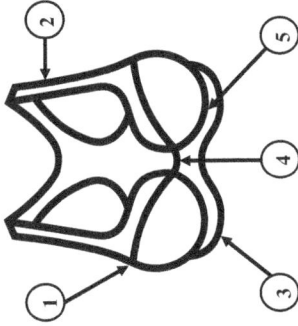

1. **The cups:** Women often wear cups that are too small, causing the breasts to spill out. If the cups are too big, the cup will hang away from the breasts. The breasts should be enclosed within the cups, with no bulging or gaping at the top or sides.

2. **The shoulder straps:** These should be adjusted to comfortably provide breast support without being too tight (digging into the skin), or too loose that they slip off the shoulders. Aim for a tension that allows two stacked fingers to fit between the shoulder and the strap.

3. **The underband:** This should be level all around the body. It should not be so tight that it is uncomfortable or makes flesh bulge over the band. The band should fit firmly around the chest and should not slide around when moving.

4. **The centre front:** This should sit flat against the body. If it does not, the cup might be too small.

5. **The underwire:** If the bra has an underwire it should follow the natural crease of the breasts and not rest on, or dig into any breast tissue, particularly tissue under the arms.

FIGURE 13.2   Professional bra-fitting criteria.

Sanchez, Jones, Hockley, et al., 2022). As a result, athletes achieved a better bra fit and selected more supportive bra styles, often switching from a compression style to a combination or encapsulation style (McGhee et al., 2010; Wakefield-Scurr, Sanchez, & Jones, 2022). Improved bra selection and fit have been successful in reducing breast pain and improving comfort (e.g. rubbing and chafing) and support (less breast movement) (McGhee et al., 2010; Wakefield-Scurr, Sanchez, & Jones, 2022), and have also been shown to have some improvements in athletes' perceptions of sporting performance (Wakefield-Scurr, Sanchez, & Jones, 2022). The benefits of breast and bra education can be long term, with athletes reporting behavioural changes, including replacing bras more frequently and seeking professional bra fitting (Wakefield-Scurr, Sanchez, & Jones, 2022).

Practitioners' perspective

Both recreational and elite women footballers may face a range of health and performance challenges related to their breasts. Establishing open, inclusive environments, where players feel comfortable enough to discuss breast-related issues, should be a priority for those working within women's football. Practitioners are encouraged to increase their own knowledge and awareness of breast health issues and of breast-support options available as these will lead to increased confidence in initiating conversations and delivering breast education sessions for players. Alternatively, there may be scope to bring in other professionals, or to identify a trusted advocate or role model within a team to support and encourage conversations and embed peer-led education. Practitioners should be cognisant of potential body image concerns that may arise when discussing breasts and avoid critical or judgemental comments. A solution-focused approach, which highlights the health and performance benefits that can be achieved with appropriate breast support, should be adopted rather than focusing on potential limitations caused by breasts.

At the game's grassroots level, simple nudges such as displaying bra fit posters in sports changing rooms may raise awareness and provide opportunities for footballers to share their experiences or concerns. If resources allow, organising professional bra fits can be considered, although empowering players to assess their own bra fit (using the criteria outlined in Figure 13.2) offers a more sustainable, long-term approach in managing breast health issues. At the elite end of the continuum, it is recommended that players be given the opportunity for a professional sports bra and bra-fit assessment to inform the selection of optimal breast support that is unconstrained by sponsors. Individual breast biomechanical assessment to inform bespoke breast-support design could also be considered, funding permitting.

Summary

Football is a dynamic sport requiring multiple and constant changes of direction, accelerations and decelerations. The breast has limited intrinsic support; therefore, a well-fitting and supportive sports bra is an important consideration for women footballers as it can reduce breast movement, improve performance and contribute to overall comfort and confidence on the pitch. Greater understanding of how the breast moves during football is needed to inform sport-specific sports bra design, and more education on breast support and bra fit is needed to allow footballers to perform optimally and in comfort. Additional focus should be given to the development of comprehensive, robust and consistent reporting procedures of sports-related breast injuries in football.

References

Ayres, B., White, J., Hedger, W., & Scurr, J. (2013). Female upper body and breast skin temperature and thermal comfort following exercise. *Ergonomics*, *56*(7), 1194–1202. https://doi.org/10.1080/00140139.2013.789554

Bowles, K. A., & Steele, J. R. (2013). Effects of strap cushions and strap orientation on comfort and sports bra performance. *Medicine and Science in Sports and Exercise*, *45*(6), 1113–1119. https://doi.org/10.1249/mss.0b013e3182808a21

Bowles, K. A., Steele, J. R., & Munro, B. J. (2012). Features of sports bras that deter their use by Australian women. *Journal of Science and Medicine in Sport*, *15*(3), 195–200. https://doi.org/10.1016/j.jsams.2011.11.248

Bridgman, C., White, J., Hedger, W., Galbraith, H., & Scurr, J. (2010). Three-dimensional kinematics of the breast during a two-step star jump. *Journal of Applied Biomechanics*, *26*, 465–472. https://doi.org/10.1123/jab.26.4.465

Brisbine, B. R., Steele, J. R., Phillips, E. J., & McGhee, D. E. (2019). The occurrence, causes and perceived performance effects of breast injuries in elite female athletes. *Journal of Sports Science & Medicine*, *18*(3), 569–576.

Brisbine, B. R., Steele, J. R., Phillips, E., & McGhee, D. E. (2020a). Breast injuries reported by female contact football players based on football code, player position and competition level. *Science and Medicine in Football*, *4*(2), 148–155. https://doi.org/10.1080/24733938.2019.1682184

Brisbine, B. R., Steele, J. R., Phillips, E. J., & McGhee, D. E. (2020b). Use and perception of breast protective equipment by female contact football players. *Journal of Science and Medicine in Sport*, *23*(9), 820–825. https://doi.org/10.1016/j.jsams.2020.02.004

Brown, N., White, J., Brasher, A., & Scurr, J. (2014). An investigation into breast support and sports bra use in female runners of the 2012 London Marathon. *Journal of Sports Sciences*, *32*(9), 801–809. https://doi.org/10.1080/02640414.2013.844348

Burbage, J., Norris, M., Horler, B., & Blackmore, T. (2018). Breast health and the exercising female. In J. Forsyth & C.-M. Roberts (Eds.), *The exercising female* (pp. 160–174). Routledge.

Burnett, E., White, J., & Scurr, J. (2015). The influence of the breast on physical activity participation in females. *Journal of Physical Activity and Health*, *12*, 588–594. https://doi.org/10.1123/jpah.2013-0236

Clarsen, B., & Bahr, R. (2014). Matching the choice of injury/illness definition to study setting, purpose and design: One size does not fit all! *British Journal of Sports Medicine*, *48*(7), 510–512. https://doi.org/10.1136/bjsports-2013-093297

Coltman, C. E., McGhee, D. E., & Steele, J. R. (2015). Bra strap orientations and designs to minimise bra strap discomfort and pressure during sport and exercise in women with large breasts. *Sports Medicine Open*, *1*(1), 1–8. https://doi.org/10.1186%2Fs40798-015-0014-z

Coltman, C. E., Steele, J. R., & McGhee, D. E. (2017). Which bra components contribute to incorrect bra fit in women across a range of breast sizes? *Clothing & Textile Research Journal*, *36*(2), 78–90. https://doi.org/10.1177/0887302X17743814

Drummond, J. L., Hostetter, K., Laguna, P. L., Gillentine, A., & Del Rossi, G. (2007). Self-reported comfort of collegiate athletes with injury and condition care by same-sex and opposite-sex athletic trainers. *Journal of Athletic Training*, *42*, 106–112.

Fong, H. B., Nelson, A. K., Storey, J. E., Hinton, J., Puppa, M., McGhee, D., Greenwood, D., & Powell, D. W. (2022). Greater beast support alters trunk and knee joint biomechanics commonly associated with anterior cruciate ligament injury. *Frontiers in Sports and Active Living*, *4*, 861553. https://doi.org/10.3389/fspor.2022.861553

Fong, H. B., & Powell, D. W. (2022). Greater breast support is associated with reduced oxygen consumption and greater running economy during a treadmill running task. *Frontiers in Sports and Active Living*, *4*, 902276. https://doi.org/10.3389/fspor.2022.902276

Griffin, J., Larsen, B., Horan, S., Keogh, J., Dodd, K., & Minahan, C. (2020). Women's football: An examination of factors that influence movement patterns. *Journal of Strength and Conditioning Research*, *34*(8), 2384–2393. https://doi.org/10.1519/jsc.0000000000003638

Haake, S., & Scurr, J. (2010). A dynamic model of the breast during exercise. *Sports Engineering*, *12*(4), 189–197. https://doi.org/10.1007/s12283-010-0046-z

Holschen, J. C. (2004). The female athlete. *Southern Medical Journal*, *97*(9), 852–859. https://doi.org/10.1097/01.SMJ.0000140124.83000.40

Jones, M., Mills, C., Exell, T., & Wakefield-Scurr, J. (2021). A novel multi-study intervention investigating the short and long term effects of a posture bra on whole body and breast kinematics. *Gait and Posture*, *83*, 194–200. https://doi.org/10.1016/j.gaitpost.2020.10.031

Lin, X., Li, Y., Zhou, J., Cao, X., Hu, J., Guo, Y., Sun, S., Lv, R., Lin, Y., Ye, Q., & Leung, H. (2015). Effects of fabrics with dynamic moisture transfer properties on skin temperature in females during exercise and recovery. *Textile Research Journal*, *85*(19), 2030–2039. https://doi.org/10.1177/0040517515580532

Lorentzen, D., & Lawson, L. (1987). Selected sports bras: A biomechanical analysis of breast motion while jogging. *The Physician and Sportsmedicine*, *15*(5), 128–139. https://doi.org/10.1080/00913847.1987.11709355

Mason, B. R., Page, K. A., & Fallon, K. (1999). An analysis of movement and discomfort of the female breast during exercise and the effects of breast support in three cases. *Journal of Science and Medicine in Sport*, *2*(2), 134–144. https://doi.org/10.1016/S14402440(99)80193-5

McGhee, D. E., & Steele, J. R. (2010). Optimising breast support in female patients through correct bra fit. A cross-sectional study. *Journal of Science and Medicine in Sport*, *13*(6), 568–572. https://doi.org/10.1016/j.jsams.2010.03.003

McGhee, D. E., & Steele, J. R. (2020). Breast biomechanics: What do we really know? *Physiology*, *35*(2), 144–156. https://doi.org/10.1152/physiol.00024.2019

McGhee, D. E., Steele, J. R., & Munro, B. J. (2010). Education improves bra knowledge and fit, and level of breast support in adolescent female athletes: A cluster-randomised trial. *Journal of Physiotherapy*, *56*(1), 19–24. https://doi.org/10.1016/S1836-9553(10)70050-3

Milligan, A., Mills, C., Corbett, J., & Scurr, J. (2015). The influence of breast support on torso, pelvis and arm kinematics during a 5 km treadmill run. *Human Movement Science*, *42*, 246–260. https://doi.org/10.1016/j.humov.2015.05.008

Milligan, A., Mills, C., & Scurr, J. (2014). The effect of breast support on upper body muscle activity during 5 km treadmill running. *Human Movement Science*, *38*, 74–83. https://doi.org/10.1016/j.humov.2014.06.001

Mills, C., Ayres, B., & Scurr, J. (2015). Breast support garments are ineffective at reducing breast motion during an aqua aerobics jumping exercise. *Journal of Human Kinetics*, *46*, 49–58. https://doi.org/10.1515%2Fhukin-2015-0033

Norris, M., Blackmore, T., Horler, B., & Wakefield-Scurr, J. (2021). How the characteristics of sports bras affect their performance. *Ergonomics*, *64*(3), 410–425. https://doi.org/10.1080/00140139.2020.1829090

Norris, M., Mills, C., Sanchez, A., & Wakefield-Scurr, J. (2020). Do static and dynamic activities induce potentially damaging breast skin strain? *BMJ Open Sport & Exercise Medicine*, *6*(1), e000770. https://doi.org/10.1136/bmjsem-2020-000770

Okholm Kryger, K., Thomson, A., Tang, A., Brown, N., Bruinvels, G., Rosenbloom, C., Carmony, S., Williamson, L., Datson, N., Jobson, E., & Mehta, R. (2022). Ten questions in sports engineering: Technology in elite women's football. *Sports Engineering*, *25*(1), 25. https://doi.org/10.1007%2Fs12283-022-00384-3

Page, K. A., & Steele, J. R. (1999). Breast motion and sports brassiere design: Implications for future research. *Sports Medicine*, *27*, 205–211. https://doi.org/10.216 5/00007256-199927040-00001

Risius, D., Milligan, A., Berns, J., Brown, N., & Scurr, J. (2016). Understanding key performance indicators for breast support: An analysis of breast support effects on biomechanical, physiological and subjective measures during running. *Journal of Sports Sciences*, *35*(9), 842–851. https://doi.org/10.1080/02640414.2016.1194523

Risius, D., Milligan, A., Mills, C., & Scurr, J. (2015). Multiplanar breast kinematics during different exercise modalities. *European Journal of Sport Science*, *15*(2), 111–117. https:// doi.org/10.1080/17461391.2014.928914

Risius, D., Thelwell, R., Wagstaff, C. R., & Scurr, J. (2014). The influence of ageing on bra preferences and self-perception of breasts among mature women. *European Journal of Ageing*, *11*(3), 233–240. https://doi.org/10.1007%2Fs10433-014-0310-3

Sánchez, M. L. M., Oliva-Lozano, J. M., García-Unanue, J., Krustrup, P., Felipe, J. L., Moreno-Pérez, V., Gallardo, L., & Sánchez-Sánchez, J. (2022). Association between fitness level and physical match demands of professional female football referees. *International Journal of Environmental Research and Public Health*, *19*(17), 10720. https://doi. org/10.3390/ijerph191710720

Schinkel-Ivy, A., & Drake, J. D. (2016). Breast size impacts spine motion and postural muscle activation. *Journal of Back and Musculoskeletal Rehabilitation*, *29*(4), 741–748. https://doi.org/10.3233/bmr-160680

Scurr, J., Brown, N., Smith, J., Brasher, A., Risius, D., & Marczyk, A. (2016). The influence of the breast on sport and exercise participation in school girls in the United Kingdom. *Journal of Adolescent Health*, *58*(2), 167–173. https://doi.org/10.1016/j. jadohealth.2015.10.005

Scurr, J., White, J., & Hedger, W. (2010). Supported and unsupported breast displacement in three-dimensions during treadmill activity. *Journal of Sports Sciences*, *29*(1), 55–61. https://doi.org/10.1080/02640414.2010.521944

Smith, L. J., Eichelberger, T. D., & Kane, E. J. (2018). Breast injuries in female collegiate basketball, soccer, softball and volleyball athletes: Prevalence, type and impact on sports participation. *European Journal of Breast Health*, *14*(1), 46–50. https://doi. org/10.5152%2Fejbh.2017.3748

Spencer, L., & Briffa, K. (2013). Breast size, thoracic kyphosis & thoracic spine pain-association & relevance of bra fitting in post-menopausal women: A correlational study. *Chiropractic & Manual Therapies*, *21*, 20. https://doi.org/10.1186/2045-709x-21-20

Starr, C. L., Branson, D., Shehab, R. L., Farr, C. A., Ownbey, S. F., & Swinney, J. L. (2005). Biomechanical analysis of a prototype sports bra. *Journal of Textile and Apparel, Technology and Management*, *4*(3), 1–14.

Wakefield-Scurr, J., Sanchez, A., & Jones, M. (2022). A multi-stage intervention assessing, advising and customising sports bras for elite female British athletes. *Research in Sports Medicine*, *31*(5), 703–718. https://doi.org/10.1080/15438627.2022.2038162

Wakefield-Scurr, J., Sanchez, A., Jones, M., Hockley, L., Biswas, A., Johnson, F., & Roberts, E. (2022). A multi-phase intervention study of sports bra prescription for elite UK female athletes preparing for the Tokyo Olympics and Paralympics. *Research in Sports Medicine*, *32*(1), 186–200. https://doi.org/10.1080/15438627.2022.2090254

Wakefield-Scurr, J., Saynor, Z. L., & Wilson, F. (2023). Tackling breast issues in contact sports. *British Journal of Sports Medicine*, *57*(18), 1160–1161. https://doi.org/10.1136/ bjsports-2023-106968

White, J. L., Lunt, H., & Scurr, J. C. (2011). *The effect of breast support on ventilation and breast comfort perception at the onset of exercise* [abstract]. Proceedings of the BASES Annual Conference, BASES, Essex.

White, J. L., & Scurr, J. C. (2012). Evaluation of professional bra fitting criteria for bra selection and fitting in the UK. *Ergonomics*, *55*(6), 704–711. https://doi.org/10.1080/00 140139.2011.647096

White, J., Scurr, J. C., & Smith, N. A. (2009). The effect of breast support on kinetics during overground running performance. *Ergonomics*, *52*(4), 492–498. https://doi. org/10.1080/00140130802707907

Wood, K., Cameron, M., & Fitzgerald, K. (2008). Breast size, bra fit and thoracic pain in young women: A correlational study. *Chiropractic & Osteopathy*, *16*(1), 1–7. https://doi. org/10.1186/1746-1340-16-1

Yick, K. L., Keung, Y. C., Yu, A., Wong, K. H., Hui, K. T., & Yip, J. (2022). Sports bra pressure: Effect on body skin temperature and wear comfort. *International Journal of Environmental Research and Public Health*, *19*(23), 157–165. https://doi.org/10.3390/ ijerph192315765

Yu, W., & Zhou, J. (2016). Sports bras and breast kinetics. *Advances in Women's Intimate Apparel Technology*, 135–146. https://doi.org/10.1016/B978-1-78242-369-0.00008-6

Zhou, J., Yu, W., & Ng, S.-P. (2012). Studies of three-dimensional trajectories of breast movement for better bra design. *Textile Research Journal*, *82*(3), 242–254. https://doi. org/10.1177/0040517511435004

Zhou, J., Yu, W., & Ng, S. (2013). Identifying effective design features of commercial sports bras. *Textile Research Journal*, *83*, 1500–1513. https://doi.org/10.1177/ 0040517512464289

14

INJURY EPIDEMIOLOGY

*Lawrence Mayhew, Lisa Hodgson, Roar Amundsen
and Solveig Thorarinsdottir*

Introduction

Epidemiology is a key scientific principle that underpins medical management in football. In this chapter, we will inform practitioners of the current patterns of injury and illness in women's football to help inform injury risk and resource management strategies. The increasing demand for monitoring illness and wellness, including tracking menstrual history, menstrual cycle and hormonal contraceptive use, in relation to the aetiology of injury and illness will be emphasised. We also include a review of current international recommendations and recent research on managing life-threatening incidents in women's football. Supported by the latest literature, these guidelines and protocols will be easily applicable for those involved in the women's game.

Professionalisation of women's football

The professionalism of women's football is rapidly developing across the globe (Fédération Internationale de Football Association [FIFA], 2018; Okholm Kryger et al., 2021) (see also Chapter 1 on global context). In 2017, 51 senior domestic leagues existed in Europe, with 3,573 women registered as professional and semi-professional players (Union of European Football Associations [UEFA], 2017). Up-to-date participation rates are difficult to obtain as they rely on retrospective survey data collated from participating football associations from the preceding season. A useful proxy measure of increased participation is the expansion of elite domestic leagues and international competitions, which allows players the opportunity to train and compete within an elite environment. More recently,

DOI: 10.4324/9781003381914-14

Cameroon, Mexico, South Africa and Thailand established national and professional leagues (FIFA, 2021), which can be considered a watershed for establishing greater opportunities for competition.

The increase in participation and professionalism has allowed players the opportunity to train and access professional sports medicine, sports science and coaching support to help maximise performance. Concomitant with the rise in participation, women's football has received increased research attention. Research related to performance, recovery, diet and female football health (Mohr et al., 2022) has facilitated medical and performance staff to prepare players for the demands of the game. With it (participation/demand) comes the inherent risk of sustaining an injury (Tischer et al., 2021). Whilst adequate physical preparedness likely is protective against some injuries (Gabbett, 2016; Soligard et al., 2016), increased training and competitive demands may result in increased injury occurrence (Soligard et al., 2010).

Injury epidemiology in women's football

Guidance exists for practitioners working in football to standardise medical reporting of injury and illness (Bahr et al., 2020; Fuller et al., 2006; Impellizzeri et al., 2022; Knowles et al., 2006; Waldén et al., 2023). This includes guidance on injury definitions and implementation and reporting standards that should be adopted when conducting prospective injury surveillance practice in football. Practitioners working in women's football should be familiar with common epidemiological terms and practices to enable medical teams to classify injury incidence, severity and burden in women's football (Nassis et al., 2021). Calculating the incidence of injury is one such metric that practitioners should familiarise themselves with, including precision estimates and the relative merits and limitations of the method chosen. In Table 14.1, a method to calculate injury incidence is provided along with a worked example. For further guidance, readers are directed to consensus recommendations (Bahr et al., 2020; Fuller et al., 2006; Waldén et al., 2023) and recent work (Impellizzeri et al., 2022).

Injury incidence in women's football

The incidence of injury in women's football has been reported in injury surveillance studies involving teams and leagues from England (Mayhew et al., 2022; Sprouse et al., 2020), Ireland (Horan et al., 2021), the Netherlands (Blokland et al., 2017), Nigeria (Owoeye et al., 2017), Norway (Amundsen et al., 2023; Nilstad et al., 2014; Tegnander et al., 2008), Korea (Joo, 2022), Spain (Del Coso et al., 2018; Larruskain et al., 2018), Sweden (Engström et al., 1991; Hägglund et al., 2009; Jacobson & Tegner, 2007; Ostenberg & Roos, 2000), Trinidad and Tobago (Babwah, 2014) and the United States (Fuller et al., 2007; Giza et al., 2005).

TABLE 14.1 Worked examples of incidence and burden which may begin to support clinicians to consider injury management strategies.

Formula for IR per 1,000 hr	Formula SE	Formula 95% CI
$\dfrac{\#\text{Injuries}}{\text{Total exposure}} \times 1,000$	$\dfrac{\sqrt{\#\text{Injuries}}}{\sum \text{Person time}}$	$(IR \pm 1.96*SE) \times 1,000$
Worked example: IR per 1,000 hr 39 injuries: 3,860 total exposure hr	**SE** $\dfrac{\sqrt{\#\text{Injuries}}}{\sum \text{Person time}} = \dfrac{\sqrt{39}}{3,860} = 0.001618$	**95% CI** $(0.0101 \pm 1.96 \times 0.001618) \times 1,000$
$\dfrac{39}{3860} \times 1,000$		
= 10.1 injuries per 1,000 hr		**= 95% CI 6.9 to 13.3**
Formula for Injury Burden per 1,000 hr	*Formula SE*	*Formula for 95% CI*
$\dfrac{\#\text{Days lost}}{\text{Total exposure}} \times 1,000$	$\dfrac{\sqrt{\#\text{Days lost}}}{\sum \text{Person time}}$	$(Burden \pm 1.96*SE) \times 1,000$
Worked example: Overall (match and training) Injury burden per 1,000 hr 1,764 days lost: 7,735 total exposure hr	**SE** $\dfrac{\sqrt{\#\text{Days lost}}}{\sum \text{Person time}} = \dfrac{\sqrt{1,764}}{7,735} = 0.00543$	**95% CI** $(0.228 \pm 1.96*0.00543) \times 1,000$
$\dfrac{1764}{7735} \approx 1000$		
= 228.1 days lost per 1,000 hr		**= 95% CI 217.4 to 238.7**

Note: CI, confidence interval; IR, injury incidence; SE, standard error.

A systematic review and meta-analysis quantified the overall injury incidence in women's football to be 6.1/1,000 hr (95% confidence interval [CI] 4.6–7.7), the match incidence to be 19.2/1,000 hr (95% CI 16.0–22.4) and training injury incidence to be 3.5/1,000 hr (95% CI 2.4–4.6) (López-Valenciano et al., 2021). Injury incidence has been reported in meta-analyses of elite women's club football by Mayhew et al. (5.7/1,000 hr, 95% CI 4.3–7.2) (Mayhew et al., 2021) and Horan et al. (5.6/1,000 hr, 95% CI 4.0–7.9) (Horan et al., 2022). Likewise, injury incidence has also been reported for club football matches (19.5/1,000 hr, 95% CI 16.2–22.8 [Mayhew et al., 2021]; 19.1/1,000 hr, 95% CI 13.7–26.5 [Horan et al., 2022]) and training (3.2/1,000 hr, 95% CI 2.1–4.3 [Mayhew et al., 2021]; 3.3/1,000 hr, 95% CI 2.2–5.0 [Horan et al., 2022]). Data pooled from international tournament matches reveal higher injury incidence compared to domestic league rates (55.7/1,000 hr, 95% CI 42.8–68.6) (Mayhew et al., 2021).

In the UEFA Women's Elite Club Injury Study conducted over four consecutive seasons (2018/2019 to 2021/2022) injury incidence was estimated to be 6.7 injuries per 1,000 hr (95% CI 6.4–7.0). There was a fourfold higher incidence during match-play compared with training (18.4, 95% CI 16.9–19.9 vs. 4.8, 95% CI 4.5–5.1; rate ratio 3.8, 95% CI 3.5–4.2) (Hallén et al., 2024).

Sites and types of injury in women's football

In a systemic review, common sites of injury were reported to be the knee (23%), thigh (21%) and ankle (18%) (Mayhew et al., 2021). When injury counts have been expressed as a rate, incidence is higher in the ankle (1.1/1,000 hr, 95% CI 0.7–1.4) compared to the knee (1.1/1,000 hr, 95% CI 0.9–1.2) and thigh (0.9/1,000 hr, 95% CI 0.6–1.2) (López-Valenciano et al., 2021). Common types of injury have been reported to be ligament sprains (37%) and muscle strains (31%) (Mayhew et al., 2021). Expressed as a rate, the incidence of muscle and tendon injuries (1.8/1,000 hr, 95% CI 1.2–2.4) are higher than joint (non-bone) and ligament injuries (1.5/1,000 hr, 95% CI 1.1–1.9) (López-Valenciano et al., 2021). In a study of elite European teams, thigh muscle injuries (hamstrings 12%, 188/1,527, and quadriceps 11%, 171/1,527) were the most frequent injury whilst anterior cruciate ligament (ACL) injury had the highest burden (38.0 days lost per 1,000 hr, inter-quartile range [IQR] 29.2–52.1) with median days loss of 292 (IQR 246–334) days (Hallén et al., 2024).

Severity of injury

Concerning severity of injury, nine studies of domestic club football were included in a pooled analysis, in which it was found that moderate time-loss injuries (8–28 days, 34%) were most common, followed by mild injuries (3–7 days, 33%), severe injuries (>28 days, 28%), minimal injuries (1–3 days, 12%) and career-ending injuries (0.7%) (Mayhew et al., 2021). In tournament football, injuries that prevented participation in match or training for up to 1 week (78%) were most common, followed by moderate (10%) and severe injuries (6%) (Mayhew et al., 2021). Across elite teams in Europe (Hallén et al., 2024), the number of slight injuries (0 days lost) was found to be more frequent than the 2% found in a recent systematic review (Mayhew et al., 2021). Slight injuries may be under-reported when using a time-loss definition. Current recommendations now advise practitioners to use the following time bins when categorising injury severity (0 days, 1–3 days, 4–7 days, 8–28 days, 29–90 days, 91–180 days and >180 days) to help communicate the consequences of injuries to stakeholders, coaching staff, national association management and media (Waldén et al., 2023). In 2023, updated guidance was provided for recording and reporting injury and illness in football and the shift to adopt broader definitions of health-related problems (rather than recording only time-loss injuries) was recommended (Waldén, et al., 2023).

Infrequent occurrence of injuries or illnesses leading to retirement from football (catastrophic injury or fatality related to training or competition), such as permanent disability, exertional heat stroke, sudden cardiac arrest (SCA) or fatality, should be recorded separately to time-loss injuries. Specifically, guidance exists on how these right-censored events can be recorded (Bahr et al., 2020; Waldén et al., 2023).

Life-threatening conditions

SCA during sports participation is a rare yet tragic event among athletes, severely impacting teams, communities and sport. Although SCA is uncommon, it is the leading cause of sport-related death in competitive athletes (Harmon et al., 2016; Maron et al., 2016). In young athletes (≤35 years of age), SCA is commonly associated within underlying structural or electrical cardiac abnormalities, such as hypertrophic cardiomyopathy or ion channel disorders (Harmon, 2022; Harmon et al., 2016; Maron et al., 2016). Blunt trauma to the chest could also cause SCA in a young athlete (Pelto & Drezner, 2020). Whilst SCA can occur at any time in any sport, nearly 75% of all cases in those under the age of 35 occur in American football, basketball and football (Harmon et al., 2015, 2016; Maron et al., 2014; Toresdahl et al., 2014).

Male athletes and black athletes are at higher risk of SCA (Harmon et al., 2015, 2016) with incidence rates higher in male athletes (1:43 348 athlete years, 95% CI 1:36 228 athlete years to 1:51 867 athlete years) than in female athletes (1:164 504 athlete years, 95% CI 1:110 552–1:244 787 athlete years) (Petek et al., 2024). Whilst the incidence of SCA in women's football is difficult to obtain, the average annual incidence of SCA in women's sport has been estimated to be 0.19 per million (95% CI 0.14–0.24), >10-fold lower compared to that in men's sport (2.63 per million [95% CI 2.45–2.83; $P < 0.0001$]) across three European regions (Weizman et al., 2023).

Policies aimed at identifying cardiac conditions (screening) and policies that increase the likelihood of successful resuscitation of cardiac arrests are currently being implemented in sport (Han et al., 2023). The American Heart Association,

American College of Cardiology and the European Society of Cardiology recommend preparticipation cardiac screening with the aim of identifying cardiac conditions that pose a risk of sudden cardiac death (SCD) (Drezner et al., 2017; Maron et al., 2015; Pelliccia et al., 2021). Whilst there is no global consensus on whether or how cardiac screening should be performed, with variability among countries, sport-governing bodies and level of competition (Han et al., 2023), American and European guidelines advise that medical history and physical examination should be part of the cardiac screening assessment (Drezner et al., 2017; Maron et al., 2015; Pelliccia et al., 2021).

The prevention of SCD relies on early recognition, calling emergency services, early cardiopulmonary resuscitation, early defibrillation (automated external defibrillator [AED] within 3 min of collapse to first shock) (Casa et al., 2013; Drezner et al., 2019) advanced life support and cardiovascular care in a hospital setting (Pelto & Drezner, 2020). For medical teams in women's football, guidelines for implementing emergency action plans for SCA have been outlined by FIFA (Patterson et al., 2022) and UEFA (UEFA, 2019); the best available evidence to respond to the unique circumstances of the football player with SCA on the field of play continues to evolve.

There are further resources in which emergency action plans in sport are considered (Pelto & Drezner, 2020). The European Resuscitation Council and UEFA (UEFA, 2023), the Resuscitation Council UK (2024) and the Football Association (England Football Learning, 2018) now provide accessible training on how to respond and manage SCA in the community and football settings.

Illness in women's football

Despite comprising a substantial part of the health problems in other cohorts (Brink et al., 2010; Clarsen et al., 2014), illnesses have not been addressed in previous epidemiological studies in women's top-level football. Team-sport athletes appear to have a lower prevalence of illness compared to athletes from other sports (Clarsen et al., 2014; Moseid et al., 2018). Endurance and technical sports have been reported to have an average weekly prevalence of 10–23%, while it has been reported to be 6–8% in Olympic and Paralympic team sport players (Clarsen et al., 2014), elite high-school team sport athletes (Moseid et al., 2018) and elite senior and junior hockey players (Nordstrøm et al., 2020, 2021). Based on recent data from the Norwegian women's premier league, an even lower average weekly prevalence of 2% was found, where players sustained 0.7 illnesses per player year with a median of 3 days lost to illness (Amundsen et al., 2023). This study was, however, conducted during two seasons with Coronavirus (COVID-19) restrictions implemented (Amundsen et al., 2023), which likely prevented transmission of infections. These data indicate that the prevalence of illnesses in team sports and women's football is generally low, and that, with good preventive measures, the burden of illnesses can be nearly eliminated. An important side note here is that the illnesses, captured with the method used in the aforementioned studies, are mostly infectious diseases, not mental health issues like anxiety, depression or eating disorders, which we know are a problem in women's football (Perry et al., 2022; Sundgot-Borgen & Torstveit, 2007). For more information on mental health, see Chapter 12.

Menstrual cycle and hormonal contraceptives

Female sex hormones (oestrogen and progesterone) are known to affect numerous parameters: cardiovascular, respiratory, thermoregulatory and metabolic (Constantini et al., 2005). The hormonal fluctuations throughout the menstrual cycle could, therefore, theoretically have both negative and positive effects on players' injury risk, as could the use of hormonal contraceptives that downregulate or alter the fluctuations of hormones (Elliott-Sale et al., 2020). However, the strength of the evidence on this topic is low. In studies on the effect of the menstrual cycle on performance (Julian et al., 2017) and injury risk in women athletes, usually assuming a natural and regular (eumenorrhoeic) cycle, it has been suggested that there is an increased risk of ACL injuries in the pre-ovulatory (Hewett et al., 2007) and ovulatory phase (Herzberg et al., 2017) and that muscle and tendon injuries may occur approximately twice as often in the days preceding ovulation compared to other phases of the cycle (Martin et al., 2021), but this does not apply for women using hormonal contraceptives. The eumenorrhoeic menstrual cycle is susceptible to external (e.g. hormonal contraceptives) and internal (e.g. menstrual dysfunction) disturbances (Elliott-Sale et al., 2020). In two studies, it has been suggested that women using hormonal contraceptives have slightly lower risk of ACL injuries (Herzberg et al., 2017) and possibly lesser risk of severe symptoms after a concussion (Porras et al., 2020). Other researchers, however, have found no effect on injury risk in addition to increased (3–11-fold) risk of deep vein thrombosis (Porras et al., 2020) and perceived negative side effects like weight gain, headaches, fatigue and mood swings (Martin et al., 2018).

On menstrual dysfunction, Martin et al. (2021) found one-fifth of the injuries in their study on English national team players (Under-15 to senior) to occur in the days after the players' next menstruation was expected, indicating that some form of menstrual irregularity or dysfunction (e.g. oligomenorrhoea or amenorrhoea) could be a factor in players' risk of injury. The negative effect of menstrual dysfunction on bone mineral density and increased risk of bone stress injuries in active women has been reported (Mountjoy et al., 2018), but this association is not as well understood in footballers (Prather et al., 2016). As up to one third of women football players (Mkumbuzi et al., 2022; Parker et al., 2022) use some form of hormonal contraceptives and one in five have a menstrual dysfunction (Prather et al., 2016), a better understanding on how they affect the players' health is crucial.

The majority of the studies on menstrual cycle and/or hormonal contraceptive use and injury risk are small and based on retrospective data (Herzberg et al., 2017;

Holtzman & Ackerman, 2019), and inconsistency in terminology makes it difficult to compare results (Elliott-Sale et al., 2020). It is, therefore, currently impossible to give certain recommendations regarding injury risk related to the menstrual cycle and contraceptive use, and it is unlikely that an approach that fits all players will ever exist. Within a football team, the timing and length of players' menstrual cycles will differ, and so will their symptoms before or during menstruation and their use of hormonal contraceptives. Use of hormonal contraceptive will also likely vary between countries and cultures (Mkumbuzi et al., 2022). Therefore, a personalised approach based on the individual player's situation should be prioritised (Datson & Okholm Kryger, 2022). Data from Australian athletes suggest that a minority of athletes discussed any menstruation-related issues with their coaches, especially if the coach was a man (Armour et al., 2020).

To succeed with a personalised approach to the player's needs, discussions about the menstrual cycle (and menstrual irregularities and dysfunction) with coaches, medical staff and teammates should be encouraged and normalised. To increase awareness on this topic and facilitate a dialogue between players, coaches and medical team, we could do the following: Educate players and coaches about the menstrual cycle, menstrual dysfunctions and hormonal contraceptive use; include questions of menstrual history and use of hormonal contraceptives in the preseason health evaluation; and use smartphone apps to track menstrual cycle data (Armour et al., 2020). Further information on menstrual cycle can be found in Chapters 5 and 6.

Practical implications

In a recent review, peer-reviewed literature was scoped to understand the current quantity of research on women's football; it was found that the head and knee were the most researched body parts (Okholm Kryger et al., 2021). The anterior thigh and ankle have received less research attention despite demonstrating higher injury incidence (Okholm Kryger et al., 2021). Understanding the incidence, prevalence, severity and burden of injury is important for practitioners to establish the extent of the sports injury problem within their own working practice environments (Nassis et al., 2021).

Guidance is readily available to support practitioners working in football to collect and interpret epidemiological-based data (Bahr et al., 2020; Fuller et al., 2006; Impellizzeri et al., 2022; Waldén et al., 2023). Guidance on emergency action planning in the event of a life-threatening event in football exists (Patterson et al., 2022; UEFA, 2023). Guidance for adopting a uniform definition of injury and illness, standardising injury and illness recording and reporting procedures, quantifying external match and training load and presenting injury incidence statistics with precision estimates (e.g. 95% CI) are available to support medical and performance staff working in football (Bahr et al., 2020; Waldén et al., 2023). In Table 14.2, we provide definitions of epidemiological terms commonly used in sports injury research; in Table 14.1 a worked example to calculate incidence per 1,000 hr with precision estimates is shown.

TABLE 14.2 Definitions of epidemiological terms commonly used in sports injury research.

Measure	Definition	Denominator	Sport Example	Range	Unit
Incidence Rate	Occurrence of new cases per unit of person-time	Person-time at risk or population-time at risk	Number of injuries divided by the total time at risk; time at risk may be computed by multiplying the total number of exposure hours (e.g. games and training hours) by the number of players participating	0 to ∞	1/time
Point Prevalence	Proportion of the study population that is a case at a single point in time	Number of individuals in the study population	Number of players within a defined population that have a specific injury (e.g. knee ligament sprain) at a specific point in time/number of players in the population at the same point in time	0 to 1	None
Period Prevalence	Proportion of the study population that is a case at any point during a specified time period	Average number of individuals in the study population over a time period	Number of players that have a specific injury over a defined period of time/number of players in the population over the same time period	0–1	None

Source: Impellizzeri et al. (2022), Knowles et al. (2006).

Summary

The surge in professionalism of women's football has opened new avenues for players, but it comes with an augmented risk of injuries, necessitating a nuanced understanding of injury and illness patterns for those practitioners working in women's football. The focus on health monitoring, including menstrual history and hormonal contraceptive use, becomes crucial in this evolving landscape. Practically, valuable guidance on emergency action planning, recording and reporting injury, illness and health problems exists. For those working in women's football, continued efforts to upskill in these areas of practice is advised and promoting awareness on menstrual health is vitally important to ensure the holistic wellbeing of women football players as the sport continues to evolve globally.

References

Amundsen, R., Thorarinsdottir, S., & Clarsen, B. (2023). #ReadyToPlay: Health problems in women's football–a two-season prospective cohort study in the Norwegian premier league. *British Journal of Sports Medicine, 58*, 4–10. https://doi.org/10.1136/bjsports-2023-107141

Armour, M., Parry, K. A., Steel, K., & Smith, C. A. (2020). Australian female athlete perceptions of the challenges associated with training and competing when menstrual symptoms are present. *International Journal of Sports Science & Coaching, 15*(3), 316–323. https://doi.org/10.1177/1747954120916073

Babwah, T. J. (2014). The incidence of injury in a Caribbean amateur women's football league. *Research in Sports Medicine, 22*(4), 327–333. https://doi.org/10.1080/15438627.2014.944304

Bahr, R., Clarsen, B., Derman, W., Dvorak, J., Emery, C. A., Finch, C. F., Hägglund, M., Junge, A., Kemp, S., Khan, K. M., Marshall, S. W., Meeuwisse, W., Mountjoy, M., Orchard, J. W., Pluim, B., Quarrie, K. L., Reider, B., Schwellnus, M., Soligard, T., . . . Chamari, K. (2020). International Olympic committee consensus statement: Methods for recording and reporting of epidemiological data on injury and illness in sport 2020 (including STROBE extension for sport injury and illness surveillance (STROBE-SIIS)). *British Journal of Sports Medicine, 54*(7), 372–389. https://doi.org/10.1136/bjsports-2019-101969

Blokland, D., Thijs, K. M., Backx, F. J., Goedhart, E. A., & Huisstede, B. M. (2017). No effect of generalized joint hypermobility on injury risk in elite female soccer players: A prospective cohort study. *American Journal of Sports Medicine, 45*(2), 286–293. https://doi.org/10.1177/0363546516676051

Brink, M. S., Visscher, C., Arends, S., Zwerver, J., Post, W. J., & Lemmink, K. A. (2010). Monitoring stress and recovery: New insights for the prevention of injuries and illnesses in elite youth soccer players. *British Journal of Sports Medicine, 44*(11), 809–815. https://doi.org/10.1136/bjsm.2009.069476

Casa, D. J., Almquist, J., Anderson, S. A., Baker, L., Bergeron, M. F., Biagioli, B., Boden, B., Brenner, J. S., Carroll, M., Colgate, B., Cooper, L., Courson, R., Csillan, D., Demartini, J. K., Drezner, J. A., Erickson, T., Ferrara, M. S., Fleck, S. J., Franks, R., . . . Valentine, V. (2013). The inter-association task force for preventing sudden death in secondary school athletics programs: Best-practices recommendations. *Journal of Athletic Training, 48*(4), 546–553. https://doi.org/10.4085/1062-6050-48.4.12

Clarsen, B., Rønsen, O., Myklebust, G., Flørenes, T. W., & Bahr, R. (2014). The Oslo sports trauma research center questionnaire on health problems: A new approach to prospective monitoring of illness and injury in elite athletes. *British Journal of Sports Medicine*, *48*(9), 754–760. https://doi.org/10.1136/bjsports-2012-092087

Constantini, N. W., Dubnov, G., & Lebrun, C. M. (2005). The menstrual cycle and sport performance. *Clinics in Sports Medicine*, *24*(2), e51–e82. https://doi.org/10.1016/j.csm.2005.01.003

Datson, N., & Okholm Kryger, K. (2022). Performance considerations in women's football. *Aspetar Sports Medicine Journal*, *11*. https://www.aspetar.com/journal/viewarticle.aspx?id=559#.ZEDkjaAzaUn

Del Coso, J., Herrero, H., & Salinero, J. J. (2018). Injuries in Spanish female soccer players. *Journal of Sport and Health Science*, *7*(2), 183–190. https://doi.org/10.1016/j.jshs.2016.09.002

Drezner, J. A., O'Connor, F. G., Harmon, K. G., Fields, K. B., Asplund, C. A., Asif, I. M., Price, D. E., Dimeff, R. J., Bernhardt, D. T., & Roberts, W. O. (2017). AMSSM position statement on cardiovascular preparticipation screening in athletes: Current evidence, knowledge gaps, recommendations and future directions. *British Journal of Sports Medicine*, *51*(3), 153–167. https://doi.org/10.1136/bjsports-2016-096781

Drezner, J. A., Peterson, D. F., Siebert, D. M., Thomas, L. C., Lopez-Anderson, M., Suchsland, M. Z., Harmon, K. G., & Kucera, K. L. (2019). Survival after exercise-related sudden cardiac arrest in young athletes: Can we do better? *Sports Health*, *11*(1), 91–98. https://doi.org/10.1177/1941738118799084

Elliott-Sale, K. J., McNulty, K. L., Ansdell, P., Goodall, S., Hicks, K. M., Thomas, K., Swinton, P. A., & Dolan, E. (2020). The effects of oral contraceptives on exercise performance in women: A systematic review and meta-analysis. *Sports Medicine*, *50*(10), 1785–1812. https://doi.org/10.1007/s40279-020-01317-5

England Football Learning. (2018, December 17). *Cardiac arrest in football: What to do if it happens*. https://learn.englandfootball.com/articles/resources/2022/cardiac-arrest-in-football-what-to-do-if-it-happens

Engström, B., Johansson, C., & Törnkvist, H. (1991). Soccer injuries among elite female players. *American Journal of Sports Medicine*, *19*(4), 372–375. https://doi.org/10.1177/036354659101900408

FIFA. (2018). *Women's football strategy*. https://digitalhub.fifa.com/m/baafcb84f1b54a8/original/z7w21ghir8jb9tguvbcq-pdf.pdf

FIFA. (2021). *Setting the pace: FIFA benchmarking report women's football*. https://digitalhub.fifa.com/m/3ba9d61ede0a9ee4/original/dzm2o61buenfox51qjot-pdf.pdf

Fuller, C. W., Dick, R. W., Corlette, J., & Schmalz, R. (2007). Comparison of the incidence, nature and cause of injuries sustained on grass and new generation artificial turf by male and female football players. Part 1: Match injuries. *British Journal of Sports Medicine*, *41*(Suppl 1), i27–i32. https://doi.org/10.1136/bjsm.2007.037267

Fuller, C. W., Ekstrand, J., Junge, A., Andersen, T. E., Bahr, R., Dvorak, J., Hägglund, M., McCrory, P., & Meeuwisse, W. H. (2006). Consensus statement on injury definitions and data collection procedures in studies of football (soccer) injuries. *British Journal of Sports Medicine*, *40*(3), 193–201. https://doi.org/10.1136/bjsm.2005.025270

Gabbett, T. J. (2016). The training—injury prevention paradox: Should athletes be training smarter or harder? *British Journal of Sports Medicine*, *50*(5), 273–280. https://doi.org/10.1136/bjsports-2015-095788

Giza, E., Mithöfer, K., Farrell, L., Zarins, B., & Gill, T. (2005). Injuries in women's professional soccer. *British Journal of Sports Medicine*, *39*(4), 212–216. https://doi.org/10.1136/bjsm.2004.011973

Hägglund, M., Waldén, M., & Ekstrand, J. (2009). Injuries among male and female elite football players. *Scandinavian Journal of Medicine & Science in Sports*, *19*(6), 819–827. https://doi.org/10.1111/j.1600-0838.2008.00861.x

Hallén, A., Tomás, R., Ekstrand, J., Bengtsson, H., Steen, E. V. d., Hägglund, M., & Waldén, M. (2024). UEFA women's elite club injury study: A prospective study on 1527 injuries over four consecutive seasons 2018/2019 to 2021/2022 reveals thigh muscle injuries to be most common and ACL injuries most burdensome. *British Journal of Sports Medicine, 58*(3), 128–135. https://doi.org/10.1136/bjsports-2023-107133

Han, J., Lalario, A., Merro, E., Sinagra, G., Sharma, S., Papadakis, M., & Finocchiaro, G. (2023). Sudden cardiac death in athletes: Facts and fallacies. *Journal of Cardiovascular Development and Disease, 10*(2), 68. https://doi.org/10.3390/jcdd10020068

Harmon, K. G. (2022). Incidence and causes of sudden cardiac death in athletes. *Clinics in Sports Medicine, 41*(3), 369–388. https://doi.org/10.1016/j.csm.2022.02.002

Harmon, K. G., Asif, I. M., Maleszewski, J. J., Owens, D. S., Prutkin, J. M., Salerno, J. C., Zigman, M. L., Ellenbogen, R., Rao, A. L., Ackerman, M. J., & Drezner, J. A. (2015). Incidence, cause, and comparative frequency of sudden cardiac death in National Collegiate Athletic Association athletes: A decade in review. *Circulation, 132*(1), 10–19. https://doi.org/10.1161/circulationaha.115.015431

Harmon, K. G., Asif, I. M., Maleszewski, J. J., Owens, D. S., Prutkin, J. M., Salerno, J. C., Zigman, M. L., Ellenbogen, R., Rao, A. L., Ackerman, M. J., & Drezner, J. A. (2016). Incidence and etiology of sudden cardiac arrest and death in high school athletes in the United States. *Mayo Clinic Proceedings, 91*(11), 1493–1502. https://doi.org/10.1016/j.mayocp.2016.07.021

Herzberg, S. D., Motu'apuaka, M. L., Lambert, W., Fu, R., Brady, J., & Guise, J.-M. (2017). The effect of menstrual cycle and contraceptives on ACL injuries and laxity: A systematic review and meta-analysis. *Orthopaedic Journal of Sports Medicine, 5*(7). https://doi.org/10.1177/2325967117718781

Hewett, T. E., Zazulak, B. T., & Myer, G. D. (2007). Effects of the menstrual cycle on anterior cruciate ligament injury risk: A systematic review. *The American Journal of Sports Medicine, 35*(4), 659–668. https://doi.org/10.1177/0363546506295699

Holtzman, B., & Ackerman, K. E. (2019). Hypothalamic-pituitary-gonadal axis in women's sport: Injuries, manipulations, and aberrations. *Current Opinion in Endocrine and Metabolic Research, 9*, 78–85. https://doi.org/https://doi.org/10.1016/j.coemr.2019.08.003

Horan, D., Blake, C., Hägglund, M., Kelly, S., Roe, M., & Delahunt, E. (2021). Injuries in elite-level women's football—a two-year prospective study in the Irish Women's National League. *Scandinavian Journal of Medicine & Science in Sports, 32*(1), 177–190. https://doi.org/10.1111/sms.14062

Horan, D., Büttner, F., Blake, C., Hägglund, M., Kelly, S., & Delahunt, E. (2022). Injury incidence rates in women's football: A systematic review and meta-analysis of prospective injury surveillance studies. *British Journal of Sports Medicine, 57*(8), 471–480. https://doi.org/10.1136/bjsports-2021-105177

Impellizzeri, F. M., McCall, A., Meyer, T., & van Smeden, M. (2022). Measures of (injury and illness) occurrence: A primer on epidemiological concepts and terminology for authors. *Science and Medicine in Football, 6*(2), 137–140. https://doi.org/10.1080/24733938.2022.2062897

Jacobson, I., & Tegner, Y. (2007). Injuries among Swedish female elite football players: A prospective population study. *Scandinavian Journal of Medicine & Science in Sports, 17*(1), 84–91. https://doi.org/10.1111/j.1600-0838.2006.00524.x

Joo, C.-H. (2022). Epidemiology of soccer injuries in Korea women national team for 5 years. *Journal of Exercise Rehabilitation, 18*(1), 68–73. https://doi.org/10.12965/jer.2142698.349

Julian, R., Hecksteden, A., Fullagar, H. H., & Meyer, T. (2017). The effects of menstrual cycle phase on physical performance in female soccer players. *PLoS One, 12*(3), e0173951. https://doi.org/10.1371/journal.pone.0173951

Knowles, S. B., Marshall, S. W., & Guskiewicz, K. M. (2006). Issues in estimating risks and rates in sports injury research. *Journal of Athletic Training, 41*(2), 207–215.

Larruskain, J., Lekue, J. A., Diaz, N., Odriozola, A., & Gil, S. M. (2018). A comparison of injuries in elite male and female football players: A five-season prospective study.

Scandinavian Journal of Medicine & Science in Sports, *28*(1), 237–245. https://doi.org/10.1111/sms.12860

López-Valenciano, A., Raya-González, J., Garcia-Gómez, J. A., Aparicio-Sarmiento, A., Sainz de Baranda, P., De Ste Croix, M., & Ayala, F. (2021). Injury profile in women's football: A systematic review and meta-analysis. *Sports Medicine*, *51*(3), 423–442. https://doi.org/10.1007/s40279-020-01401-w

Maron, B. J., Haas, T. S., Ahluwalia, A., Murphy, C. J., & Garberich, R. F. (2016). Demographics and epidemiology of sudden deaths in young competitive athletes: From the United States national registry. *The American Journal of Medicine*, *129*(11), 1170–1177. https://doi.org/https://doi.org/10.1016/j.amjmed.2016.02.031

Maron, B. J., Haas, T. S., Murphy, C. J., Ahluwalia, A., & Rutten-Ramos, S. (2014). Incidence and causes of sudden death in U.S. college athletes. *Journal of the American College of Cardiology*, *63*(16), 1636–1643. https://doi.org/https://doi.org/10.1016/j.jacc.2014.01.041

Maron, B. J., Levine, B. D., Washington, R. L., Baggish, A. L., Kovacs, R. J., & Maron, M. S. (2015). Eligibility and disqualification recommendations for competitive athletes with cardiovascular abnormalities: Task force 2: Preparticipation screening for cardiovascular disease in competitive athletes: A scientific statement from the American Heart Association and American college of cardiology. *Journal of the American College of Cardiology*, *66*(21), 2356–2361. https://doi.org/10.1016/j.jacc.2015.09.034

Martin, D., Sale, C., Cooper, S. B., & Elliott-Sale, K. J. (2018). Period prevalence and perceived side effects of hormonal contraceptive use and the menstrual cycle in elite athletes. *International Journal of Sports Physiology and Performance*, *13*(7), 926–932. https://doi.org/10.1123/ijspp.2017-0330

Martin, D., Timmins, K., Cowie, C., Alty, J., Mehta, R., Tang, A., & Varley, I. (2021). Injury incidence across the menstrual cycle in international footballers. *Frontiers in Sports and Active Living*, *3*. https://doi.org/10.3389/fspor.2021.616999

Mayhew, L., Johnson, M. I., Francis, P., Lutter, C., Alali, A., & Jones, G. (2021). Incidence of injury in adult elite women's football: A systematic review and meta-analysis. *BMJ Open Sport & Exercise Medicine*, *7*(3), e001094. https://doi.org/10.1136/bmjsem-2021-001094

Mayhew, L., Johnson, M. I., Lutter, C., & Jones, G. (2022). The epidemiology of injury in English women's domestic club football: A single site prospective cohort study. *Journal of Elite Sport Performance*, *2*(1), 1–10. https://doi.org/10.54080/RFAA9612

Mkumbuzi, N. S., Dlamini, S. B., Chibhabha, F., Govere, F. M., & Manda-Taylor, L. (2022). The menstrual cycle and football: The experiences of African women football players. *Science and Medicine in Football*, *6*(5), 626–632. https://doi.org/10.1080/24733938.2021.2005252

Mohr, M., Brito, J., de Sousa, M., & Pettersen, S. A. (2022). Executive summary: Elite women's football—performance, recovery, diet, and health. *Scandinavian Journal of Medicine & Science in Sports*, *32*(S1), 3–6. https://doi.org/10.1111/sms.14145

Moseid, C. H., Myklebust, G., Fagerland, M. W., Clarsen, B., & Bahr, R. (2018). The prevalence and severity of health problems in youth elite sports: A 6-month prospective cohort study of 320 athletes. *Scandinavian Journal of Medicine & Science in Sports*, *28*(4), 1412–1423. https://doi.org/10.1111/sms.13047

Mountjoy, M., Sundgot-Borgen, J. K., Burke, L. M., Ackerman, K. E., Blauwet, C., Constantini, N., Lebrun, C., Lundy, B., Melin, A. K., Meyer, N. L., Sherman, R. T., Tenforde, A. S., Torstveit, M. K., & Budgett, R. (2018). IOC consensus statement on relative energy deficiency in sport (RED-S): 2018 update. *British Journal of Sports Medicine*, *52*(11), 687–697. https://doi.org/10.1136/bjsports-2018-099193

Nassis, G. P., Brito, J., Tomás, R., Heiner-Møller, K., Harder, P., Kryger, K. O., & Krustrup, P. (2021). Elite women's football: Evolution and challenges for the years ahead. *Scandinavian Journal of Medicine & Science in Sports*, *32*(S1), 7–11. https://doi.org/10.1111/sms.14094

Nilstad, A., Andersen, T. E., Bahr, R., Holme, I., & Steffen, K. (2014). Risk factors for lower extremity injuries in elite female soccer players. *American Journal of Sports Medicine, 42*(4), 940–948. https://doi.org/10.1177/0363546513518741

Nordstrøm, A., Bahr, R., Clarsen, B., & Talsnes, O. (2021). Prevalence and burden of self-reported health problems in junior male elite ice hockey players: A 44-week prospective cohort study. *American Journal of Sports Medicine, 42*(12), 3379–3385. https://doi.org/10.1177/03635465211032979

Nordstrøm, A., Bahr, R., Talsnes, O., & Clarsen, B. (2020). Prevalence and burden of health problems in male elite ice hockey players: A prospective study in the Norwegian professional league. *Orthopaedic Journal of Sports Medicine, 8*(2). https://doi.org/10.1177/2325967120902407

Okholm Kryger, K., Wang, A., Mehta, R., Impyellizzeri, F. M., Massey, A., & McCall, A. (2021). Research on women's football: A scoping review. *Science and Medicine in Football, 6*(5), 549–558. https://doi.org/10.1080/24733938.2020.1868560

Ostenberg, A., & Roos, H. (2000). Injury risk factors in female European football. A prospective study of 123 players during one season. *Scandinavian Journal of Medicine & Science in Sports, 10*(5), 279–285. https://www.ncbi.nlm.nih.gov/pubmed/11001395

Owoeye, O. B. A., Aiyegbusi, A. I., Fapojuwo, O. A., Badru, O. A., & Babalola, A. R. (2017). Injuries in male and female semi-professional football (soccer) players in Nigeria: Prospective study of a national tournament. *BMC Research Notes, 10*(1), 133. https://doi.org/10.1186/s13104-017-2451-x

Parker, L. J., Elliott-Sale, K. J., Hannon, M. P., Morton, J. P., & Close, G. L. (2022). An audit of hormonal contraceptive use in Women's Super League soccer players; implications on symptomology. *Science and Medicine in Football, 6*(2), 153–158. https://doi.org/10.1080/24733938.2021.1921248

Patterson, M., Gordon, J., Boyce, S. H., Lindsay, S., Seow, D., Serner, A., Thomson, K., Jones, G., & Massey, A. (2022). Set-piece approach for medical teams managing emergencies in sport: Introducing the FIFA poster for emergency action planning (PEAP). *British Journal of Sports Medicine, 56*(13), 715–717. https://doi.org/10.1136/bjsports-2021-105126

Pelliccia, A., Sharma, S., Gati, S., Bäck, M., Börjesson, M., Caselli, S., Collet, J. P., Corrado, D., Drezner, J. A., Halle, M., Hansen, D., Heidbuchel, H., Myers, J., Niebauer, J., Papadakis, M., Piepoli, M. F., Prescott, E., Roos-Hesselink, J. W., Graham Stuart, A., . . . Wilhelm, M. (2021). 2020 ESC guidelines on sports cardiology and exercise in patients with cardiovascular disease. *European Heart Journal, 42*(1), 17–96. https://doi.org/10.1093/eurheartj/ehaa605

Pelto, H. F., & Drezner, J. A. (2020). Design and implementation of an emergency action plan for sudden cardiac arrest in sport. *Journal of Cardiovascular Translational Research, 13*(3), 331–338. https://doi.org/10.1007/s12265-020-09988-1

Perry, C., Chauntry, A. J., & Champ, F. M. (2022). Elite female footballers in England: An exploration of mental ill-health and help-seeking intentions. *Science and Medicine in Football, 6*(5), 650–659. https://doi.org/10.1080/24733938.2022.2084149

Petek, B. J., Churchill, T. W., Moulson, N., Kliethermes, S. A., Baggish, A. L., Drezner, J. A., Patel, M. R., Ackerman, M. J., Kucera, K. L., Siebert, D. M., Salerno, L., Zigman Suchsland, M., Asif, I. M., Maleszewski, J. J., & Harmon, K. G. (2024). Sudden cardiac death in national collegiate athletic association athletes: A 20-year study. *Circulation, 149*(2), 80–90. https://doi.org/10.1161/circulationaha.123.065908

Porras, L., Mangutz, N. J., Boyd, M. O., Newby-Goodman, M., Jones, J. M., & Stafford, H. C. (2020). Effects of hormonal contraceptives on non-bone related injury risk and athletic performance in female athletes: A systematic review of the literature. *Annals of Sports Medicine and Research, 7*(5), 1162.

Prather, H., Hunt, D., McKeon, K., Simpson, S., Meyer, E. B., Yemm, T., & Brophy, R. (2016). Are elite female soccer athletes at risk for disordered eating attitudes, menstrual dysfunction, and stress fractures? *PM & R*, *8*(3), 208–213. https://doi.org/10.1016/j.pmrj.2015.07.003

Resuscitation Council UK. (2024). *Resources including guidelines and quality standards.* https://www.resus.org.uk/professional-resources

Soligard, T., Grindem, H., Bahr, R., & Andersen, T. E. (2010). Are skilled players at greater risk of injury in female youth football? *British Journal of Sports Medicine*, *44*(15), 1118–1123. https://doi.org/10.1136/bjsm.2010.075093

Soligard, T., Schwellnus, M., Alonso, J.-M., Bahr, R., Clarsen, B., Dijkstra, H. P., Gabbett, T., Gleeson, M., Hägglund, M., Hutchinson, M. R., Janse van Rensburg, C., Khan, K. M., Meeusen, R., Orchard, J. W., Pluim, B. M., Raftery, M., Budgett, R., & Engebretsen, L. (2016). How much is too much? (Part 1) International Olympic committee consensus statement on load in sport and risk of injury. *British Journal of Sports Medicine*, *50*(17), 1030–1041. https://doi.org/10.1136/bjsports-2016-096581

Sprouse, B., Alty, J., Kemp, S., Cowie, C., Mehta, R., Tang, A., Morris, J., Cooper, S., & Varley, I. (2020). The Football Association injury and illness surveillance study: The incidence, burden and severity of injuries and illness in men's and women's international football. *Sports Medicine*, *54*(1), 213–232. https://doi.org/10.1007/s40279-020-01411-8

Sundgot-Borgen, J., & Torstveit, M. K. (2007). The female football player, disordered eating, menstrual function and bone health. *British Journal of Sports Medicine*, *41*(Suppl 1), i68–i72. https://doi.org/10.1136/bjsm.2007.038018

Tegnander, A., Olsen, O. E., Moholdt, T. T., Engebretsen, L., & Bahr, R. (2008). Injuries in Norwegian female elite soccer: A prospective one-season cohort study. *Knee Surgery, Sports Traumatology, Arthroscopy*, *16*(2), 194–198. https://doi.org/10.1007/s00167-007-0403-z

Tischer, T., Besenius, E., Lutter, C., & Seil, R. (2021). Primary prevention of sports injuries and overuse. *Sports Orthopaedics and Traumatology*, *37*(1), 4–9. https://doi.org/https://doi.org/10.1016/j.orthtr.2021.01.011

Toresdahl, B. G., Rao, A. L., Harmon, K. G., & Drezner, J. A. (2014). Incidence of sudden cardiac arrest in high school student athletes on school campus. *Heart Rhythm*, *11*(7), 1190–1194. https://doi.org/10.1016/j.hrthm.2014.04.017

UEFA. (2017). *Women's football across the national associations.* https://www.uefa.com/MultimediaFiles/Download/OfficialDocument/uefaorg/Women'sfootball/02/43/13/56/2431356_DOWNLOAD.pdf

UEFA. (2019). *Guide to minimum medical requirements.* https://www.uefa.com/MultimediaFiles/Download/uefaorg/Medical/02/61/67/19/2616719_DOWNLOAD.pdf

UEFA. (2023, January 31). *UEFA and European resuscitation council team up to promote CPR training and education.* https://www.uefa.com/insideuefa/mediaservices/mediareleases/news/027d-1733b06a0a23-88a88c5edaf1-1000-uefa-and-european-resuscitation-council-team-up-to-promote-c/

Waldén, M., Mountjoy, M., McCall, A., Serner, A., Massey, A., Tol, J. L., Bahr, R., Hooghe, M., Bittencourt, N., Della Villa, F., Dohi, M., Dupont, G., Fulcher, M., Janse van Rensburg, D. C., Lu, D., & Andersen, T. E. (2023). Football-specific extension of the IOC consensus statement: Methods for recording and reporting of epidemiological data on injury and illness in sport 2020. *British Journal of Sports Medicine*, *57*(21), 1341–1350. https://doi.org/10.1136/bjsports-2022-106405

Weizman, O., Empana, J.-P., Blom, M., Tan, H. L., Jonsson, M., Narayanan, K., Ringh, M., Marijon, E., & Jouven, X. (2023). Incidence of cardiac arrest during sports among women in the European Union. *Journal of the American College of Cardiology*, *81*(11), 1021–1031. https://doi.org/https://doi.org/10.1016/j.jacc.2023.01.015

15

CONCUSSION

Craig Rosenbloom, Katrine Okholm Kryger, Sean Carmody, Ritan Mehta, Charlotte Cowie, Millie Bright, OBE and Daniel Broman

Vignette by Millie Bright, OBE, Chelsea Football Club Women Captain and England Women's Senior National Team Player

I have experienced two concussions a few years ago; my reflections are different on both as I had two different experiences. With my first concussion, I played on, but on reflection, I probably should have come off. My eye swelled very quickly but I answered all questions correctly on pitch and felt fine in myself. My symptoms were increasing with time after the game. I started to be affected by noise and light. Over the next few days, I was only comfortable when lying down and in the dark. My head felt full of pressure and very uncomfortable. My second concussion was another collision in a game but this time my symptoms were instant. I remember a heavy fall and hitting my head on the floor and when I tried to stand up, I felt off balance. I tried to play on and shake it off, but I struggled with my sight, which had become blurred, and my hearing was muffled so that's when I knew I needed to go down as I could not continue.

Returning back to play took longer on the first concussion, as I needed a little longer to recover, but the usual protocol was in place and as a player you need to be really honest if you try to progress and you feel something isn't right. I feel it is massively important and I would like to see more educational work done on concussions. We talk about protocol and the steps but concussions, like my first one, can look fine instantly, but as the days went by, my symptoms developed. It is not always as simple as you may think as a player to fully understand the risks you are taking by playing on or rushing returning to play.

We are seeing more players suffering from concussions and it is a topic that needs to be spoken about. I also do understand it is part of sport and ultimately, it is

DOI: 10.4324/9781003381914-15

the risk we take when participating, but I think more educational bits can be done that are more realistic to what we experience as players.

I honestly would say the best education I've had is experiencing two different concussions and learning that you don't have to have immediate symptoms to be concussed. It has made me more aware of the risks if you play on, return too quickly or ignore symptoms. I take concussion very seriously and now advise other players to do the same and not to risk your health for any sport.

Introduction

Background and overview of concussion in women's football

The recognition around the importance of early diagnosis, appropriate management and the long-term impact to brain health is growing, with discussions about sports-related concussion (SRC) now being mainstream and in the public eye. Much of the research and attention has focused on sports dominated by men with the lack of research in women's compared to men's football being highlighted in a review (Okholm Kryger et al., 2022).

As participation in women's football grows globally at both a professional and an amateur level, so should the understanding regarding the specific issues surrounding SRC in women's football. As these specific considerations become clearer, promoting player safety and long-term player brain health should be the focus of all players, healthcare professionals, coaching staff and governing bodies. In this chapter, we aim to provide an overview of SRC in women's football, and we explore the unique challenges, prevalence, assessment, management and future directions regarding SRC.

Prevalence of concussion

The reported incidence of SRC in women's football is higher than that of men's, with elite women's footballers sustaining 1.5–4 times more diagnosed concussions when compared to men (McGroarty et al., 2020; Prien et al., 2018; Walshe et al., 2022). In elite Swedish women's football, it was found that, on average, one concussion occurred every 25 games played (Vedung et al., 2020).

Understanding SRC

Definition of SRC

Although there is no universally agreed definition, SRC has been described as a traumatic brain injury caused by a direct blow to the head, neck or body resulting in an impulsive force being transmitted to the brain that occurs in sport and exercise-related activities (Patricios et al., 2023). Following such an injury, a metabolic and neurotransmitter cascade begins, which can lead to axonal injury, cerebral blood flow change and neuro-inflammation. Symptoms of SRC can present immediately post-trauma and can develop and evolve over the subsequent hours or days. The majority of SRC cases self-resolve within days, but some episodes can be prolonged with ongoing symptomology being present weeks after the initial injury.

It is important to recognise that SRC sits on a spectrum of brain injuries, sitting at the mild end. Significant traumatic brain injuries, although rare, can occur in football. A loss of consciousness for more than 30 min, a Glasgow Coma Scale (GCS) of <13 completed 30 min post-injury or post-traumatic amnesia ≥24 hr would indicate the injury being more than a mild traumatic brain injury, which should be investigated and managed accordingly (Silverberg et al., 2023). Sports-related concussion is characterised by having normal standard structural neuroimaging (computed tomography [CT] or magnetic resonance imaging [MRI]). The terms *concussion* and *mild-traumatic brain injury* are interchangeable when neuroimaging is normal or not indicated. Those with abnormal CT and/or MRI imaging can be referred to as a mild traumatic brain injury, "with neuroimaging evidence of structural intracranial injury" (Silverberg et al., 2023).

Causes of SRC

The mechanism of injury could be from an external force striking the head or body (such as a football) or from the head or body hitting a hard object or surface such as a goal post, the ground or surrounding objections (Silverberg et al., 2023, p. 1347).

In women's football, the most common mechanism for SRC is head-to-head contact when challenging for a header (Dvorak et al., 2007). This is different to men's football, where the most common cause is the head contacting with an elbow (Beaudouin et al., 2021). In women's football, the rates of SRC are equally distributed amongst outfield playing positions (29–34%), whilst goalkeepers are injured less often (9%). In men's football, 40% of SRCs have been found to occur in defenders, whilst forwards and midfielders are impacted 22–23% of the time and goalkeepers 15% of the time (Dvorak et al., 2007; Fuller et al., 2005).

Signs and symptoms

SRC can present with a range of clinical signs and symptoms that may or may not be accompanied by loss of consciousness, with some being outlined in Table 15.1. A commonly quoted figure is that less than 10% of those with SRC had a loss of consciousness or were "knocked out". However, this figure is based on data published in the early 2000s from mostly a professional and collegiate American Football population (Delaney et al., 2002; Guskiewicz et al., 2003). It is important to remember that signs and symptoms of concussion could also be caused

TABLE 15.1 Signs and symptoms of concussion.

Visible signs of concussion—what you might see

Loss of consciousness or responsiveness.
Lying motionless on ground/slow to get up.
Unsteady on feet/balance problems or falling over/incoordination.
Dazed, blank or vacant look.
Slow to respond to questions.
Confused/not aware of plays or events.
Grabbing/clutching of head.
An impact seizure/convulsion.
Tonic posturing—lying rigid/motionless due to muscle spasm (may appear to be unconscious).
More emotional/irritable than normal for that person.
Vomiting.

Symptoms of concussion—what they might feel (UK Government, 2023)

Disoriented (not aware of their surroundings; e.g. opponent, period, score).
Headache.
Dizziness/feeling off balance.
Mental clouding, confusion or feeling slowed down.
Drowsiness/feeling like "in a fog"/difficulty concentrating.
Visual problems.
Nausea.
Fatigue.
"Pressure in head".
Sensitivity to light or sound.
More emotional.
"Don't feel right."
Concerns expressed by parent, official, spectators about a player.

by medication, alcohol, drug use or other pre-existing comorbidities or injuries (Patricios et al., 2023).

Clinical signs of SRC are because of acute disruption of brain function. These clinical signs could include one or more of the signs discussed in the following and could be directly observed in person or on video review (Davis et al., 2019; Silverberg et al., 2023):

- Loss of consciousness immediately following an injury, characterised by not taking protective action when falling after impact or lying motionless or unresponsive on the ground.
- Altered mental status immediately following the injury or on regaining consciousness; this might be demonstrated in a reduced responsiveness or inappropriate responses when asked questions or when giving instructions, with

the individual demonstrating agitated behaviour, inability to follow basic commands or being disorientated to place, time and situation.
- Complete or partial amnesia for events immediately before or after the injury or on regaining consciousness.
- Acute neurological signs including motor inco-ordination upon standing, or seizure immediately following injury.

Symptoms of SRC are caused by brain function being disrupted and are subjectively reported by the athlete. The symptoms must be new or worsened post-injury and could include cognitive, emotional and physical symptoms. The onset can occur immediately following the impact or after regaining consciousness but symptom development can be delayed, usually appearing within 72 hr post-injury (Echemendia et al., 2023; Patricios et al., 2023; Silverberg et al., 2023; "Sport Concussion Assessment Tool 6 (SCAT6)", 2023).

Risk factors for concussion

There are several factors that are thought to increase an individual's risk of sustaining a SRC (Abrahams et al., 2014). These factors are usually cited as being young, being a woman and being someone with a previous history of concussive episodes, but the published evidence around risk factors is limited.

Previous concussions: There is a high level of certainty that having a history of previous concussion(s) is an established risk factor for an individual's susceptibility to future concussions; however, it is unclear exactly how much this increases someone's risk (Abrahams et al., 2014).

Sex-related differences: Concussive risk between men and women varies depending on what sport is being participated in, but within football, women have a 1.5–4 times increased rate of diagnosed concussions compared to that of men (Abrahams et al., 2014; Prien et al., 2018). It is important to recognise that these figures are based on diagnosed concussions rather than actual sex-driven increased risk factors.

Genetic factors: There is a growing interest in the genetic factors that might predispose an athlete to concussion (Antrobus et al., 2021). This is an area of growing research that, in the future, may allow identification of individuals who are at high risk of concussive events; but how such information is utilised could raise ethical challenges.

Age: It is felt that younger athletes have an increased concussive risk, but how significant age is as a concussive risk factor is unclear (Abrahams et al., 2014).

Behaviour: An athlete's behaviour while playing football could increase their risk of concussion. Players deemed to have an aggressive style of play or those who put their heads into more high-risk areas while challenging for the ball could be involved in more potentially concussive events; however, there is limited published evidence to substantiate this.

Match play: There is a higher risk of sustaining a concussion in a competitive match versus in a training session due to matches having more high-impact and high-risk situations compared to those in training (Prien et al., 2018).

Assessment and diagnosis of concussion

Recognition of SRC is the first step in managing athletes with concussion. Protecting the player from further injury is paramount, with removal from activity being recommended for any player where there is even a suspicion of a possible concussion. Suspicion alone meets the threshold for further assessment and removal. The English Football Association promotes the approach of "If in doubt, sit them out", encouraging the removal of any player in whom there is even a suspicion of a concussion (England Football, 2023). Once a player is removed from play, they should not re-enter the game. Due to the evolving nature of concussions, footballers should be re-evaluated over the hours and days post-injury.

Sideline assessment

Development of signs or symptoms of concussion would raise concern, and this information may be offered by the athletes themselves, or visualised by other athletes, medical staff, referees/other officials or members of the coaching staff. Increasingly, video replay is available in elite sports; however, availability in domestic elite women's football is variable and reliance of video replay for concussion detection might not be appropriate.

In elite settings, medical staff are pitchside during games and at training sessions. In amateur settings, no medical staff may be present, and the assessment and removal decision becomes the collective responsibility of the player themselves, other players, the coaching staff, parents of athletes or the match officials. Increasingly, non-medical staff are educated about concussion in first-aid courses, but this may not be mandatory. There are several free-to-access educational resources online aimed at non-medical professionals, parents and athletes, which can be found on (but limited to) the Fédération Internationale de Football Association (FIFA), Union of European Football Associations (UEFA), the English Football Association and US Soccer websites. Encouraging engagement in concussion education is an area of growing interest.

On-field, Maddocks questions can be used for footballers over the age of 12 without clear signs or symptoms of concussion. Five questions are asked: What venue are we at today? What half is it? Who scored last in this match? Whom did you play last week? Did your team win the last game? Any incorrect answers would warrant further off-field assessment; however, there is concern regarding a high false-negative rate when using Maddocks as a stand-alone assessment, with some researchers finding that it missed up to 9 out of 10 concussions (Fuller et al., 2020; Maddocks et al., 1995).

Current FIFA guidelines allow for 3 min for an "on-pitch, in-game" concussion assessment at FIFA tournaments, with permanent concussion substitutes being trialled by some confederations. Guidelines and protocols around the on-pitch assessment and substitution of concussions are an area that is likely to change with time, with the guidance most likely to change since this chapter was written. Future guidelines will be dependent on the national governing body and confederation in which the team or nation is based (Patricios et al., 2023).

Sport Concussion Assessment Tool

The most widely recognised multimodal concussion evaluation tool is the Sport Concussion Assessment Tool (SCAT), with the most recent version—the SCAT6—published in 2023 (Echemendia et al., 2023). The previous SCATs were most effective at differentiating between athletes who are concussed or not if used within 72 hr of injury, with utility after a week being limited (the SCAT6 is too new to be commented upon on effectiveness). There is a Child SCAT6 for use in athletes aged 8–12, with SCAT6 used for those over 12 years. Assessing children under 8 years of age poses clinical challenges due to difficulties in the children understanding the assessment. All SCATs are open access and available freely online. An experienced clinician can perform a SCAT in around 10 min, which should be completed in a quiet setting. This procedure has in-match limitations and would be reserved for after the match once the player has been removed from play.

Further assessment

The diagnosis of SRC can usually be made based on the history, video replay review (if available), sideline assessment and SCAT testing. There will be a minority of cases in which the diagnosis is less clear with more assessment being required. Player baseline testing is important, with footballers in elite settings usually completing SCAT testing and/or other neuro-psychometric testing pre-season. Post-injury, these tests are compared to the player's baseline with any discrepancies adding weight to the diagnosis of a concussion. Specialists in SRC are available to give advice; however, if there is that much uncertainty, based on current guidance, it is recommended that the player should be treated as if they were concussed.

Neuroimaging, such as MRI and CT scanning, should not be used to diagnose concussion. Neuroimaging has a role in assessing brain and head injuries that might require acute neuro-surgical intervention or monitoring in an acute care setting (Silverberg et al., 2023).

The development of objective diagnostic tools is the focus of much interest, with salivary biomarker and involuntary eye-movement testing being two areas of note, neither of which are validated currently to diagnose SRC.

Management and treatment of concussion

The overall management and treatment of SRC outlined in the following are the same, regardless of the age or sex of the athlete; however, guidelines specific for children and adolescent footballers do exist. There is a lack of current evidence to support individualised approaches for child, adolescent or adult footballers with all following a standardised graduated return to play. Please note the following information is based on the 6th Consensus Statement on Concussion in Sport (Amsterdam, October 2022) and will change following the publication of future Consensus Statements.

Immediate management

Once an SRC has been confirmed or suspected, the immediate management is to remove the footballer from play. The player should be monitored by a suitably qualified member of staff and given concussion care advice. Due to the cognitive impairment some experience post-injury, it is important to recommend that the player not drive a motor vehicle (car or motorcycle), ride a bicycle, operate machinery, drink alcohol or be left unaccompanied for the first 24 hr post-injury (UK Government, 2023). Should their symptoms worsen, or the player becomes unwell, urgent assessment should be recommended in an acute care medical setting. It is advisable to give concussed athletes a post-injury information leaflet and to speak to the person who will be observing them for the next 24 hr.

Although rare, athletes who sustain more than one head injury can suffer from second impact syndrome, which is also known as repetitive head injury syndrome (May et al., 2023). If an individual experiences a second head injury before they have recovered from the initial head injury, they could develop this potentially fatal second impact syndrome, emphasising the importance of immediate removal of concussed athletes from play.

Initial management

Once the athlete has been removed from play, they need time to rest and recover. Current evidence no longer supports resting until the complete resolution of concussion-related symptoms (Patricios et al., 2023). Relative rest from activities of daily living and screen time is recommended for the first 48 hr (Patricios et al., 2023). After 48 hr, light-intensity exercise such as walking or stationary cycling can be performed, assuming that it does not more than mildly exacerbate symptoms. Physical activity intensity can be increased in the first 10 days post-injury, assuming there is not more than mild concussive symptom exacerbation with exercise. Individualised rehabilitation plans are recommended to take into account the athlete's history and symptoms post-injury (Patricios et al., 2023).

In some elite settings, teams will have access to complex concussion specialist services. These services are of significant value in players who have a history of multiple concussions (especially in short succession) and those with persistent symptoms for more than four weeks. Specific symptomology, such as cervicogenic symptoms, migraine and headache, cognitive and psychological difficulties, balance disturbances, vestibular signs or oculomotor issues, may need management. Multidisciplinary working may include input from sports medicine physicians, physiotherapists, occupational therapists, neurologists, neurosurgeons, neuropsychologists, ophthalmologists, optometrists, rehabilitation physicians, psychologists and psychiatrists (Patricios et al., 2023).

Return-to-play protocols

One of the first questions players ask after any injury is, When can I play again? Increasingly, at a professional level the decision around SRC return to play is set out by the country's governing body rather than the club's individual medical team.

Return to learning is an important consideration for footballers in education and can start 24–48 hr post-injury with an incremental increase in cognitive load. Most players post-SRC will be able to quickly return to education with minimal or no issues. Those with more severe concussions, scoring highly on symptom scoring or those with pre-existing learning difficulties, may require more support. In these cases, discussion with the parents and educators is paramount. Modifications to school attendance, rest opportunities, adjustments to academic workloads and limiting electronic screen time may be helpful. Players should be excluded from any physical activity lessons and at break times should not participate in any physical activity other than walking.

Graduated return-to-sport guidance has evolved over time with the objective of allowing athletes adequate time to recover fully. The exact specific guidance varies within each national governing body; however, a stepwise approach with the first stage being one of rest should be followed. An extract from the English Football Association return-to-play guidance published in 2023 is displayed in Table 15.2, demonstrating a "non-enhanced" care setting protocol. Additional guidance is available for players over the age of 17, who in exceptional circumstance could be considered for an earlier return to play if they fulfil strict criteria (England Football, 2023). Following an initial rest period of 24–48 hr post-injury, athletes can return to light aerobic exercise if it does not worsen existing concussive symptoms or produce new symptoms. In elite settings, concussed athletes' return to exercise should be supervised by an appropriate healthcare professional. Athlete's symptom reporting guides a stepwise progression towards a return to full competitive participation, with minimum time requirements being in place to stop an accelerated and expedited return. The initial return-to-sport stages avoid head impact or contact. Players who have difficulty in progressing towards their return may benefit from further evaluation or specialist input. Having a minimum timeframe advised by an

TABLE 15.2 The English Football Association's Non-Enhanced Care Setting Graduated Return-to-Play Guidelines.

	Stage 1 Initial relative rest period	Stage 2 Light exercise	Stage 3 Football-specific exercise	Stage 4 Non-contact training	Stage 5 Full contact practice	Stage 6 RTP
	Combined progression through stages 1–4 must take a minimum of 14 days				Stage 5 must only start after a minimum period of 14 days symptom free	Earliest RTP at day 21
	48 hr	Minimum 24 hr	Minimum 24 hr	Minimum 24 hr		
Exercise allowed	Stage 1 is an initial relative rest period of 48 hr. In the first 48 hr, it is okay to perform mental activities (e.g. reading) and normal activities of daily living, as well as walking for no more than 15 min at a time	Light jogging, swimming, stationary cycling or equivalent. No football, resistance training, weightlifting, jumping or hard running	Simple movement activities (e.g. running drills). Limit body and head movement. No head impact activities including no heading	Progression to more complex training activities with increased intensity, co-ordination and attention (e.g. passing, change of direction, shooting, small-side games). No head impact activities including no heading. Goalkeeper activities should avoid diving and any risk of head being hit by the ball	Normal training activities (e.g. tackling, heading, diving saves)	Player rehabilitated and cleared to participate in match play
				Review by doctor/healthcare professional		
% max heart rate	No training	<70%	<80%	<90%		
Duration (min)		<15	<45	<60		
Objective	Recovery	Increase heart rate	Add movement	Exercise, co-ordination and skills/tactics	Restore confidence and assess functional skills by coaching staff.	Return to play

Source: Adapted from England Football, *The Football Association Concussion Guidance* (2023).
Note: RTP, return to play.

external governing body can prevent any potential conflict directed towards medical staff by the players themselves, or other non-medical stakeholders within the club who may want the footballer returned quicker.

Women footballers might show more concussion symptoms post-injury than men footballers and may take longer to recover and return to sport than male players (Master et al., 2021). There is growing evidence to suggest that the recovery difference between male and female athletes is not as significant as previously thought (Master et al., 2021).

Psychological support

Footballers who have sustained an SRC should have their mental health and wellbeing closely monitored. The psychological impact of having sustained a concussion can be significant and, in an elite setting, their injury might be very public. It is not uncommon for athletes post-concussion to experience anxiety, depression or emotional disturbances as outlined in a study in former male professional athletes across a range of sports (Gouttebarge et al., 2017). Providing psychological support through counselling, education and access to mental health resources may significantly assist in a player's recovery and overall wellbeing.

Impact of concussion on athlete health

Short-term effects

Footballers suffering from SRC may experience one or more of the signs and symptoms outlined earlier in the chapter; symptoms can present immediately or may develop over the following hours or days. These signs and symptoms can affect the player's ability to perform in a sporting context as well as in their private life and at their job/school.

Cognitive impairment such as difficulties with memory, attention and processing speed are the reason why concussed individuals are recommended not to drive a vehicle, operate machinery, drink alcohol or be left unaccompanied for the first 24 hr post-injury (UK Government, 2023) In men's football, players with SRC are at an increased risk of sustaining a musculoskeletal injury within a year following their concussion, thought to be due to a change in their proprioceptive and oculomotor processing (Nordström et al., 2014). There is a lack of published evidence from a women's cohort, but the assumption is that this risk would also apply to women.

Long-term effects

There is increasing concern about possible long-term effects of athletes who have sustained previous SRCs, such as mental health problems, cognitive impairment and neurological diseases. This was an area of discussion within the recent Consensus Statement on Concussion in Sport in 2022, with the majority of literature in this area being from male populations; however, this is still highly relevant to women's sports (Patricios et al., 2023). The suggested outcomes of the meeting, based on the literature available at the time, are as follows:

- Former amateur athletes were not at increased risk for cognitive impairment, neurological disorders or neurodegenerative diseases compared with the general population.
- Former professional athletes had greater mortality rates from neurological diseases and dementia in former professional American football and football players (men) compared to the general public.
- Former amateur athletes were not at an increased risk for depression or suicide during early adulthood or as older adults.
- Former professional athletes were not at increased risk for death associated with having a psychiatric disorder or as a result of suicide.
- Former professional athletes were not at increased risk for psychiatric hospitalisation during their adult life.

Repetitive brain injury can cause a progressive neurological condition now recognised and called chronic traumatic encephalopathy (McKee et al., 2015). Chronic traumatic encephalopathy is a neuropathological condition, which currently is only diagnosable after death and can cause behavioural and mood changes, memory loss, cognitive impairment and dementia. The majority of research is currently focused on cohorts from within men's American football, but as elite women's football participation is increasing, it is important to include women players in the discussion about this important topic.

Although they do not cause concussions, some researchers have suggested that repetitive heading may have a negative effect on long-term brain health. Although not from a female population, there have been several works in which retired male professional footballers have been studied, which raises the possibility of the long-term effect of heading and the link between the development of neurodegenerative conditions (Espahbodi et al., 2023; Macnab et al., 2023; Russell et al., 2021). It is not possible at present to establish a clear causation between sports participation and SRC incidence or repetitive head impact early in life and the risk of cognitive impairment or dementia late in life. This area of concussion care is of significant importance and is the focus of global, prospective research projects (Patricios et al., 2023).

Prevention of concussion

Rule changes

Football is an impact sport and therefore SRCs are not completely preventable; however, efforts have been and are being made to improve safety. Rule changes have helped to reduce the rates of SRC in football, the most notable being in 2006, when the International Football Association Board changed rules stating that direct and deliberate elbow-to-head blows were punishable with a red card, which led to a reduction of elbow-to-head contacts by 23% in elite players in men's football in Germany (Beaudouin et al., 2019). Supporting medical teams in their ability to assess and remove players is an important development, with medical teams having the final say on player removal; some national governing bodies have recognised this and amended their policies accordingly. At FIFA tournaments, FIFA gives medical teams 3 min to assess a concussion on pitch, but what is included in this 3-min assessment is not specified. In most domestic leagues, elite match officials are increasingly sensitive to SRC, and the growing expectation is that they will allow the medical team to complete an appropriate on-pitch assessment.

With a growing concern about the cumulative effect of repetitive ball heading, limits on heading are being introduced, applying precautionary principles in some countries by their national governing body. These guidelines can be hugely variable but may include banning heading below a certain age, limiting the number of balls that can be headed during training, reducing ball pressure and/or size, reducing the size of pitches for younger age groups and banning heading immediately before and after matches.

There is no current evidence to support the widespread routine use of protective equipment, such as headgear or mouthguards, in preventing SRC within football (Abrahams et al., 2014). More research is required to explore the possible benefits of different headgear design and material for use in football, but there is no evidence to support mouthguard use or external jugular vein compressive devices (Eliason et al., 2023). There is concern that usage of protective equipment could change athletes' perceptions of risk and danger, which could negate any positive effect of protective equipment.

Education and awareness

Concussion-specific education is important in increasing the awareness and knowledge of SRC and to change the attitude towards concussions. Individualising education for athletes, coaching staff, parents of younger athletes and match officials can engage and influence stakeholders. Elite women footballers in England who had previous SRC education demonstrated an increased knowledge about concussion, but previous education did not change their concussion attitudes, demonstrating that education alone is not enough (Shafik et al., 2022). Although concussion education is recommended, it is not always mandated for players or coaching staff. Education rates in elite women's football in England were significantly lower than those of men's teams (Rosenbloom et al., 2021). The English professional football leagues are in the process of implementing mandatory concussion education across all their teams and the English Football Association includes it in all medical staff pitchside emergency training courses.

Risk mitigation strategies

Risk mitigation strategies, such as optimising athlete health, can be important to detect medical issues that could limit concussion recovery. Undiagnosed visual or vestibulo-ocular problems could worsen SRC symptomology, as can undiagnosed or untreated headache syndromes. Psychological and psychiatric health can play an important role post-injury in those who develop persistent and prolonged concussive symptoms. A history of mental health problems, such as anxiety and depression, has been found to be strongly associated with poorer recovery outcomes post-SRC (Resch et al., 2017).

Neck strength may be related to SRC rates in female athletes. Increasing women footballers' cervical spine strength has been shown to reduce contact force transmission with head contact, but whether this reduces the risk of SRC is currently unknown and needs further exploration (Elliott et al., 2021). Neuromuscular training warm-up programmes have been shown to reduce the rates of concussion in rugby union and could be implemented into women's football (Patricios et al., 2023).

Unique challenges in elite women's football

Gender- and sex-specific factor variations between men's and women's football

Being a woman is thought to increase an individual's risk of sustaining a concussive event (Abrahams et al., 2014; Prien et al., 2018). The reasons behind this are multifactorial and poorly understood but thought to be partly as a result of sex-based biological and pathophysiological differences between male and female athletes.

Symptom report

There is a difference in reporting concussive symptoms between men and women at baseline and post-injury, due to either women being more willing to report symptoms or men more frequently under-reporting symptoms (Prien et al., 2018). This difference is important, given the significance player reporting has when using a tool such as the SCAT to diagnose concussion and monitor recovery. Without a baseline comparison, higher post-injury symptom reporting could be perceived as persistent symptoms and could prolong an athlete's return unnecessarily (Resch et al., 2017). Post-injury, athletes in women's sport report more disrupted sleep, emotional change, cognitive functional difficulties and somatic symptoms than do men, which may be due to women being more honest when volunteering information. Given the reliance on subjective symptom reporting on return-to-sport progression, it is important to be aware of this possible gender difference (Resch et al., 2017).

Game play

Women's matches have more free kicks, corners, duels and passes, but fewer fouls when compared to those in men's matches (Pappalardo et al., 2021). A greater number of free kicks and corners could increase the potential for SRC-inducing mechanisms such as head-to-head or head-to-body contact.

Provision of medical team services

Within women's football, medical provision is known to be different to that of men's football, although this is changing with the growth of women's football and the increased resources that this brings. Whether the differences in medical provision influence the SRC diagnosis rate and player care post-injury is unknown but is an important factor to consider.

Concussion education

Rates of concussion education in elite English football were found to be significantly lower in women's football compared to rates in men's (Rosenbloom et al., 2021). This point is important as concussion education was shown to significantly improve knowledge of concussion in elite women footballers (Shafik et al., 2022).

Biomechanical factors

Female athletes have different head and neck biomechanics compared to those in male athletes. Female athletes cannot tolerate as much head and neck biomechanical force when compared to male athletes, possibly reducing the force required to cause an SRC (Beckwith et al., 2013; McGroarty et al., 2020). Head-to-ball size ratio is increased in women's/girls' football, which may be a factor in increasing SRC risk, but more research is required.

Hormonal factors

Hormonal factors are unlikely to be a main determinant in SRC recovery, but hormonal factors unique to female athletes have been attributed to poorer outcomes after SRC compared to those in male athletes. Although alterations in pituitary function post-concussion have been documented in both male and female athletes, luteinising hormone and follicle-stimulating hormone are important determinants for the production of oestrogen and progesterone, which are thought to be protective post-SRC. As a result, disruption of the hypothalamic–pituitary–gonadal axis is thought to more negatively affect female athletes (Resch et al., 2017). The timing of the concussive injury may have significance in relation to the athlete's menstrual cycle due to the cyclical levels of progesterone, with poorer outcomes being seen in those sustaining a concussion during the luteal phase (Wunderle et al., 2014).

Equity and access to care

Equitable access to healthcare and resources is important for effective concussion management. Players, particularly those competing in teams with fewer allocated healthcare resources, might face barriers in accessing specialised care and rehabilitation services.

Research and future directions

There is much to be done in the field of SRC research in women, with the majority of current evidence relating to populations in men's sport. As participation in women's football grows, so does the need for targeted research focusing on SRC within this group. Specific research gaps include the incidence and prevalence of concussions at an elite and amateur level, women-specific risk factors, differences in injury mechanisms, differences in return-to-sport post-SRC and the long-term brain health consequences. Exploration of the impact of hormonal involvement on concussion recovery and developing specific rehabilitation programmes for footballers post-concussion should be a research focus.

Emerging technologies, such as advanced neuroimaging, fluid-based biomarkers and genetic testing, may have a significant role in the future of SRC care. It is important that players from women's football are given the opportunity to participate in this research.

Conclusion

In this chapter, we have explored the current evidence and practice around SRC, as well as the unique challenges posed within women's football. Concussion is becoming one of the most important topics in athlete care with a fast-moving landscape that is constantly evolving. While the long-term impact and consequences of SRC are being explored, those working with footballers have a duty of care to create a safe environment for participation. Evidence-based practice should be mandated in elite women's football and should not be seen as something that is merely desirable.

References

Abrahams, S., McFie, S., Patricios, J., Posthumus, M., & September, A. (2014). Risk factors for sports concussion: An evidence-based systematic review. *British Journal of Sports Medicine, 48*(2), 91–97. https://doi.org/10.1136/bjsports-2013-092734

Antrobus, M. R., Brazier, J., Stebbings, G. K., Day, S. H., Heffernan, S. M., Kilduff, L. P., Erskine, R. M., & Williams, A. G. (2021). Genetic factors that could affect concussion risk in elite rugby. *Sports, 9*(2), 19. https://doi.org/10.3390/sports9020019

Beaudouin, F., Aus der Fünten, K., Tröß, T., Reinsberger, C., & Meyer, T. (2019). Head injuries in professional male football (soccer) over 13 years: 29% lower incidence rates after a rule change (red card). *British Journal of Sports Medicine, 53*(15), 948–952. https://doi.org/10.1136/bjsports-2016-097217

Beaudouin, F., Demmerle, D., Fuhr, C., Tröß, T., & Meyer, T. (2021). Head impact situations in professional football (soccer). *Sports Medicine International Open*, *5*(2), e37–e44. https://doi.org/10.1055/a-1338-1402

Beckwith, J. G., Greenwald, R. M., Chu, J. J., Crisco, J. J., Rowson, S., Duma, S. M., Broglio, S. P., McAllister, T. W., Guskiewicz, K. M., & Mihalik, J. P. (2013). Head impact exposure sustained by football players on days of diagnosed concussion. *Medicine and Science in Sports and Exercise*, *45*(4), 737–746. https://doi.org/10.1249/MSS.0b013e3182792ed7

Davis, G. A., Makdissi, M., Bloomfield, P., Clifton, P., Echemendia, R. J., Falvey, É. C., Fuller, G. W., Green, G., Harcourt, P., Hill, T., McGuirk, N., Meeuwisse, W., Orchard, J., Raftery, M., Sills, A. K., Solomon, G. S., Valadka, A., & McCrory, P. (2019). International consensus definitions of video signs of concussion in professional sports *British Journal of Sports Medicine*, *53*(20), 1264–1267. https://doi.org/10.1136/bjsports-2019-100628

Delaney, J. S., Lacroix, V. J., Leclerc, S., & Johnston, K. M. (2002). Concussions among university football and soccer players. *Clinical Journal of Sport Medicine*, *12*(6), 331–7338. https://doi.org/10.1097/00042752-200211000-00003

Dvorak, J., McCrory, P., & Kirkendall, D. T. (2007). Head injuries in the female football player: Incidence, mechanisms, risk factors and management. *British Journal of Sports Medicine*, *41*(Suppl 1), i44–i46. https://doi.org/10.1136/bjsm.2007.037960

Echemendia, R. J., Brett, B. L., Broglio, S., Davis, G. A., Giza, C. C., Guskiewicz, K. M., Harmon, K. G., Herring, S., Howell, D. R., Master, C. L., Valovich McLeod, T. C., McCrea, M., Naidu, D., Patricios, J., Putukian, M., Walton, S. R., Schneider, K. J., Burma, J. S., & Bruce, J. M. (2023). Introducing the sport concussion assessment tool 6 (SCAT6). *British Journal of Sports Medicine*, *57*(11), 619–621. https://doi.org/10.1136/bjsports-2023-106849

Eliason, P. H., Galarneau, J.-M., Kolstad, A. T., Pankow, M. P., West, S. W., Bailey, S., Miutz, L., Black, A. M., Broglio, S. P., Davis, G. A., Hagel, B. E., Smirl, J. D., Stokes, K. A., Takagi, M., Tucker, R., Webborn, N., Zemek, R., Hayden, A., Schneider, K. J., & Emery, C. A. (2023). Prevention strategies and modifiable risk factors for sport-related concussions and head impacts: A systematic review and meta-analysis. *British Journal of Sports Medicine*, *57*(12), 749–761. https://doi.org/10.1136/bjsports-2022-106656

Elliott, J., Heron, N., Versteegh, T., Gilchrist, I. A., Webb, M., Archbold, P., Hart, N. D., & Peek, K. (2021). Injury reduction programs for reducing the incidence of sport-related head and neck injuries including concussion: A systematic review. *Sports Medicine*, *51*(11), 2373–2388. https://doi.org/10.1007/s40279-021-01501-1

England Football. (2023). *The FA concussion guidelines: If in doubt sit them out*. https://cdn.englandfootball.com/-/media/EnglandFootball/Files/learn/Brain-Health/Sep-2023/Concussion-Guidelines-110923/The-FA-Concussion-Guidelines.pdf?rev=baeae2d524ab491ca40fad7ffd75d9f8

Espahbodi, S., Hogervorst, E., Macnab, T. P., Thanoon, A., Fernandes, G. S., Millar, B., Duncan, A., Goodwin, M., Batt, M., Fuller, C. W., Fuller, G., Ferguson, E., Bast, T., Doherty, M., & Zhang, W. (2023). Heading frequency and risk of cognitive impairment in retired male professional soccer players. *JAMA Network Open*, *6*(7), e2323822. https://doi.org/10.1001/jamanetworkopen.2023.23822

Fuller, C. W., Junge, A., & Dvorak, J. (2005). A six year prospective study of the incidence and causes of head and neck injuries in international football. *British Journal of Sports Medicine*, *39*(Suppl 1), i3–i9. https://doi.org/10.1136/bjsm.2005.018937

Fuller, G. W., Tucker, R., Starling, L., Falvey, E., Douglas, M., & Raftery, M. (2020). The performance of the world rugby head injury assessment screening tool: A diagnostic accuracy study. *Sports Medicine—Open*, *6*(1), 2. https://doi.org/10.1186/s40798-019-0231-y

Gouttebarge, V., Aoki, H., Lambert, M., Stewart, W., & Kerkhoffs, G. (2017). A history of concussions is associated with symptoms of common mental disorders in former male professional athletes across a range of sports. *The Physician and Sports Medicine*, *45*(4), 443–449. https://doi.org/10.1080/00913847.2017.1376572

Guskiewicz, K. M., McCrea, M., Marshall, S. W., Cantu, R. C., Randolph, C., Barr, W., Onate, J. A., & Kelly, J. P. (2003). Cumulative effects associated with recurrent concussion in collegiate football players: The NCAA concussion study. *Journal of the American Medical Association, 290*(19), 2549–2555. https://doi.org/10.1001/jama.290.19.2549

Macnab, T.-M. P., Espahbodi, S., Hogervorst, E., Thanoon, A., Fernandes, G. S., Millar, B., Duncan, A., Goodwin, M., Batt, M., Fuller, C. W., Fuller, G., Ferguson, E., Bast, T., Doherty, M., & Zhang, W. (2023). Cognitive impairment and self-reported dementia in UK retired professional soccer players: A cross sectional comparative study. *Sports Medicine—Open, 9*(1), 43. https://doi.org/10.1186/s40798-023-00588-2

Maddocks, D. L., Dicker, G. D., & Saling, M. M. (1995). The assessment of orientation following concussion in athletes. *Clinical Journal of Sport Medicine, 5*(1), 32–35. https://doi.org/10.1097/00042752-199501000-00006

Master, C. L., Katz, B. P., Arbogast, K. B., McCrea, M. A., McAllister, T. W., Pasquina, P. F., Lapradd, M., Zhou, W., & Broglio, S. P. (2021). Differences in sport-related concussion for female and male athletes in comparable collegiate sports: A study from the NCAA-DoD concussion assessment, research and education (CARE) consortium. *British Journal of Sports Medicine, 55*(24), 1387–1394. https://doi.org/10.1136/bjsports-2020-103316

May, T., Foris, L. A., & Donnally, C. J. (2023, July 3). Second impact syndrome. In *StatPearls* [Internet]. StatPearls Publishing. https://www.ncbi.nlm.nih.gov/books/NBK448119/

McGroarty, N. K., Brown, S. M., & Mulcahey, M. K. (2020). Sport-related concussion in female athletes: A systematic review. *Orthopaedic Journal of Sports Medicine, 8*(7). https://doi.org/10.1177/2325967120932306

McKee, A. C., Stein, T. D., Kiernan, P. T., & Alvarez, V. E. (2015). The neuropathology of chronic traumatic encephalopathy. *Brain Pathology, 25*(3), 237–375. https://doi.org/10.1111/bpa.12248

Nordström, A., Nordström, P., & Ekstrand, J. (2014). Sports-related concussion increases the risk of subsequent injury by about 50% in elite male football players. *British Journal of Sports Medicine, 48*(19), 1447–1450. https://doi.org/10.1136/bjsports-2013-093406

Okholm Kryger, K., Wang, A., Mehta, R., Impellizzeri, F. M., Massey, A., & McCall, A. (2022). Research on women's football: A scoping review. *Science and Medicine in Football, 6*(5), 549–558. https://doi.org/10.1080/24733938.2020.1868560

Pappalardo, L., Rossi, A., Natilli, M., & Cintia, P. (2021). Explaining the difference between men's and women's football. *PLoS One, 16*(8), e0255407. https://doi.org/10.1371/journal.pone.0255407

Patricios, J. S., Schneider, K. J., Dvorak, J., Ahmed, O. H., Blauwet, C., Cantu, R. C., Davis, G. A., Echemendia, R. J., Makdissi, M., McNamee, M., Broglio, S., Emery, C. A., Feddermann-Demont, N., Fuller, G. W., Giza, C. C., Guskiewicz, K. M., Hainline, B., Iverson, G. L., Kutcher, J. S., . . . Meeuwisse, W. (2023). Consensus statement on concussion in sport: The 6th international conference on concussion in sport-Amsterdam, October 2022. *British Journal of Sports Medicine, 57*(11), 695–711. https://doi.org/10.1136/bjsports-2023-106898

Prien, A., Grafe, A., Rössler, R., Junge, A., & Verhagen, E. (2018). Epidemiology of Head injuries focusing on concussions in team contact sports: A systematic review. *Sports Medicine, 48*(4), 953–969. https://doi.org/10.1007/s40279-017-0854-4

Resch, J. E., Rach, A., Walton, S., & Broshek, D. K. (2017). Sport concussion and the female athlete. *Clinics in Sports Medicine, 36*(4), 717–739. https://doi.org/10.1016/j.csm.2017.05.002

Rosenbloom, C., Broman, D. D., Chu, W., Chatterjee, R., & Okholm Kryger, K. (2021). Sport-related concussion practices of medical team staff in elite football in the United Kingdom, a pilot study. *Science and Medicine in Football, 6*(1), 127–135. https://doi.org/10.1080/24733938.2021.1892174

Russell, E. R., Mackay, D. F., Stewart, K., MacLean, J. A., Pell, J. P., & Stewart, W. (2021). Association of field position and career length with risk of neurodegenerative disease in male former professional soccer players. *JAMA Neurology*, *78*(9), 1057–1063. https://doi.org/10.1001/jamaneurol.2021.2403

Shafik, A., Bennett, P., Rosenbloom, C., Okholm Kryger, K., Carmody, S., & Power, J. (2022). Sport-related concussion attitudes and knowledge in elite English female footballers. *Science and Medicine in Football*, 1–7. https://doi.org/10.1080/24733938.2022.2161613

Silverberg, N. D., Iverson, G. L., Cogan, A., Dams-O-Connor, K., Delmonico, R., Graf, M. J. P., Iaccarino, M. A., Kajankova, M., Kamins, J., McCulloch, K. L., McKinney, G., Nagele, D., Panenka, W. J., Rabinowitz, A. R., Reed, N., Wethe, J. V., Whitehair, V., Anderson, V., Arciniegas, D. B., . . . Zemek, R. (2023). The American congress of rehabilitation medicine diagnostic criteria for mild traumatic brain injury. *Archives of Physical Medicine and Rehabilitation*, *104*(8), 1343–1355. https://doi.org/10.1016/j.apmr.2023.03.036

Sport Concussion Assessment Tool 6 (SCAT6). (2023). *British Journal of Sports Medicine*, *57*(11), 622–631. https://doi.org/10.1136/bjsports-2023-107036

UK Government. (2023, April). *If in doubt, sit them out: UK concussion guidelines for non-elite (grassroots) sport*. https://sramedia.s3.amazonaws.com/media/documents/9ced1e1a-5d3b-4871-9209-bff4b2575b46.pdf

Vedung, F., Hänni, S., Tegner, Y., Johansson, J., & Marklund, N. (2020). Concussion incidence and recovery in Swedish elite soccer—prolonged recovery in female players. *Scandinavian Journal of Medicine & Science in Sports*, *30*(5), 947–957. https://doi.org/10.1111/sms.13644

Walshe, A., Daly, E., & Ryan, L. (2022). Epidemiology of sport-related concussion rates in female contact/collision sport: A systematic review. *BMJ Open Sport & Exercise Medicine*, *8*(3), e001346. https://doi.org/10.1136/bmjsem-2022-001346

Wunderle, K., Hoeger, K. M., Wasserman, E., & Bazarian, J. J. (2014). Menstrual phase as predictor of outcome after mild traumatic brain injury in women. *The Journal of Head Trauma Rehabilitation*, *29*(5), e1–e8. https://doi.org/10.1097/htr.0000000000000006

16

INJURY PREVENTION AND REHABILITATION

Mark De Ste Croix, Francisco Ayala, Ross Julian, Debby Sargent and Jonathan Hughes

Introduction

There has been a rapid growth in women's football and thus there is greater need to develop injury screening, risk prevention strategies and rehabilitation modalities. All of these are key factors in ensuring the health and wellbeing of players, enhancing their performance and sustaining the long-term success of the sport across all levels of participation. Injury epidemiology has been described in Chapter 14, and the information from these studies forms the foundation of screening, prevention and rehabilitation models in women's football. Data from the current chapter highlight the importance of injury risk screening and prevention, given the severity and burden of anterior-cruciate ligament (ACL) injuries in women players. Such injuries are associated with increased risk of end-stage osteoarthritis resulting in total knee arthroplasties (Khan et al., 2019), considerable financial contributions per injury to gain a quality-adjusted life (Eggerding et al., 2022) and psychological barriers that may affect recovery, return to sport and an increased risk of sustaining a subsequent injury (Ardern et al., 2016). Likewise, match demands in women's football (see Chapter 3) are important to understand, in terms of preparing players for the demands of the game, which must be considered alongside injury risk-management strategies. Understanding and exploring loading and accumulated fatigue, in terms of injury risk, are paramount in the prevention strategy, but data on players from the women's game are severely lacking. By implementing comprehensive injury prevention measures, teams and players can mitigate the risk of injuries and ensure a sustainable and thriving future for women's football. Recent advances in using machine learning and artificial intelligence to predict injury risk have provided greater insight into the possible mechanisms associated with injury risk in women's football (Nassis et al., 2022). As part of the Van Mechelen et al.

DOI: 10.4324/9781003381914-16

injury model (1992), the first stage of understanding injury, and subsequently trying to reduce incidence, is understanding the surveillance and risk data. Only then can appropriate screening, prevention and rehabilitation strategies be developed that are designed for players in women's football. The aims of this chapter are to describe appropriate injury risk screening strategies, review the efficacy of prevention programmes and outline rehabilitation processes for women's football.

Screening strategies for injury risk

Sport-related injuries in women's football have complex, multifactorial causes and occur frequently, with significant negative consequences on players' health and career development, in both the short and long terms (McKay & Mellalieu, 2021). Through numerous systematic reviews and meta-analyses, it has been demonstrated that the likelihood of these injuries occurring in the women's game can be minimised through injury prevention programmes (IPPs) if routinely implemented during training sessions (Crossley et al., 2020; Lemes et al., 2021). These IPPs typically target evidence-based modifiable risk factors for lower extremity injuries including high-risk biomechanical movement strategies (e.g. excessive dynamic knee valgus motion at landing and cutting) and neuromuscular deficits (e.g. muscle weakness and poor dynamic joint stability).

For exercise-based interventions to be highly effective in mitigating modifiable risk factors of injury, they must meet specific requirements, including a design tailored to the specific characteristics and needs of each player and their context (Olivares-Jabalera et al., 2021). Therefore, the initial step for practitioners in designing individualised IPPs is the careful selection and application of assessment tests targeting the key modifiable risk factors associated with the most burdensome injuries in women's football, that is muscle strains of the hamstring and quadriceps, ankle sprains and ACL tears (Robles-Palazón, Cejudo, et al., 2021). Moreover, the information gathered from testing in healthy players can greatly assist in decision-making regarding a safe return to competition following rehabilitation post-injury.

Systematic analysis of video in women's football has established identifiable patterns in non-contact soft-tissue injuries among players (Aiello et al., 2023; Lucarno et al., 2021). As a result, an effective test battery for assessing football-related neuromuscular capacities and movement mechanics should include jump, sprint and changes-of-direction tests. These tests have demonstrated valid, reliable and independent kinetic and kinematic measures, providing rich data with minimal testing in players. Given the time and resource constraints commonly encountered in applied environments, it is recommended that the tests incorporated be portable, cost-effective and technically simple to administer, to enable the assessment of players within a short timeframe. Therefore, it is paramount that an evidence-based approach to testing the key neuromuscular parameters and biomechanical movement patterns involved in the occurrence mechanisms of the most burdensome women's football injuries is implemented. We discuss two such screening frameworks.

The "Stop-&-Go" programme

The Stop-&-Go programme was designed on the basis of the research in women's and girls' football of the "Locomotor System and Sports" (University of Murcia) and the "Move Well Be Strong" (https://www.movewellbestrong.net/) research groups. The programme consists of three blocks of field-based tests that allow the assessment in applied scenarios of several factors related to the incidence of injuries in football:

1 Personal or individual factors (e.g. age, sex, maturation status, history of previous injuries).
2 Psychological factors related to emotional wellbeing and sports performance (e.g. sleep quality and quantity, anxiety and stress, emotional regulation and cognitive functioning).
3 Factors related to physical performance, neuromuscular capacity and motor competence.

For this chapter, we will focus solely on the third block of tests, which includes vertical and horizontal jump tests, maximal speed running assessment and postural assessment. For more information on the other blocks, please refer to Robles-Palazón, Cejudo, et al. (2021).

Jumping assessment

Jump landings have consistently been identified as primary movement patterns associated with some of the most burdensome knee and ankle injuries in women's football (Lucarno et al., 2021). Given that neuromuscular strategies and lower extremity biomechanics adopted during jumps and landings are task specific (Taylor et al., 2016), a range of different jump methodologies have been proposed. The proposed jump assessment protocol encompasses six vertical and two horizontal jump tests to provide a comprehensive evaluation of players' physical performance, landing mechanics and neuromuscular capacity during this primary motor skill (Table 16.1) (Flanagan & Comyns, 2008; Lloyd et al., 2009; Myer et al., 2008).

In the Drop Vertical Jump (DVJ) (typically from 30 cm) and Countermovement Jump (CMJ) tests, simultaneous assessment of some kinetic (Bishop et al., 2021) and kinematic measures can by conducted using two force platforms (for calculating bilateral differences in kinetic measures) and three two-dimensional cameras positioned in the frontal and sagittal planes. The captured images from the DVJ and CMJ tests are subsequently analysed using software packages (e.g. Kinovea, Quintic, ImageJ and Dartfish), which allow kinematic analysis in a plane that is perpendicular to the camera (Robles-Palazón et al., Ruiz-Perez, et al., 2021). In the absence of force platforms, cost-effective alternatives, such as the "My Jump" app, are available to assess jumping performance (Balsalobre-Fernández et al., 2015).

TABLE 16.1 Jump tests included in the Stop-&-Go programme and the measures extracted from them.

Jump protocol	Vertical jump tests	
	Neuromuscular capacity	Landing mechanic
Drop vertical jump	Peak landing force (first and second landings). Modified reactive strength index. Ratio of peak landing force to peak take-off force. Asymmetries (%). Jump height.	Frontal plane projection angle. Hip, knee and ankle flexion angles at initial contact and peak flexion and their respective ranges of motion.
Countermovement jump	Peak landing force. Modified reactive strength index. Time to take off. Jump momentum. Countermovement jump depth Leg stiffness. Asymmetries (%). Jump height.	
Tuck jump	Ligament dominance (yes/no). Quadriceps dominance (yes/no). Leg dominance (yes/no). Trunk dominance (yes/no). Neuromuscular fatigue (yes/no). Feedforward mechanism deficits (yes/no).	
20 submaximal vertical hops	Leg stiffness.	
Five maximum vertical hops	Modified reactive strength index.	
Horizontal jump tests		
Bilateral broad jump	Distance reached.	
Single hop (horizontal) test	Distance reached. Asymmetries (%).	

Note: All measures must be taken in the dominant and non-dominant legs.
Stop-&-Go programme: https://www.stopandgosport.com/.

The qualitative information extracted (ligament dominance, quadriceps dominance, leg dominance, trunk dominance, feedforward mechanisms, deficits and neuromuscular fatigue [Fort-Vanmeerhaeghe et al., 2017]) from the Tuck Jump Assessment (TJA) regarding players' neuromuscular capacity could be enriched with kinematic assessment of each landing performed during the 10-s test, following the same methodology as described earlier for DVJ and CMJ (Robles-Palazón, Ruiz-Perez, et al., 2021). Additionally, the 20 submaximal, bilateral hop test, as described by Lloyd et al. (2009), allows relative leg stiffness, normalised to the player's body mass, to be calculated (Dalleau et al., 2004). Finally, the five-maximum hop test (Flanagan & Comyns, 2008) and the modified reactive strength index (McMahon et al., 2022) allow stretch-shortening-cycle capability to be determined.

It is advisable to perform three to five valid attempts of the DVJ and CMJ tests and select the one with the highest jump height for subsequent kinetic and kinematic analyses to ensure accurate measurements and a true representativeness of the players' neuromuscular capability. For the vertical hop tests, two to three valid attempts should be performed, and those with the greatest relative leg stiffness and modified reactive-strength-index values selected. However, due to the physical demands of the TJA, only one valid attempt is recommended to avoid fatigue-related responses. In the horizontal jump tests, only the distance reached is recorded, which must be normalised with respect to the player's leg length. For the single hop test (Munro & Herrington, 2011), the differences between the distances reached by the dominant and the non-dominant legs are also calculated.

Sprint assessment

The Stop-&-Go programme incorporates two sprint tests: (1) A 30-m straight-line sprint test (Lahti et al., 2020) and (2) a 90° change-of-direction test (Aparicio-Sarmiento et al., 2022). These two tests aim to assess the physical performance, neuromuscular function and mechanics of sprinting (including acceleration, maximal speed and deceleration).

In the straight-line sprint test, the time recorded at 5, 10, 15, 20, 25 and 30 m using timing gates is incorporated into the spreadsheet designed by Samozino et al. (2016), to calculate the players' mechanical capacity to generate force during maximum speed running (Table 16.2). Concurrently, the players' sprint mechanics (sagittal plane) are assessed to record hip, knee and ankle flexion angles (Lahti et al., 2020). An alternative, cost-effective and reliable option for those who do not have access to timing gates is to video record the 30-m sprint and analyse data using the "My Sprint" app (Romero-Franco et al., 2017).

The change-of-direction test (modified by Aparicio-Sarmiento et al., 2022) allows determination of both qualitative (using the cutting movement assessment score) and quantitative (Weir et al., 2019) assessment of players' change-of-direction mechanics. The time taken by participants to complete the change-of-direction test is also recorded using timing gates as a measure of performance.

Postural assessment

The shortened version of the postural fitness test battery includes a series of tests aimed at assessing neuromuscular constructs, such as dynamic and static trunk stability, trunk muscle endurance, maximal isometric strength of the hip muscles and range of motion of the lower extremity. Specifically, postural assessment should

TABLE 16.2 Maximum speed running tests included in the Stop-&-Go programme and the measures extracted from them.

Maximum speed running	Neuromuscular capacity	Landing mechanic
30-m sprint	Time (physical performance): 5-, 10-, 15-, 20-, 25- and 30-m split times. Force–velocity profile measures: Theoretical maximal force, maximal ratio of forces, mean ratio of forces at 10 m, maximal power and velocity.	Early acceleration and upright sprint (maximal) kinematic measures in the toe-off and touchdown phases: Centre of mass distance (m body-length^{-1}), hip angle (ipsilateral and contralateral legs), trunk angle and step length (m/body length).
90° change of direction	Time (physical performance): 5- and 10-m split times.	Initial and final (weight acceptance phase) contact time, trunk and knee flexion angles and ranges of motion of both the penultimate and final footsteps of each change of direction (left and right). Frontal plane projection angle and trunk inclination angle and ranges of motion of the final footstep.

include the rotary stability and trunk stability push-up tests (Cook et al., 2006), for assessing the dynamic stability of the trunk musculature during a combined upper and lower extremity motion and a closed-chain upper body movement.

For the trunk muscle endurance assessment, the flexion rotation trunk test (Brotons-Gil et al., 2013) is proposed, while the protocol described by Ruiz-Pérez et al. (2021) is preferred for assessing isometric hip abduction and adduction strength. The players' results for each hip abduction and adduction isometric strength measurement are normalised to body mass and tibia length (isometric strength [N] × tibial length [m] ÷ body mass [kg]) (Cejudo et al., 2021). Finally, the maximum passive range of motion for hip flexion and extension with the knee extended, hip abduction, knee flexion and ankle dorsiflexion with the knee extended is evaluated using the methodology and instrumentation described by Cejudo et al. (2020).

Considerations for the implementation of screening in applied environments

In applied contexts, where there is a need to assess several players within the same training session, it is proposed to carry out the tests using a circuit approach to optimise the time available. Normally the circuit consists of six stations, requiring approximately six to eight experienced testers (Figure 16.1), which needs consideration if resource is limited. Each station includes one or several tests to maximise the time spent screening players.

Prevention strategies

Given the benefits of screening athletes for injury risk, it is imperative that effective injury prevention strategies are put in place. Over the last three decades, mitigation of injury risk has seen the implementation of validated IPPs, with the vast majority designed specifically to address ACL injury in girls and women (De Ste Croix et al., 2018; Waldén et al., 2012).

With the demands of football including high-intensity running (made up of rapid accelerations and decelerations), changes in direction and contact through tackling, the adoption of evidence-based IPPs reduces incidence and severity of injuries (Crossley et al., 2020). These programmes typically consist of a combination of strength and conditioning exercises, flexibility training, balance and proprioception drills and education of coaches and players on how to best mitigate injury risk. A criteria-driven approach should be used (see Figure 16.2) to support the player on their developmental journey to reduce injury risk.

Strength and conditioning training

Strength and conditioning training has been shown to significantly reduce injury risk in footballers (Crossley et al., 2020). De Ste Croix et al. (2018) implemented an injury prevention programme consisting of strength, plyometric and balance exercises in girls aged 13–17 years. It was reported that markers of injury risk (knee valgus, leg stiffness and peak knee adduction moment) were all improved with the programme. Further, it was identified that there were significant beneficial effects of such training for those players who were identified as high risk through screening, as opposed to those classified as low risk. This finding highlights the importance of incorporating strength and conditioning exercises tailored to women's football in IPPs.

Flexibility training

Flexibility training plays a crucial role in injury prevention by improving joint range of motion and muscle extensibility (Ayala et al., 2012). Most evidence focuses on the implications of dynamic stretching embedded in IPPs such as the Fédération Internationale de Football Association (FIFA) 11+ on lower-extremity range of motion, measured either through joint angular change (e.g. passive knee extension, passive dorsiflexion or the modified Thomas test [Curry et al., 2009; Matsuo et al., 2019; Pamboris et al., 2019]) or through posterior-chain flexibility tests such as the sit-and-reach test (Ayala et al., 2012). The implementation of

Total duration: 90–120 min approx.
Players should move to the next station every 15–20 min

Three players per station

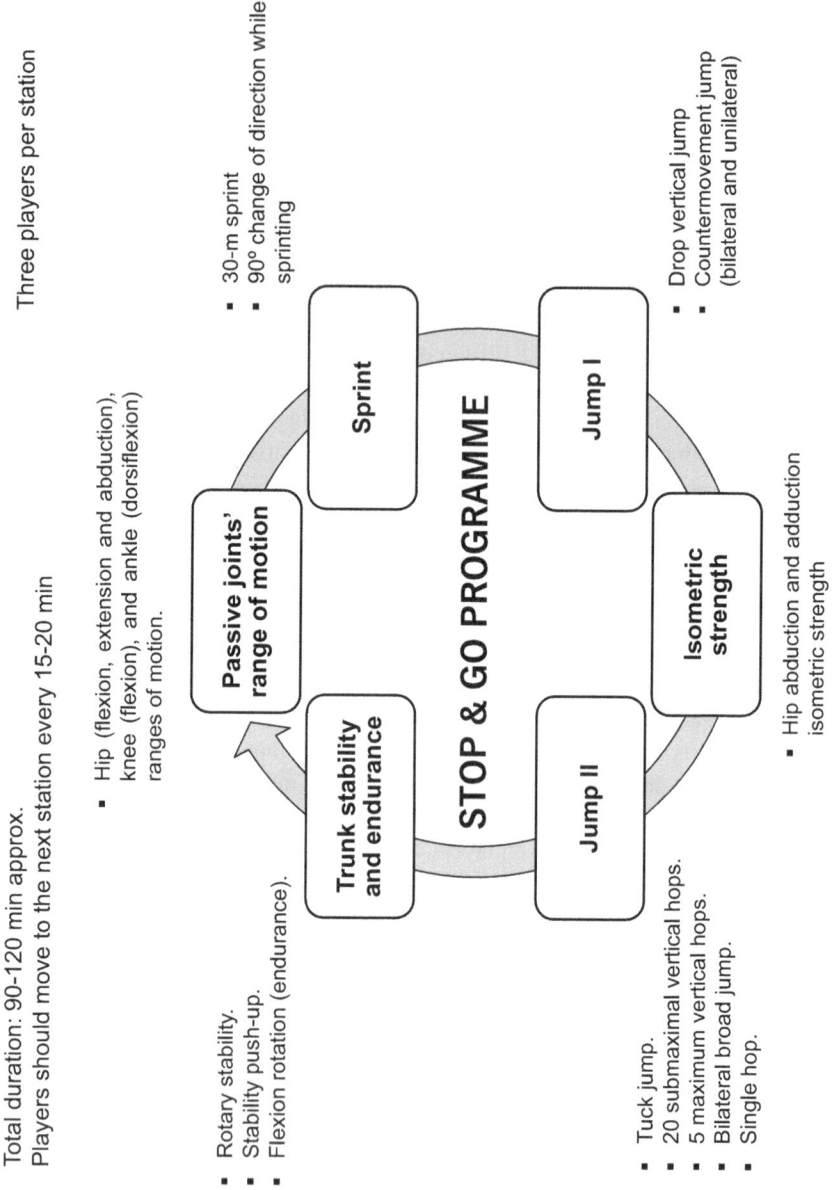

STOP & GO PROGRAMME

Sprint
- 30-m sprint
- 90° change of direction while sprinting

Passive joints' range of motion
- Hip (flexion, extension and abduction), knee (flexion), and ankle (dorsiflexion) ranges of motion.

Trunk stability and endurance
- Rotary stability.
- Stability push-up.
- Flexion rotation (endurance).

Jump II
- Tuck jump.
- 20 submaximal vertical hops.
- 5 maximum vertical hops.
- Bilateral broad jump.
- Single hop.

Isometric strength
- Hip abduction and adduction isometric strength

Jump I
- Drop vertical jump
- Countermovement jump (bilateral and unilateral)

FIGURE 16.1 Jump tests included in the Stop-&-Go programme (https://www.stopandgosport.com/) and the measures extracted from them. All measures must be taken in the dominant and the non-dominant leg

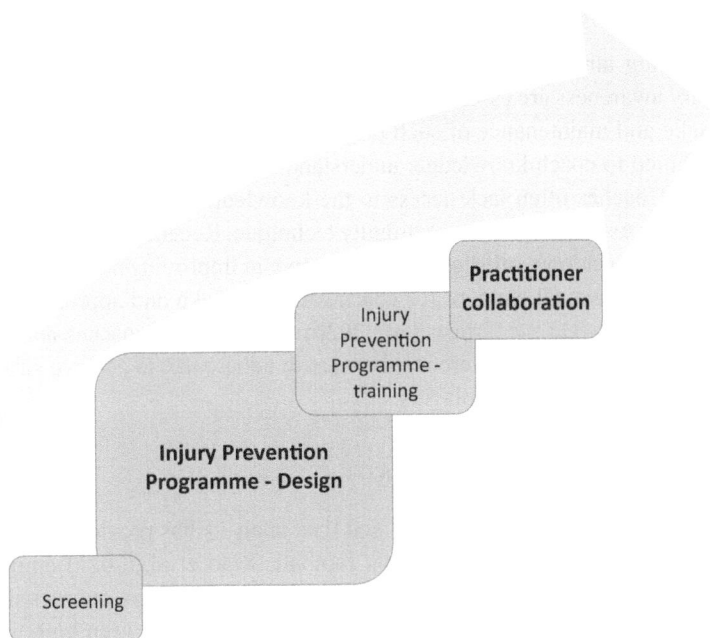

FIGURE 16.2   Maximum speed running tests included in the Stop-&-Go programme and the measures extracted from them.

comprehensive IPPs, including flexibility training, in elite women football players demonstrated reductions in the incidence of injuries by 27% (Crossley et al., 2020). These findings underscore the significance of flexibility training in reducing the risk of specific injuries in women's football.

Balance and proprioception training

Balance and proprioception training are vital in enhancing neuromuscular control and preventing injuries, particularly in lower limb joints (Crossley et al., 2020). Steffen et al. (2008) investigated the effectiveness of balance training in elite girls' football (13–18 years), with players who undertook the training exhibiting a 35% reduction in the incidence of ankle sprains compared to that of the control group. Moreover, a multitude of researchers have integrated various forms of balance training into their IPPs, highlighting the significance of including exercises focused on balance and proprioception in injury prevention initiatives for girls' and women's football (Emery & Meeuwisse, 2010; Foss et al., 2018; Söderman et al., 2000).

Injury prevention education

Educating athletes and coaches on injury prevention techniques and promoting injury awareness are essential. However, there is an ongoing concern regarding the uptake and maintenance of such programmes (Emery et al., 2020), which may be attributed to coach knowledge, understanding and attitude towards such interventions. Coaches often lack access to the knowledge and skills that are required to teach the exercises or to correct faulty technique. Recently it has been reported that a coach education workshop can be effective in improving adherence to IPPs when there is a practical element for coaches to undertake and appreciate what quality movement is (De Ste Croix et al., 2020). Empowering coaches and athletes with this training may help overcome barriers to adherence, to achieve sustained injury reduction in the football players.

Sports science and data analysis

The integration of sports science and data analysis has provided valuable insights into injury prevention in women's football. Xiao et al. (2021) employed global positioning systems to monitor training loads and assess injury risk in football players. The results of their research revealed a link between high training loads spanning two, three and four weeks and an elevated risk of injury. This study demonstrates the significance of data-informed decision-making and load-management strategies in minimising injury risk, which is a growth area in the development of sport science support in women's football (Costa et al., 2022).

Rehabilitation for football players

Given the previously noted greater injury incidence rates in women's football, inevitably the rehabilitation process needs to be effective in terms of return to play. In a recent report into gender inequality in football, it was suggested that the disparity in resource between men's and women's football places the woman player at a potential disadvantage in this process (Philippou et al., 2022), but, to date, this assumption is largely anecdotal, with little data to support such claims. There is no suggestion that rehabilitation programmes should be fundamentally different across the men's and the women's game (Cerulli et al., 2002); however, linking back to the injury prevention elements, women may wish to focus on specific types of training within the rehabilitation process. Cerulli et al. (2002) suggest that rehabilitation processes after ACL injury in women athletes should focus on neuromuscular capability, plyometrics, postural balance, biomechanics of movement and functional agility, all within a sport-specific context. As with prevention programmes, it is important that rehabilitation strategies are specific for women and are focused on their biology, anatomy, physiology and movement competency, as well as the access that they have to resources. In a study exploring hip and core strengthening on patellofemoral pain syndrome, an eight-week programme in women players reduced pain, reduced knee abduction and improved neuromuscular control (Earl et al., 2011). This finding is supported by López-Valenciano et al. (2019), who stressed that players' rehabilitation should include exercises for strength and mobility of the hip abductors and core stability (especially in the frontal plane).

The key to a successful rehabilitation process is compliance (Johnson, 1997), and many researchers have examined the psychosocial elements of successful return to play in women athletes, probably due to the high burden associated with serious injuries. Those women footballers ($n = 43$) who are most successful in their rehabilitation demonstrate autonomous motivation that results in rehabilitation adherence (Johnson, 1997), as well as high levels of self-confidence and mindfulness (Mosewich et al., 2014). It has been identified that those less successful in the rehabilitation process are younger women, with limited injury experience, negative emotions and with perceived isolation (Forsdyke et al., 2016), noting that there is a gender bias with little data on women compared to men (Forsdyke et al., 2016)

Return to play post-injury

Given the greater propensity of players in women's football to suffer serious injuries, the rehabilitation process can often be long, and it might be perceived that players will not be able to return to pre-injury levels of performance. However, most data indicate good return-to-play outcomes for football players with most returning to the same pre-injury levels (Webster, 2021), often back to the highest level of competition. This positive outcome is evident in a recent case study by Taberner et al. (2020), who used the "control-chaos continuum" as a framework for return to play for an elite player, which resulted in a return to above pre-injury training load demands and who achieved her goal of representing her country at the World Cup.

Nordahl et al. (2014) found that the main characteristics of women skiers who did not return to sport post-ACL injury were young women with no previous experience of injury and who demonstrated risk and fear of re-injury. However, Johnson et al. (2016) found that women footballers displayed resilient behaviours during ACL rehabilitation, and that they were more successful if they had rich interactions with significant others, strong belief in one's own actions and ability to set clear goals.

Re-injury rates in women's football

Around one in four women who have returned to play following an ACL injury will go onto either re-injure the same or other ACL, and this is around 23% higher than it is in men (Wong et al., 2023). Faude et al. (2006) reported that 26.3% of German professional players went on to have a second ACL injury. Webster (2021) noted that data regarding level of performance after return to play are severely lacking in women's sport. There are limited data, but based on data from one study, it has been shown that hamstring eccentric training after hamstring injury in women players resulted in no re-injuries 12 months after return to play (Tyler et al., 2017).

Psychosocial aspects in return to play post-injury

Many researchers have explored the psychosocial aspects needed for successful return to play in women's sport, and a range of mechanisms have been identified. These mechanisms include motivation, goal setting, social support and managing internal and external pressures (Hildingsson et al., 2018). One of the mechanisms that most often appear in the literature is the effectiveness of social-support mechanisms in the rehabilitation process for players, and this might be due to the reduced formal support that players get in women's club settings (Hildingsson et al., 2018). Forsdyke et al. (2022) noted that increasing positive perceptions of social support is important in preparing players to be more psychologically ready to return to sport. Managing emotions, anxiety regarding performance and re-injury fears, alongside building confidence and sound social-support mechanisms appear essential if productive rehabilitation outcomes are desired in women's football. For those interested in this area, the reader is guided to the extensive work of Forsdyke and colleagues (2016, 2022).

Practitioners' perspective

With the practitioner at the frontline of screening, prevention and rehabilitation work, it is important that any continuation and carry-over of improved kinematics need to transfer into sports performance (i.e. when they are stressed and under fatigue), and this needs to be reinforced by the technical coaches and other support staff, so there is no disconnect between strength and conditioning/physiotherapy practices and technical training. This disconnect highlights the need for technical coaches to be educated in how their players should be moving, so they can also reinforce good movement patterns and manage training load when required. Thus, technical coaches need to work with the multidisciplinary team to identify sports-specific technical models to both minimise injury and maximise effectiveness in football. Movement screening (Tables 16.1 and 16.2) is an efficient way to get to know "new players" and identify training needs quickly, but players need to be motivated to perform at their best in movement screens, so player education may also be needed. Movement screening can be effective as a player education tool by raising awareness of their own movement competency. However, it is important that any data are presented to athletes in a clear and impactful way.

Technical coaches should know what strategies they can use in a warm-up that effectively improve movement competency (e.g. mobility drills improve range of motion) for each player that may form part of the individualised warm-up but these strategies should be developed using objective movement screening data (refer to the section on prevention strategies). Given that we often find clubs that are resource poor in the women's game, it is important that coach and player education is effective in reducing injury risk. Keeping prevention training fun and engaging is important for player compliance and subsequently minimising risk.

Summary

In this chapter, we have highlighted the growing popularity of women's football and the need for injury screening, risk prevention and rehabilitation strategies to ensure athletes' wellbeing and long-term success in the sport. Non-contact ACL injury incidence is higher in women than it is in men, causing personal, societal and economic burdens. Screening strategies for injury risk are crucial, including strength and conditioning training, flexibility training, balance and proprioception exercises and education on injury prevention. Rehabilitation for players in women's football should focus on neuromuscular capability, plyometrics, postural balance and functional agility. Successful return to play relies on compliance, psychosocial support and managing emotions and anxiety and appropriate goal setting.

References

Aiello, F., Impellizzeri, F. M., Brown, S. J., Serner, A., & McCall, A. (2023). Injury-inciting activities in male and female football players: A systematic review. *Sports Medicine*, *53*(1), 151–176. https://doi.org/10.1007/s40279-022-01753-5

Aparicio-Sarmiento, A., Hernández-García, R., Cejudo, A., Palao, J. M., & Sainz de Baranda, P. (2022). Reliability of a qualitative instrument to assess high-risk mechanisms during a 90° change of direction in female football players. *International Journal of Environmental Research and Public Health*, *19*(7), 41–43. https://doi.org/10.3390/ijerph19074143

Ardern, C. L., Kvist, J., & Webster, K. E. (2016). Psychological aspects of anterior cruciate ligament injuries. *Operative Techniques in Sports Medicine*, *24*(1), 77–83. https://doi.org/10.1053/j.otsm.2015.09.006

Ayala, F., de Baranda, P. S., De Ste Croix, M. B. A., & Santonja, F. (2012). Absolute reliability of five clinical tests for assessing hamstring flexibility in professional futsal players. *Journal of Science and Medicine in Sport*, *15*(2), 142–147. https://doi.org/10.1016/j.jsams.2011.10.002

Balsalobre-Fernández, C., Glaister, M., & Lockey, R. A. (2015). The validity and reliability of an iPhone app for measuring vertical jump performance. *Journal of Sports Sciences*, *33*(15), 1574–1579. https://doi.org/10.1080/02640414.2014.996184

Bishop, C., Read, P., McCubbine, J., & Turner, A. (2021). Vertical and horizontal asymmetries are related to slower sprinting and jump performance in elite youth female soccer players. *The Journal of Strength & Conditioning Research*, *35*(1), 56–63. https://doi.org/10.1519/JSC.0000000000002544

Brotons-Gil, E., García-Vaquero, M. P., Peco-González, N., & Vera-García, F. J. (2013). Flexion-rotation trunk test to assess abdominal muscle endurance: Reliability, learning effect, and sex differences. *Journal of Strength and Conditioning Research*, *27*(6), 1602–1608. https://doi.org/10.1519/JSC.0b013e31827124d9

Cejudo, A., Armada-Zarco, J. M., Izzo, R., & Sainz de Baranda, P. (2021). Perfil de fuerza isométrica máxima de los rotadores de la cadera de un equipo senior de fútbol. *Journal of Universal Movement and Performance*, *4*, 1–9. https://doi.org/10.17561/jump.n4.1

Cejudo, A., Sainz de Baranda, P., Ayala, F., De Ste Croix, M., & Santonja-Medina, F. (2020). Assessment of the range of movement of the lower limb in sport: Advantages of the ROM-sport I battery. *International Journal of Environmental Research and Public Health*, *17*(20), 7606. https://doi.org/10.3390/ijerph17207606

Cerulli, G., Caraffa, A., & Ponteggia, F. (2002). Rehabilitation issues in women with anterior cruciate ligament deficiency. *Sports Medicine and Arthroscopy Review*, *10*(1), 76–82.

Cook, G., Burton, L., & Hoogenboom, B. (2006). Pre-participation screening: The use of fundamental movements as an assessment of function—part 2. *North American Journal of Sports Physical Therapy*, *1*(3), 132–139.

Costa, J. A., Rago, V., Brito, P., Figueiredo, P., Sousa, A., Abade, E., & Brito, J. (2022). Training in women soccer players: A systematic review on training load monitoring. *Frontiers in Psychology*, *13*, 943857. https://doi.org/10.3389/fpsyg.2022.943857

Crossley, K. M., Patterson, B. E., Culvenor, A. G., Bruder, A. M., Mosler, A. B., & Mentiplay, B. F. (2020). Making football safer for women: A systematic review and meta-analysis of injury prevention programmes in 11773 female football (soccer) players. *British Journal of Sports Medicine*, *54*(18), 1089–1098. https://doi.org/10.1136/bjsports-2019–101587

Curry, B. S., Chengkalath, D., Crouch, G. J., Romance, M., & Manns, P. J. (2009). Acute effects of dynamic stretching, static stretching, and light aerobic activity on muscular performance in women. *Journal of Strength and Conditioning Research*, *23*(6), 1811–1819. http://doi.org/10.1519/JSC.0b013e3181b73c2b

Dalleau, G., Belli, A., Viale, F., Lacour, J. R., & Bourdin, M. (2004). A simple method for field measurements of leg stiffness in hopping. *International Journal of Sports Medicine*, *25*(3), 170–176. http://doi.org/10.1055/s-2003-45252

De Ste Croix, M., Ayala, F., Sanchez, S. H., Lehnert, M., & Hughes, J. (2020). Grass-root coaches' knowledge, understanding, attitude and confidence to deliver injury prevention training in youth soccer: A comparison of coaches in three EU countries. *Journal of Science in Sport and Exercise*, 367–374. https://doi.org/10.1007/s42978-020-00075-0

De Ste Croix, M., Hughes, J. D., Ayala, F., Taylor, L., & Datson, N. (2018). Efficacy of injury prevention training is greater for high-risk vs low-risk elite female youth soccer players. *The American Journal of Sports Medicine*, *46*(13), 3271–3280. https://doi.org/10.1177/0363546518795677

Earl, J. E., & Hoch, A. Z. (2011). A proximal strengthening program improves pain, function, and biomechanics in women with patellofemoral pain syndrome. *The American Journal of Sports Medicine*, *39*(1), 154–163. https://doi.org/10.1177/0363546510379967

Eggerding, V., Reijman, M., Meuffels, D. E., van Es, E., van Arkel, E., van den Brand, I., van Linge, J., Zijl, J., Bierma-Zeinstra, S. M., & Koopmanschap, M. (2022). ACL reconstruction for all is not cost-effective after acute ACL rupture. *British Journal of Sports Medicine*, *56*(1), 24–28. https://doi.org/10.1136/bjsports-2020-102564

Emery, C. A., & Meeuwisse, W. H. (2010). The effectiveness of a neuromuscular prevention strategy to reduce injuries in youth soccer: A cluster-randomised controlled trial. *British Journal of Sports Medicine*, *44*(8), 555–562. https://doi.org/10.1136/bjsm.2010.074377

Emery, C. A., van den Berg, C., Richmond, S. A., Palacios-Derflingher, L., McKay, C. D., Doyle-Baker, P. K., McKinlay, M., Toomey, C. M., Nettel-Aguirre, A., Verhagen, E., Belton, K., Macpherson, A., & Hagel, B. E. (2020). Implementing a junior high school-based programme to reduce sports injuries through neuromuscular training (iSPRINT): A cluster randomised controlled trial (RCT). *British Journal of Sports Medicine*, *54*(15), 913–919. https://doi.org/10.1136/bjsports-2019-101117.

Faude, O., Junge, A., Kindermann, W., & Dvorak, J. (2006). Risk factors for injuries in elite female soccer players. *British Journal of Sports Medicine*, *40*(9), 785–790. https://doi.org/10.1136/bjsm.2006.027540

Flanagan, E. P., & Comyns, T. M. (2008). The use of contact time and the reactive strength index to optimize fast stretch-shortening cycle training. *Strength and Conditioning Journal, 30*(5), 32–38. http://doi.org/10.1519/SSC.0b013e318187e25b

Forsdyke, D., Smith, A., Jones, M., & Gledhill, A., (2016). Psychosocial factors associated with outcomes of sports injury rehabilitation in competitive athletes: A mixed studies systematic review. *British Journal of Sports Medicine, 50*(9), 537–544. https://doi.org/10.1136/bjsports-2015-094850

Forsdyke, D., Madigan, D., Gledhill, A., & Smith, A. (2022). Perceived social support, reinjury anxiety, and psychological readiness to return to sport in soccer players. *Journal of Sport Rehabilitation, 31*(6), 749–755. https://doi.org/10.1123/jsr.2021-0181

Fort-Vanmeerhaeghe, A., Montalvo, A. M., Lloyd, R. S., Read, P., & Myer, G. D. (2017). Intra-and inter-rater reliability of the modified tuck jump assessment. *Journal of Sports Science and Medicine, 16*(1), 117–124.

Foss, K. D. B., Thomas, S., Khoury, J. C., Myer, G. D., & Hewett, T. E. (2018). A school-based neuromuscular training program and sport-related injury incidence: A prospective randomized controlled clinical trial. *Journal of Athletic Training, 53*(1), 20–28. https://doi:10.4085/1062-6050-173-16

Hildingsson, M., Fitzgerald, U. T., & Alricsson, M. (2018). Perceived motivational factors for female football players during rehabilitation after sports injury-a qualitative interview study. *Journal of Exercise Rehabilitation, 14*(2), 199. https://doi.org/10.12965%2Fjer.1836030.015

Johnson, U. (1997). Coping strategies among long-term injured competitive athletes: A study of 81 men and women in team and individual sports. *Scandinavian Journal of Medicine and Science in Sports, 7*(6), 367–372. https://doi.org/10.1111/j.1600-0838.1997.tb00169.x

Johnson, U., Ivarsson, A., Karlsson, J., Hägglund, M., Waldén, M., & Börjesson, M. (2016). Rehabilitation after first-time anterior cruciate ligament injury and reconstruction in female football players: A study of resilience factors. *BMC Sports Science, Medicine & Rehabilitation, 8*(1), 20. https://doi.org/10.1186/s13102-016-0046-9

Khan, T., Alvand, A., Prieto-Alhambra, D., Culliford, D. J., Judge, A., Jackson, W. F., Scammell, B. E., Arden, N. K., & Price, A. J. (2019). ACL and meniscal injuries increase the risk of primary total knee replacement for osteoarthritis: A matched case–control study using the clinical practice research datalink (CPRD). *British Journal of Sports Medicine, 53*(15), 965–968. https://doi:10.1136/bjsports-2017-097762

Lahti, J., Mendiguchia, J., Ahtiainen, J., Anula, L., Kononen, T., Kujala, M., Matinlauri, A., Peltonen, V., Thibault, M., Toivonen, R-M., Edouard, P., & Morin, J. B. (2020). Multifactorial individualised programme for hamstring muscle injury risk reduction in professional football: Protocol for a prospective cohort study. *BMJ Open Sport and Exercise Medicine, 6*(1), e000758. https://doi/10.1136/bmjsem-2020-000758

Lemes, I. R., Pinto, R. Z., Lage, V. N., Roch, B. A., Verhagen, E., Bolling, C., Aquino, C. F., Fonseca, S. T., & Souza, T. R. (2021). Do exercise-based prevention programmes reduce non-contact musculoskeletal injuries in football (soccer)? A systematic review and meta-analysis with 13 355 athletes and more than 1 million exposure hours. *British Journal of Sports Medicine, 55*(20), 1170–1178. https://doi.org/10.1136/bjsports-2020-103683

Lloyd, R. S., Oliver, J. L., Hughes, M. G., & Williams, C. A. (2009). Reliability and validity of field-based measures of leg stiffness and reactive strength index in youths. *Journal of Sports Sciences, 27*(14), 1565–1573. https://doi.org/10.1080/02640410903311572

López-Valenciano, A., Ayala, F., De Ste Croix, M., Barbado, D., & Vera-Garcia, F. J. (2019). Different neuromuscular parameters influence dynamic balance in male and female football players. *Knee Surgery, Sports Traumatology, Arthroscopy, 27*, 962–970. https://doi.org/10.1007/s00167-018-5088-y

Lucarno, S., Zago, M., Buckthorpe, M., Grassi, A., Tosarelli, F., Smith, R., & Della Villa, F. (2021). Systematic video analysis of anterior cruciate ligament injuries in professional female soccer players. *American Journal of Sports Medicine*, *49*(7), 1794–1802. https://doi.org/10.1177/03635465211008169

Matsuo, S., Iwata, M., Miyazaki, M., Fukaya, T., Yamanaka, E., Nagata, K., Tsuchida, W., Asai, Y., & Suzuki, S. (2019). Changes in flexibility and force are not different after static versus dynamic stretching. *Sports Medicine International Open*, *3*(03), e89–e95. https://doi.org/10.1055/a-1001-1993

McKay, C. D., & Mellalieu, S. (2021). When injuries lead to retirement: Calling it a day. In C. D. McKay (Ed.), *The mental impact of sports injury* (pp. 153–166). Routledge.

McMahon, J. J., Ripley, N. J., & Comfort, P. (2022). Force plate-derived countermovement jump normative data and benchmarks for professional rugby league players. *Sensors*, *22*(22), 8669. https://doi.org/10.3390/s22228669

Mosewich, A. D., Crocker, P. R., & Kowalski, K. C. (2014). Managing injury and other setbacks in sport: Experiences of (and resources for) high-performance women athletes. *Qualitative Research in Sport, Exercise and Health*, *6*(2), 182–204. https://doi.org/10.1080/2159676X.2013.766810

Munro, A. G., & Herrington, L. C. (2011). Between-session reliability of four hop tests and the agility T-test. *Journal of Strength and Conditioning Research*, *25*(5), 1470–1477. https://doi.org/10.1519/JSC.0b013e3181d83335

Myer, G. D., Ford, K. R., & Hewett, T. E. (2008). Tuck jump assessment for reducing anterior cruciate ligament injury risk. *International Journal of Athletic Therapy and Training*, *13*(5), 39–44. https://doi.org/10.1123/att.13.5.39

Nassis, G., Verhagen, E., Brito, J., Figueiredo, P., & Krustrup, P. (2022). A review of machine learning applications in soccer with an emphasis on injury risk. *Biology of Sport*, *40*(1), 233–239. https://doi.org/10.5114/biolsport.2023.114283

Nordahl, B., Sjöström, R., Westin, M., Werner, S., & Alricsson, M. (2014). Experiences of returning to elite alpine skiing after ACL injury and ACL reconstruction. *International Journal of Adolescent Medicine and Health*, *26*(1), 69–77. https://doi.org/10.1515/ijamh-2012-0114

Olivares-Jabalera, J., Fílter-Ruger, A., Dos' Santos, T., Afonso, J., Della Villa, F., Morente-Sánchez, J., Soto-Hermoso, V., & Requena, B. (2021). Exercise-based training strategies to reduce the incidence or mitigate the risk factors of anterior cruciate ligament injury in adult football (soccer) players: A systematic review. *International Journal of Environmental Research and Public Health*, *18*(24), 13351. https://www.mdpi.com/1660-4601/18/24/13351#

Pamboris, G. M., Noorkoiv, M., Baltzopoulos, V., & Mohagheghi, A. A. (2019). Dynamic stretching is not detrimental to neuromechanical and sensorimotor performance of ankle plantar flexors. *Scandinavian Journal of Medicine and Science in Sports*, *29*(2), 200–212. https://doi.org/10.1111/sms.13321

Philippou, C., Clarkson, B., Pope, S., Jain, S., Parry, K. D., Huang, X., Plumley, D., & Cox, A. (2022 March). *The gender divide that fails football's bottom line: The commercial case for gender equality* [Technical Report]. Fair Game. https://static1.squarespace.com/static/6047aabc7130e94a70ed3515/t/6225fcd351786a64ba4421b0/1646656733257/The+Gender+Divide+That+Fails+Football%27s+Bottom+Line+-+Fair+Game+Report+March+2022.pdf

Robles-Palazón, F. J., Cejudo, A., Aparicio-Sarmiento, A., de Baranda, P. S., & Ayala, F. (2021). Programa Stop & Go: Pruebas de campo para la identificación del riesgo de lesión en jugadores jóvenes de deportes de equipo. *JUMP*, *4*, 59–86. https://doi.org/10.17561/jump.n4.6

Robles-Palazón, F. J., Ruiz-Pérez, I., Oliver, J. L., Ayala, F., & de Baranda, P. S. (2021). Reliability, validity, and maturation-related differences of frontal and sagittal plane landing kinematic measures during drop jump and tuck jump screening tests in male youth soccer players. *Physical Therapy in Sport*, *50*, 206–216. https://doi.org/10.1016/j.ptsp.2021.05.009

Romero-Franco, N., Jiménez-Reyes, P., Castaño-Zambudio, A., Capelo-Ramírez, F., Rodríguez-Juan, J. J., González-Hernández, J., Javier, J., Toscano-Bendala, F., Cuadrado-Peñafiel,V.,&Balsalobre-Fernández,C.(2017).Sprintperformanceandmechanical outputs computed with an iPhone app: Comparison with existing reference methods. *European Journal of Sport Science*, *17*(4), 386–392. https://doi.org/10.1080/17461391. 2016.1249031

Ruiz-Pérez, I., Elvira, J. L., Myer, G. D., De Ste Croix, M. B., & Ayala, F. (2021). Criterion related validity of 2-dimensional measures of hip, knee and ankle kinematics during bilateral drop-jump landings. *European Journal of Human Movement*, *47*, 100–120. https://doi.org/10.21134/eurjhm.2021.47.10

Samozino, P., Rabita, G., Dorel, S., Slawinski, J., Peyrot, N., Saez de Villarreal, E., & Morin, J. B. (2016). A simple method for measuring power, force, velocity properties, and mechanical effectiveness in sprint running. *Scandinavian Journal of Medicine and Science in Sports*, *26*(6), 648–658. https://doi.org/10.1111/sms.12490

Söderman, K., Werner, S., Pietilä, T., Engström, B., & Alfredson, H. (2000). Balance board training: Prevention of traumatic injuries of the lower extremities in female soccer players? A prospective randomized intervention study. *Knee Surgery, Sports Traumatology, and Arthroscopy*, *8*, 356–363. https://doi.org/10.1007/s001670000147

Steffen, K., Myklebust, G., Olsen, O. E., Holme, I., & Bahr, R. (2008). Preventing injuries in female youth football—a cluster-randomized controlled trial. *Scandinavian Journal of Medicine and Science in Sports*, *18*(5), 605–614. https://doi.org/10.1111/j.1600-0838.2007.00703.x

Taberner, M., Van Dyk, N., Allen, T., Jain, N., Richter, C., Drust, B., Betancur, E., & Cohen, D. D. (2020). Physical preparation and return to performance of an elite female football player following ACL reconstruction: A journey to the FIFA Women's World Cup. *BMJ Open Sport and Exercise Medicine*, *6*(1), 1–24. https://doi.org/10.1136/bmjsem-2020-000843

Taylor, J. B., Ford, K. R., Nguyen, A. D., & Shultz, S. J. (2016). Biomechanical comparison of single-and double-leg jump landings in the sagittal and frontal plane. *Orthopaedic Journal of Sports Medicine*, *4*(6). https://doi.org/10.1177/2325967116655158

Tyler, T. F., Schmitt, B. M., Nicholas, S. J., & McHugh, M. P. (2017). Rehabilitation after hamstring-strain injury emphasizing eccentric strengthening at long muscle lengths: Results of long-term follow-up. *Journal of Sport Rehabilitation*, *26*(2), 131–140. https://doi.org/10.1123/jsr.2015-0099

Van Mechelen, W., Hlobil, H., & Kemper, H. C. (1992). Incidence, severity, aetiology and prevention of sports injuries: A review of concepts. *Sports Medicine*, *14*, 82–99. https://doi.org/10.2165/00007256-199214020-00002

Waldén, M., Atroshi, I., Magnusson, H., Wagner, P., & Hägglund, M. (2012). Prevention of acute knee injuries in adolescent female football players: Cluster randomised controlled trial. *British Medical Journal*, *344*, 1–11. https://doi.org/10.1136/bmj.e3042

Webster, K. E. (2021). Return to sport and reinjury rates in elite female athletes after anterior cruciate ligament rupture. *Sports Medicine*, *51*(4), 653–660. https://doi.org/10.1007/s40279-020-01404-7

Weir, G., Alderson, J., Smailes, N., Elliott, B., & Donnelly, C. (2019). A reliable video-based ACL injury screening tool for female team sport athletes. *International Journal of Sports Medicine*, *40*(3), 191–199. https://doi.org/10.1055/a-0756-9659

Wong, C. Y., Mok, K. M., & Yung, S. H. (2023). Secondary anterior cruciate ligament injury prevention training in athletes: What is the missing link? *International Journal of Environmental Research and Public Health*, *20*(6), 4821. https://doi.org/10.3390/ijerph20064821

Xiao, M., Nguyen, J. N., Hwang, C. E., & Abrams, G. D. (2021). Increased lower extremity injury risk associated with player load and distance in collegiate women's soccer. *Orthopaedic Journal of Sports Medicine*, *9*(10). https://doi.org/10.1177/23259671211048248

17

REFLECTION AND REFLECTING ON FOOTBALL COACH EDUCATION IN CONNECTION WITH IDENTITY, PROCESS AND PRACTICE

Dave Lawrence and Hanya Pielichaty

Introduction

Football as "work" is framed by Culvin (2021) in connection with the professionalisation of women's football in England. This iteration of professionalisation has brought with it significant opportunities for transformation, along with sustained social, cultural, economic and financial challenges (Clarkson et al., 2022; Culvin, 2021; Koukiadaki & Pearson, 2019). Women's football is of global significance and the 2023 World Cup broke records in terms of viewing figures and ticket sales (Snape, 2023). The international professionalisation of women's football has developed unevenly but has shaped migration and labour markets (Williams, 2013). For example Agergaard and Botelho (2014) explore immigration into the Scandinavian women's football environment and highlight social mobility and player development as key benefits of professionalisation. The professionalisation of women's football has also significantly influenced coaching practice, whereby professional status is drawn upon as a progress marker, often in comparison to boys' and men's football setups (Sleeman & Ronkainen, 2020).

Not all women players believe being a professional footballer is an option for them, causing tension for some coaches, who try to influence the mentality of players in the professional pathway (Sleeman & Ronkainen, 2020). The English Football Association (the FA) has outlined ambitious plans for the girls' and women's game, asserting that by 2024 there will be "exceptional coaches at every level of the game who are representative of our society" (The FA, 2020, October, p. 37). Coaching is also a focus area across the football pyramid, with the FA Women's National League strategy outlining priority areas for progress, which include support, leadership and culture, and a focus on the coaching pathway (The FA, 2022). Furthermore, the Coaching Excellence Initiative, launched in 2021, can be viewed as one way in

DOI: 10.4324/9781003381914-17

which high-performance coaching in women's football is being strategically targeted (The FA, 2021, February). This strategy complements academic literature acknowledging the quality of the relationship between coach and athlete as fundamental (Jowett, 2017), but the emphasis on winning makes it difficult to define what effective coaching is (Nash & Mallet, 2019). Women's national team football coaches in Sweden were able to navigate the pressure to win medals by treating players with respect and emphasising wellbeing and voice (Lindgren & Barker-Ruchti, 2017).

There has been an increase in football coaches across levels in the Women's Super League (The FA, 2020, May). Despite this positive trend, women are pressurised to navigate sexist and discriminatory coaching spaces and practices (Clarkson et al., 2019), which reflect issues in coach education more broadly (Lewis et al., 2018). Sawiuk et al. (2021, p. 124) explain that coaching courses sustain discriminatory practices despite increased numbers: "It could be that women are now hardened to the androcentric nature of the delivery or have found new and robust ways to 'put up' with the sexist dialogue and the marginalisation of their own practice."

Knoppers et al. (2022) explain that women coaches must negotiate "sovereign" power (established within football associations) that automatically equate men to higher knowledge states. As such, coach education courses "constructed football as a sport played primarily by men and discursively made women invisible" (Knoppers et al., 2022, p. 886). In an exploration of women coach-learners undertaking the Union of European Football Associations (UEFA) A licence, voice and language were platforms for exclusion (Sawiuk et al., 2021). A hierarchy of knowledge, privileging men's football, is significant, whereby women are in the minority in terms of physical presence (tutors, learners and administrators) and in relation to curriculum content and delivery (Sawiuk et al., 2021). This situation is consolidated by Fasting et al. (2019), who suggested that women coaches believed men's experiences were more valued in the job market, and that respect and authority came more easily.

Football has a history of social exclusion making it difficult for women coaches to enter the sport and thrive within it due to multilevel issues of marginalisation (see Schlesinger et al., 2022). Pfister's (2013) examination of European coaches found that stereotypes about women's abilities in sport and society were problematic and influenced women coaches' decision-making. Coach education is pivotal to the success and development of strategies in relation to professionalisation and success. In this chapter, we will offer practical guidance for coach educators and coaches in women's football. We will examine reflective practice and coach identity in the following section before drawing upon empirical research to provide a practical model for coach educators.

Reflective practice and coach identity

Reflection is a contested term (Voldby & Klein-Døssing, 2020) but in essence can be understood as a process that links professional knowledge and practice. This connection, in turn, raises the consciousness of a practitioner's personal or craft knowledge (Knowles et al., 2001) and consequently improves practice effectiveness (Ghaye, 2010). Reflexivity is "an ability to locate yourself in the picture, is complemented by a process of reflectivity" (Fook, 1999, p. 11), and is valuable to coach education research (Townsend & Cushion, 2021) and effective coach education experience (Nelson et al., 2014).

Within general reflective research, there exists a recognition, in which values and the importance of self are a justifiable inclusion in reflective practice. For example Ghaye (2010) deems facets such as exercising care and compassion, respecting human diversity, professional demeanour and developing a sense of community as being integral to consider within the reflection process. Reflective thinking may evoke images of mistakes and errors (Ghaye, 2010), which can challenge the efficiency and commitment to being a confident reflective practitioner. Reflection and identity are entangled within the human condition and are enabled and stifled by many internal and external factors within the sporting context.

The term *identity* is contentious (Zehntner & McMahon, 2014), with some researchers preferring *self-awareness* (Hughes, 2010), and others focusing on aligning coach identity with a "true" self (Blackett et al., 2021, p. 670). Lally (2007, p. 86) suggests that identity is "a multidimensional view of oneself that is both enduring and dynamic", whereby these multiple dimensions may be affected by psychological and sociological processes (Carless & Douglas, 2013). Examples of psychological factors are self-efficacy and esteem (Kelchtermans, 2009), whilst sociological factors, such as community, context, gender and ethnic background, are also impactful (Stets & Burke, 2000). A coach may showcase an identity of characteristics such as assertiveness, self-esteem, charisma and courage (Ghaye, 2010), but the journey of becoming self-aware, and of understanding that these traits or others are present in their coaching identity, is a challenging process (Lally, 2007). Coach identity leadership is also of importance and linked to self-efficacy but not significantly connected with perceived control or social support (Miller et al., 2020).

The former elite players-turned-coaches in Blackett et al.'s (2021) study demonstrated the interconnection between coaching philosophy and identity, although the former was deemed difficult to articulate. Furthermore, the importance of personal values to facilitate an "honest" coach identity was significant and the need for self-reflexivity as a tonic to manage fixed coach identities was suggested (Blackett et al., 2021). Cultural proficiency and contextual intelligence are regarded as highly significant to football practitioner development (Champ et al., 2021). Emotion is also central to sports coaching and should not be underplayed in terms of its importance in identity-making, embodied experiences and reflective practice (Potrac et al., 2017).

The difficulty with changes to practice in connection to reflection is described here relating to elite coaches and gymnasts: "Not everyone enjoys change, as it involves reframing and reimagining things, ideas, situations, and—most of all— our own selves, which is rarely easy" (Cavallerio et al., 2020, p. 56). Generally, it is suggested that engaging in reflective practice may develop self-awareness and, as a result, better understanding to change current behaviours (Leduc et al., 2012). Ideological assumptions (linked to sociocultural and/or individual levels) can occur in a myriad of environments and contexts that may shape a person's identity (Cushion, 2018). It is important to recognise the presence of assumptions in coaching, and trying to make sense of them within an environment facilitates a constant process of identity development (Watts & Cushion, 2017). This process is particularly important for coaches of women athletes who may reproduce and be influenced by binary, gendered coaching practices that perpetuate male superiority (de Haan & Knoppers, 2020; Levi et al., 2022). Champ et al. (2021), in connection to trainee sport psychology consultants, whose professional identities were shaped by cultural assertions, also noted a link to the masculine domain of football. Experiences of coach education whereby "masculine ideals are uncritically reproduced" were also highlighted in the elite swimming coaching environment (Graham & Blackett, 2022, p. 811).

Despite the vast literature surrounding general reflective practice and coach reflections through scholarship, it is not entirely known what capabilities reflective practice has to *positively* impact on the coaching process (Hall & Gray, 2016). This means that coaches are not fully aware of the benefits of reflective coaching or even what it means to implement it. Academically, there is also a lack of detail on coaching in women's football, information often relating to player, rather than coach, identities (Christensen, 2013; Pielichaty, 2019, 2021). Given the masculine hegemonic, sociocultural backdrop of football, it is crucial that reflective practice becomes embedded in effective coach identity-making.

Voice from industry: navigating the coach identity in women's football

Similar to Sleeman and Ronkainen (2020, p. 329), I will use my lived experiences as the first author to provide a reflexive "personal history" to frame the findings. My personal history involves 22 years of coaching football predominantly in the UK and 20 of those years have been spent specifically coaching girls and women footballers within the emerging professional leagues. This section is co-created using my industry voice alongside findings from empirical research undertaken as part of a larger study. As such, industry reflections will be interlaced with empirical data taken from one focus group of seven men and two women coaches, and then four follow-up, semi-structured interviews with three men and one woman, each with experience of coaching girls and women. The participants have been given pseudonyms for this chapter. "I" will be used at times in this section to situate the first author's experiences alongside data gathered. This approach is similar to Townsend and Cushion's (2021) study on disability sport that used reflexive practice in connection with "crossing fields" (and crossing back), between the empirical and research context. Reflective practice in this section refers to the crossing fields of industry practice and research, each underlined by author reflection.

(Un)taught reflective practice

Reflection does not always follow a formal pedagogical process. Whilst face-to-face coach education *can* include time to discuss things with peers, teaching on "how" to reflect can be sparse. Instead, methods and approaches tend to develop organically, some perceiving it to be natural:

> I think I do it . . . probably without even thinking or recognising that I do it. . . . (Callum).
>
> It's natural, isn't it, whether you perform as a player or as a coach, because you are performing as a coach, that you naturally reflect on the way home, you talk about it, when you probably don't even know you're talking about it (Louise).

As such, reflection is considered something we just "do". Rather than being a taught and formal process, reflection becomes embroiled in daily life and frequent tasks. Similar to Stone's (2007) work on football as permeating various contexts, reflective practice does the same. For example introspecting may happen as part of a travel routine, through contemplation at mealtimes or to end the day. The continual presence of reflection gives the illusion it is formulaic, taught and routine but in fact it drifts in and out of coach consciousness. A consequence of this is that it can be unsupported, without instruction and lacking direction.

From personal experience, higher-level qualifications, such as the UEFA A licence, now dedicate more time to supporting a coach with reflection. Fortunately, as an advocate of reflection, I found this process enjoyable and impactful, but some coaches either disregarded the reflective stage or were unsure about how to use it effectively. If reflection was treated as more purposeful practice earlier on in coach education, better strategies and understanding would be more apparent prior to higher-level qualifications. Coaches I have engaged with around the topic also commented on the fact that a tutor with a commitment or passion for reflection would heavily influence their understanding of it.

Informal learning

Reflection is significantly beneficial in supporting the professional development of the coach, as well as in-player development. In general, it was accepted and valued across the empirical data collected by women and men coaches who perceived it as a beneficial informal learning strategy: "It's helped me massively because sometimes I kind of panic with sessions. But then when I reflect afterwards, I think actually it's not gone as bad as I thought" (Daniel). This statement relates to the position of hot versus cold reflection, but also the concept of reflecting on negatives (Ghaye, 2010), which may impact self-esteem. There is also a link between reflection and effective feedforward strategies to positively shape future sessions, as Catherine explains: "Reflection allows for me to reflect upon what has happened and what improvement could be made going forward" (Catherine). Reflection was also discussed as a strategy to develop self-awareness, an important discovery when connecting to identity construction: "As you reflect, you become more self-aware. And I think that's really important as a coach, especially if you've got biases that you not aware of, if you're doing things that you're not aware of" (Adam).

Removing yourself from the coaching role and reflecting may give an opportunity to ascertain what is important to you, whilst also removing bias to allow a coach to see things from other perspectives or paradigms. Such a process, however, needs commitment from the coach to embed reflection as a constant practice. An issue with informal learning is that without structure and tutor facilitation, the self-guided nature of learning may not receive the time and quality required to add benefit.

Self-esteem

The two women coaches involved in the data collection confirmed that they tended to "over-think" sessions. They spent a lot of time analysing their respective coaching sessions and dived "cognitively deep" into the architecture and delivery of the activities. This approach can leave the reflective process lacking clarity about whether the session was effective. This overthinking may also be linked to other factors such as a perceived lack of time, overcomplicating the process and not knowing what to reflect on. Coaches explained that the absence of learning outcomes, a focused curriculum and coaching across multiple contexts were barriers to their development. This could be explained through the ongoing challenges women coaches face due to anxiety, self-doubt and pressure to represent when operating in male-dominated coaching environments (Norman & Simpson, 2022). It would be inappropriate to make assertions about women coaches' reflective practices based on a small sample size, but it is important to register the significance this has had for these coaches involved. In my coaching experiences, the desire for conformity complicated issues of self-esteem, whereby women coaches would either adapt their behaviours to fit in or otherwise keep quiet from expressing their views and ideas. Norman and Simpson (2022) found that high-performance women coaches, however, sought to resist conformity but that there was a lack of united, collective support to do so. The gendered coaching landscape is difficult for women to navigate due to the "fine line between challenge and negative stress" (Carson et al., 2018, p. 65).

I believe the lack of clarity concerning "what worked well" in coaches' processing styles results in uncertainty around how effective we can be. Tutors and mentors should aim to articulate honest, kind and helpful feedback to enhance self-esteem, whilst highlighting areas that may benefit from critical analysis. From a coach perspective, I would reverse the "what went well, even better if . . ."-method of reflection. For example begin a reflective coach activity with the "even better if" to forefront the more negative reflections and then follow these with clear strategies for improvement. This approach facilitates a better engagement with the "what-went-well" aspect of the session's reflection that may cover practice design, player engagement and coach behaviour. It is vital to spend plentiful time dissecting this area, rather than skipping past it to get to the areas of development. Consequently, engaging with the positives at the planning phase will develop a feeling of esteem and confidence, resulting in momentum for coaching well.

How to embed reflective practice into women's football coaching

Previously, coaching was criticised for applying reflective models from other contexts rather than generating its own sport-specific frameworks (Downham & Cushion, 2021). In this section, we look to address this omission by offering a practical guide to reflective practice for coaches in women's football. Previous theoretical models such as those of Gibbs (1988) and Schön (1983) were mentioned by two coaches in the empirical data but were not acknowledged more widely. More popular approaches, cited by the coaches in the study, included the aforementioned "what went well, even better if" strategy, as well as the use of a mentor, critical friend or sounding board. Both women coaches confirmed they had access to a coach-mentor to support their learning: "That's how I started to reflect as well as when I first started coaching, I . . . used quite a lot of critical friends" (Steven). Interestingly, three coaches discussed mentorship external to their peer coaching group to assist with their development, such as support from a family member. Such a person may, due to familiarity, be in a positive position to support the construction or progression of coach identity.

I have mentored many women coaches and a central theme I have discovered is the prominent pattern of negative thinking (things that were missed, sessions that did not go so well) and reflection. But, with a mentor who has an intention to help, be kind and offer critical feedback, the coach soon becomes compelled and motivated to be better, to create action plans, to plug gaps in knowledge and further improve coaches' professional learning. Many of these conversations should reconnect with the self: Why is this important to you? Why did you coach the way you coached? This focus improves authenticity and confirms that sessions are delivered in line with how we want to see ourselves as practitioners. The "even better if" here is having a mentor who knows you both on and off the coaching pitch, so they know what is important to you and why.

An inclusive model to reflection in football coach education

Synthesising the personal experiences articulated in the previous section along with previous academic literature, the model, shown in Figure 17.1, has been developed:

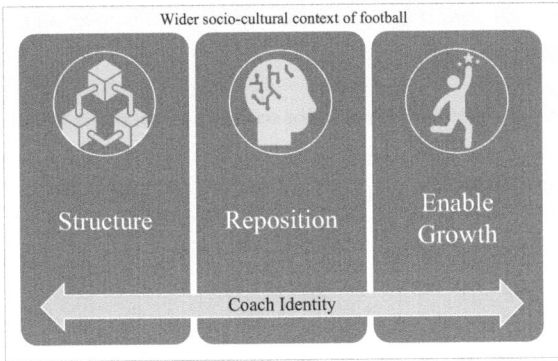

FIGURE 17.1   An inclusive model to reflection in football coach education.

The entire model is underpinned by an inclusive coaching framework that acknowledges the sociocultural, patriarchal history of football but takes effective steps to challenge this history at every level. This model encapsulates a "how-to" process for embedding reflection and reflective practice into coach education, utilising experience from women's football.

Stage 1: structure, formality and process

Whilst coaches may prefer to adopt a reflection process grounded in theory, others may benefit effectively with a basic "even better if" and "what went well". In essence, reflective practice should include the following:

- Structured thoughts: Consider these based on a pre-arranged process or training plan.
- Formality: Create a formal setting/environment for reflection and then structure this into training sessions.
- Routine: Be methodical about how, when and where reflection is carried out and make it a regular feature of coaching practice.
- Recording of reflections: This could include informal notes and actions for development, which will create greater impact on coaching competence long-term.

Stage 2: repositioning

Sometimes negative, and heavily critical, reflections can overpower the positive. In basic reflective models, a coach will consider the "good" elements of the session first, followed by the "even better if" reflections later, which can result in leaving the process with negative feelings about what has been delivered, ultimately impacting on self-esteem. It is, therefore, important to reposition the negativity by doing the following:

- Process the "even better if" first, prior to completing the reflective exercise.
- Directly utilise the positive elements to feature centrally in the reflective exercise. Consider unpacking the positives and utilising them purposefully.
- Use the positive elements to shape an action plan for the next session whilst being mindful (but not absorbed by) the "even-better-if" elements.
- Seek to create more productive emotions of confident affirmation by following these steps.

Stage 3: enabling growth

Approaching the first two stages can be an insular and independent action. We only know what we know. We create subjective opinions on success or failure based on what we think and believe, aligned to our knowledge level, identity and values. It is important, therefore, to enable personal growth in the following ways:

- Acquire and/or utilise a critical friend or mentor: This provides access to alternative opinions and reveals more about the session delivery than introversion. A mentor with effective observation skills, knowledge and an understanding of rapport and teaching can provide much deeper feedback to support reflection, as well as potentially having some opinions and insight into reflective practice itself.
- Add formality and structure to your relationship with the critical friend/mentor. Observers tend to see things the deliverer has missed, so ask them to take notes on a set area of themes linked to your own areas of aspired development.

Coach identity

Remembering who we are, why we coach and why we coach the way we coach across all phases of the reflection model is vital. It is important to celebrate your coach identity and be aware of the gendered barriers that may inhibit women coaches (Carson et al., 2018) and their associated identity development. A coach who identifies themselves as having a growth mindset will use all these phases to be vulnerable in their critical analysis of success and of failure. They will aim to access a mentor because supporting player development is important to them. Coaches who value the power of positive thoughts and affirmations will consider stage 2 as being a key area for reflection to ensure they continue to be motivated and constructive in their coaching role. As such, there must be continual evaluation across stages whereby these are not understood as discrete levels and instead cross over and permeate one another.

Summary

In this chapter, we have provided a practical way in which to examine the role of reflective practice within women's football. We have focused on the application of reflective practice as an effective learning tool, providing a model for implementation. A limitation of this work, however, is the lack of intersectionality provided, a drawback stated in other literature (Rankin-Wright et al., 2019; Townsend et al., 2020), which therefore should be prioritised in future explorations. It is also important to note that women coaches are not a homogenous group and instead reflective practice is presented here as a significant facilitator to progressive coach education. Future examinations could develop this model by further exploring the experiences of coaching within the socio-historical context of football. We have showcased the importance of reflection within coach education by developing a new model for effective application and identity development.

References

Agergaard, S., & Botelho, V. (2014). The way out? African players' migration to Scandinavian women's football. *Sport in Society*, *17*(4), 523–536. https://doi.org/10.1080/17430437.2013.815512

Blackett, A. D., Evans, A. B., & Piggott, D. (2021). Negotiating a coach identity: A theoretical critique of elite athletes' transitions into post-athletic high performance coaching roles. *Sport, Education and Society*, *26*(6), 663–675. https://doi.org/10.1080/13573322.2020.1787371

Carless, D., & Douglas, K. (2013). "In the boat" but "selling myself short": Stories, narratives, and identity development in elite sport. *The Sport Psychologist*, *27*(1), 27–39. https://doi.org/10.1123/tsp.27.1.27

Carson, F., McCormack, C., & Walsh, J. (2018). Women in sport coaching: Challenges, stress and wellbeing. *Journal of Physical Education, Sport, Health and Recreations*, *7*(2), 63–67. https://doi.org/10.15294/active.v7i2.22100

Cavallerio, F., Wadey, R., & Wagstaff, C. R. D. (2020). Member reflections with elite coaches and gymnasts: Looking back to look forward. *Qualitative Research in Sport, Exercise and Health*, *12*(1), 48–62. https://doi.org/10.1080/2159676X.2019.1625431

Champ, F., Ronkainen, N., Tod, D., Eubank, A., & Littlewood, M. (2021). A tale of three seasons: A cultural sport psychology and gender performativity approach to practitioner identity and development in professional football. *Qualitative Research in Sport, Exercise and Health*, *13*(5), 847–863. https://doi.org/10.1080/2159676X.2020.1833967

Christensen, M. K. (2013). Outlining a typology of sports coaching careers: Paradigmatic trajectories and ideal career types among high-performance sports coaches. *Sports Coaching Review*, *2*(2), 98–113. https://doi.org/10.1080/21640629.2014.898826

Clarkson, B. G., Cox, E., & Thelwell, R. C. (2019). Negotiating gender in the English football workplace: Composite vignettes of women head coaches' experiences. *Women in Sport and Physical Activity Journal*, *27*(2), 73–84. https://doi.org/10.1123/wspaj.2018-0052

Clarkson, B. G., Culvin, A., Pope, S., & Parry, K. D. (2022). Covid-19 reflections on threat and uncertainty for the future of elite women's football in England. *Managing Sport and Leisure*, *27*(1–2), 50–61. https://doi.org/10.1080/23750472.2020.1766377

Culvin, A. (2021). Football as work: The lived realities of professional women footballers in England. *Managing Sport and Leisure*, *28*(6), 684–697. https://doi.org/10.1080/23750472.2021.1959384

Cushion, C. J. (2018). Reflection and reflective practice discourses in coaching: A critical analysis. *Sport, Education and Society, 23*(1), 82–94. http://doi.org10.1080/13573322.2 016.1142961

De Haan, D., & Knoppers, A. (2020). Gendered discourses in coaching high-performance sport. *International Review for the Sociology of Sport, 55*(6), 631–646. https://doi. org/10.1177/1012690219829692

Downham, L., & Cushion, C. (2021). Reflection and reflective practice in high-performance sport coaching: A heuristic device. *Physical Education & Sport Pedagogy,* 1–20. https:// doi.org/10.1080/17408989.2022.2136369

Fasting, K., Sand, T. S., & Nordstrand, H. R. (2019). One of the few: The experiences of female elite-level coaches in Norwegian football, *Soccer & Society, 20*(3), 454–470. https://doi.org/10.1080/14660970.2017.1331163

Fook, J. (1999). Reflexivity as method. *Annual Review of Health Social Science, 9*(1), 11–20. https://doi.org/10.5172/hesr.1999.9.1.11

The Football Association. (2020, October). *Inspiring positive change: The FA strategy for women's and girls' football: 2020–2024.* https://www.thefa.com/news/2020/oct/19/new-fa-womens-strategy-launched-191020

The Football Association. (2020, May). *We continue to look at the impact of our women's football strategy on coaching.* https://www.thefa.com/news/2020/may/28/gameplan-for-growth-coaching-280520

The Football Association. (2021, February). *New initiative for top coaches in elite women's football.* https://www.thefa.com/news/2021/feb/18/audrey-cooper-launches-coaching-excellence-initiative-20210218

The Football Association. (2022, May). *New FA WNL strategy announced to bolster women's football pyramid in England.* https://www.thefa.com/news/2022/may/24/fa-womens-national-league-strategy-2022-25-launched-20222405

Ghaye, T. (2010). *Teaching and learning through reflective practice: A practical guide for positive action.* Routledge.

Gibbs, G. (1988). *Learning by doing: A guide to teaching and learning methods.* Further Education Unit.

Graham, L. C., & Blackett, A. D. (2022). "Coach, or female coach? And does it matter?": An autoethnography of playing the gendered game over a twenty-year elite swim coaching career. *Qualitative Research in Sport, Exercise and Health, 14*(5), 811–826. https://doi. org/10.1080/2159676X.2021.1969998

Hall, E.T., & Gray, S. (2016). Reflecting on reflective practice: A coach's action research narratives. *Qualitative Research in Sport, Exercise and Health, 8*(4), 365–379. https:// doi.org/10.1080/2159676X.2016.1160950

Hughes, G. (2010). Identity and belonging in social learning groups: The importance of distinguishing social, operational and knowledge-related identity congruence. *British Educational Research Journal, 36*(1), 47–63. https://www.jstor.org/stable/27823586

Jowett, S. (2017). Coaching effectiveness: The coach-athlete relationship at its heart. *Current Opinion in Psychology, 16,* 154–158. https://doi.org/10.1016/j.copsyc.2017.05.006

Kelchtermans, G. (2009). Who I am in how I teach is the message: Self-understanding, vulnerability and reflection. *Teachers and Teaching, 15*(2), 257–272. https://doi. org/10.1080/13540600902875332

Knoppers, A., de Haan., Norman, L., & LaVoi, N. (2022). Elite women coaches negotiating and resisting power in football. *Gender, Work & Organization, 29*(3), 880–896. https:// doi.org/10.1111/gwao.12790

Knowles, Z., Gilbourne, D., Borrie, A., & Nevill, A. (2001). Developing the reflective sports coach: A study exploring the processes of reflective practice within a higher education coaching programme. *Reflective Practice, 2*(2), 185–207. https://doi. org/10.1080/14623940123820

Koukiadaki, A., & Pearson, G. (2019, July 5). Women's football may be growing in popularity but the game is still fighting for survival. *The Conversation.* https://

theconversation.com/womens-football-may-be-growing-in-popularity-but-the-game-is-still-fighting-for-survival-119888

Lally, P. (2007). Identity and athletic retirement: A prospective study. *Psychology of Sport and Exercise*, *8*(1), 85–99. https://doi.org/10.1016/j.psychsport.2006.03.003

Leduc, M., Culver, D. M., & Werthner, P. (2012). Following a coach education programme: Coaches' perceptions and reported actions. *Sports Coaching Review*, *1*(2), 135–150. https://doi.org/10.1080/21640629.2013.797752

Levi, H., Wadey, R., Bunsell, T., Day, M., Hays, K., & Lampard, P. (2022). Women in a man's world: Coaching women in elite sport. *Journal of Applied Sport Psychology*, *35*(4), 571–597. https://doi.org/10.1080/10413200.2022.2051643

Lewis, C. J., Roberts, S. J., & Andrews, H. (2018). "Why am I putting myself through this?" Women football coaches' experiences of the Football Association's coach education process. *Sport, Education and Society*, *23*(1), 28–39. https://doi.org/10.1080/13573322.2015.1118030

Lindgren, E.-C., & Barker-Ruchti, N. (2017). Balancing performance-based expectations with a holistic perspective on coaching: A qualitative study of Swedish women's national football team coaches' practice experiences. *International Journal of Qualitative Studies on Health and Well-being*, *12*(2), 1–11. https://doi.org/10.1080/17482631.2017.1358580

Miller, A. J., Slater, M. J., & Turner, M. J. (2020). Coach identity leadership behaviours are positively associated with athlete resource appraisals: The mediating roles of relational and group identification. *Psychology of Sport & Exercise*, *51*, 101755. https://doi.org/10.1016/j.psychsport.2020.101755

Nash, C., & Mallet, C. J. (2019). Effective coaching in football. In E. Konter, J. Beckmann, & T. M. Loughead (Eds.), *Football psychology: From theory to practice* (pp. 101–116). Routledge. https://doi.org/10.4324/9781315268248-9

Nelson, L., Potrac, P., & Groom, R. (Eds.). (2014). *Research methods in sports coaching*. Routledge.

Norman, L., & Simpson, R. (2022). Gendered microaggressions towards the "only" women coaches in high-performance sport. *Sports Coaching Review*, *12*(3), 302–322. https://doi.org/10.1080/21640629.2021.2021031

Pfister, G. (2013). Outsiders: Female coaches intruding upon a male domain? In G. Pfister & M. K. Sisjord (Eds.), *Gender and sport: Changes and challenges* (pp. 71–99). Waxman.

Pielichaty, H. (2019). Identity salience and the football self: A critical ethnographic study of women and girls in football. *Qualitative Journal of Sport, Exercise and Health*, *11*(4) 527–542. https://doi.org/10.1080/2159676X.2018.1549094

Pielichaty, H. (2021). *Football, family, gender and identity: The football self*. Routledge.

Potrac, P., Mallett, C., Greenough, K., & Nelson, L. (2017). Passion and paranoia: An embodied tale of emotion, identity, and pathos in sports coaching. *Sports Coaching Review*, *6*(2), 142–161. https://doi.org/10.1080/21640629.2017.1367067

Rankin-Wright, A. J., Hylton, K., & Norman, L. (2019). Negotiating the coaching landscape: Experiences of Black men and women coaches in the United Kingdom. *International Review for the Sociology of Sport*, *54*(5), 603–621. https://doi.org/10.1177/1012690217724879

Sawiuk, R., Lewis, C. J., & Taylor, W. G. (2021). "Long ball" and "balls deep": A critical reading of female coach-learners' experiences of the UEFA A licence. *Sports Coaching Review*, *10*(1), 110–127. https://doi.org/10.1080/21640629.2021.1874688

Schön, D. A. (1983). *The reflective practitioner: How professionals think in action*. Basic Books.

Schlesinger, T., Ingwersen, F., & Weigelt-Schlesinger, Y. (2022). Gender stereotypes as mechanisms of social exclusion of women as football coaches. In L. Norman (Ed.), *Improving gender equity in sports coaching*. Routledge.

Sleeman, E. J., & Ronkainen, N. J. (2020). The professionalization of women's football in England and its impact on coaches' philosophy of practice. *International Sport Coaching Journal*, *7*(3), 326–334. https://doi.org/10.1123/iscj.2019-0018

Snape, J. (2023, August 4). Women's World Cup 2023 hailed as 'most successful in history' at halfway point. *The Guardian.* https://www.theguardian.com/football/2023/aug/04/womens-world-cup-2023-hailed-as-most-successful-in-history-at-halfway-point#:~:text=6%20months%20old-,Women's%20World%20Cup%202023%20hailed%20as%20'most,in%20history'%20at%20halfway%20point&text=Channel%20Seven's%20coverage%20of%20the,the%20most%20successful%20in%20history

Stets, J. E., & Burke, P. J. (2000). Identity theory and social identity theory. *Social Psychology Quarterly, 63*(3), 224–237. https://doi.org/10.2307/2695870

Stone, C. (2007). The role of football in everyday life. *Soccer & Society, 8*(2–3), 169–184. https://doi.org/10.1080/14660970701224319

Townsend, R. C., & Cushion, C. J. (2021). "Put that in your fucking research": Reflexivity, ethnography and disability sport coaching. *Qualitative Research, 21*(2), 145–309. https://doi-org.proxy.library.lincoln.ac.uk/10.1177/1468794120931349

Townsend, R. C., Huntley, T., Cushion, C. J., & Fitzgerald, H. (2020). "It's not about disability, I want to win as many medals as possible": The social construction of disability in high-performance coaching. *International Review for the Sociology of Sport, 55*(3), 344–360. https://doi.org/10.1177/1012690218797526

Voldby, C. R., & Klein-Døssing, R. (2020). "I thought we were supposed to learn how to become better coaches": Developing coach education through action research. *Educational Action Research, 28*(3), 534–553. https://doi.org10.1080/09650792.2019.1605920

Watts, D. W., & Cushion, C. J. (2017). Coaching journeys: Longitudinal experiences from professional football in Great Britain. *Sports Coaching Review, 6*(1), 76–93. https://doi.org/10.1080/21640629.2016.1238135

Williams, J. (2013). *Globalising women's football: Europe, migration and professionalization.* Peter Lang.

Zehntner, C., & McMahon, J. A. (2014). Mentoring in coaching: The means of correct training? An autoethnographic exploration of one Australian swimming coach's experiences. *Qualitative Research in Sport, Exercise and Health, 6*(4), 596–616. https://doi.org/10.1080/2159676X.2013.809376

INDEX

Note: Page numbers in *italics* indicate a figure and page numbers in **bold** indicate a table on the corresponding page.